A FIELD GUIDE TO THE MAJOR NATIVE AND
INTRODUCED SPECIES NORTH OF MEXICO

TREES

OF NORTH AMERICA

by C. FRANK BROCKMAN

PROFESSOR OF FORESTRY, EMERITUS
COLLEGE OF FOREST RESOURCES
UNIVERSITY OF WASHINGTON

Illustrated by REBECCA MERRILEES

Under the Editorship of
HERBERT S. ZIM

GOLDEN PRESS • NEW YORK
Western Publishing Company, Inc.
Racine, Wisconsin

FOREWORD

Reasons for the study of trees can be given by the score. All of them—scientific, cultural, economic, and aesthetic—are justifiable. Yet reasons are hardly necessary. Trees are too large, too majestic, too important, and too much a part of nature to be ignored. Man's dependence on trees, directly and indirectly, goes back to those distant times when the human species was first making its mark. The dependence continues into this age of synthetics. On a planet covered in good part by forests it is almost impossible to understand fully the many other groups of plants and animals without taking into account the natural biological role of trees. From the human point of view, trees are a multipurpose natural resource without equal.

TREES is the second volume of the Golden Field Guide series, developed to play a unique role in the natural sciences. Without the cooperation of dedicated individuals and organizations, the preparation of this guide would have been an impossible task. Special thanks are due E. S. Harrar, for his early review of the manuscript; Sally Kaicher, who did the illustrations of palms and yuccas; the Native Plant Workshop of South Florida, for checking the art of plants that grow in South Florida and in the Florida Keys. Daniel B. Ward checked range maps for the Southeast; Arturo Gomez Pompa, the maps for the Southwest and Mexico. Conrad Byrd, B. O. Mulligan, Carl English, Julia F. Morton, George B. Stevenson, Hugh B. Wycoff, Percy C. Everett, and Donald E. Stone were among those who supplied specimens. The U. S. Forest Service furnished many photographs to assist the artist.

C.F.B.

GOLDEN®, GOLDEN FIELD GUIDE, and GOLDEN PRESS® are trademarks of Western Publishing Company, Inc.

HOW TO USE THIS BOOK

This is a field guide to the identification of 594 of some 865 species of trees native to North America north of Mexico. Included are the most common and most important species and also many that are less familiar but no less interesting. In addition, important foreign species that have become naturalized and some that are grown commercially or as ornamentals are also described and illustrated. In total, the guide includes more than 730 species in 76 families.

The criteria used to determine which species to describe and illustrate and which to only mention are based on the definition of a tree (p. 13). Native woody plants that regularly attain a height of 20 feet have been included, as have major introduced and naturalized species. A more difficult group were those woody plants that are treelike in only part of their range, in optimum habitats, or under special conditions. The more widespread, abundant, and important the plant, the better its chances for inclusion. Many of these smaller trees (to 15 feet) and some species that have limited ranges are mentioned, however.

Willows and hawthorns include many local species difficult to identify. Those that are of unquestionable tree size or that are the only representative in an area have been included.

To make this book most useful in the field, the text, range maps, and illustrations have been brought together so that all pertinent information can be seen at a glance. Because of limited space, the text is necessarily brief and therefore not complete in every detail, but the combination of text, range map, and illustrations will aid greatly in making identifications in the field.

Some trees have such distinctive forms that they can be identified at a glance, even at a considerable distance or from a moving car. A number of trees may be recognized quickly by their bark or by some unique character of the twigs, such as thorns or spines. Others may require a careful study of their flowers, fruits, buds, or detailed features of the foliage to confirm an identification. The range maps indicate the probability of finding a species in a particular area and, except for ornamentals planted outside their natural environment, are important, too, in tree identification. Range maps are especially helpful in identifying trees in such groups as the willows and hawthorns. These maps give only a general picture of where the species may be found, for within its range each species typically grows in a particular habitat, as in swamps, along rivers, or on alpine slopes. Some species are so tolerant of soil, moisture, and sunlight requirements that they are very widely distributed.

Each person develops his own method of tree identification. Often this is a combination of some characteristics that can be observed at a distance and others that need closer study. In most places, except in parks, a specimen of a leafy twig can be taken for study later at home or to show to a local authority on trees. A Bibliography (p. 271) is included to aid your further study.

Practice is the best way to learn to recognize trees. By observing the varied characteristics of different species and by reading further about them, distinctive features and descriptive botanical terms become commonplace. An awareness of the variations that might be expected of a species also develops with observation, for though leaves and other features of each species have a typical basic form, size, color, or other characteristic, often there is considerable variation in individuals of the same species. With field experience, the pleasure and satisfaction gained from this fascinating hobby is greatly increased. As a suggestion, underline in this book those field marks that are most helpful to you, especially those useful in differentiating a species from a similar species.

Technical terms have been held to a minimum in this field guide. In fact, an effort has been made to simplify terms wherever possible in the very brief descriptions and to emphasize only the most obvious field characteristics that may not be obvious in the illustration. Comparing a specimen with the illustrations and the description reduces considerably the need for these technical terms. Some of the most commonly used terms for parts of trees are given on pages 13-17, however. If a tree cannot be identified by quick reference to this guide, the use of such terminology will be of great help in conferring with tree experts or in using more technical references.

As a further aid to finding information quickly, this guide has a complete index to common and scientific names (pp. 272-280). And the illustrated guide to family characteristics on pages 5-12 will help in fitting a tree to its group and also in comparing features of the various families.

Common and scientific names in this book are based largely on the *Check List of Native and Naturalized Trees of the United States,* by Elbert L. Little, prepared under the direction of the Forest Service Tree and Range Plant Name Committee (see Bibliography, p. 271). Major departures from the *Check List* in this book are the division of Pinaceae into three families: Pinaceae, Taxodiaceae, and Cupressaceae; and the division of Cornaceae into two families: Cornaceae and Nyssaceae. Recognized botanical publications were consulted to determine the names for ornamental or naturalized species included in this guide but not in the *Check List.*

Many trees, as well as other plants, have several common names, varying with different localities. For this reason, botanists use scientific names that are written in Latin, a language that is no longer spoken and hence does not change with time. Each name consists of two parts——the genus and the species. Thus the scientific name of Sugar Maple is *Acer saccharum;* of Eastern Redcedar, *Juniperus virginiana;* of White Oak, *Quercus alba.* Regardless of nationality or native language, botanists anywhere in the world can recognize trees, as well as other plants and animals, by this naming system. Tree species also have varietal forms. A few examples of these are included in this book, as in Lodgepole Pine, *Pinus contorta* var. *latifolia.*

4

A GUIDE TO THE FAMILIES OF TREES

This is a guide to the families of trees in this book, presenting in abbreviated form their principal features. Major families are described in greater detail later; smaller families are described only here. In this condensed treatment, comparison of families is made easy. Often, of course, the precise botanical characteristics by which plants are classified are too small—flower details, for example—to be useful in field identification by the amateur. These are omitted.

GYMNOSPERMS

Gymnosperms do not have flowers in the commonly accepted sense; they produce naked seeds, usually on the scale of a cone. Many are evergreen, with needle-like, linear, or scalelike foliage.

Pages 20-65

YEW FAMILY (Taxaceae): leaves evergreen, linear (sides parallel), growing separately on twigs and not clustered; fruit one-seeded and drupaceous (plumlike) or with red, fleshy cup at base. *Yews, Torreyas.*   **Page 20**

CYCAD FAMILY (Cycadaceae): tree-sized members palmlike; large, pinnate leaves; conelike male and female strobiles on separate trees; fruit a cone. *Sago Palm, Fern Palm.*   **Page 20**

PINE FAMILY (Pinaceae): leaves evergreen (deciduous in larches), either needle-like or linear, single, in bundles (fascicles) or clusters; fruit a woody cone. *Pines, Larches, Spruces, Hemlocks, True Firs, Douglas-firs.*   **Page 22**

REDWOOD FAMILY (Taxodiaceae): leaves linear or awl-like, single and in spirals on twig; most species evergreen; small woody cones. *Redwood, Sequoia, Baldcypress.*   **Page 50**

CEDAR OR CYPRESS FAMILY (Cupressaceae): foliage evergreen, opposite or whorled, usually scalelike and overlapping, or awl-like and spreading, occasionally in 3's, sometimes both on same tree; fruit a woody, leathery, or semi-fleshy cone. *Cedars, Cypress, Junipers.*   **Page 54**

GINKGO FAMILY (Ginkgoaceae): one species (not native to N.A.); fanlike leaves; male and female strobiles on separate trees—male in catkinlike cluster, paired female on spurlike shoots; fruit drupaceous (plumlike), with foul odor. **Page 64**

ARAUCARIA FAMILY (Araucariaceae): not native to N.A.; evergreen; cone disintegrates when mature. *Monkey Puzzle, Norfolk Island Pine.* **Page 64**

PODOCARP FAMILY (Podocarpaceae): evergreens; no native N.A. species.   **Page 64**

ANGIOSPERMS

Angiosperms, true flowering plants, bear seeds within a closed vessel, often fleshy. Divided into Monocotyledons and Dicotyledons. **Pages 66-269**

Monocotyledons: leaves evergreen, with parallel veins; flower parts in 3's; woody fibers irregularly distributed in stems, hence no annual rings. **Pages 66-75**

PALM FAMILY (Palmae): tropical and subtropical trees; compound leaves, large and pinnate (feather-like) or palmate (fan-shaped) in a cluster at top of an unbranched trunk; fruits are berries (dates) or drupes (coconuts). *Palms, Palmettos.* **Page 66**

LILY FAMILY *(Liliaceae)*: a large family with only a few tree-sized members; leaves tough, long, slim, and sharp-pointed; flowers in large, terminal panicles; fruit a papery, leathery, or woody capsule in some, berry-like in others. Yuccas. **Page 74**

Dicotyledons: leaves net-veined, mostly deciduous but some evergreen; stems increase in diameter by annual layers of wood of varying thickness, forming rings. **Pages 76-269**

WILLOW FAMILY (Salicaceae): leaves simple, alternate, deciduous (leaves of *Willows* slender; leaves of most *Poplars* broad); staminate and pistillate catkins on different trees; fruits a capsule, with many small, tufted seeds. **Page 76**

WAXMYRTLE FAMILY (Myricaceae): shrubs or small trees; leaves evergreen, simple, alternate, aromatic, and with tiny resin dots; flowers in catkins; fruit a waxy drupe. *Bayberries.* **Page 90**

WALNUT FAMILY (Juglandaceae): large trees; leaves deciduous, alternate, pinnately compound; monoecious, staminate flowers in drooping catkins, pistillate, solitary or in small spikes; pith of twigs chambered in walnuts, solid in hickories; fruit a nut in husk. *Walnuts, Hickories.* **Page 92**

CORKWOOD FAMILY (Leitneriaceae): leaves deciduous, alternate, simple, hairy below; flowers dioecious, in catkins; fruit dry; wood light; one species, in Southeast. *Corkwood.* **Page 100**

BIRCH FAMILY (Betulaceae): leaves deciduous, simple, alternate, toothed; monoecious—staminate flowers in catkins, pistillate in catkins, clusters, or spikes; fruit a nutlet or nut, in a conelike strobile, leafy cluster, or husk. *Birches, Alders, Hornbeams, Hophornbeams, Hazelnut.* **Page 102**

BEECH FAMILY (Fagaceae): leaves mostly deciduous, simple, alternate; staminate and pistillate flowers on same tree—staminate in catkins or heads, pistillate in spikes—or in some genera both sexes in same catkin; fruit a nut or an acorn. *Beeches, Chestnuts, Chinkapins, Oaks, Tanoak.*
Page 114

ELM FAMILY (Ulmaceae): leaves deciduous (except in *Florida Trema*), simple, alternate, toothed; flowers inconspicuous, in greenish clusters; fruit dry, wafer-like *(Elms)*, nutlike *(Planertree)*, or a thin-fleshed drupe *(Hackberry, Trema)*. **Page 138**

MULBERRY FAMILY (Moraceae): leaves simple and alternate, deciduous or evergreen; milky sap; flowers in spikes, heads, or hollow receptacles; multiple fruits in spikes, heads, or fleshy receptacles. *Mulberries, Osage-orange, Figs.* **Page 144**

OLAX (TALLOWWOOD) FAMILY (Olacaceae): leaves evergreen, simple, alternate; axillary clusters of small, bell-shaped flowers; twigs thorny; fleshy fruit. *Tallowwood.* **Page 148**

BUCKWHEAT FAMILY (Polygonaceae): low, sprawling shrubs or small trees, largely tropical; leaves leathery, evergreen, alternate, simple, oval to circular, margins smooth; edible, grapelike fruits. *Seagrapes.* **Page 148**

FOUR-O'CLOCK FAMILY (Nyctaginaceae): largely tropical, with few trees; one tree species in Florida; leaves evergreen, simple, alternate or opposite, margins smooth; small flowers in clusters; fruit a nutlet in a fleshy, ribbed covering. *Longleaf Blolly.* **Page 148**

MAGNOLIA FAMILY (Magnoliaceae): leaves alternate, simple, entire *(Magnolias)* or lobed *(Yellow-poplar)*, mostly deciduous; large, showy flowers; conelike, aggregate fruits; stipule scars encircle twigs. **Page 150**

CUSTARD-APPLE (ANNONA) FAMILY (Annonaceae): small trees, largely in southeastern U.S.; leaves simple, alternate, entire; deciduous *(Pawpaw)* or evergreen *(Pond-apple)*; flowers large, solitary, yellow, white, or purple; large, fleshy fruits. **Page 154**

LAUREL FAMILY (Lauraceae): mostly tropical and subtropical trees; leaves evergreen or deciduous, simple, alternate, lobed or unlobed with smooth margins, aromatic; flowers small, greenish yellow or white; fruit one-seeded berry or drupe. *Sassafras, California Laurel, Redbay.* **Page 156**

7

WITCH-HAZEL FAMILY (Hamamelidaceae): leaves deciduous, alternate, simple, unlobed or palmately lobed; flowers in clusters or globose heads; fruit a woody capsule borne separately or in bur-like heads. *Witch-hazel, Sweetgum.*   **Page 158**

CAPER FAMILY (Capparidaceae): leaves evergreen, alternate, simple, scaly below, smooth margins; flowers, with elongated stamens, in terminal clusters; fruit an elongated berry-like pod; shrubs or small trees of tropics and subtropics. *Jamaica Caper.*   **Page 158**

SYCAMORE FAMILY (Platanaceae): leaves deciduous, alternate, simple, palmately lobed; flowers tiny, in heads; fruit a tight ball of achenes, each with a tuft of hair at its base; buds encircled by leaf scars, stipule scars encircling twigs. *Sycamores, Planetrees.*   **Page 160**

ROSE FAMILY (Rosaceae): a large family of trees, shrubs, herbs; leaves usually alternate, toothed, simple or pinnately compound, deciduous or evergreen; flower parts typically in 5's; fruit a drupe, pome, capsule, achene. *Apples, Plums, Cherries, Hawthorns, and others.*   **Page 162**

LEGUME FAMILY (Leguminosae): a large family; leaves alternate, simple, pinnate, or bipinnate; flowers regular or sweetpea-shaped; fruit a legume. *Acacias, Redbuds, Locusts, others.*   **Page 182**

RUE FAMILY (Rutaceae): leaves alternate (opposite in *Sea Amyris*), pinnately compound, evergreen or deciduous; twigs of some spiny; flowers small, clustered; fruit a capsule, samara, or thin-fleshed drupe. *Prickly-ashes and others.*   **Page 194**

BURSERA FAMILY (Burseraceae): tropical and subtropical trees and shrubs; leaves deciduous, alternate, pinnately compound; flowers in clusters; fruit small, with single seed. *Gumbo-limbo.* **Page 196**

CALTROP FAMILY (Zygophyllaceae): leaves evergreen, opposite, pinnately compound; fruit a capsule; one U.S. species. *Lignumvitae.* **Page 196**

AILANTHUS (QUASSIA) FAMILY (Simaroubaceae): tropical and subtropical trees; leaves evergreen (deciduous in *Ailanthus*), alternate, pinnately compound; fruit winged or thin-fleshed. *Paradise-tree and others.*   **Page 198**

MAHOGANY FAMILY (Meliaceae): shrubs and trees of tropics and subtropics; leaves alternate, pinnately compound, evergreen or deciduous. *West Indies Mahogany, Chinaberry.* **Page 200**

8

SPURGE FAMILY (Euphorbiaceae): a large family of mainly tropical and subtropical herbs, shrubs, and trees with acrid sap. Few native to U.S.; leaves evergreen or tardily deciduous, simple, alternate; flowers in terminal spikes or axillary clusters; fruit a 3-lobed capsule or fleshy drupe. *Oysterwood, Guianaplum, Manchineel.*

Page 200

CASHEW (SUMAC) FAMILY (Anacardiaceae): deciduous or evergreen leaves, alternate, pinnately compound (simple in *American Smoketree*); flower clusters conspicuous. *Sumacs and others.*

Page 202

CYRILLA FAMILY (Cyrillaceae): a small family, with evergreen or tardily deciduous, simple, alternate, smooth-margined leaves; flowers in terminal racemes; fruit a capsule. *Swamp Cyrilla, Buckwheat-tree.* **Page 204**

HOLLY FAMILY (Aquifoliaceae): leaves alternate, simple, usually evergreen with spiny-toothed (occasionally smooth) margins; mostly dioecious; flowers small, greenish white, in axillary clusters; fruit a red or purple drupe. *Hollies.* **Page 206**

BITTERSWEET FAMILY (Celastraceae): leaves simple, opposite or alternate (leafless with spiny twigs in *Canotia*); flowers in stalked, axillary clusters; fruit a dry capsule or a thin-fleshed drupe. *Wahoo, Falsebox.* **Page 208**

MAPLE FAMILY (Aceraceae): leaves deciduous, opposite, usually simple and palmately lobed (pinnately compound in *Boxelder*); flowers small, usually polygamous or dioecious, clustered; fruit double-seeded, each seed with propeller-like wing (samara). *Maples.* **Page 210**

HORSECHESTNUT FAMILY (Hippocastanaceae): leaves deciduous, opposite, palmately compound; showy, tubular flowers in large clusters; fruit a leathery capsule with 1 or 2 large brown seeds. *Buckeyes, Horsechestnuts.* **Page 218**

PAPAYA FAMILY (Caricaceae): leaves large, alternate, simple, palmately lobed; flowers unisexual, yellowish, clustered (staminate clusters elongated, many-flowered; pistillate short-stemmed, few-flowered); fruit large, fleshy, many-seeded; one N.A. species in Florida. *Papaya.* **Page 220**

BUCKTHORN FAMILY (Rhamnaceae): leaves simple, alternate or opposite, deciduous or evergreen; small flowers in clusters; fruit drupaceous or capsular. *Buckthorns, Ceanothus, Leadwood, and others.* **Page 222**

CANELLA (WILD CINNAMON) FAMILY (Canellaceae): leaves evergreen, simple, alternate, smooth margins; small flowers in clusters; fruit a red berry; tropical and subtropical trees, one N.A. species. *Canella.* **Page 226**

SOAPBERRY FAMILY (Sapindaceae): mainly tropical trees, shrubs, and herbs; leaves mostly evergreen, alternate, pinnately compound; flowers small, clustered; fruit fleshy, with one or many seeds or a 3-valved capsule. *Soapberry, Butterbough, and others.* **Page 226**

LINDEN FAMILY (Tiliaceae): leaves deciduous, alternate, simple, toothed, heart-shaped and unequal at base; pale-yellow, fragrant flowers in long-stemmed clusters, attached to a narrow leaflike bract; small, woody, nutlike fruit. *Basswoods* or *Lindens.* **Page 228**

TEA FAMILY (Theaceae): leaves mostly evergreen, alternate, simple, toothed; large, showy flowers; fruit a woody capsule. *Loblolly-bay, Mountain Stewartia, Franklinia.* **Page 230**

CACTUS FAMILY (Cactaceae): typically no leaves; spiny, fleshy trunks and stems; large, showy flowers; fruit a fleshy berry. *Saguaro and other cacti.* **Page 230**

MYRTLE FAMILY (Myrtaceae): leaves evergreen, usually opposite, simple, mostly smooth-margined and aromatic; flowers of most species showy; fruit a berry *(Cajeput-tree, Guava, Eugenias)* or capsule, *Eucalyptus.* **Page 232**

MANGROVE FAMILY (Rhizophoraceae): leaves evergreen, oval, leathery, opposite, smooth-margined; yellow flowers in clusters; fruit cone-shaped, leathery apex perforated by germinating embryo; roots stiltlike; in brackish coastal waters of tropics and subtropics. *Red Mangrove.* **Page 234**

COMBRETUM (WHITE-MANGROVE) FAMILY (Combretaceae): leaves evergreen, simple, alternate (opposite in *White-mangrove)*; small flowers in spikes or heads; fruit leathery, one-seeded. *Button-mangrove, White-mangrove.* **Page 234**

DOGWOOD FAMILY (Cornaceae): leaves deciduous, simple, usually opposite; small, greenish-white flowers in terminal clusters, or in heads surrounded by showy bracts; the fruit is drupaceous. *Dogwoods.* **Page 236**

TUPELO FAMILY (Nyssaceae): leaves deciduous, simple, alternate; small, greenish flowers in clusters; fruit thin-fleshed, ovoid to oblong, the simple seed ridged or winged. *Tupelos.*   **Page 238**

HEATH FAMILY (Ericaceae): leaves evergreen or deciduous, simple, alternate; flowers usually tubular to urn-shaped, solitary or in clusters; fruit fleshy and one-seeded (drupe), many-seeded (berry), or capsular. *Madrones, Rhododendrons, and others.*   **Page 240**

GINSENG FAMILY (Araliaceae): leaves deciduous, alternate, bipinnately compound, toothed; small flowers in large clusters; fruit berry-like; twigs spiny. *Devils-walkingstick.*   **Page 244**

MELASTOME (MEADOW BEAUTY) FAMILY (Melastomataceae): leaves evergreen, simple, opposite; flowers in clusters; fruit berry-like or capsular; mainly tropical species; rare in N.A. *Florida Tetrazygia.*   **Page 244**

MYRSINE FAMILY (Myrsinaceae): leaves evergreen, simple, alternate, smooth-margined; flowers in clusters, fragrant in *Marbleberry;* fruit thin-fleshed, one-seeded; mainly tropical, rare in N.A. *Guiana Rapanea.*   **Page 244**

SAPOTE (SAPODILLA) FAMILY (Sapotaceae): tropical and subtropical trees and shrubs; leaves simple, alternate, smooth-margined, evergreen (deciduous in *Bumelias);* milky sap; inconspicuous flowers in axillary clusters; fruit berry-like. *False-mastic, Willow Bustic, Satinleaf, Wild-dilly.*   **Page 246**

THEOPHRASTA (JOEWOOD) FAMILY (Theophrastaceae): leaves evergreen, alternate, simple, smooth-margined, glandular-dotted; bell-shaped flowers in loose clusters; fruit an orange-red berry; small tropical family. *Joewood.*   **Page 248**

SWEETLEAF FAMILY (Symplocaceae): leaves deciduous, simple, alternate, margins smooth or finely toothed; small flowers in small clusters; fruit thin-fleshed, one-seeded; one N.A. species is limited to South. *Common Sweetleaf.*   **Page 248**

EBONY FAMILY (Ebenaceae): leaves deciduous, simple, alternate, smooth-margined; flowers dioecious (male in loose clusters, female solitary) or polygamous; fruit an orange-red or black edible berry; found mostly in warm climates. *Persimmons.*   **Page 250**

11

SNOWBELL (STORAX) FAMILY (Styracaceae): southern trees; leaves deciduous, simple, alternate, margins smooth to finely toothed, hairy below; bell-shaped flowers in clusters; fruit single-seeded, ovoid (*Bigleaf Snowbell*), or elongated and winged (*Silverbells*). **Page 250**

OLIVE FAMILY (Oleaceae): leaves mostly deciduous, opposite, simple or, in ashes, pinnately compound; flowers perfect, dioecious or polygamous; fruit a dry, single-winged samara, or single-seeded, fleshy. *Ashes and others.* **Page 252**

BORAGE FAMILY (Boraginaceae): leaves evergreen or tardily deciduous, alternate, simple, margins smooth or toothed; showy flowers in clusters; fruit single-seeded and thin-fleshed; mostly herbs. *Bahama Strongbark, Geiger-tree, Anaqua.* **Page 260**

VERBENA FAMILY (Verbenaceae): leaves simple, opposite, entire, evergreen; flowers in clusters, fragrant in *Fiddlewood*; fruit a drupe or capsule; mainly herbs. *Black-mangrove.* **Page 262**

NIGHTSHADE FAMILY (Solanaceae): mostly herbs, a few trees; leaves of single native species (Florida) evergreen, simple, alternate, hairy, smooth-margined; flowers in clusters; fruit berry-like. *Mullein Nightshade.* **Page 262**

BIGNONIA (TRUMPET CREEPER) FAMILY (Bignoniaceae): leaves simple, mostly deciduous, opposite and whorled, or alternate; large flowers in showy clusters or solitary; fruit an elongated or ovoid capsule or berry; mostly tropical trees, shrubs, vines, herbs. *Catalpa, Black-Calabash, Desertwillow.* **Page 264**

HONEYSUCKLE FAMILY (Caprifoliaceae): leaves deciduous, opposite, simple or pinnately compound; flowers in showy clusters; fruits drupaceous; mainly shrubs and herbs of temperate regions, a few trees. *Elders, Viburnums.* **Page 266**

COMPOSITE (SUNFLOWER) FAMILY (Compositae): a very large family of mostly herbs and few shrub or small-tree-sized members; small flowers in compact heads. *Big Sagebrush.* **Page 266**

MADDER FAMILY (Rubiaceae): leaves simple, opposite or whorled, smooth-margined, deciduous or evergreen; flowers tubular, in clusters or globose heads; fruit a capsule or dry drupe. *Buttonbush and others.* **Page 268**

MISCELLANEOUS FAMILIES: Casuarinaceae, Stericuliaceae, Proteaceae, Elaeagnaceae, Moringaceae, and Tamaricaceae. **Page 270**

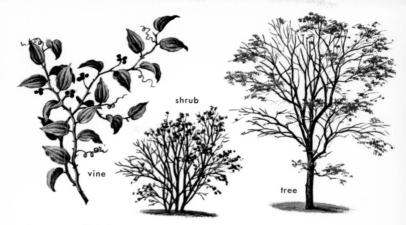

shrub

vine

tree

BASIC FEATURES OF TREES

Trees are woody plants at least 15 feet tall at maturity, with a well-developed crown and a single stem, or trunk, at least several inches in diameter. Shrubs, also woody plants, have several stems growing from a clump and are usually smaller than trees. Vines may have woody stems but do not have a distinct crown of upright branches.

Trees usually develop their typical shapes only when they grow in the open. Owing mainly to competition for light, those that grow in crowded forest conditions have a much greater "clear length" of trunk. Many trees that grow at timberline on high mountains are sprawling. Their irregular and twisted forms are a result of short growing seasons, deep snows, poor soils, and constant buffeting by strong winds. Many tree species have a characteristic shape, however, and with field experience it is possible to recognize them at a considerable distance. Some examples are shown below.

Leaves, flowers, fruits, bark, twigs, and buds are also important identification features. These parts are described and illustrated on the following pages. Although most technical terms are avoided in this book, an acquaintance with some of the most commonly used may be valuable in talking to tree specialists or in using other botanical references.

White Pine Blue Spruce Royal Palm Sugar Maple American Elm Live Oak

LEAVES may be deciduous (shed annually), or they may be evergreen or persistent (remaining on tree one to many years). Most cone-bearing trees and some broad leaved trees are evergreen. Leaf arrangement may be obscure at growing tips, where leaves may not have reached full size. Leaves of some trees bear stipules (not shown), small leaflike appendages at base of petiole.

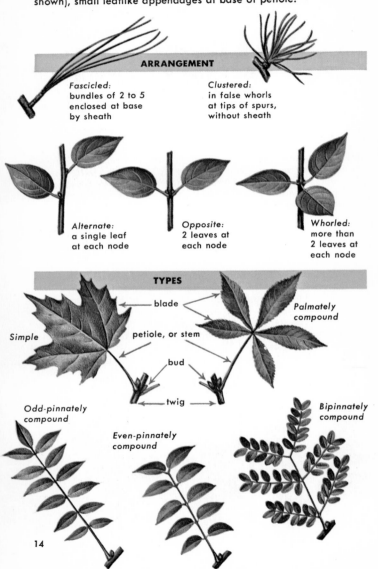

ARRANGEMENT

Fascicled:
bundles of 2 to 5
enclosed at base
by sheath

Clustered:
in false whorls
at tips of spurs,
without sheath

Alternate:
a single leaf
at each node

Opposite:
2 leaves at
each node

Whorled:
more than
2 leaves at
each node

TYPES

blade

Simple

Palmately compound

petiole, or stem

bud

twig

Odd-pinnately compound

Even-pinnately compound

Bipinnately compound

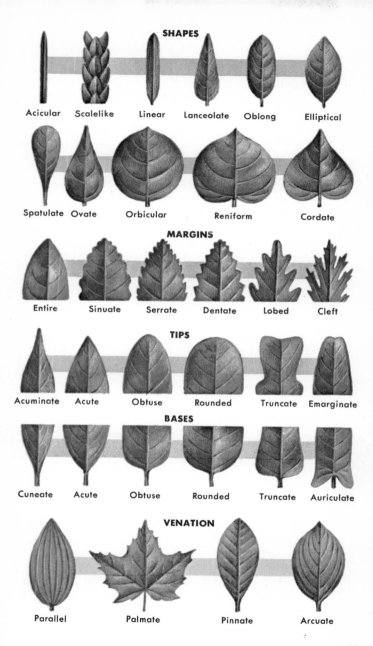

SHAPES

Acicular Scalelike Linear Lanceolate Oblong Elliptical

Spatulate Ovate Orbicular Reniform Cordate

MARGINS

Entire Sinuate Serrate Dentate Lobed Cleft

TIPS

Acuminate Acute Obtuse Rounded Truncate Emarginate

BASES

Cuneate Acute Obtuse Rounded Truncate Auriculate

VENATION

Parallel Palmate Pinnate Arcuate

15

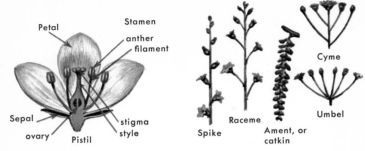

Petal
Stamen
anther
filament
Cyme
Sepal
stigma
style
Umbel
ovary
Pistil
Spike
Raceme
Ament, or
catkin

FLOWERS are a plant's reproductive organs. Those of some trees are small and inconspicuous; others are large and showy. *Complete* flowers have sepals, petals, and the two vital reproductive parts—the pollen-producing stamens (male) and pistils (female) with basal ovary enclosing ovules. *Incomplete* flowers lack one or more of these four parts. *Perfect* flowers have both stamens and pistils; sepals and petals may be present or not. *Imperfect,* or *unisexual,* flowers have either stamens or pistils. *Monoecious* species bear both sexes on the same tree—together in either complete or incomplete flowers, or separately in imperfect or unisexual flowers. *Dioecious* species have staminate and pistillate flowers on different trees. *Polygamous* species bear both perfect and unisexual flowers.

FRUITS bear the seeds. Seeds of gymnosperms are naked. In conifers they are borne in cones at the base of scales; in others a single seed is partly or wholly within a fleshy covering (aril). Angiosperm fruits bear seeds enclosed within the ripened ovary (sometimes including accessory parts). A *simple* fruit originates from a single pistil. Compound fruits are *aggregates* from two or more pistils of the same flower on a common receptacle, or *multiples* from pistils of separate flowers, often in a head.

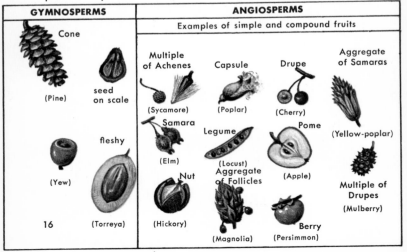

GYMNOSPERMS	ANGIOSPERMS

Examples of simple and compound fruits

Cone

seed on scale

(Pine)

fleshy

(Yew)

16

(Torreya)

Multiple of Achenes

(Sycamore)

Samara

(Elm)

Nut

(Hickory)

Capsule

(Poplar)

Legume

(Locust)
Aggregate of Follicles

(Magnolia)

Drupe

(Cherry)

Pome

(Apple)

Berry

(Persimmon)

Aggregate of Samaras

(Yellow-poplar)

Multiple of Drupes

(Mulberry)

Smooth
Amer.
Beech

Furrowed
Black
Oak

Scaly
White
Pine

Plated
Ponderosa
Pine

Warty
Common
Hackberry

Shaggy
Shagbark
Hickory

Fibrous
Coast
Redwood

BARK often changes in appearance between small, young trees and larger, older specimens of the same species, between the trunk and twigs on the same tree, or even between individuals of the same species growing under different conditions. The bark of some trees is so distinctive that they can be easily identified, however.

Papery
Paper
Birch

TWIGS may be distinctive in color, odor, taste, lenticels (warty tissues for aeration), thorns, or spines, but the most helpful for identification are the position, size, and shape of the buds, leaf scars, vascular bundle scars, and pith. Buds of several types are scaly (or naked), gummy, fragrant, smooth, hairy, or, in some species, submerged beneath leaf scars. Buds are especially useful in identifying species in winter.

Red Maple

Terminal buds: at apex of twig; usually larger than lateral buds

Pseudo-terminal bud: actually a lateral bud located at apex of the twig

American Sycamore

Imbricate scales: overlapping like shingles

Valvate scales: joined along edges; as in clam shell

Red Alder

Lateral buds: along twigs, in axils of previous season's leaves, at leaf scars

Leaf Scars indicate point of attachment of leaf stem. Shape may be distinctive

Pith forms core of twig. It varies in color, texture, and shape in cross section. May be solid,

chambered (open spaces with thin partitions), or diaphragmed (spongy with denser partitions)

pith solid

pith chambered

Black Walnut

FOREST REGIONS occurring in North America are based largely on climatic differences at different latitudes. Each of the major divisions may be divided into smaller areas, also with distinctive groups of trees. Species that have similar needs occur together, so learning these common associations of trees often helps in tree identification.

Variation in temperature, moisture, and soils are the principal factors that determine where trees grow. These climatic variations occur also with changes in altitude, which accounts for the extension in ranges of some northern trees into the southern Appalachians and, similarly, far southward in high western mountain ranges.

The map on the next page shows six basic forest regions. Also shown are the largely treeless regions (grasslands, desert, desert scrub and grass, and tundra).

NORTHERN Forest Region is typified by a short growing season and low temperatures. Far northern tree associations (boreal) consist largely of a few conifers, birches, and willows. To the southeast, especially where this region merges with adjacent areas, milder climates favor more complex mixtures of both cone-bearing and deciduous, broadleaved trees.

Typical cone-bearing trees include White and Black spruces; Balsam Fir; Eastern Hemlock; Eastern White, Red, and Jack pines; Northern White Cedar; Tamarack. The principal broad-leaved trees are Paper, Sweet, and Yellow birches; Sugar Maple; Northern Red and other oaks; Quaking and Bigtooth aspens; American Beech; American Elm; Black Cherry.

SOUTHEASTERN Forest Region occurs mainly on the sandy coastal plain which is relatively dry despite the ample annual rainfall. The pines and broad-leaved trees here are adapted to drier soils than those of the coast and Mississippi Basin.

Shortleaf, Longleaf, Loblolly, and Slash pines, with Baldcypress in swamps and lowlands, are typical cone-bearers. Broad-leaved trees are magnolias; tupelos; Winged and Cedar elms; Sugarberry; Pecan and other hickories; oaks and hollies.

CENTRAL HARDWOOD Forest Region has a variable climate, rich soils, and fairly even precipitation. Much of the original forest cover of the area has been cleared for agriculture and other developments.

Typical trees of the many complex associations include Black Walnut; American Sycamore; Yellow-poplar; Sweetgum; Yellow Buckeye; and a variety of oaks, maples, ashes, hickories, basswoods, and some conifers.

ROCKY MOUNTAIN Forest Region, occurring chiefly on higher mountain slopes, is typified by cold winters and a short but warm growing season. A summer dry period is most pronounced in southern latitudes. Cone-bearing trees predominate.

Typical are Ponderosa, Lodgepole, Western White, Limber, and Pinyon pines; Engelmann and Blue spruces; Subalpine Fir; Douglas-fir; Western Larch; and a number of junipers. Quaking Aspen is the most conspicuous broad-leaved tree.

SUBTROPICAL Forest Region occurs along Florida's tip and the mouth of the Rio Grande in Texas. Tropical forests of broad-leaved, deciduous and evergreen trees occur southward.

Among the trees typical of the Florida subtropics are West Indies Mahogany; several mangroves; Sapodilla; Lignumvitae; and a number of species of palms.

Northern	Subtropical
Southeastern	Rocky Mountain
Central Hardwood	Pacific Coast
Tundra	Desert
Grasslands	Desert scrub and grass

PACIFIC COAST Forest Region from Alaska to northern California has a mild climate and abundant precipitation along the coasts. Here are dense forests, primarily of cone-bearing trees. Some typical coastal species range inland in the Pacific Northwest. Southward and inland the warmer, drier climate favors mixtures of cone-bearing trees on mountain slopes and broad-leaved trees at lower elevations.

Typical cone-bearing trees include Douglas-fir; true firs; Western and Mountain hemlocks; cedars (Western red, Port-Orford, and Alaska); Sugar, Ponderosa, Whitebark, and other pines; Western Larch; Redwood and Giant Sequoia; junipers and cypresses. Among the broad-leaved trees are Black Cottonwood and Quaking Aspen; several oaks; Pacific Dogwood; Bigleaf Maple; Red Alder; and Oregon Ash.

19

GYMNOSPERMS

Gymnosperms bear naked seeds, often on a scale; angiosperm seeds, in contrast, are enclosed by the ovary (p. 66). Most familiar of the gymnosperms are pines, firs, and others of the pine family, but included in the nearly 700 species are the yews and cycads (below), plus the redwood family (p. 50), cedar family (p. 54), the Ginkgo and others (p. 64).

YEW FAMILY (Taxaceae)

Yews and torreyas are small trees and shrubs without cones but with flat, linear evergreen needles. Yews *(Taxus)* include about seven species. Three grow in North America; others in Europe, North Africa, and Asia. English Yew *(T. baccata)* and varieties are widely grown as ornamentals. Of five species of torreyas *(Torreya)*, two grow in North America; others in Japan and China.

PACIFIC (WESTERN) YEW *(Taxus brevifolia)* needles are 0.5 to 1 inch long, dark green above and light green below. Break from twig cleanly; similar Coast Redwood needles (p. 50) tear from twig and have two silvery bands below. Greenish seed, 0.3 of an inch, protrudes from scarlet, gelatinous cup (aril). Reddish-purple bark scales off in thin, irregular patches. Not abundant but widely distributed; grows 20 to 40 feet tall (rarely to 75), 1 to 2 feet in diameter, in moist forests. Florida Yew (*T. floridana*) is a rare, smaller, bushy tree, with short trunk and spreading branches.

CALIFORNIA TORREYA *(Torreya californica)* needles are 1 to 3.5 inches long, with a sharp tip. The plumlike fruit, streaked with purple, is 1 to 1.5 inches long and contains a large, brown seed. Sometimes called California Nutmeg. Bark is gray-brown, fissured to loosely scaly. Grows 30 to 90 feet tall, 1 to 3 feet in diameter, usually along streams. The rare Florida Torreya (*T. taxifolia*), also called Stinking-cedar because of the odor of its leaves, is smaller and has darker fruit.

CYCAD FAMILY (Cycadaceae)

CYCADS of about 100 species in 9 genera are primitive, palmlike plants of warm regions. A cluster of large, pinnate leaves is borne either on an erect trunk or on an underground stem. Staminate and pistillate flowers are in conelike structures on different plants. Four species of *Zamia,* or Coontie, grow in Florida. The Sago Palm (*Cycas revoluta*), from Java, and the slightly larger Fern Palm (*C. circinalis*), from southeastern Asia, East Africa, and the South Pacific islands, are cycads that are grown in southern U.S. as ornamentals.

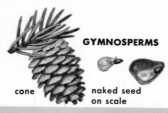

GYMNOSPERMS

cone

naked seed on scale

branchlet with fruit

seed protected by ovary wall

ANGIOSPERMS

COMPARISONS

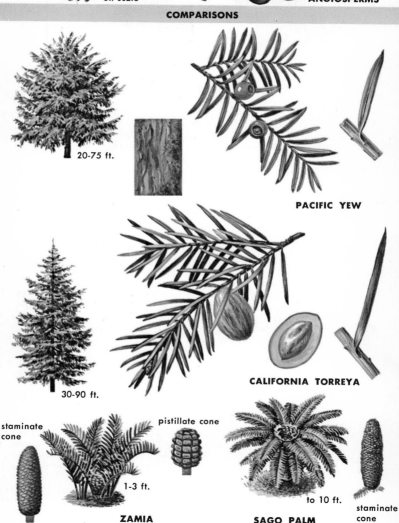

20-75 ft.

PACIFIC YEW

30-90 ft.

CALIFORNIA TORREYA

staminate cone

pistillate cone

1-3 ft.

ZAMIA

to 10 ft.

SAGO PALM

staminate cone

21

PINE FAMILY (Pinaceae)

Pines, larches, spruces, hemlocks, douglas-firs, and true firs represent the pine family in North America. Three other genera occur elsewhere. Needles of pines are in bundles (fascicles); those of larches (p. 36) in brushlike clusters on spur shoots; in other genera (pp. 38-48) needles are produced singly, either growing from persistent woody bases or directly from twigs. Based on wood and other features, about 35 species of North American pines *(Pinus)* are separated into two groups: soft (p. 22-25) and hard (p. 26-35).

SOFT PINES

EASTERN WHITE PINE *(Pinus strobus)* needles, in bundles of 5, are 3 to 5 inches long, soft, and flexible. They remain on the branches one to two years. Fine white lines of stomata are on two surfaces of each needle. The stalked, curved cones are 4 to 8 inches long (usually 5), and their scales lack spines. On young trees the bark is smooth and gray; on mature trunks it is broken into small rectangular blocks. This largest conifer in the Northeast grows 75 to 100 feet tall, 2 to 4 feet in diameter, with a pyramidal crown of whorled, horizontal branches. Prefers moist, sandy loam soils; often forms pure stands.

WESTERN WHITE PINE *(Pinus monticola)* needles resemble those of Eastern White Pine but may remain on the tree for as long as four years, making the crown denser. The stalked cones, which may be slightly curved, are 5 to 15 inches long (usually 8) with spineless scales. The bark resembles that of the Eastern White Pine. Grows 100 to 175 feet tall, 2 to 5 feet in diameter. Crown is open, with pyramidal whorls of horizontal branches.

SUGAR PINE *(Pinus lambertiana)* needles, usually twisted, resemble those of Eastern White Pine but have fine white lines on all surfaces. The stalked, columnar cones, with spineless scales, are 10 to 26 inches long (usually 16), the longest cones of any American conifer. The smooth, gray-green bark of young trees becomes grayish brown to purplish and is broken into scaly ridges. Sugar Pine grows 175 to 200 feet tall and 3 to 5 feet in diameter, the tallest American pine. Its pyramidal crown has whorls of horizontal branches, with several conspicuously longer than others. Its sap contains a sugary substance.

SOFT PINES

needles usually in bundles of 5, occasionally 1-4; sheath is shed

seeds

cones usually stalked and scales without prickles

HARD PINES

needles usually in bundles of 2 or 3, occasionally 5-8; sheath persists

cones usually with thick woody scales armed with prickles

COMPARISONS

EASTERN WHITE PINE

75-100 ft.

WESTERN WHITE PINE

100-175 ft.

175-200 ft.

SUGAR PINE

23

WHITEBARK PINE *(Pinus albicaulis)* has stout, stiff needles, 1 to 2.5 inches long, in bundles of 5. The ovoid cones, about 2.5 inches long, have scales with blunt, triangular tips. Unlike cones of other pines, they disintegrate when mature. The thin bark is scaly and gray to brown. An alpine tree, from altitudes of about 5,000 feet in the north to 10,000 feet or higher in California, Whitebark Pine may grow 50 to 60 feet tall and 1 to 2 feet in diameter. In rocky, exposed places, often a sprawling shrub. It grows slowly, requiring 200 years or longer to mature.

LIMBER PINE *(Pinus flexilis)* is a timberline tree of dry, rocky soil. Similar in appearance to Whitebark Pine. Cones are columnar, 3 to 8 inches long; they do not disintegrate and scales are thickened but not pointed at the ends. Bark scaly, dark brown to black. Limber Pine grows 25 to 50 feet tall and 1 to 2 feet in diameter. Like Whitebark Pine, it becomes twisted and dwarfed when growing in exposed locations.

FOXTAIL PINE *(Pinus balfouriana)* needles are 1 to 2 inches long and remain on the branches 10 to 12 years, giving them a bushy, foxtail appearance. Cones, 3 to 5 inches long, have scales tipped with a small, curved prickle. Bark of mature trees is gray to reddish brown, in scaly plates. Grows in poor, rocky soils at high elevations and is often contorted and windblown. On best sites, may grow 20 to 50 feet tall.

BRISTLECONE PINE *(Pinus aristata)* is a western alpine tree that may grow 20 to 60 feet tall and 1 to 2 feet in diameter. It resembles Foxtail Pine, but its needles remain on the branches even longer. Tiny, gray droplets of resin mark the needles and the 3-inch-long cones. Cone scales are tipped with long, stiff, incurved prickle. A gnarled specimen in California is believed to be 4,000 years old.

Singleleaf

Mexican

Pinyon

Parry

PINYONS have large, edible seeds. All four species are small trees, 20 to 60 feet tall, with rounded crowns. They are typical of dry, rocky, or gravelly soils in semi-arid regions of the West. Needles are 1 to 1.5 inches long; cones round, resinous, and about 2 inches long. Single-leaf Pinyon *(Pinus monophylla)* bears needles singly. Parry Pinyon *(P. quadrifolia)* has needles in 4's. Pinyon *(P. edulis)* needles are in 2's, with smooth margins; Mexican Pinyon *(P. cembroides)* needles are in 2's or 3's, more slender, and have finely toothed margins.

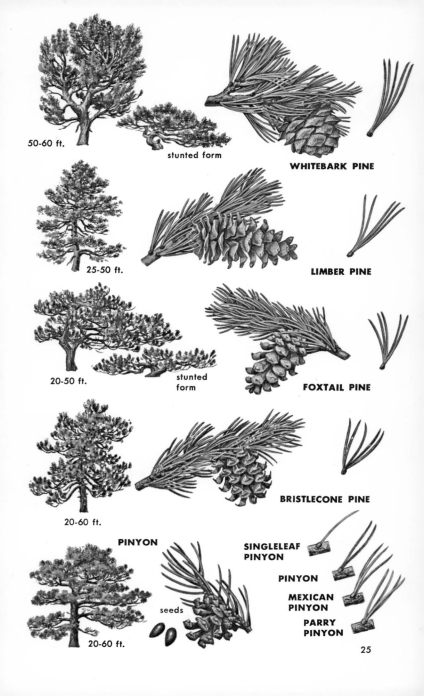

50-60 ft.

stunted form

WHITEBARK PINE

25-50 ft.

LIMBER PINE

20-50 ft.

stunted form

FOXTAIL PINE

20-60 ft.

BRISTLECONE PINE

PINYON

seeds

20-60 ft.

SINGLELEAF PINYON

PINYON

MEXICAN PINYON

PARRY PINYON

25

HARD PINES

JACK PINE *(Pinus banksiana)* needles, in bundles of 2, are 1 to 1.5 inches long, stiff, and dark green. The cones, which may stay on the tree for many years, are 1 to 2 inches long and generally curve toward the tip of the branch. Each scale is tipped with a short, slender prickle. The scaly bark is dark gray to reddish brown. Jack Pine is a small to medium-sized tree, 70 to 80 feet tall and 1 to 1.5 feet in diameter. It is usually ragged in appearance, especially in the poor soils in which it commonly grows.

RED PINE *(Pinus resinosa)* needles, in bundles of 2, are 4 to 6 inches long, slender and flexible, but break readily when doubled. The 1- to 2.5-inch, conical-ovoid cones have unarmed scales. Twigs yellowish at first, changing to reddish brown. On mature trees, bark forms irregular, diamond-shaped, scaly plates. An important timber tree, 50 to 100 feet tall and 2 to 3 feet in diameter, Red Pine has a symmetrically oval crown. Another common name for this tree is Norway Pine, though it is a native of North America.

LODGEPOLE PINE *(Pinus contorta)* needles, in bundles of 2, are 1 to 3 inches long, stiff, and dark green. They stay on the branches for three years or longer. Each scale on the 1- to 2-inch cones is tipped with a stiff prickle. Cones remain closed and attached for years, but open when heated. Areas destroyed by ground fire are often reseeded quickly. The scaly bark is black to straw-colored. Lodgepole Pine grows in sandy soils, in bogs, and at high elevations in a wide range of conditions that also influence tree's form. Coastal form is 25 to 30 feet tall and 1 to 1.5 feet in diameter, with a ragged crown. A slender form of Lodgepole Pine *(P. contorta* var. *latifolia)* is 75 to 80 feet tall and 1 to 3 feet in diameter. In California, it is also called Tamarack Pine.

SHORTLEAF PINE *(Pinus echinata)* has needles 3 to 5 inches long, mostly in bundles of 2; they are dark yellow-green, slender, and flexible. The cones are 1.5 to 2.5 inches long, each scale tipped with a prickle. The bark is dark brown and in irregular, scaly plates. Grows 80 to 100 feet tall and 2 to 3 feet in diameter, with a narrow, pyramidal crown. An important timber tree, it grows in light, dry soils.

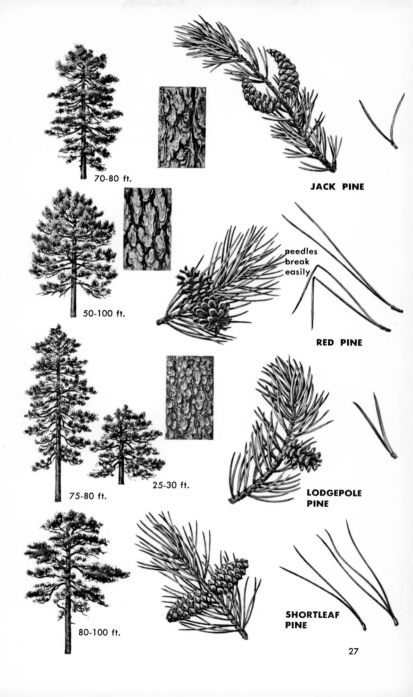

70-80 ft.

JACK PINE

50-100 ft.

needles
break
easily

RED PINE

75-80 ft.   25-30 ft.

**LODGEPOLE
PINE**

80-100 ft.

**SHORTLEAF
PINE**

27

SLASH PINE *(Pinus elliottii)* needles are mostly in bundles of 2. They are stiff, 8 to 10 inches long, and dark blue-green. The scales on the 3- to 6-inch cones are tipped with prickles, and the gray to reddish-brown bark occurs in irregular, scaly plates. Slash Pine grows 80 to 100 feet tall, 2 to 3 feet in diameter, with a dense, rounded crown. It prefers relatively moist soils. Because of its vigor and rapid growth, Slash Pine is used in reforestation not only in southeastern United States but also in Australia, New Zealand, and South Africa.

BISHOP PINE *(Pinus muricata)* needles, in bundles of 2, are thick, rigid, and about 5 inches long. The 2- to 4-inch cones are usually in clusters of 3 to 5, the scales tipped with a stout, spurlike prickle. Bark is dark purple-brown and scaly or ridged. Bishop Pine grows 40 to 50 feet tall, 2 to 3 feet in diameter, with a spreading, pyramidal to flat-topped crown. Found in either dry or swampy soils, in pure stands.

SAND PINE *(Pinus clausa)* has slender, flexible needles, about 3 inches long, in bundles of 2. The ovoid-conical cones are 2 to 3.5 inches long. Bark is reddish brown, forming scaly plates and ridges. The Sand Pine is a scrubby tree, 15 to 20 feet tall, 1 foot in diameter, with a flat-topped crown; generally grows in poor soils.

VIRGINIA PINE *(Pinus virginiana)* is a small tree, 30 to 40 feet tall, 1 to 1.5 feet in diameter, with a ragged, flat-topped crown. Generally grows in poor soils. Needles, in bundles of 2, are 1 to 3 inches long and stiff. The 1.5- to 2.5-inch cones have a prickle on each scale; reddish-brown bark is scaly.

SPRUCE PINE *(Pinus glabra)* needles are 3 inches long, slender, flexible, and in bundles of 2. The globose cones, 2 to 3.5 inches long, have scales tipped with a minute prickle (often deciduous). Bark is dark gray and furrowed. Grows 80 to 100 feet tall and 2 to 2.5 feet in diameter. Generally found with hardwoods.

TABLE-MOUNTAIN PINE *(Pinus pungens)* grows to 60 feet tall, 2 to 3 feet in diameter, with a narrow, round-topped crown. Its needles, in bundles of 2, are 1.5 to 2.5 inches long, rigid, and twisted. Cones are 2.5 to 3.5 inches long, clustered, and persistent.

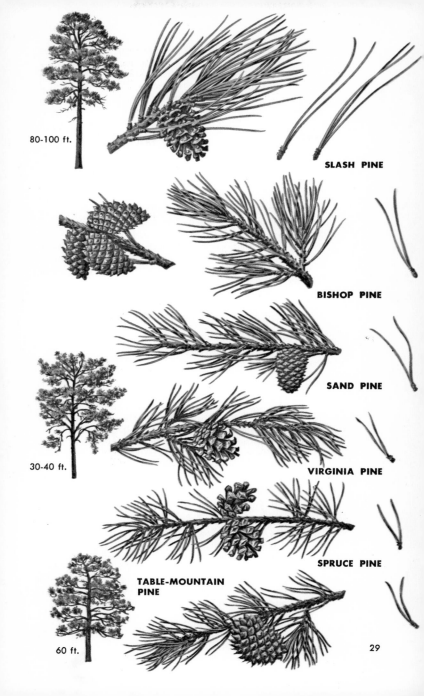

80-100 ft.

SLASH PINE

BISHOP PINE

SAND PINE

30-40 ft.

VIRGINIA PINE

SPRUCE PINE

TABLE-MOUNTAIN PINE

60 ft.

29

PONDEROSA PINE *(Pinus ponderosa)* needles may be in bundles of 3 or in 2's and 3's on same tree. They are 5 to 10 inches long, dark yellow-green, and form tufts near the end of the branches. Cones are oval, 3 to 6 inches long, the scales tipped with a stiff prickle. Bark on young, vigorous trees is dark brown or black. On mature trees, bright reddish-orange bark is in broad, irregular, scaly plates; scales fit together like jigsaw puzzle pieces. Grows 150 to 180 feet tall, 3 to 4 feet in diameter, with a broad, open crown. Ponderosa Pine is common throughout the West and is an important timber tree.

JEFFREY PINE *(Pinus jeffreyi)* resembles Ponderosa Pine but has darker needles that remain on the branches six to nine years, giving the tree a denser crown. Cones are 5 to 15 inches long, with incurved prickles on the scales. Bark of mature trees forms elongated plates. It has a distinctive odor of vanilla or pineapple. Jeffrey Pine is generally smaller than Ponderosa Pine and is found at a higher elevation. Washoe Pine *(P. washoensis)* is a closely related, rare species that grows only on the high eastern slopes of the Sierra Nevada.

KNOBCONE PINE *(Pinus attenuata)* has slender, stiff, yellow-green needles about 5 inches long, in bundles of 3. They cover the branches sparsely. The narrowly conical cones are 4 to 5 inches long, their scales tipped with a prickle and the basal scales knoblike. The cones remain closed and attached in clusters on the branches for long periods but open when heated, like Lodgepole Pine. Occasionally cones are found imbedded in wood as a branch has increased in diameter and grown around them. The gray-brown bark forms scaly ridges. Knobcone Pine grows 40 to 75 feet tall and 1 to 2 feet in diameter, with a sparse, irregular crown. It grows on dry foothill slopes.

COULTER PINE *(Pinus coulteri)* has stiff, blue-green needles, 10 inches long and in bundles of 3. The large, oval cones, heaviest of all pine cones, are 10 inches long, with thick, woody scales, each ending in a long, narrow, sharp, curved claw. Bark is black, scaly, and ridged. Generally found in dry, gravelly, or loamy soil at low elevations. Coulter Pine grows 40 to 80 feet tall and 1 to 3 feet in diameter, with a dense, broadly rounded crown.

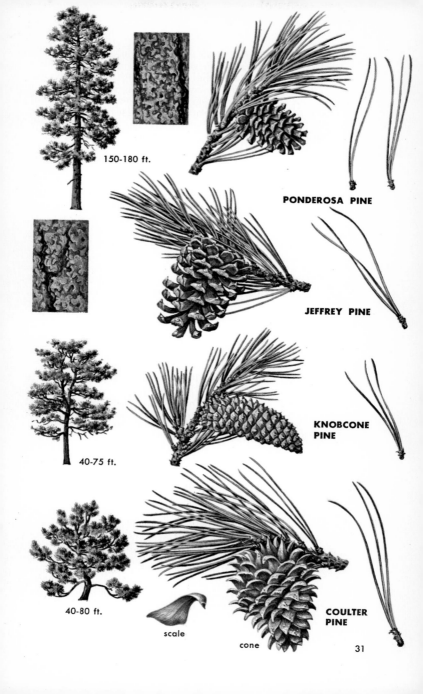

150-180 ft.

PONDEROSA PINE

JEFFREY PINE

40-75 ft.

KNOBCONE PINE

40-80 ft.

scale

cone

COULTER PINE

31

DIGGER PINE *(Pinus sabiniana)* needles, in bundles of 3, are stiff, gray-green, and 8 to 10 inches long. The oval cones are 5 to 8 inches long, with thick, woody scales that end in a broad, triangular claw. The scaly bark is black to reddish brown. Digger Pine grows 40 to 60 feet tall and 1 to 2 feet in diameter; trunk often forked. Common in Sierra foothills. The seeds were part of the diet of California Indians.

APACHE PINE *(Pinus engelmannii)* has 10- to 14-inch, dark-green needles, usually in 3's but sometimes in bundles of 2's or 5's. The oval cones, 4 to 6 inches long, are often asymmetrical at base; scales narrowly flattened at apex and tipped with a tiny prickle. The dark-brown bark is fissured. Grows 50 to 60 feet tall and 1 to 2 feet in diameter.

PITCH PINE *(Pinus rigida)* has stiff, yellow-green needles, 3 to 5 inches long, in 3's. Oval cones are 2 to 3.5 inches long, each scale tipped with a prickle. On mature trees the yellowish-brown bark is in scaly plates. Pitch Pine is a ragged, small to medium-sized tree, 50 to 60 feet tall and 1 to 2 feet in diameter. It generally grows in poor soils but may also have limited occurrence on better sites. Occasionally, and unusual for a conifer, it sprouts from base, especially after fire.

LOBLOLLY PINE *(Pinus taeda)* needles, usually in bundles of 3, are 6 to 9 inches long, slender but stiff, and yellow-green. The oval to conical cones are 2 to 6 inches long, each scale tipped with a prickle. Bark on mature trees is reddish brown and in scaly plates. Loblolly Pine is an important timber tree in southeastern United States. It grows 90 to 100 feet tall and 2 to 3 feet in diameter, with a relatively dense crown.

LONGLEAF PINE *(Pinus palustris)* has bright-green needles, 8 to 18 inches long, in 3's (or 5's in some parts of Gulf region), and tufted near ends of branches. Except early in the growing season, Longleaf Pine can be recognized by its white buds. Young trees grow slowly, forming deep roots and only a tuft of foliage near the ground; this is known as the "grass stage." Mature trees have cones 6 to 10 inches long, each scale tipped with a prickle. Bark is dark reddish brown in rough, scaly plates. Longleaf Pine grows 75 to 120 feet tall and 2 to 2.5 feet in diameter, with an open crown. It is important for lumber, pulp, and resin.

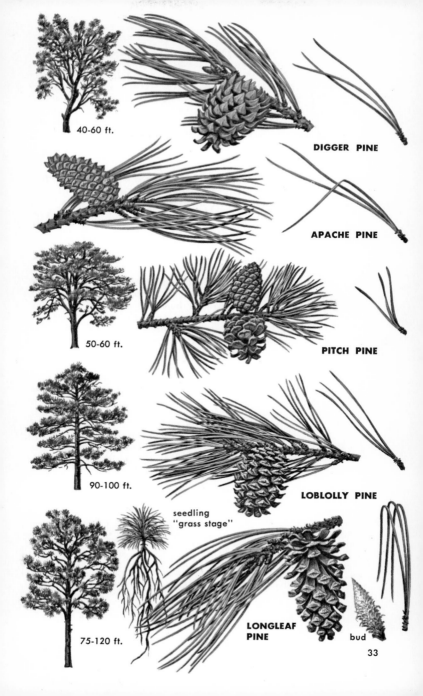

40-60 ft.

DIGGER PINE

APACHE PINE

50-60 ft.

PITCH PINE

90-100 ft.

LOBLOLLY PINE

seedling "grass stage"

75-120 ft.

LONGLEAF PINE

bud

33

MONTEREY PINE *(Pinus radiata)* has slender, flexible, bright blue-green needles, 5 inches long, in bundles of 3 (rarely 2). Oval cones are 3 to 7 inches long, with light-brown, rounded scales tipped with a minute prickle. Bark is brown to black and fissured. Monterey Pine grows 40 to 100 feet tall and 1 to 3 feet in diameter, with a dense crown. Used for reforestation and as a timber tree in New Zealand, Australia, and South Africa, though in its native range the wood has little commercial value.

POND PINE *(Pinus serotina)* needles are 6 to 8 inches long, slender, flexible, and dark yellow-green; in 3's (occasionally 4's). Oval cones, 2 to 2.5 inches long, have flattened scales tipped with a prickle. Bark is dark reddish brown, scaly, and fissured. Usually grows in moist to swampy places. Pond Pine grows to an average height of 25 feet and occasionally 40 to 70 feet, with an open, round-topped crown.

CHIHUAHUA PINE *(Pinus leiophylla* var. *chihuahuana)* needles are in bundles of 3 and, unlike other hard pines, sheaths around bundles are shed. Needles 2 to 4 inches long, slender, and pale green. Cones 1.5 to 2.5 inches long, scales tipped with tiny, deciduous prickles; require three years to mature. Bark is dark reddish brown to black, scaly, and ridged. Grows 40 to 50 feet tall and 1 to 2 feet in diameter.

TORREY PINE *(Pinus torreyana)* needles, in bundles of 5, are 7 to 11 inches long, stiff, and dark green. The nearly round, chocolate-brown cones are 4 to 6 inches long and have scales ending in a thickened triangle with a rigid point. Bark is reddish brown, scaly, and fissured. Torrey Pine, a rare, protected tree, grows 20 to 60 feet tall and 1 to 1.5 feet in diameter, with a dense, bushy, round-topped crown.

SOME INTRODUCED PINES

SCOTCH PINE *(Pinus sylvestris)*, an important European timber tree, is widely planted in North America. Needles are stiff, yellow-green, 1.5 to 3 inches long, in bundles of 2. Cones, 2 to 5 inches long, have flat-topped scales tipped with a slender prickle. Bark scaly, bright orange-red; darker on older trees. Trunk often crooked. To 50 feet tall, 1.5 feet in diameter.

AUSTRIAN PINE *(Pinus nigra)*, a European species grown as an ornamental in North America, has dark-green needles, to 6 inches long, 2 per bundle; resemble those of Red Pine but are darker, heavier, and do not break cleanly. Cones, 2 to 4 inches long, have scales tipped with a tiny prickle. To 100 feet tall and 2.5 feet in diameter; stout branches, pyramidal crown.

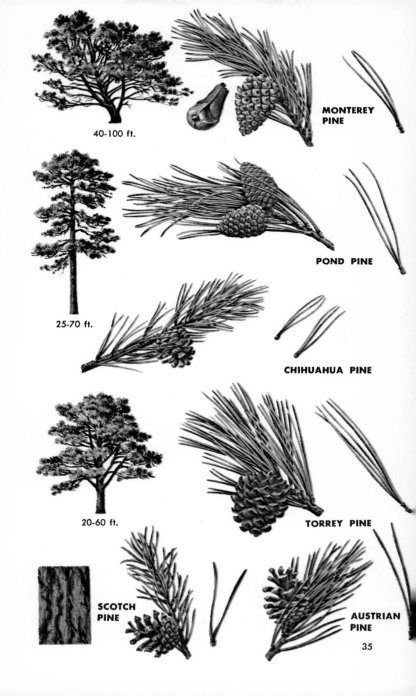

MONTEREY PINE

40-100 ft.

POND PINE

25-70 ft.

CHIHUAHUA PINE

20-60 ft.

TORREY PINE

SCOTCH PINE

AUSTRIAN PINE

35

LARCHES OR TAMARACKS *(Larix)*

Unlike most conifers, larches are deciduous. Their soft, flat needles grow in dense, brushlike clusters at tips of short, spurlike shoots (singly on new growth). Cones, 0.5 to 2 inches long, grow upright and may cling for several years. Needles resemble those of true cedars (see below), but true cedar needles are evergreen and plump in cross section. Ten species grow in cooler parts of Northern Hemisphere—three in Canada and northern United States. European Larch *(L. decidua)* is commonly planted as an ornamental.

TAMARACK *(Larix laricina)* has flat to slightly 3-angled, blue-green needles, 0.8 to 1.3 inches long; turn yellow in fall. Cones ovoid, 0.5 to 0.8 of an inch long, the 12 to 15 scales usually longer than broad and bracts shorter than scales. Bark thin, scaly, and gray to reddish brown. Grows 40 to 80 feet tall, 1 to 2 feet in diameter, usually in moist to boggy soils.

WESTERN LARCH *(Larix occidentalis)* needles are similar to Tamarack's but 1 to 1.8 inches long. Also, the 1- to 1.5-inch cones have more scales, usually broader than long; bracts are longer than scales. Bark thick, reddish brown, and in elongated, scaly plates. Grows to 150 feet tall, 3 to 4 feet in diameter. An important timber tree, it prefers moist mountain slopes but will grow in dry soils.

SUBALPINE LARCH *(Larix lyallii)* needles are somewhat 4-angled in cross section, otherwise resemble those of other larches. New-growth twigs are covered with white, cottony hairs. Cones, 2 inches long, appear bristly because bracts extend well beyond end of scales. Grows 15 to 60 feet tall and a foot in diameter. Branches often crooked and somewhat pendant, forming an irregularly shaped crown. Subalpine Larch is generally found in poor, rocky soils near timberline, often in pure stands.

TRUE CEDARS *(Cedrus spp.)* are not native to North America, but three species, and their varieties, are planted as ornamentals. Foliage resembles that of larches but is evergreen. Cones are upright, 3 to 5 inches long, barrel-shaped, and disintegrate after maturity (two years). Deodar Cedar *(C. deodara)*, from the Himalayas, has needles 1 to 2 inches long, downswept branches and a drooping tip. Both Atlas Cedar *(C. atlantica)*, from northern Africa, and Lebanon Cedar *(C. libani)*, from Asia Minor, have needles to 1.3 inches long, horizontal to uplifted branches, and a rather erect tip. All three grow to 100 feet tall. (See p. 54 for native species known as cedar.)

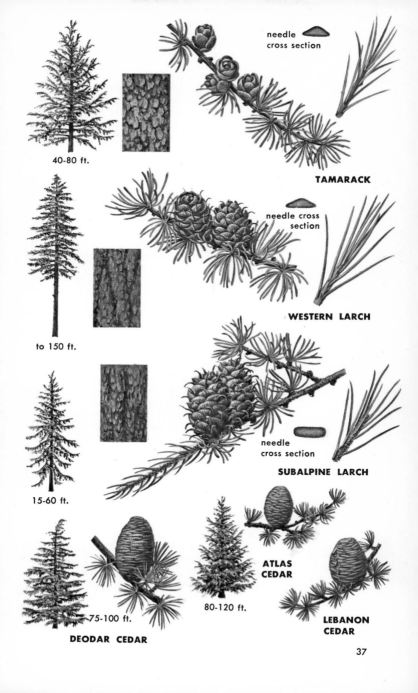

needle
cross section

TAMARACK

needle cross
section

WESTERN LARCH

40-80 ft.

to 150 ft.

15-60 ft.

needle
cross section

SUBALPINE LARCH

**ATLAS
CEDAR**

80-120 ft.

75-100 ft.

DEODAR CEDAR

**LEBANON
CEDAR**

SPRUCES *(Picea)*

Spruces have sessile, rigid, often prickly, evergreen needles that grow singly from persistent, woody, peglike bases. Naked twigs are rough and warty. The pendant cones are composed of thin to light, woody scales. Seeds are ovoid or oblong. Bark typically thin and scaly. Spruces grow best in relatively moist soils, their crowns characteristically dense and spirelike.

About 40 species of spruces grow in the cooler and temperate parts of the Northern Hemisphere. Seven are native to the United States and Canada; others are found in Europe and Asia, most abundantly in China where there are about 18 species. Many spruces are commercially important, especially for paper pulp. Some spruces, including a number of introduced species, are planted as ornamentals.

BLACK SPRUCE *(Picea mariana)* needles are rigid but not prickly, dark green, plump to 4-sided in cross section and 0.3 to 0.5 of an inch long. Numerous short, brown hairs are typical on new growth of the twigs. The ovoid cones, 0.5 to 1 inch long, have brittle scales, rough along the outer margin. They often hang on branches for many years. The outer bark is reddish brown; the inner bark is olive green when freshly exposed. Black Spruce grows best in boggy situations, where it becomes 30 to 40 feet tall and a foot in diameter.

RED SPRUCE *(Picea rubens)* needles are similar to those of Black Spruce but are 0.5 to 0.7 of an inch long. New-growth twigs have only a few short, brown hairs. Cones, which fall soon after maturity, are 1.3 to 2 inches long and have thin, woody scales, generally smooth and rounded on the margin. Bark dark gray to brown; inner bark reddish brown. Red Spruce often grows along the edge of streams and bogs, where it attains a height of 60 to 70 feet and a diameter of 1 to 2 feet.

WHITE SPRUCE *(Picea glauca)* needles are similar to those of Black Spruce but are 1 inch long and generally crowded on the upperside of the branch. New twigs are not hairy. Cones are 1 to 2.5 inches long with thin, woody, but flexible scales, smooth on the rounded margin. Outer bark is ash brown; inner bark silvery when freshly exposed. White Spruce is found along the shores of streams and lakes, growing 75 feet tall and 2 feet in diameter.

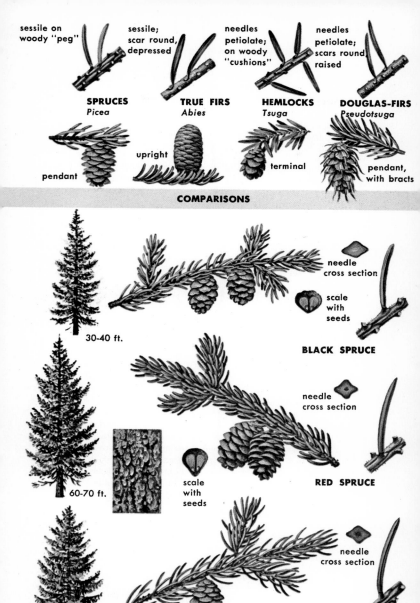

sessile on woody "peg"

sessile; scar round, depressed

needles petiolate; on woody "cushions"

needles petiolate; scars round raised

SPRUCES
Picea

TRUE FIRS
Abies

HEMLOCKS
Tsuga

DOUGLAS-FIRS
Pseudotsuga

pendant

upright

terminal

pendant, with bracts

COMPARISONS

30-40 ft.

needle cross section

scale with seeds

BLACK SPRUCE

60-70 ft.

needle cross section

scale with seeds

RED SPRUCE

75 ft.

needle cross section

WHITE SPRUCE

39

ENGELMANN SPRUCE (*Picea engelmannii*) foliage resembles White Spruce's, but the needles (plump to 4-sided in cross section) are often prickly; twigs minutely hairy. Cones, 1 to 2.5 inches long, are light chestnut-brown, the scales papery thin, stiff, ragged along outer edge. Bark scaly, purplish to reddish brown. Grows 100 to 125 feet tall, 1 to 3 feet in diameter, at high elevations in western mountains. Important timber tree.

BLUE SPRUCE (*Picea pungens*) needles are 1 to 1.5 inches long and stick out in all directions from branch. They are silvery blue, diamond-shaped in cross section, stiff, and very prickly. Twigs not hairy. Cones are similar to those of the Engelmann Spruce but 3.5 inches long. Bark dark gray. A medium-sized tree, 80 to 100 feet tall and 1 to 2 feet in diameter, Blue Spruce occurs on mountain slopes in Rocky Mountain regions, generally near streams. This tree is also widely used as an ornamental.

SITKA SPRUCE (*Picea sitchensis*) needles are flat in cross section, 0.5 to 1.5 inches long, extremely prickly and often silvery. Twigs not hairy. Cones resemble those of Engelmann Spruce, and the scaly bark is silvery to purplish gray. An important timber tree, grows 150 to 200 feet tall and 3 to 6 feet in diameter, occasionally larger. Crown of somewhat drooping branches. Grows at low elevations near sea level.

BREWER SPRUCE (*Picea breweriana*) needles are 0.8 to 1.3 inches long and flattened to 3-sided. The cones, 2 to 5 inches long, have thin, purplish-green scales, smooth and rounded on margin; later turn brown. Bark reddish brown. Brewer Spruce grows at elevation of 5,000 to 7,000 feet and reaches a height of 80 to 100 feet and a diameter of 2 to 3 feet. The long, pendant branches may touch the ground.

SOME INTRODUCED SPRUCES

NORWAY SPRUCE (*Picea abies*), from Europe, is planted in the U.S. and Canada; many varieties. Needles are stiff, dark green, 0.5 to 0.8 of an inch long, flattened to triangular, usually point forward. Cones brown, 4 to 7 inches long. Bark reddish brown. Grows 125 feet tall, 2 feet in diameter.

TIGERTAIL SPRUCE (*Picea polita*), from Orient, has spiny, dark-green, 1-inch needles, curved and often sticking out from stout branches that turn up—like "a tiger's tail." The 3- to 4-inch cones have broad scales with wavy or toothed margins; bark is dark. To 90 feet tall, 2 feet in diameter.

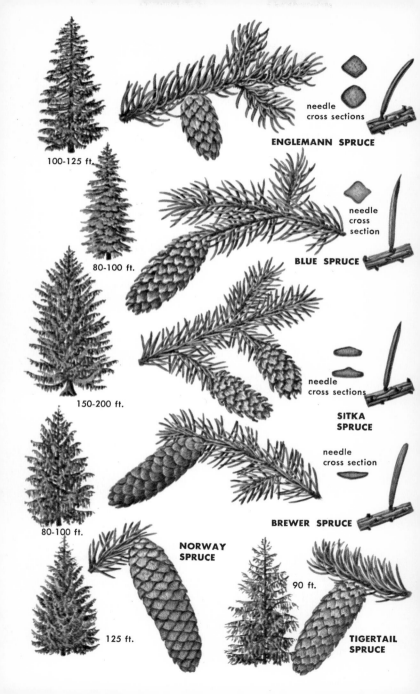

100-125 ft.

needle
cross sections

ENGLEMANN SPRUCE

80-100 ft.

needle
cross
section

BLUE SPRUCE

150-200 ft.

needle
cross sections

**SITKA
SPRUCE**

needle
cross section

80-100 ft.

BREWER SPRUCE

**NORWAY
SPRUCE**

90 ft.

125 ft.

**TIGERTAIL
SPRUCE**

HEMLOCKS *(Tsuga)*

Hemlocks are graceful trees, usually with soft, "lacy" foliage, and a drooping tip. The linear needles, generally flat and variable in length, are narrowed at the base into a short, slender stem. They grow from small, persistent, woody "cushions" on the twigs, as opposed to the more prominent woody "pegs" of spruces. Naked twigs are slightly roughened. The oval to oblong cones hang from the tips of the branchlets. Four of the 10 species are native to temperate North America; others grow in Japan, Taiwan, China, and the Himalayas. Some species are important for lumber and paper pulp, and because of their beauty, a number are planted as ornamentals.

EASTERN HEMLOCK *(Tsuga canadensis)* has flat needles, 0.3 to 0.7 of an inch long, tapering from base to apex, with two white bands of stomata below. Ovoid cones, 0.5 to 0.8 of an inch long, are attached by a short, slender stalk; outer margin of scales is smooth. Bark on mature trees is dark purplish brown, scaly, and deeply furrowed. Eastern Hemlock grows 60 to 75 feet tall and 1 to 3 feet in diameter, with a dense, pyramidal, "lacy" crown. It grows best in cool, moist locations.

CAROLINA HEMLOCK *(Tsuga caroliniana)* needles are flat but not tapered, about 0.8 of an inch long, grooved above, and with two white bands of stomata below. Oblong, stalked cones are 1 to 1.5 inches long. Bark is dark reddish brown, scaly, and furrowed. In rocky locations; to 50 feet tall, 2 feet in diameter.

WESTERN HEMLOCK *(Tsuga heterophylla)* needles resemble those of Eastern Hemlock but are not tapered. The cones, 0.8 to 1 inch long, are attached directly to branchlets, and their scales have wavy margins. Bark is dark reddish brown, scaly, and fissured; inner bark is reddish purple. Western Hemlock may grow 125 to 175 feet tall and 2 to 5 feet in diameter.

MOUNTAIN HEMLOCK *(Tsuga mertensiana)* needles are flat or plump in cross section, 0.8 of an inch long, curved, grooved and ribbed, and densely crowded on branches. Oblong cones, 0.8 to 3 inches long, at first green to purple, but turn brown to black with age. Dark purplish-brown bark. Where protected, Mountain Hemlock may be 75 to 100 feet tall, 2 to 3 feet in diameter; where exposed, may be a sprawling shrub.

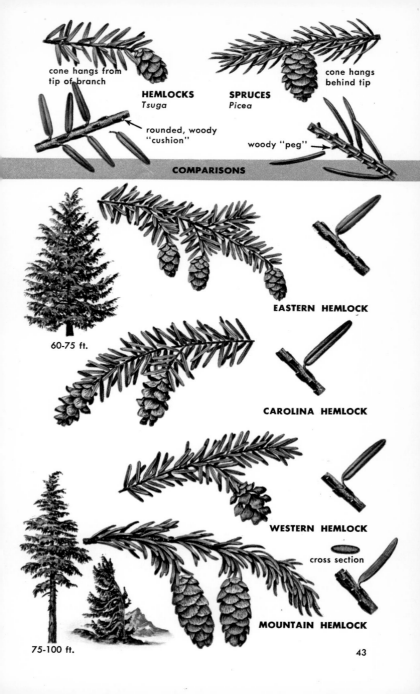

cone hangs from
tip of branch

HEMLOCKS
Tsuga

SPRUCES
Picea

cone hangs
behind tip

rounded, woody
"cushion"

woody "peg"

COMPARISONS

EASTERN HEMLOCK

60-75 ft.

CAROLINA HEMLOCK

WESTERN HEMLOCK

cross section

MOUNTAIN HEMLOCK

75-100 ft.

43

DOUGLAS-FIRS *(Pseudotsuga)*

Douglas-firs have flat, linear needles, with blunt to pointed tips. They grow directly from the branch and are narrowed at the base into a short, slender stem (petiole). When shed, a small, raised scar remains on the twig (see top of p. 39 and p. 45). Buds are ovoid, pointed, and shiny brown. The pendant, oblong-ovoid cones have distinctive 3-pointed bracts. Two douglas-fir species are native to western North America; three others grow in the Orient.

DOUGLAS-FIR *(Pseudotsuga menziesii)* needles, 1 to 1.5 inches long, stick out in all directions from the branches. Cones, 3 to 4 inches long, have 3-pointed bracts extending beyond ends of scales. Buds "cigar-shaped." Bark of young trees smooth and gray, with resin blisters; on mature trees, thick and furrowed, black to reddish brown outside and marbled cream-and-brown beneath. The compact, conical crown has drooping side branches. Forest trees have long, clear trunk. Grows rapidly, attaining greatest size—250 feet tall, 8 feet in diameter—in moist Pacific Coast region. In drier inland areas, grows slower and smaller —100 to 130 feet tall, 2 to 3 feet in diameter. Inland form sometimes considered a separate species; smaller cones, with bracts bent backward. Douglas-fir is an important timber tree; its strong, durable wood has many uses. One of the most distinctive trees in the Pacific Northwest, it is also prized as an ornamental, as a Christmas tree, and for reforestation.

BIGCONE DOUGLAS-FIR *(Pseudotsuga macrocarpa)* resembles Douglas-fir, but foliage is more nearly 2-ranked and the cones, 4 to 6 inches long, have bracts extending only to about the ends of the scales. Bigcone Douglas-fir grows 60 to 75 feet tall and 1 to 2 feet in diameter. Limited in distribution, Bigcone Douglas-fir is of no economic importance and is primarily of botanical interest.

SEEDS OF TREES IN PINE FAMILY

These seeds are borne in pairs at the base of cone scales. They vary in shape and weight; they also differ in how long they can remain dormant and still germinate. Seeds of some species in the pine family are wingless, but most are winged. Wings aid in dispersal by the wind. Cone-hoarding squirrels also help to spread and to plant the seeds. Good seed crops are produced every few years. At such times foresters collect seeds for use in reforestation of burned and logged-off lands. (Also see pp. 52-53 for comparisons of seeds of other conifers.)

leaf scar large, round, and depressed; needle lacks petiole

TRUE FIRS
Abies

leaf scar small, raised; needle with petiole

DOUGLAS-FIRS
Pseudotsuga

COMPARISONS

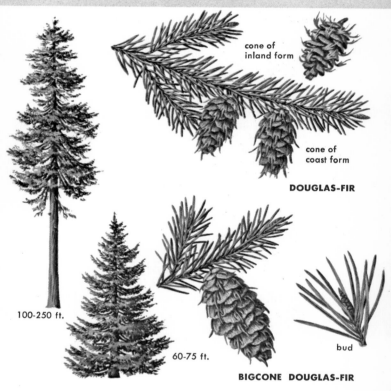

cone of inland form

cone of coast form

DOUGLAS-FIR

100-250 ft.

60-75 ft.

bud

BIGCONE DOUGLAS-FIR

Red Pine

Balsam Fir

Western Larch

Pinyon

Noble Fir

Western Hemlock

Ponderosa Pine

Red Spruce

Douglas-fir

TRUE FIRS (Abies)

True firs have dense, compact, often spirelike crowns. Needles, flat to plump in cross section, grow directly from the branch. They have an expanded base, like a suction cup, and leave a distinctive, round, depressed scar on the twig. Location of silvery lines or bands of stomata on needles is an aid in identifying species. Erect cone disintegrates at maturity leaving a spikelike axis on branch. Buds plump, blunt at apex, often resinous. Though not highly regarded for lumber many true firs are sources of paper pulp. Others are prized as ornamentals or as Christmas trees. About 40 species of true firs grow in various parts of the world; nine are native to the area covered by this book (p. 3).

BALSAM FIR (Abies balsamea) needles are flat, 0.8 to 1.5 inches long, usually blunt or notched at the tip, with 2 silvery bands of stomata on the underside only. Needles 2-ranked except where they are crowded on upperside of the twigs. Cylindrical, purplish cones are 2 to 4 inches long, the bracts shorter than the scales. On young trees, bark has many resin blisters; on mature trees, it is gray to reddish brown and in scaly plates. Balsam Fir may be 40 to 60 feet tall and 1 to 1.5 feet in diameter, attaining its best growth in moist soils near lakes and streams.

FRASER FIR (Abies fraseri) resembles Balsam Fir, but bracts of cones are longer than scales.

GRAND FIR (Abies grandis) needles, 0.5 to 2 inches long, are flat, blunt, or notched at tip, with stomata on the lower surface only. Distinctly 2-ranked and variable in length on lower branches. The cylindrical, greenish cones, 2 to 4 inches long, have bracts shorter than the scales. Bark on mature trees is gray to reddish brown, ridged, and furrowed. Grows 125 to 150 feet tall, 2 to 4 feet in diameter, the crown becoming rounded in older trees.

PACIFIC SILVER FIR (Abies amabilis) needles are flat and uniform in length (1 to 1.5 in.), with stomata on lower surface only; clothe top and sides of twigs. Purple, barrel-shaped cones, 3 to 6 inches long, have bracts shorter than scales. Bark, silvery to ash gray, is smooth, rarely furrowed. Pacific Silver Fir grows 100 to 150 feet tall, 1 to 3 feet in diameter; crown dense, spirelike.

cone upright, disintegrates at maturity

TRUE FIRS
Abies

cone pendant; does not disintegrate at maturity

DOUGLAS-FIRS
Pseudotsuga

COMPARISONS

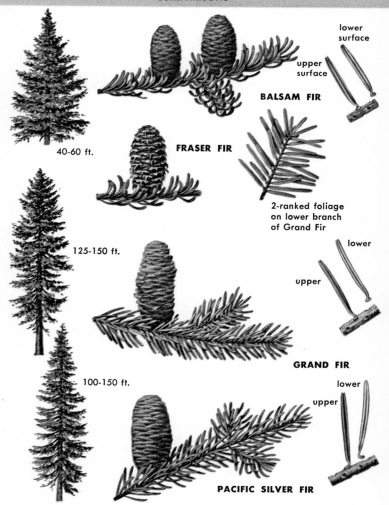

lower surface

upper surface

BALSAM FIR

40-60 ft.

FRASER FIR

2-ranked foliage on lower branch of Grand Fir

125-150 ft.

lower

upper

GRAND FIR

100-150 ft.

lower

upper

PACIFIC SILVER FIR

47

WHITE FIR *(Abies concolor)* has bluish-green needles that are 2 to 3 inches in length. They are flat, blunt to pointed, loosely 2-ranked, with stomata on both surfaces. The oblong, olive-green to purple cones are 3 to 5 inches long, their bracts shorter than their scales. The dark-gray bark is heavily ridged. White Fir grows 125 to 150 feet tall and 2 to 4 feet in diameter, with a dome-shaped crown. It occurs at low elevations, usually in drier soils than other firs.

BRISTLECONE FIR *(Abies bracteata)* has flat, often curved needles, 1.5 to 2.5 inches long, with stomata on lower surface only. Oval, purple-brown cones, 3 to 4 inches long, appear bristly due to long, slender bracts. Bark reddish brown. Bristlecone Fir is usually small but may grow 150 feet tall and 3 feet in diameter. The sharp spire of its crown is one of this tree's distinctive features.

NOBLE FIR *(Abies procera)* has 1- to 1.5-inch needles, flat on lower branches and plump to 4-angled on upper branches; on topmost branches erect and crowded on upper side. Needles silvery, stomata occurring on all surfaces. Cylindrical cones, 4 to 6 inches long, are "shingled" with long, reflexed greenish-brown bracts. Bark dark gray, in small, rectangular blocks. Grows 100 to 150 feet tall, 3 to 5 feet in diameter, with a dense, domelike crown. Noble Fir prefers deep, moist soils, at 2,000 to 5,000 feet.

CALIFORNIA RED FIR *(Abies magnifica)* needles resemble Noble Fir's, but the cones are 6 to 9 inches long, cylindrical to barrel-shaped, purple, with bracts shorter than the scales. Outer bark is reddish brown; inner bark reddish purple. Grows 100 to 150 feet tall, 2 to 4 feet in diameter, with a spirelike crown. California Red Fir grows between elevations of 5,000 and 10,000 feet, reaching its maximum size in moist, well-drained soils. A variety, Shasta Red Fir *(A. magnifica shastensis)*, has cones with reflexed bracts that are longer than the scales.

SUBALPINE FIR *(Abies lasiocarpa)* needles are flat, 1 to 1.8 inches long, with silvery lines of stomata on both surfaces. Cones, with bracts shorter than scales, are 2 to 4 inches long, purple, and cylindrical. Bark on mature trees is gray-brown, scaly, and furrowed. At timberline, often twisted and contorted; elsewhere grows 40 to 100 feet tall and 1 to 2 feet in diameter, with a compact, spirelike crown.

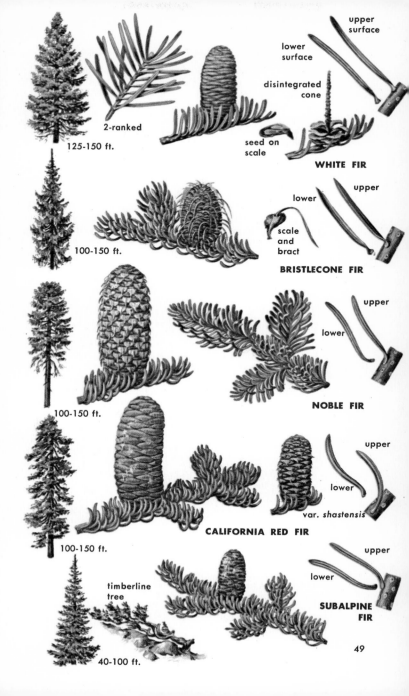

125-150 ft.

2-ranked

upper surface

lower surface

disintegrated cone

seed on scale

WHITE FIR

100-150 ft.

upper

lower

scale and bract

BRISTLECONE FIR

100-150 ft.

upper

lower

NOBLE FIR

100-150 ft.

upper

lower

var. *shastensis*

CALIFORNIA RED FIR

40-100 ft.

timberline tree

upper

lower

SUBALPINE FIR

49

REDWOOD FAMILY (Taxodiaceae)

About 40 species of sequoias (Sequoia) flourished in Northern Hemisphere forests some 60 million years ago. Only two species survive. Both are evergreen trees found principally in California; both have a high resistance to fire, insects, and disease, which accounts largely for their great age. Baldcypresses (Taxodium) are the only other native North American members of the redwood family. Other genera occur in Asia.

GIANT SEQUOIA (Sequoia gigantea) foliage is blue-green; leaves awl-like, 0.2 of an inch long (at ends of branches lance-shaped, 0.5 of an inch long). The egg-shaped cones, 2 to 3.5 inches long and with 24 to 40 woody, wedge-shaped, roughly flattened scales, reach full size in one season. Seeds do not mature until second season. Bark is fibrous, reddish brown, and furrowed; it may be 2 feet thick at base of columnar trunk of large trees. Young trees have a tapered trunk. Limited to groves on west side of Sierra Nevada, between 4,000 and 8,000 feet. The General Sherman Tree, in Sequoia National Park, is 272 feet tall, has an average basal diameter of 30.7 feet, and is estimated to be 3,800 years old. Placed in separate genus, Sequoiadendron, by some botanists.

REDWOOD (Sequoia sempervirens) needles are flat, 0.5 to 1 inch long, with a pointed tip; base extends down twig. Foliage resembles Pacific Yew's (p. 21), but Redwood needles tear rather than break from the branch and have two prominent, silvery bands on their underside. The cones are 0.8 to 1 inch long and have 15 to 20 scales; they mature in one season. Seeds do not germinate well, but the tree reproduces readily by sprouts from the stump, uncommon in conifers. The fibrous, reddish-brown bark is 3 to 10 inches thick. Commonly grows 200 to 275 feet tall, 8 to 10 feet in diameter, with a narrow, conical crown; exceptional specimens have exceeded 350 feet.

INTRODUCED RELATIVES OF SEQUOIA

JAPANESE CEDAR, SUGI, OR CRYPTOMERIA (Cryptomeria japonica) is a common and highly important evergreen tree native to Japan. Grown as an ornamental in parts of U.S. and southern Canada. The foliage resembles the Giant Sequoia's, and the oval, bristly cones are 0.8 to 1 inch long.

METASEQUOIA OR DAWN REDWOOD (Metasequoia glyptostroboides) was thought to be extinct until living specimens were found in an isolated valley in central China in 1948. The foliage resembles the Redwood's, but it is deciduous and the linear needles are somewhat longer.

REDWOOD
Sequoia sempervirens
p. 50

needles tear from branch

silvery bands on underside

PACIFIC YEW
Taxus brevifolia
p. 20

needles break from branch

underside greenish

COMPARISONS

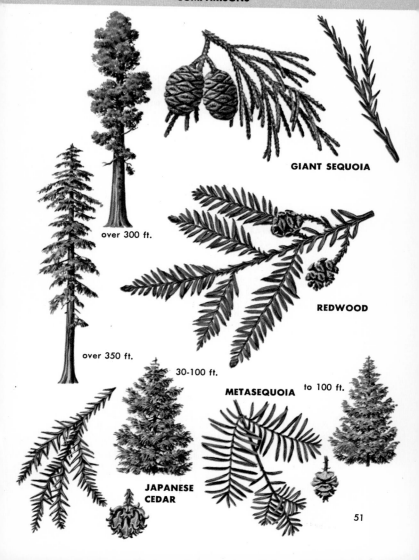

GIANT SEQUOIA

over 300 ft.

REDWOOD

over 350 ft.

30-100 ft.

METASEQUOIA

to 100 ft.

JAPANESE CEDAR

51

BALDCYPRESSES (*Taxodium*)

Like the redwoods (p. 51), baldcypresses are of ancient lineage, attain large size, and reach venerable age. There are only two species, found in southern United States and Mexico.

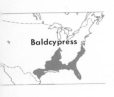

BALDCYPRESS (*Taxodium distichum*) has yellow-green 2-ranked, linear needles 0.5 to 0.8 of an inch long on lateral branchlets; they turn brown before falling with the branchlets in autumn. The tree also has shorter scalelike foliage, usually on fertile branchlets. Cones nearly round, 0.8 to 1 inch in diameter, the surface wrinkled; mature in one season, then usually disintegrate. Bark ash gray to reddish brown, fibrous or scaly. Baldcypress grows 100 to 125 feet tall and 3 to 5 feet in diameter. Trunk swollen, fluted, tapered; crown pyramidal to irregular. Typical of swamplands of southeastern U.S., but not confined to that environment. Branches often draped with Spanish Moss. Woody "knees," from a few inches to several feet tall, protrude above water from shallow, wide-spreading root system.

Pondcypress (*T. distichum* var. *nutans*) is a smaller variety of Baldcypress. Its branches are horizontal or ascending, and the shorter foliage is mostly awl-like and closely appressed to the slender twigs.

MONTEZUMA BALDCYPRESS (*Taxodium mucronatum*) resembles Baldcypress but has slightly larger cones and lacks "knees." Except in colder parts of range essentially an evergreen, as new needles develop before older needles drop. Not a swamp species, but needs ample moisture. Seeds germinate only in water or wet soil. Usually in small groups, or as single trees above 1,000 feet. Mexico's national tree, the largest and most famous is the Tule Cypress in Santa Maria del Tule, near Oaxaca. Although only 140 feet tall, this giant is between 35 and 40 feet in diameter, and its age has been estimated variously at from 2,000 to 5,000 years.

SEED COMPARISONS OF CONIFERS

Redwood and cypress trees bear from 1 to about 20 seeds on each cone scale. Each seed usually has two narrow, lateral wings. Juniper seeds are wingless; Baldcypress seeds have ridges rather than wings and are spread by water. Giant Sequoia seeds range from about 3,000 to more than 8,000 per ounce, yet each has the potential to become the largest of all living things.

Trees of the yew family do not bear cones. They produce single, relatively large seeds, either fully or partly enclosed by a fleshy covering, or aril. (See pp. 44-45.)

COMPARISONS

leaves 2-ranked, deciduous; cones round, disintegrate

needle clusters on spur shoots; deciduous; cones oblong, persist

BALDCYPRESS
Taxodium

LARCHES
Larix

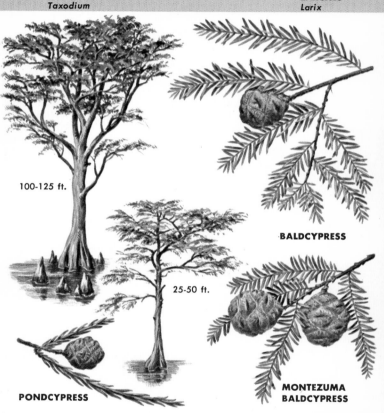

100-125 ft.

25-50 ft.

BALDCYPRESS

PONDCYPRESS

MONTEZUMA
BALDCYPRESS

CYPRESS FAMILY

Western
Redcedar

Incense
Cedar

Common
Juniper

Port-Orford-
Cedar

REDWOOD FAMILY

Redwood

Giant
Sequoia

Baldcypress

YEW FAMILY

Pacific
Yew

California
Torreya

53

CEDAR OR CYPRESS FAMILY (Cupressaceae)

Cedar is the common name given trees of various genera in several families. Most familiar are native American species of the genera *Libocedrus, Thuja, Chamaecyparis* (pp. 54–57) and several junipers (pp. 60–64). All, together with cypresses (p. 58), also in this family, have scalelike foliage on flattened or rounded branchlets. Species in the genus *Cedrus* (p. 36) of the pine family and *Cryptomeria* (p. 50) of the redwood family are also called cedar. The wood of most trees known as cedar is aromatic.

INCENSE-CEDAR *(Libocedrus decurrens)* has flattened branchlets covered with elongated (0.1 to 0.5 of an inch) closely overlapping, lustrous, dark-green scales in whorls of 4. The oblong cones, 0.8 to 1.5 inches long, are at first bright green, turning brown and opening wide when mature. They hang from the tips of the branchlets. On mature trees, the bark is dark brown, fibrous, deeply and irregularly furrowed. Young trees have a dense, conical crown; in older trees, which may grow 100 to 150 feet tall and 3 to 4 feet in diameter, crown becomes rounded.

NORTHERN WHITE-CEDAR *(Thuja occidentalis)* has flattened branchlets clothed by alternate pairs (at right angles to the pairs above and below) of closely overlapping, yellowish-green, aromatic scales, 0.1 to 0.3 of an inch long and glandular below. Oblong cones, 0.3 to 0.5 of an inch long, stand erect on branchlets; fibrous, gray to reddish-brown bark is ridged and furrowed. Typical of limestone soils but common also in moist or boggy situations. Usually has a compact, conical crown and may grow 40 to 50 feet tall, 2 to 3 feet in diameter.

WESTERN REDCEDAR *(Thuja plicata)* foliage is similar to Northern White-cedar's but a darker, more lustrous green. The cones, similar in size to those of Northern White-cedar, have a small spine just below tip of outer scales. Dark reddish-brown bark is fibrous, shreddy, and vertically ridged. In moist bottomland soils, this tree reaches its largest size—150 to 200 feet tall and 3 to 8 feet in diameter. The downswept branches that form the dense crown turn up at the ends; they look like giant fern fronds. Because of its durable, straight-grained wood, Western Redcedar is an important timber tree.

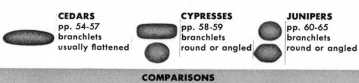

CEDARS
pp. 54-57
branchlets
usually flattened

CYPRESSES
pp. 58-59
branchlets
round or angled

JUNIPERS
pp. 60-65
branchlets
round or angled

COMPARISONS

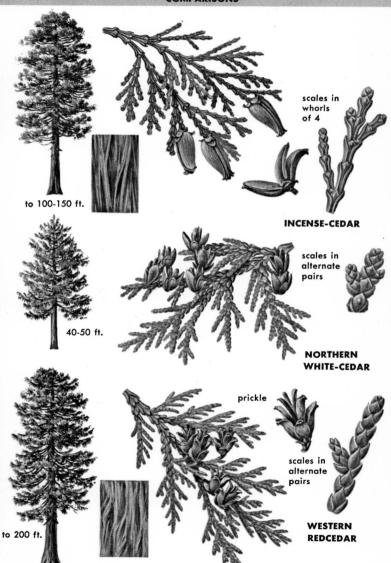

to 100-150 ft.

scales in whorls of 4

INCENSE-CEDAR

40-50 ft.

scales in alternate pairs

NORTHERN WHITE-CEDAR

to 200 ft.

prickle

scales in alternate pairs

WESTERN REDCEDAR

PORT-ORFORD-CEDAR *(Chamaecyparis lawsoniana)* has flattened branchlets with closely overlapping, lustrous, dark-green scales, 0.1 of an inch long, in alternate pairs. Foliage similar to Western Redcedar's, but the smaller scales are marked on underside by stomata in conspicuous silvery X's. Round cones, 0.3 of an inch in diameter, have several wedge-shaped scales, each with a small, curved point in the center. At first bright green, cones turn brown at maturity. Bark on mature trunks is silver-brown, fibrous, and vertically ridged. Grows 140 to 180 feet tall and 4 to 6 feet in diameter, with a dense crown of short, somewhat pendant branches. An important timber tree and also planted as an ornamental, with several varieties developed especially for this purpose. Port-Orford-Cedar is often called Lawson Cypress.

ALASKA-CEDAR *(Chamaecyparis nootkatensis)* has scale-like, yellow-green foliage without silvery X's on underside and with a rougher texture (scales loose at ends) than Port-Orford-Cedar's. The cones resemble those of Port-Orford-Cedar but mature in two seasons and point in center of cone scales is usually erect. On mature trees, gray, shaggy bark is in thin, elongated, vertical scales loose at the ends. A medium-sized tree, 70 to 100 feet tall and 2 to 3 feet in diameter, the drooping branches give Alaska-cedar a "wilted" appearance. Lemon-yellow wood used for interior finish.

ATLANTIC WHITE-CEDAR *(Chamaecyparis thyoides)* has small, bluish-green scales, 0.06 to 0.1 of an inch long. The branchlets are not conspicuously flattened. The cones, 0.3 of an inch in diameter, are somewhat fleshy and wrinkled (raisin-like). On mature trees, the thin bark is ash gray to reddish brown. Usually grows in coastal fresh-water swamps or bogs. It may be 80 to 85 feet tall and 1 to 1.5 feet in diameter, with a crown of short, horizontal branches.

SOME INTRODUCED "CEDARS"

CHINESE, OR ORIENTAL, ARBORVITAE *(Thuja orientalis)* has foliage like American trees in the same genus (p. 55). Oblong cones, 0.5 to 1 inch long, have curved, hornlike projections near scale ends. Native to China and Taiwan; numerous varieties. May reach 60 feet.

HIBA ARBORVITAE *(Thujopsis dolobrata)* scales are nearly 0.3 of an inch long, lustrous dark green above and with silvery patches of stomata below. Cones are ovoid but flat-topped. Native to Japan, several varieties are grown in U.S. To 50 feet tall.

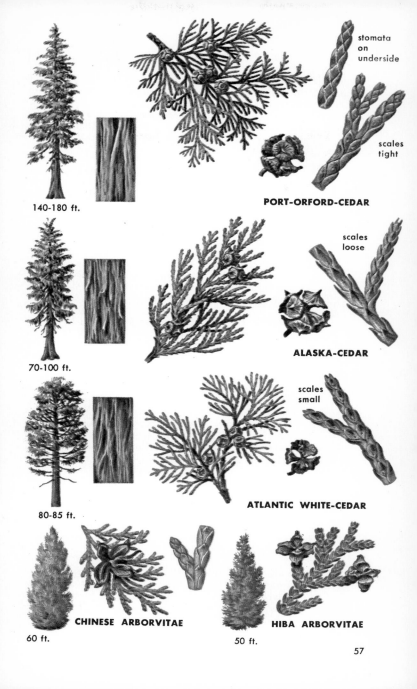

stomata on underside

scales tight

140-180 ft.

PORT-ORFORD-CEDAR

scales loose

70-100 ft.

ALASKA-CEDAR

scales small

80-85 ft.

ATLANTIC WHITE-CEDAR

CHINESE ARBORVITAE

60 ft.

HIBA ARBORVITAE

50 ft.

57

CYPRESSES (Cupressus)

Cypresses are evergreen trees or shrubs with round to 4-sided branchlets clothed with small, closely overlapping, alternate pairs of scalelike foliage; surface of scales often glandular. The cones, 0.5 to 1.5 inches in diameter, are composed of woody, wedge-shaped scales. All species of cypress native to the United States occur in the West. A number of these, as well as some foreign species, are cultivated as ornamentals.

Monterey Cypress

MONTEREY CYPRESS (Cupressus macrocarpa) has dark blue-green foliage without glandular pits; woody cones 1 to 1.5 inches in diameter. It grows 20 to 70 feet tall and 3 to 4 feet in diameter, with dark-brown to light-gray, scaly, ridged bark. In the Monterey Bay region of California, this picturesque tree occurs on rocky headlands where it is often misshapen by the buffeting of high winds. Old trees have broad, flat-topped crowns with stout branches. Crowns of young trees growing in sheltered places are narrower, bushy, and pyramidal. This tree is extensively planted as an ornamental or for a windbreak.

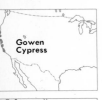
Gowen Cypress

GOWEN CYPRESS (Cupressus goveniana) has dark-green, nonglandular foliage, and cones 0.5 to 0.8 of an inch in diameter. It is a many-stemmed shrub or small tree, to 25 feet tall and 1.5 feet in diameter, with reddish-brown, scaly, ridged bark. Usually grows in dry, alkaline soils. (Sargent Cypress, C. sargentii, is a synonym of this species in Check List.)

MacNab Cypress

MACNAB CYPRESS (Cupressus macnabiana) has light-green foliage with glandular pits. Cones, 0.5 to 0.8 of an inch in diameter, have long projections on scales. Bark reddish brown, fibrous, often with a purplish tinge. MacNab Cypress, often a shrub, may be a small tree to 40 feet tall and 3 feet in diameter. Modoc Cypress (C. bakeri) is similar, more northern.

Tecate Cypress

TECATE CYPRESS (Cupressus guadalupensis) has blue-green, obscurely glandular foliage and cones 0.8 to 1.5 inches in diameter. The purplish to reddish-brown bark sheds in scales or strips. To 20 or 25 feet tall, 2 to 3 feet in diameter.

Arizona Cypress

ARIZONA CYPRESS (Cupressus arizonica) has gray-green, generally glandless foliage; cones are 0.8 to 1 inch in diameter. Mature trees have brown, fibrous bark. In protected sites, grows 60 feet tall and 2 feet in diameter, with a dense, conical crown.

BALDCYPRESS

large woody cones; needle-like foliage deciduous with lateral branchlets

CYPRESS

large woody cones; scalelike, evergreen foliage on plump or angled branchlets

CHAMAECYPARIS

small woody cones; scalelike evergreen foliage on flattened branchlets

JUNIPER

small fleshy cones; scalelike evergreen foliage on plump or angled branchlets

20-70 ft.

MONTEREY CYPRESS

GOWEN CYPRESS

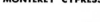

MACNAB CYPRESS

TECATE CYPRESS

ARIZONA CYPRESS

to 60 ft.

59

JUNIPERS *(Juniperus)*

About 70 species of evergreen trees and shrubs. They are widely distributed in the Northern Hemisphere, with 13 species native to the United States. Several are called "cedars." Junipers usually grow in dry, rocky soils. Their foliage is either scalelike and variously glandular, covering the rounded or 4-sided branchlets in closely overlapping, alternate pairs (occasionally 3's), or is awl-like and pointed outward. In some cases both kinds of foliage are found on the same tree. The semi-fleshy, bluish or reddish-brown cones are often called "juniper berries." They are 0.2 of an inch in diameter, covered with a gray, waxy substance, and reach maturity in from one to three seasons.

ROCKY MOUNTAIN JUNIPER *(Juniperus scopulorum)* has scalelike, obscurely glandular foliage about 0.1 inch long covering the rounded to 4-sided branchlets in closely overlapping, alternate pairs. On new growth, the foliage is pointed and awl-like. The fleshy cones, 0.2 inch in diameter, are blue with a gray, waxy covering; they mature in two seasons. Rocky Mountain Juniper grows 30 to 40 feet tall and 1 to 3 feet in diameter, with a short, stout, often divided trunk and a bushy crown of horizontal or ascending branches. Its gray-brown to reddish-brown bark is broken into narrow, flat, interlacing ridges with shreddy scales on the surface. Rocky Mountain Juniper is found widely throughout the Rocky Mountain region and, unusually, in a localized dry area of the Puget Sound region noted for its moist climate.

WESTERN JUNIPER *(Juniperus occidentalis)* resembles Rocky Mountain Juniper, but the foliage is conspicuously glandular, occurring both in pairs and in 3's. Also the bark is cinnamon brown and divided into large, irregular, scaly plates. A small tree, 20 to 60 feet tall and 1 to 3 feet in diameter, with a short, twisted trunk and a broad crown of stout, horizontal to ascending branches. Found on rocky slopes. Ashe Juniper *(J. ashei)* resembles Western Juniper but has less conspicuously glandular foliage and is more southern in distribution.

ONE-SEED JUNIPER *(Juniperus monosperma)* foliage is commonly glandular. The cones resemble those of Western Juniper but usually contain only one seed. Common on semi-arid, rocky soils. Usually grows as a much-branched shrub on very poor sites. In suitable locations, grows 20 to 30 feet tall and 1 to 3 feet in diameter, with a short, often twisted trunk and an open crown of stout branches.

JUNIPER

cones
fleshy
about 0.2 in.
in diameter

CYPRESS

cones woody,
0.5-1.5 in.
in diameter

COMPARISONS

30-40 ft.

ROCKY MOUNTAIN JUNIPER

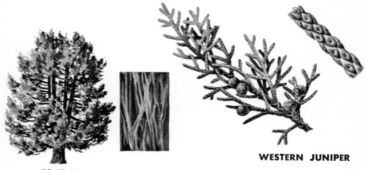

20-60 ft.

WESTERN JUNIPER

to 30 ft.

ONE-SEED JUNIPER

61

UTAH JUNIPER *(Juniperus osteosperma)* has scale-like, yellow-green, usually glandular foliage. Its oblong cones, 0.2 to 0.3 of an inch long, are reddish brown beneath their gray, waxy covering; mature in two seasons. The gray bark is broken into thin, fibrous, elongated scales. Grows to 20 feet tall and 1.5 feet in diameter, with a short, twisted trunk and slender, ascending branches that form a broad, open crown. California Juniper *(J. californica)* resembles Utah Juniper, but foliage is in 3's, not pairs.

ALLIGATOR JUNIPER *(Juniperus deppeana)* has blue-green, occasionally glandular, scalelike foliage. Its cones resemble Utah Juniper's. On mature trees, the reddish-brown bark may be 4 inches thick and divided by deep fissures into scaly squares, 1 to 2 inches long, like an alligator's hide. The trunk is short, and the tree's slender branches form a pyramidal or round-topped crown. Alligator Juniper may grow 50 to 60 feet tall and 3 to 5 feet in diameter.

COMMON JUNIPER *(Juniperus communis)* has lanceolate, sharp-pointed, concave needles, 0.3 to 0.5 of an inch long, marked with silvery bands of stomata above. They grow in whorls of 3. The cones, 0.2 inch in diameter, are blue beneath their gray, waxy covering; mature in three seasons. A sprawling shrub and very rarely a small tree, it usually grows on rocky soils. Common Juniper is widely distributed in the Northern Hemisphere. Some of the many varieties of this species are planted as ornamentals.

PINCHOT JUNIPER *(Juniperus pinchotii)* has dark yellow-green, conspicuously glandular, scalelike foliage. The scales, usually in 3's, are 0.1 inch long. Red cones, 0.2 of an inch in diameter, mature in one season. Light-brown bark has distinctive long, narrow, thin scales. To 20 feet tall and a foot in diameter, with stout, wide-spreading branches.

DROOPING JUNIPER *(Juniperus flaccida)* foliage may or may not have glands. The scales are 0.1 inch long, sometimes longer on young, rapidly growing branchlets and somewhat spreading at the apex. Dull, reddish-brown cones, 0.5 of an inch in diameter, are covered with a waxy bloom. Bark is cinnamon brown with thin, narrow scales. Drooping Juniper grows 30 feet tall and 1 foot in diameter. The wide-spreading crown of hanging branchlets give the tree a "weeping" appearance that is unique among the junipers.

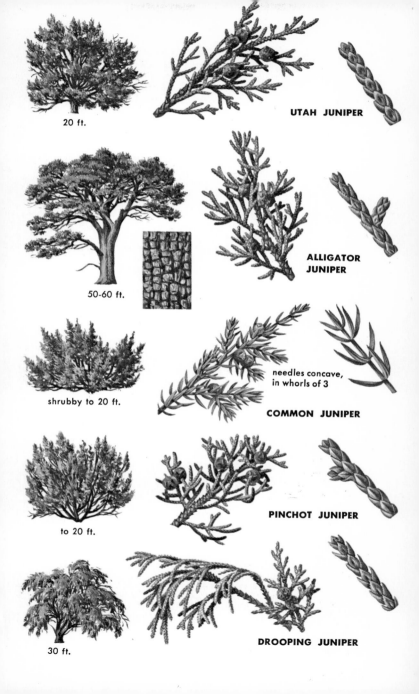

UTAH JUNIPER

20 ft.

ALLIGATOR JUNIPER

50-60 ft.

shrubby to 20 ft.

needles concave, in whorls of 3

COMMON JUNIPER

to 20 ft.

PINCHOT JUNIPER

30 ft.

DROOPING JUNIPER

Eastern Redcedar

Southern Redcedar

EASTERN REDCEDAR *(Juniperus virginiana)* has rounded to 4-sided branchlets covered by closely overlapping, dark-green, occasionally glandular scales about 0.06 of an inch long and in alternate pairs. New foliage near tips of branches is pointed and prickly. Round cones, 0.3 of an inch in diameter, are somewhat fleshy; green at first, turning blue at maturity, and covered with a gray, waxy substance. Ash-gray to reddish-brown bark is fibrous or in long, narrow, fringed scales. Small to medium-sized, 40 to 50 feet tall and 1 to 2 feet in diameter, with a dense, pyramidal crown. Common in poor soils, but grows best in limestone regions. Many varieties grown as ornamentals. Southern Redcedar *(J. silicicola)* resembles Eastern Redcedar, but has somewhat pendant branches and smaller cones. Prefers moist to swampy soils.

SOME INTRODUCED GYMNOSPERMS

GINKGO FAMILY
(Ginkgoaceae)

GINKGO *(Ginkgo biloba)* is the only remaining species of a group of trees widely distributed in prehistoric times. Fan-shaped leaves are deciduous, 2 to 3.5 inches wide, and bright yellow in fall. Dioecious; the plumlike fruit is about 1 inch long, orange-yellow when ripe. Its thin, pulpy flesh encloses a large white seed and gives off a foul odor as it disintegrates. Native to the Orient, where it is cultivated. Often planted as an ornamental in the United States. Grows to 100 feet tall, 3 feet in diameter.

PODOCARP FAMILY
(Podocarpaceae)

PODOCARPS *(Podocarpus spp.),* about 100 species of evergreen trees and shrubs, grow mainly in the Southern Hemisphere. Foliage linear to ovate, dark green above and lighter below; commonly alternate. Usually dioecious, staminate flowers yellow, in catkin-like spikes; pistillate greenish, solitary. Single-seeded fruit at apex of a swollen base. Ornamentals in warmer parts of U.S. include *P. nagi,* with opposite, elliptical leaves, and *P. macrophyllus,* with alternate, linear foliage. Both native to Japan.

ARAUCARIA FAMILY (Araucariaceae)

MONKEY PUZZLE *(Araucaria imbricata)* is a striking evergreen with stiff, leathery, dark-green, scalelike foliage. Sharp-tipped, overlapping scales are 1 inch long or less on branchlets, to 2 inches on large branches. Dioecious, producing ovoid to globose cones, 5 to 8 inches long, which disintegrate at maturity. Monkey Puzzle's pyramidal crown is formed of whorls of long, stiff branches. Grows to 100 feet tall. Native to South America but is grown as an ornamental in U.S.

NORFOLK ISLAND PINE *(Araucaria excelsa)* has evergreen foliage to 0.5 of an inch long—curved, sharp-pointed, spreading, and overlapping on the branches. Subglobose cones are 4 to 6 inches broad. Norfolk Island Pine grows to 70 feet tall, its slightly upturned branches in regular whorls of 4 to 7 and with pendant side branchlets. Native of Norfolk Island, northernmost of the New Zealand group; grown outdoors in warmer parts of the U.S. or indoors as a potted plant.

new foliage

old foliage

EASTERN REDCEDAR

40-50 ft.

GINKGO

PODOCARPS

P. nagi

to 100 ft.

P. macrophyllus

MONKEY PUZZLE

NORFOLK ISLAND PINE

to 100 ft.

to 70 ft.

ANGIOSPERMS

Angiosperms include most of the common flowering plants. This large group, composed of about 300 families and nearly 200,000 species, dominates the earth's vegetation. Angiosperms are divided into two classes: monocots (Monocotyledoneae) and dicots (Dicotyledoneae). Their differences are compared in the examples illustrated at the top of p. 67.

MONOCOTS include members of the grass, palm, lily, pineapple, banana, and orchid families. In northern North America, only the palm and lily families contain plants that attain tree size.

DICOTS include members of the oak, willow, ash, maple, hickory, birch, elm, and other families. Most of the tree-sized angiosperms that grow in northern North America are members of the dicot group.

PALM FAMILY (Palmae)

The palm family contains about 4,000 species of vines, shrubs, and trees in a wide range of sizes and forms. They are most abundant in the tropics of America and Asia; a few occur in tropical Africa, in the Mediterranean region, and in Chile, Japan, and Korea. Palms provide food, shelter, and clothing for people living in the tropics. Copra, coconuts, dates, oils, and waxes are familiar palm products. Native North American species and many exotics are grown as ornamentals in warm parts of the United States.

Palms are separated into two groups: fan palms, the leaf segments (pinnae) of the broad, fanlike leaves radiating from a common point; and feather palms, the numerous narrow, pinnate segments arising at right angles to the central leaf stalk.

JAMAICA THATCHPALM (*Thrinax parviflora*) has fan-shaped leaves, 2 to 3 feet wide, lustrous green above and pale below. The many narrow, tapering, pointed segments extend nearly to the center. Stiff, flat stems are about 4 feet long. New foliage densely covered with gray hairs. In early spring, white, fragrant, short-stalked flowers occur in narrow clusters about 3 feet long. Fruits, which mature in the fall, are smooth, ivory-white, nearly round, and about 0.5 inch in diameter; single chestnut-brown seed is enclosed in dry, thick flesh. Jamaica Thatchpalm grows 30 feet tall and 4 to 8 inches in diameter. The foliage is clustered at the top of the slender, gray trunk, which is commonly thatched with dead leaf bases.

BRITTLE THATCHPALM (*Thrinax microcarpa*) is similar to Jamaica Thatchpalm but foliage silvery below and fruits smaller, about 0.1 of an inch in diameter.

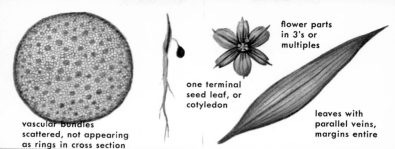

flower parts in 3's or multiples

one terminal seed leaf, or cotyledon

leaves with parallel veins, margins entire

vascular bundles scattered, not appearing as rings in cross section

MONOCOTS

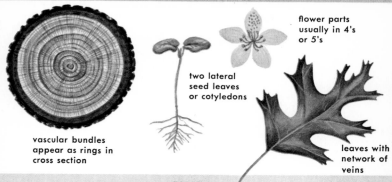

flower parts usually in 4's or 5's

two lateral seed leaves or cotyledons

vascular bundles appear as rings in cross section

leaves with network of veins

DICOTS

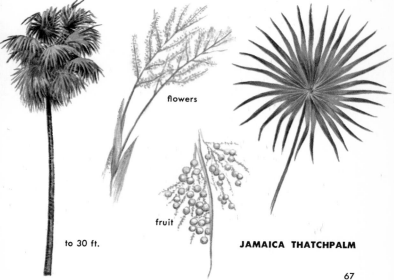

flowers

fruit

to 30 ft.

JAMAICA THATCHPALM

FLORIDA SILVERPALM *(Coccothrinax argentata)* has drooping foliage similar to that of thatchpalms, but somewhat smaller and with orange midribs. Flowers are produced in clusters about 2 feet long. Fruit, 0.5 to 0.8 of an inch in diameter, turns lustrous black when mature. Each contains a single brown seed. Florida Silverpalm grows 15 to 25 feet tall and 4 to 6 inches in diameter. Its smooth trunk is gray-blue to brownish.

CABBAGE PALMETTO *(Sabal palmetto)* has costate leaves (midway between pinnate and palmate) with stiff, half-rounded stems 6 to 7 feet long. Margins of lustrous, dark-green blades, 5 to 8 feet long, are cut into numerous long, drooping segments, bearing many threadlike fibers. Fragrant, white flowers, about 0.3 inch in diameter, are produced in spring, in drooping clusters about 2 to 2.5 feet long. Fruits, which ripen in fall, are smooth, round to oval, almost black and about 0.3 inch in diameter; each encloses a single chestnut-brown seed. Cabbage Palmetto may grow to 80 feet tall and 1 to 2 feet in diameter, with a brownish to gray trunk. At first the leaf bases cling to the trunk, or it is ringed with leaf scars. Trunk eventually becomes smooth. Texas Palmetto *(S. texana)* resembles Cabbage Palmetto but is smaller, 30 to 50 feet tall and 2 feet in diameter, with flower clusters to 8 feet long and fruits often lobed. Louisiana Palmetto *(S. louisiana)* ordinarily grows from an underground stem but occasionally develops a short, upright trunk to 8 feet tall. Palmettos are among the most abundant of our native tree palms.

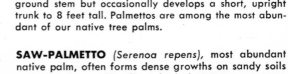

SAW-PALMETTO *(Serenoa repens),* most abundant native palm, often forms dense growths on sandy soils or in pine forests. Usually a shrub, but stems may grow to 25 feet tall. Leaves fan-shaped, about 2 feet in diameter, the leafstalks armed with sharp, rigid, curved spines.

PAUROTIS *(Paurotis wrightii)* has fan-shaped leaves 2 to 3 feet in diameter, light yellow-green above, bluish to silver-green below, and split almost to their base. Leaf stems, 18 to 24 inches long, are bordered with stout, flattened, orange-colored teeth. Small, greenish flowers are in drooping, branched clusters 4 to 6 feet long; the fruit, 0.3 of an inch in diameter, is orange-red, turning black when ripe. Paurotis, a native of the Florida Everglades, grows to 30 feet tall, often less, with clustered stems 4 inches in diameter.

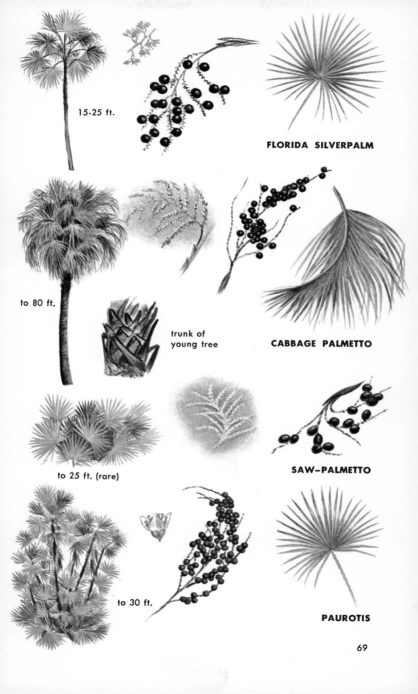

15-25 ft.

FLORIDA SILVERPALM

to 80 ft.

trunk of
young tree

CABBAGE PALMETTO

to 25 ft. (rare)

SAW-PALMETTO

to 30 ft.

PAUROTIS

CALIFORNIA WASHINGTONIA *(Washingtonia fili-fera)* has fan-shaped leaves, 5 to 6 feet long and 3 to 6 feet broad. The leaves are light green, with numerous folds and narrow, recurved segments that extend half to two-thirds of the way to the base and have many threadlike fibers along their margins. The stout, spiny leaf stems are 3 to 5 feet long and 1 to 3 inches wide. The somewhat fragrant flowers, which open from May to June, occur in branched clusters 8 to 10 feet long. The fruits are oval, 0.3 of an inch long and black at maturity. This is a large palm, 20 to 75 feet tall and 2 to 3 feet in diameter, with a thick, reddish-brown trunk. The dead leaves commonly hang on the tree, forming a brown skirt around the trunk. Both the California Washingtonia and a Mexican species *(W. robusta)* are grown as ornamentals.

FLORIDA CHERRYPALM *(Pseudophoenix sargentii)* has feather-like leaves, 5 to 6 feet long. They are dark yellow-green above, but paler and somewhat silvery below, with a short fibrous stem that is concave on its upper surface. Narrow, pointed leaflets are about 18 inches long and an inch wide, longest and widest at the center of the leaf. Yellowish flowers are widely spaced in loose clusters, and the orange to red fruits are 0.3 to 0.8 of an inch in diameter. Grows to 25 feet tall but usually shorter, with a ringed trunk.

FLORIDA ROYALPALM *(Roystonea elata)* has dark-green leaves, 10 to 12 feet long. The pointed leaflets are 2.5 to 3 feet long, becoming shorter toward end of the leaf. They extend in two ranks from the round leaf stalk that is flattened to concave at its base. In late winter to early spring, white, fragrant flowers, 0.3 of an inch in diameter, occur in densely branched, drooping clusters about 2 feet long. The smooth, purple fruits, about 0.5 of an inch long, are rounded at the tip and narrowed at the base. The thin, light-brown seed is embedded in fibrous flesh. This striking palm grows 80 to 100 feet tall. Its smooth, concrete-gray trunk, often conspicuously and abruptly swollen along its length, may be 2 feet in diameter. The Cuban Royalpalm *(R. regia)*, Caribbean Royalpalm *(R. oleracea)*, and Puerto Rican Palm *(R. borinquena)* are introduced species planted as ornamentals. All are stately trees much like the Florida Royalpalm in appearance.

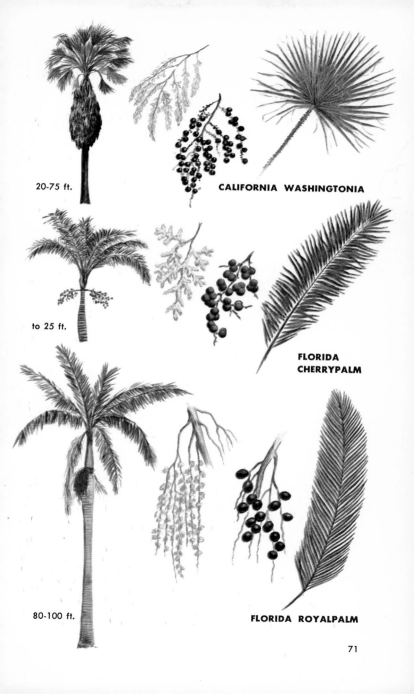

20-75 ft.

CALIFORNIA WASHINGTONIA

to 25 ft.

FLORIDA CHERRYPALM

80-100 ft.

FLORIDA ROYALPALM

71

SOME INTRODUCED PALMS

COCONUT PALM *(Cocos nucifera)* has feather-like leaves up to 18 feet long, with numerous long, linear, gracefully drooping leaflets. The creamy-white to yellowish flowers are in large, dense clusters (panicles). The familiar fruit is oval to somewhat 3-sided, 10 to 12 inches long and 6 to 8 inches in diameter. The large seed, or nut, is enclosed in a thick, fibrous husk. Inside the woody shell of the seed is a layer of creamy-white meat; inside that, the whitish "milk." The Coconut Palm may reach a height of 100 feet, its smooth trunk as much as 2 feet in diameter, often curved. The Coconut Palm's precise origin is not known; some say the Indo-Pacific, others the American tropics. It was naturalized before the discovery of America by Europeans.

MANILA PALM *(Veitchia merrillii)* has a stocky, usually straight trunk to 20 feet tall and 10 inches in diameter. It is crowned with strongly arched, feather-like leaves, each with numerous upswept leaflets that are widest at their middle. Clusters of white flowers form below the leaves. The striking, crimson fruit, more than 1 inch long, ripen in December or January. Manila Palm is one of 18 species of a genus native to South Pacific.

MADAGASCAR PALM *(Chrysalidocarpus lutescens)* forms an attractive loose clump consisting of several smooth, yellow-ringed stems, each up to 2 inches in diameter and 20 feet tall. These bear an elongated crown of long, graceful, arching, glossy-green, feather-like leaves, each with 30 or more pointed pinnae along central shaft. Small, yellowish flowers occur in clusters among the foliage; fruit is yellowish or red. Native to the island of Madagascar and quite sensitive to cold. Often cultivated in southern Florida, where it is known also as Areca Palm.

DATE PALM *(Phoenix dactylifera)* has feather-like, gray-green leaves, 15 to 20 feet long. The upper leaves stand more or less upright; the lower leaves arch outward and downward. Dioecious, the small, yellowish flowers produced in large clusters (panicles). Fruits, about 3 inches long, consist of a hard, grooved seed in a soft, pulpy, edible flesh. Grows 75 feet tall and 1 to 5 feet in diameter, the trunk usually roughened by bases of dead leaves. Native to northern Africa and western Asia, the Date Palm grows commonly as an ornamental in the warm parts of North America. The similar Canary Island Date Palm *(P. canariensis)* has inedible fruit but more graceful, arching foliage. Date Palm is the most common species of palm planted in Florida.

QUEEN PALM *(Arecastrum romanzoffianum)* has a slender trunk to 40 feet tall and 12 inches in diameter. It has a crown of erect, loosely spread, and somewhat recurved, feather-like leaves to 15 feet long. The soft, flexible leaf segments are about 18 inches long and 1 inch wide. Clusters of yellow flowers, 2 to 3 feet long, occur among the leaves. Orange fruits, about 1 inch long, are nearly round. Native to South America.

FISHTAIL PALM *(Caryota urens)* has a single stout, ringed trunk, to 50 feet tall and 1.5 feet in diameter. It bears an elongated terminal cluster of gracefully spreading, bipinnate leaves, to 20 feet long, with pinnae as much as 6 feet wide. Segments of pinnae are wedge-shaped with toothed tips, resembling a fish's tail. Clusters of flowers, to 12 feet long and 2 feet wide, form first in leaf axils near top of trunk, then develop progressively downward. Fruit is globular and red. A smaller species, C. *mitis,* has clustered trunks, black fruit.

to 100 ft.

ripe

green

COCONUT PALM

to 75 ft.

DATE PALM

to 40 ft.

to 20 ft.

MANILA PALM

QUEEN PALM

to 20 ft.

MADAGASCAR PALM

to 50 ft.

FISHTAIL PALM

73

LILY FAMILY (Liliaceae)

YUCCAS (Yucca)

Yuccas have light to dark-green, stiff, bayonet-like, often concave leaves. Bases may be thickened and clasping, margins toothed or fibrous; tips sharp-pointed. Clusters of cup-shaped flowers open during the night, the 6 white segments often streaked with green or purple. Fruit is an oval to oblong capsule containing numerous smooth, flat, black seeds. Yuccas occur only in Western Hemisphere, in dry soils. Of about 30 species, 11 reach tree size; the 4 most common are described here. The closely related Bigelow Nolina (Nolina bigelovii), which resembles a yucca, grows to tree size in southwestern Arizona and southeastern California.

JOSHUA-TREE (Yucca brevifolia) has dark-green leaves, 6 to 10 inches long, with pointed tips and finely toothed margins. They are clustered at ends of thick, irregularly formed branches. White flowers, about 2 inches long, produced in dense clusters about a foot long. Fruit somewhat 3-angled; bark divided into oblong plates. Grows 15 to 30 feet tall, 1 to 3 feet in diameter.

SOAPTREE YUCCA (Yucca elata) has pale yellow-green, grasslike leaves, 1 to 2.5 feet long and less than 0.5 inch wide; tipped with a sharp spine; smooth margins fringed with fine filaments. Flowers, 1.5 to 2 inches long, produced in branched clusters, 3 to 6 feet long. Fruit 3-celled, about 2 inches long and 1 to 1.5 inches in diameter; tipped with a stout point. Soaptree Yucca usually grows 3 to 6 feet tall; occasionally to 20 feet. Trunk gray.

SCHOTTS YUCCA (Yucca schottii) has flat, blue-green, bayonet-like leaves, 1.5 to 2.5 feet long and 1 to 2 inches wide, with a sharp-tipped spine and smooth, reddish-brown margins without threads. Flowers, 1 to 1.5 inches long, are in erect, branched clusters 1 to 2.5 feet long. Fleshy fruit, 4 to 5 inches long and 1.3 to 2 inches in diameter, has a pointed tip. Often branched, to 20 feet tall; trunk gray to brown.

ALOE YUCCA (Yucca aloifolia) has slightly concave, dark-green leaves, 18 to 32 inches long. Tips stiff and brown, margins toothed. Flowers, 1 to 1.5 inches long and 3 to 4 inches wide, in clusters 18 to 24 inches long. Oblong, light-green fruit about 3 to 4 inches long, black when ripe. Aloe Yucca grows 25 feet tall, 6 inches in diameter.

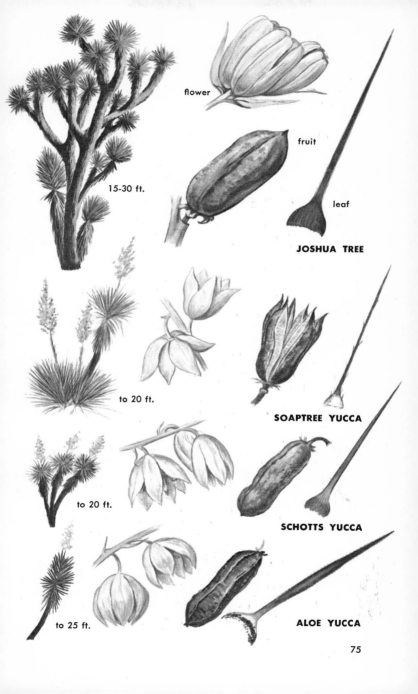

flower

fruit

leaf

15-30 ft.

JOSHUA TREE

to 20 ft.

SOAPTREE YUCCA

to 20 ft.

SCHOTTS YUCCA

to 25 ft.

ALOE YUCCA

75

WILLOW FAMILY (Salicaceae)

More than 325 species of willows (*Salix*), poplars or cottonwoods, and aspens (*Populus*) are widely distributed in the world but occur most abundantly in the cooler parts of the Northern Hemisphere. All are deciduous, rapid-growing but relatively short-lived, and dioecious——that is, staminate and pistillate flowers, both in aments, or catkins, are produced on separate plants.

WILLOWS (*Salix*)

Willow leaves are alternate, have short stems, and are usually much longer than broad. Each tiny flower of the staminate or pistillate aments is attached to a nectar-producing, hairy bract. The fruit is a small, 2-valved capsule that contains many minute, hairy seeds. Buds, excellent features for winter identification, usually hug the twigs and are covered by a single scale. More than 100 species are native to North America. Most are shrubs, but about 40 species attain tree size, 15 of them described and illustrated here. Willows root easily and occasionally form dense thickets. They are often planted to help hold stream banks in danger of erosion by floods. Bees obtain nectar from the blossoms in early spring, and the flexible twigs of some are used in basketry. A few kinds are planted as ornamentals; the catkins of those called "pussy willows" are used in decorations.

Willows generally grow along streams or in similar places where the soil is moist. As the many species of willows are so similar that exact identification is extremely difficult, check range maps carefully to determine where the species can be expected to occur.

BLACK WILLOW (*Salix nigra*) has lanceolate leaves, 3 to 6 inches long, 0.5 to 0.8 of an inch wide, with finely toothed margins. They are smooth and green, more lustrous above and slightly paler below. Twigs of the current year are a reddish to gray-brown. Capsule about 0.3 of an inch long. Bark of large trees is dark brown to black and heavily ridged. Usually grows 30 to 40 feet tall and 12 to 14 inches in diameter, with an irregular crown and often several trunks. This is the only willow important for lumber, used for boxes and similar purposes not requiring strength.

PACIFIC WILLOW (*Salix lasiandra*) resembles Black Willow, but the leaves are gray-green on the underside, with glands at the base of the blade. Twigs of the current year are yellow. Grows 15 to 50 feet tall and 12 to 14 inches in diameter, with an irregular crown of ascending, spreading branches.

WILLOWS
Salix

leaves usually longer than wide

buds covered by a single scale

POPLARS
Populus

leaves usually as broad as long

buds covered by several overlapping scales

30-40 ft.

staminate

capsular fruit

pistillate

BLACK WILLOW

PACIFIC WILLOW

77

PEACHLEAF WILLOW (*Salix amygdaloides*) has broadly lanceolate leaves, 2 to 5 inches long and 0.8 to 1.3 inches wide, with finely toothed margins. They are light green above and grayish below, with a yellow or orange midrib. Bark of large trunks is black, ridged, and furrowed. Peachleaf Willow grows 10 to 60 feet tall, 12 to 15 inches in diameter, and has a crown of ascending branches. It is commonly found along prairie watercourses.

RED WILLOW (*Salix laevigata*) leaves are broadly lanceolate, 2 to 7 inches long and 0.8 to 1.5 inches wide, with obscurely toothed margins. Leaves are shiny green above, gray-green below, with yellow midrib. Red Willows grow 20 to 50 feet tall and 1 to 2 feet in diameter, with a spreading crown of slender, reddish-brown branches. The black, furrowed bark is somewhat scaly.

SANDBAR WILLOW (*Salix interior*) has narrowly lanceolate leaves, 2 to 6 inches long and 0.3 to 0.5 inch wide. Somewhat curved, the leaves are yellow-green but darker than below, with a yellowish midrib and wide-spaced marginal teeth. The dark, reddish-brown bark is scaly. Sandbar Willow is commonly shrubby, often forming dense, riverside thickets. Occasionally it grows to 30 feet tall and 3 to 6 inches in diameter, with short, slender, orange to purplish-red, erect branches.

ARROYO WILLOW (*Salix lasiolepis*) leaves are lanceolate to oblanceolate, 3 to 6 inches long and 0.5 to 1 inch wide, dark green above and somewhat hairy and gray below. Their margins are slightly curled under and smooth or occasionally toothed. Bark is gray-brown on branches and on young trees; thick, ridged, and black on mature trees. Arroyo Willow is a large shrub or small tree, to 30 feet tall and 6 inches in diameter, with a loose open crown of slender, erect branches.

MACKENZIE WILLOW (*Salix mackenzieana*) has lanceolate to elliptical leaves, 1.5 to 4 inches long and 0.8 to 1.5 inches wide. They are light green above and pale green below, with small, rounded, marginal teeth. A shrub or small tree, 15 to 20 feet tall and 6 inches in diameter, the Mackenzie Willow has a narrow crown of slender, upright, yellowish to lustrous reddish-brown branches. Bark gray.

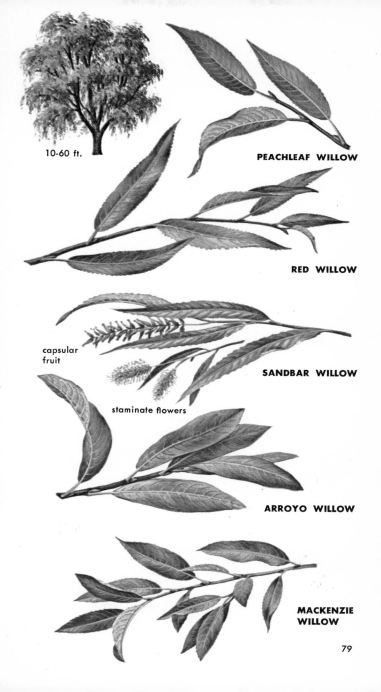

10-60 ft.

PEACHLEAF WILLOW

RED WILLOW

capsular
fruit

SANDBAR WILLOW

staminate flowers

ARROYO WILLOW

**MACKENZIE
WILLOW**

79

PUSSY WILLOW *(Salix discolor)* leaves are lanceolate to elliptical, 3 to 5 inches long and 0.8 to 1.5 inches wide, with wide-spaced marginal teeth and a yellow midrib. They are light green above, somewhat silvery below and often hairy. The flowers appear in late winter or early spring, the staminate flowers (aments, or catkins) soft and silky. Pussy Willow may be a shrub or a small tree, to 25 feet tall and 6 inches in diameter, with an open, rounded crown of stout branches.

BONPLAND WILLOW *(Salix bonplandiana)* has lanceolate leaves, 4 to 6 inches long and 0.5 to 0.8 of an inch wide. They are a lustrous yellow-green above and silvery white below, with a yellowish midrib and usually toothed margins somewhat curled under. On larger trees, the dark-brown to black bark is ridged and fissured. Bonpland Willow grows to 30 feet tall and 1 foot in diameter, with a rounded crown of slender, erect branches that usually droop toward the ends. An interesting feature of this species is that it can be considered semi-evergreen; its leaves, instead of being early deciduous in the fall like other willows, drop irregularly from the branches during the winter.

COASTAL PLAIN WILLOW *(Salix caroliniana)* has lanceolate leaves, 2 to 4 inches long and 0.5 to 0.8 inch wide, with finely toothed margins. They are green above, paler and hairy below. On large trees, the bark is black, ridged, and scaly. Coastal Plain Willow grows as a shrub or small tree, to 30 feet tall and 1 foot in diameter.

YEWLEAF WILLOW *(Salix taxifolia)* has small, linear-lanceolate leaves, 0.5 to 1.3 inches long and 0.1 of an inch wide, usually with smooth margins. As they unfold, the leaves are white and hairy; later they become pale green. Yewleaf Willow grows 40 to 50 feet tall and 1.5 feet in diameter, with a broad, open crown of erect branches usually drooping toward the ends.

BEBB WILLOW *(Salix bebbiana)* has elliptical, oblong or lanceolate leaves, 1 to 3 inches long and 0.5 to 1 inch wide. They are often toothed above the middle. At first pale green, they later become dull and usually hairy, especially along the midrib and veins on the undersurface. A shrub or small bushy tree, to 25 feet tall and 6 to 8 inches in diameter, Bebb Willow has a rounded crown of slender, reddish-brown branches. The bark is greenish gray tinged with red.

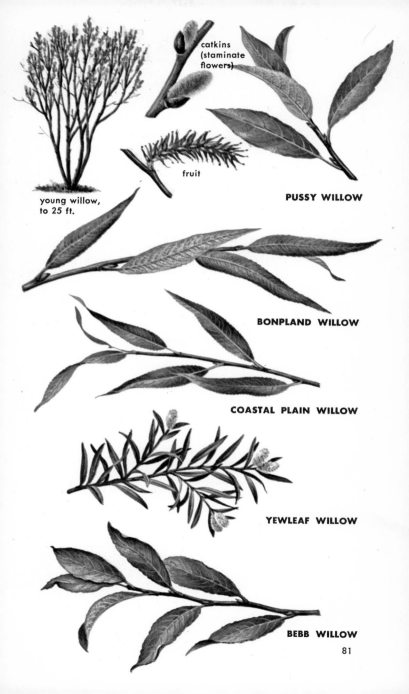

catkins
(staminate
flowers)

fruit

young willow,
to 25 ft.

PUSSY WILLOW

BONPLAND WILLOW

COASTAL PLAIN WILLOW

YEWLEAF WILLOW

BEBB WILLOW

81

FELTLEAF WILLOW *(Salix alaxensis)* leaves are narrowly elliptical to obovate, 2 to 4 inches long and 1 to 1.5 inches wide. Dull yellowish green above and white and hairy below, they have smooth margins, a yellow midrib, and may be somewhat wrinkled. Grows to 30 feet tall and 6 inches in diameter, with a crown of stout branches hairy during tree's early years.

HOOKER WILLOW *(Salix hookeriana)* leaves are 2 to 6 inches long and 1 to 1.5 inches wide. They have coarse marginal teeth, are bright green above, paler and hairy below, especially along the midrib. Usually a shrub; sometimes 25 to 30 feet tall, 6 to 8 inches in diameter, often with several stems. Bark light reddish brown.

SCOULER WILLOW *(Salix scouleriana)* leaves are dark yellow-green above, paler and usually hairy below. Widest above the middle, they are 1 to 4 inches long and 0.5 to 1.5 inches wide, with a yellowish-green midrib. One of the "pussy willows," the staminate flowers are furry and silky. Scouler Willow grows 50 feet tall and 12 to 14 inches in diameter or is a large shrub.

SOME COMMON INTRODUCED WILLOWS

WEEPING WILLOW *(Salix babylonica)* is native to China but is now widely planted throughout the world. This large handsome tree, 30 to 70 feet tall and 1 to 3 feet in diameter, has a broad, rounded crown of slender, pendulous branches. Bark on large trees heavily ridged, furrowed, and dark brown to black. Narrow, lanceolate leaves are 3 to 6 inches long, 0.5 to 1 inch wide; finely toothed margins. Smooth, glossy above; paler below.

WHITE WILLOW *(Salix alba)*, introduced from Europe into eastern U.S., grows 50 to 80 feet tall and 1 to 3 feet in diameter. It has a crown of olive-green branches and furrowed, dull-brown bark. The finely toothed, lanceolate leaves are 2 to 4 inches long and 0.5 to 1.5 inches wide. They are pale green above and silvery white below with fine silky hairs on both sides.

CRACK WILLOW *(Salix fragilis)*, native to Eurasia and introduced from Europe during Colonial days, grows 50 to 80 feet tall and 1 to 3 feet in diameter, with a broad crown of relatively upright branches; the glossy, yellow-green, brittle twigs snap off readily. Large trees have heavily ridged, dark-brown to black bark. The smooth, bright-green, lanceolate leaves are 4 to 6 inches long and 0.5 to 1.3 inches wide; finely toothed margins.

BASKET WILLOW *(Salix viminalis)* is a small shrubby tree, to 20 feet tall. Its slender green twigs were once important in basketry. The linear to narrowly lanceolate leaves are 2.5 to 3.5 inches long and up to 1 inch wide. They usually have smooth margins, are dark green above, and silky white with fine hairs below. Introduced from Europe, it is now common in eastern U.S.

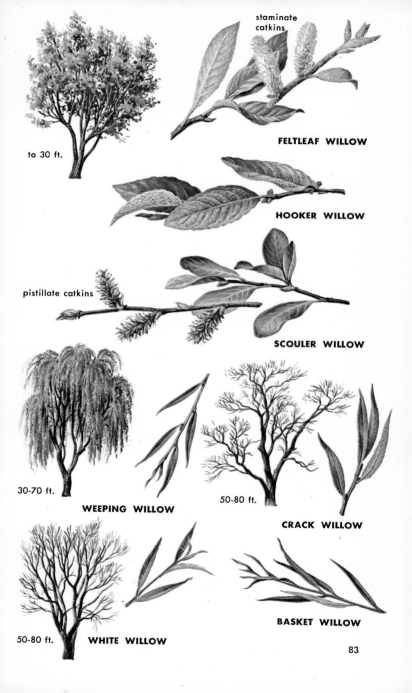

staminate catkins

to 30 ft.

FELTLEAF WILLOW

HOOKER WILLOW

pistillate catkins

SCOULER WILLOW

30-70 ft.

WEEPING WILLOW

50-80 ft.

CRACK WILLOW

50-80 ft. **WHITE WILLOW**

BASKET WILLOW

83

POPLARS AND ASPENS *(Populus)*

About 15 species of poplars, or cottonwoods, and aspens are native to North America. Both have broad, usually coarsely toothed, alternate leaves with long stems. Staminate and pistillate flowers are in aments, or catkins, on separate trees. The seeds are borne within small, green, flask-shaped capsules clustered along short, slender stems that hang from the branches in narrow, elongated clusters. When ripe, fruits split open and release the many tiny, dark-brown seeds. Each seed is attached to a tuft of cottony hairs and is blown by the wind. Twigs have long, pointed buds covered by several overlapping scales (p. 77); the buds extend at an angle from branches. Buds of some species are resinous and fragrant in early spring.

Poplars prefer moist soils and are often found along streams. Because they grow rapidly they are planted for quick shade or for wind protection. The soft wood of some species is used for veneers, boxes, matches, excelsior, and paper. The name poplar is also used for Yellow-poplar (p. 154) of the magnolia family.

EASTERN COTTONWOOD *(Populus deltoides)* leaves are roughly triangular, 3 to 6 inches long and 4 to 5 inches wide, with coarsely rounded marginal teeth. They are smooth and lustrous green above and paler below with a flattened stem, 1.5 to 3 inches long. The seed-bearing capsules are 3- to 4-valved, 0.3 of an inch long. Bark of mature trunks is dark gray and furrowed or ridged; on the upper branches and on young trees, smooth and greenish yellow. Eastern Cottonwood commonly attains a height of 75 to 100 feet and 3 to 4 feet in diameter.

PLAINS COTTONWOOD *(Populus sargentii)* has ovate leaves, 3 to 3.5 inches long and 3.5 to 4 inches wide, with coarsely rounded marginal teeth and flattened stems. Bark pale, ridged. Plains cottonwood grows to 80 feet tall and 3 feet in diameter. This species is the principal cottonwood along streams of the prairie country in west-central United States and Canada.

NARROWLEAF COTTONWOOD *(Populus angustifolia)* leaves are 2 to 3 inches long and 0.5 to 1 inch wide, bright yellow-green above and paler below, with toothed margins and nearly round stems. Capsules 2-valved. On young trees, bark yellowish green, becoming thick, dark brown, and furrowed on older trunks. Narrowleaf Cottonwood grows 50 to 60 feet tall and 1 to 1.5 feet in diameter.

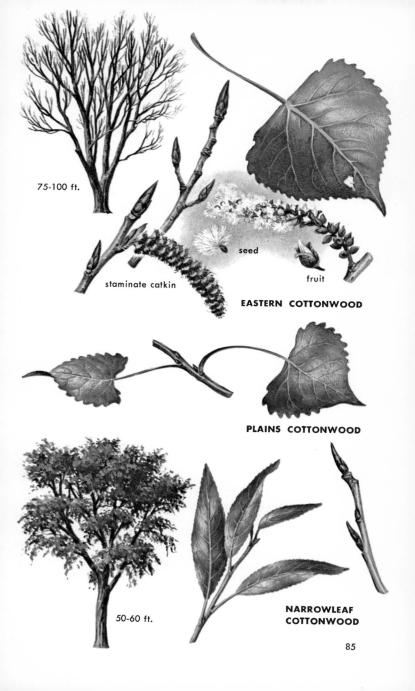

75-100 ft.

staminate catkin

seed

fruit

EASTERN COTTONWOOD

PLAINS COTTONWOOD

50-60 ft.

**NARROWLEAF
COTTONWOOD**

BLACK COTTONWOOD *(Populus trichocarpa)* leaves are 5 to 6 inches long, 2 to 4 inches wide, tapering from a broad, rounded base. The marginal teeth are small and rounded; stems also round. They are dark green above, veiny and pale green, silvery white, or rusty brown below. The 3-valved capsules are hairy. Resinous buds are fragrant in early spring. Bark on old trees is dark to black and deeply furrowed; smooth and greenish gray on branches or on young trees. Black Cottonwood grows 80 to 125 feet tall and 2 to 4 feet in diameter. Its wood is used for paper pulp and also for veneer.

BALSAM POPLAR *(Populus balsamifera)* resembles Black Cottonwood but is smaller, 60 to 80 feet tall and 1 to 2 feet in diameter. Capsules are 2-valved and not hairy. Like those of Black Cottonwood, its buds are sticky, fragrant, and resinous in spring.

SWAMP COTTONWOOD *(Populus heterophylla)* has ovate leaves, 4 to 7 inches long and 3 to 6 inches wide. They have a gradually narrowed or rounded apex, a rounded to heart-shaped base, coarsely rounded marginal teeth, and round stems. They are dark green above and paler below, with a yellow midrib. The capsules are 2- to 3-valved. Bark of older trees is reddish brown, scaly, and somewhat shaggy. Swamp Cottonwood may attain a height of 70 to 90 feet and 2 to 3 feet in diameter. It has a narrow, rounded crown of stout branches.

PALMER COTTONWOOD *(Populus palmeri)* leaves are thin, ovate, 2.5 to 5 inches long and 1.5 to 2.5 inches wide, with small, incurved marginal teeth and slender, flattened stems. The seed-bearing capsules are 4-valved. Bark of old trunks is gray-brown and deeply fissured; on branches or on small trees, smooth and gray to reddish brown. Palmer Cottonwood grows 40 to 60 feet tall and 1 to 3 feet in diameter. It has an open, pyramidal crown.

FREMONT COTTONWOOD *(Populus fremontii)* leaves are roughly triangular, 2 to 2.5 inches long and 2.5 to 3 inches wide. They are shiny green with a thin, yellow midrib, a coarsely toothed margin, and yellow, flattened stem. Seed-bearing capsules are usually 3-, sometimes 4-valved. On older trees, bark is thick, deeply furrowed, dark reddish brown; on branches or on young trees, thin, smooth, and gray-brown. Grows 50 to 75 feet tall and 2 to 5 feet in diameter, with a broad crown.

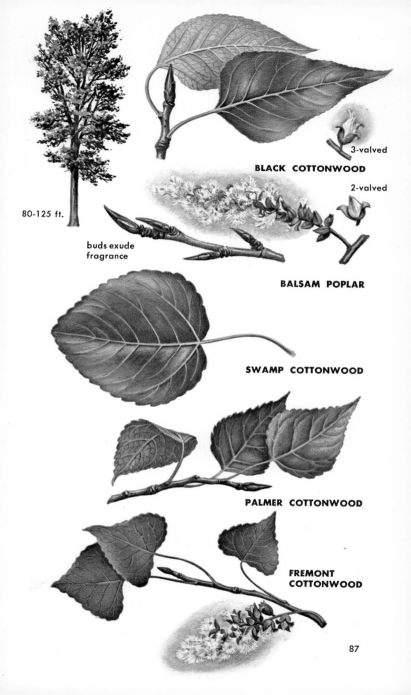

80-125 ft.

3-valved

BLACK COTTONWOOD

2-valved

buds exude
fragrance

BALSAM POPLAR

SWAMP COTTONWOOD

PALMER COTTONWOOD

**FREMONT
COTTONWOOD**

87

QUAKING ASPEN *(Populus tremuloides)* leaves are nearly circular, 1 to 3 inches in diameter, with small, rounded marginal teeth and long, slender, flattened stems. They are lustrous green above, pale silvery below. The foliage quivers in the slightest breeze, hence the common name. In fall, the leaves turn brilliant gold or yellow. The smooth, greenish-white to cream-colored bark is marked by black, warty patches, and unlike most other poplars, buds are essentially nonresinous. Quaking Aspen grows 20 to 60 feet tall and 1 to 2 feet in diameter, with a narrow, rounded crown of slender branches.

BIGTOOTH ASPEN *(Populus grandidentata)* leaves are ovate to nearly round, 2 to 3.5 inches long and 2 to 2.5 inches wide, with coarse, rounded marginal teeth. Dark green above and paler below, they have a yellow midrib and a slender, flattened stem. The buds are minutely haired (Quaking Aspen buds smooth) and essentially nonresinous. On younger trees, the bark is dark green; on older trees, it is brown and furrowed. Bigtooth Aspen grows 30 to 60 feet tall and 1 to 2 feet in diameter, with a narrow, round-topped crown of rather stout branches.

SOME INTRODUCED POPLARS

WHITE POPLAR *(Populus alba)* leaves are usually 3- to 5-lobed, 2 to 5 inches long and 1.5 to 3.5 inches wide, with wavy or coarsely toothed margins; occasionally heart-shaped, with flattened base. Leaves are dark green above and woolly white below. On branches and on small trees, bark is greenish gray; on older trunks, black and furrowed. A medium-sized to large tree, 50 to 80 feet tall and 2 to 3 feet in diameter, White Poplar often has several trunks forming a broad, rounded crown. A native of Eurasia, White Poplar, with several varieties, is now widespread in the U.S.

LOMBARDY POPLAR *(Populus nigra var. italica)* has triangular to somewhat diamond-shaped leaves, 2 to 3.5 inches long and 1.5 to 3 inches wide. They have rounded marginal teeth and flattened stems. Bark thin and greenish gray on upper branches and on young trees; at base of larger trunks, black and furrowed. The slender, columnar crown of short, sharply ascending branches makes Lombardy Poplar easy to recognize from a distance. Grows 40 to 80 feet tall and 1 to 3 feet in diameter. Introduced from Europe, it is now planted throughout the United States, especially for windbreaks.

SIMON POPLAR *(Populus simonii)*, a native of China, is planted as an ornamental in the U.S. There are several varieties. The leaves, 2 to 5 inches long and 1 to 3 inches wide, taper from the center to a rounded base and long-pointed apex. They are bright green above, paler or whitish below, with numerous small, rounded, marginal teeth. Simon Poplar has a narrow crown and slender, reddish-brown branchlets. It commonly attains a height of about 40 feet and may have a diameter of about 2 feet.

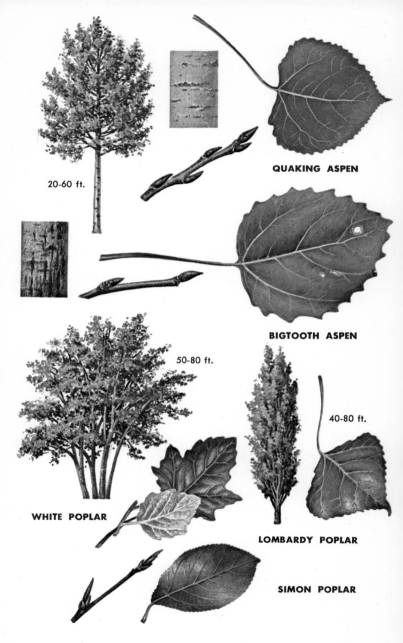

20-60 ft.

QUAKING ASPEN

BIGTOOTH ASPEN

50-80 ft.

40-80 ft.

WHITE POPLAR

LOMBARDY POPLAR

SIMON POPLAR

WAXMYRTLE FAMILY (Myricaceae)

Bayberries, or waxmyrtles *(Myrica)*, are widely distributed in temperate and warm climates. Five species, all with alternate leaves, occur in the U.S. and Canada, usually in sterile, sandy soils; two are usually shrubs. Northern Bayberry *(M. pensylvanica)*, found from Newfoundland south to North Carolina and Ohio, has tardily deciduous to evergreen foliage and white buds on twigs covered with gray hair. Evergreen Bayberry *(M. heterophylla)*, of coastal plains from New Jersey to Louisiana, has evergreen foliage and twigs covered with black hair.

SOUTHERN BAYBERRY *(Myrica cerifera)* has short-stemmed, evergreen leaves, 1.5 to 4 inches long and 0.3 to 0.5 of an inch wide, usually widest and with coarse marginal teeth above the middle. Aromatic when crushed, they are yellow-green, spotted with small dark glands above and orange glands below. Staminate and pistillate flowers are in leaf axils of separate plants, in oblong catkins 0.2 to 0.7 of an inch long. Fruits are globose, light-green drupes, about 0.1 of an inch in diameter, thickly coated with pale-blue wax, sometimes used to make candles. Bark is thin, smooth, and gray-green. Grows to 40 feet tall and 8 inches in diameter, with a narrow, round-topped crown of slender, upright, or slightly spreading reddish branches.

ODORLESS BAYBERRY *(Myrica inodora)* leaves are dark lustrous green above and bright green below, with a glandular midrib slightly hairy below. Broader than leaves of Southern Bayberry, they usually have smooth curled-under margins and are not aromatic. Dioecious; the fruit, about 0.5 of an inch in diameter, is black and covered with white wax. The bark is ash gray to white. Odorless Bayberry is usually a shrub, but occasionally grows 15 to 20 feet tall.

PACIFIC BAYBERRY *(Myrica californica)* has oblong to oblanceolate, leathery, aromatic leaves, 2 to 4 inches long and 0.5 to 0.8 of an inch wide, with smooth or toothed, recurved margins; dark green above, yellow-green with black glandular dots below. Flowers resemble those of other bayberries, but both sexes are on the same plant (monoecious). The dark-purple fruit, 0.3 of an inch in diameter, is thinly coated with a granular gray wax. Branchlets are somewhat hairy. Pacific Bayberry is most commonly a shrub but is occasionally a small tree 20 to 30 feet tall.

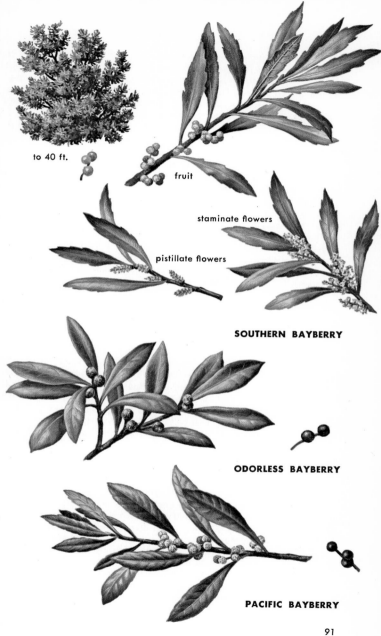

to 40 ft.

fruit

staminate flowers

pistillate flowers

SOUTHERN BAYBERRY

ODORLESS BAYBERRY

PACIFIC BAYBERRY

91

WALNUT FAMILY (Juglandaceae)

In addition to walnuts and hickories, most of which are native to North America, four wholly foreign groups of trees and shrubs belong to this family—*Pterocarya* (Wingnut, occasionally planted in the United States), *Engelhardtia, Platycarya,* and *Alfaroa.* Many species of the walnut family, valued for the wood's strength and resilience, are used in fine cabinet work.

WALNUTS *(Juglans)*

Walnuts have deciduous, alternate, pinnately compound leaves, the numerous oblong-lanceolate leaflets with toothed margins; in North American species, the leaflets midway along the stem are largest. Staminate and pistillate flowers are in different inflorescences on the same tree (monoecious); the staminate in tassel-like, un-branched catkins, the pistillate in few-flowered, erect, terminal spikes. Fruit, a drupaceous nut, is enclosed in a thick leathery husk, which does not split open when ripe. Pith of twigs is chambered. Six species are native to the United States. About 15 other members of this genus occur in South America, the West Indies, southern Europe, and Asia.

BLACK WALNUT *(Juglans nigra)* leaves are 12 to 24 inches long, with 15 to 23 almost sessile leaflets, smooth above and hairy below. The nearly spherical fruit, 1.5 to 2 inches in diameter, has a thick, semi-fleshy, yellowish-green husk enclosing the woody, corrugated nut and its sweet, oily seed. The husk contains a dark-brown dye. The stout twigs have 3-lobed leaf scars, blunt buds covered by a few hairy scales, and a buff-colored chambered pith. Bark of mature trees is furrowed and dark brown to black. Black Walnut grows 70 to 100 feet tall and 2 to 3 feet in diameter. It is valued for its beauty, its fruit, and its rich-brown, fine-grained wood.

BUTTERNUT *(Juglans cinerea)* leaves are 18 to 30 inches long, larger than those of Black Walnut, but have only 11 to 17 leaflets. Butternut leaflets are also more hairy on the underside. The oval fruit, 1.5 to 2.5 inches long, has a greenish-brown husk with a sticky surface. The husk contains a yellow or orange dye. Butternut twigs are hairy above the leaf scar, and have dark, chocolate-colored diaphragms dividing the pith chambers. On mature trees, the bark is gray and furrowed. Butternut grows 50 to 60 feet tall and 1 to 2 feet in diameter. Its wood is a much lighter brown than is the wood of Black Walnut.

usually many leaflets

staminate catkins not branched

husk does not split when ripe

shell corrugated

pith chambered

WALNUTS *Juglans*

few leaflets,

staminate catkins branched

husk splits when ripe

shell smooth between ridges

pith solid

HICKORIES *Carya*

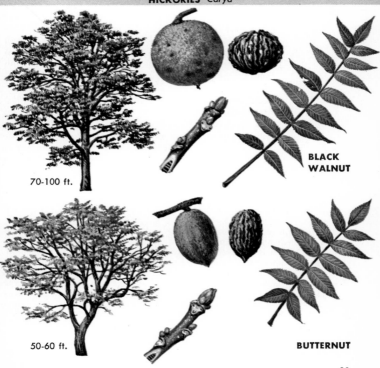

70-100 ft.

BLACK WALNUT

50-60 ft.

BUTTERNUT

93

CALIFORNIA WALNUT *(Juglans californica)* is a round-crowned, bushy tree, 15 to 50 feet tall and 1 to 2 feet in diameter, often with several stems. Leaves, 6 to 9 inches long, usually have 11 to 15 leaflets. Small, round fruits, 0.3 to 0.8 of an inch in diameter, have dark-colored, finely haired husks and nuts, with longitudinally grooved shells. California Walnut generally shows a preference for the moist soils along streams or in fertile bottomlands.

HINDS WALNUT *(Juglans hindsii)* grows 50 to 60 feet tall and 2 feet in diameter, with a single trunk and narrow, round-topped crown. The leaves are 9 to 12 inches long and have 15 to 19 leaflets with relatively coarse, wide-spaced marginal teeth. Leaflets are often slightly curved toward the ends. Round fruits, 1.3 to 2 inches in diameter, have thin, dark-brown, slightly hairy husks enclosing nuts, with longitudinally grooved shells. Usually occurs in moist soils.

LITTLE WALNUT *(Juglans microcarpa)* is a small, shrubby, often several-stemmed tree, 20 to 30 feet tall and 18 to 30 inches in diameter, with a rounded crown. Its leaves are 9 to 12 inches long, with 13 to 23 narrow, finely toothed, curved leaflets. The small fruits, about 0.5 to 0.8 of an inch in diameter, have thin, rusty-brown, slightly hairy husks and nuts with longitudinally ridged or grooved shells.

ARIZONA WALNUT *(Juglans major)* may grow 50 feet tall and 3 feet in diameter with a single trunk, but it is often shrubby. Leaves are 8 to 12 inches long, with 9 to 13 coarsely toothed leaflets. The round fruits, 1 to 1.5 inches in diameter, have thin, brown-haired husks and nuts with a deeply grooved shell.

AN INTRODUCED WALNUT

ENGLISH WALNUT *(Juglans regia)*, is native to southeastern Europe, India, and China. Its wood, known also as Circassian Walnut, is used for furniture and cabinet work. In the United States it is grown as an ornamental and for commercial nut production; there are many varieties. The leaves, 8 to 16 inches long, are pinnately compound with 7 to 9 leaflets. The leaflets differ from those of native American species in that they are oblong, with smooth rather than toothed margins and rounded rather than long-pointed tips, and the terminal leaflets are the largest. The round fruit, 1.5 to 2 inches in diameter, has a smooth green husk surrounding a thin-shelled nut that has rounded surface ridges. English Walnut may attain a height of 70 feet and a trunk diameter of 3 feet; it has a broad, rounded crown.

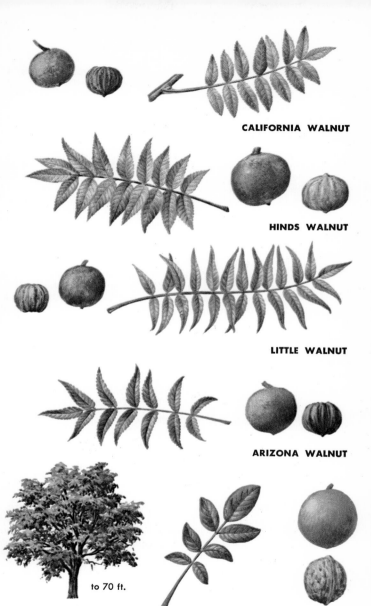

CALIFORNIA WALNUT

HINDS WALNUT

LITTLE WALNUT

ARIZONA WALNUT

to 70 ft.

ENGLISH WALNUT

95

HICKORIES (Carya)

Hickories are found mainly in eastern United States. One species grows in the Mexican highlands, two in eastern and southeastern Asia. Hickories are generally slow-growing trees with a long taproot. Like walnuts, they have alternate, odd-pinnately compound leaves, but the leaflets are usually fewer and broader, with the terminal leaflets largest. Staminate flowers are in 3-branched catkins; the husk of the nut splits open when ripe and the pith of twigs is solid (p. 93). Pecan hickories, a subgroup, usually have more and narrower leaflets, and "winged" husks; the buds have valvate rather than overlapping scales.

Nuts of most hickories are edible, the Pecan grown commercially. Hickories are also grown as ornamentals and their strong, tough, resilient wood is used for tool handles, athletic equipment, and similar items. Green hickory wood is used to flavor meat in smoking or barbecuing.

SHAGBARK HICKORY (Carya ovata) leaves are 8 to 14 inches long, with 5 (occasionally 9) smooth, broadly lanceolate leaflets. The nut, nearly round and with a smooth, 4-ribbed, light-brown shell, is enclosed in a reddish-brown to black, 4-ribbed husk, about 1 to 2.5 inches in diameter and 0.3 to 0.5 inch thick. The husk splits into four parts when ripe. Mature trees have distinctive shaggy bark composed of thin, narrow scales, curved outward at ends. Young trees have smooth gray bark. Shagbark Hickory grows 70 to 90 feet tall and 1 to 2 feet in diameter, with a rather narrow crown except when growing in open situations.

SHELLBARK HICKORY (Carya laciniosa) resembles Shagbark Hickory, but the leaves are 15 to 22 inches long and the 5 to 9 leaflets (usually 7) are softly hairy below. In addition, the nuts are 4- to 6-ribbed. Shellbark Hickory grows 80 to 100 feet tall and 3 to 4 feet in diameter.

MOCKERNUT HICKORY (Carya tomentosa) has fragrant leaves, 8 to 12 inches long, with a hairy stalk and 7 to 9 relatively narrow leaflets, which are hairy below. The nut is ovoid, thick-shelled, and 4-ribbed, enclosed in a thick, reddish-brown, deeply 4-grooved husk, depressed at the apex. The husk splits nearly to the base when ripe. The kernel is sweet but is hard to extract. Mockernut Hickory grows to 80 feet tall and 2 feet in diameter; it is most common in the South, especially in drier soils.

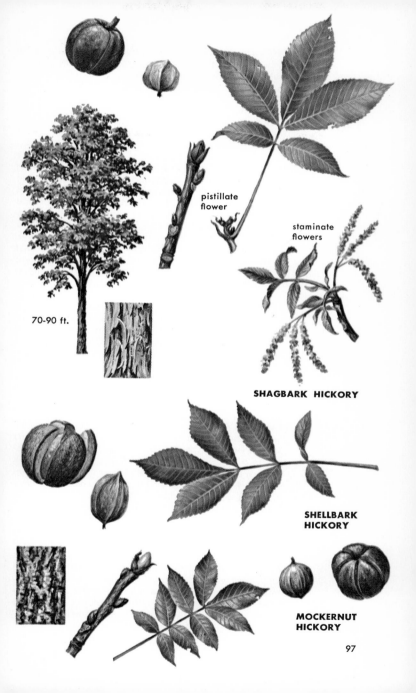

pistillate flower

staminate flowers

70-90 ft.

SHAGBARK HICKORY

SHELLBARK HICKORY

MOCKERNUT HICKORY

97

PIGNUT HICKORY *(Carya glabra)* leaves are 6 to 12 inches long, with 5 (occasionally 7) lanceolate leaflets. Nuts, not ribbed, are thick-shelled, enclosed in pear-shaped husks about 1.3 inches long. Husks, 0.1 of an inch thick, split only part way to the base when the nut is ripe. On mature trees, the scaly ridges of the bark form a rough, diamond-shaped pattern. Usually found in dry soils; grows 50 to 75 feet tall and 2 to 3 feet in diameter.

WATER HICKORY *(Carya aquatica)* leaves are 9 to 15 inches long and have reddish, hairy stems. The 7 to 13 narrow, curved leaflets are brownish and somewhat hairy below. The 4-ribbed, oblong, flattened nut has bitter "meat" and is enclosed in a thin, conspicuously 4-winged husk, 1.5 inches long and 1 to 1.3 inches in diameter, with yellow scales. Buds have valvate scales. Water Hickory is most common in moist to swampy soils, where it grows 60 to 80 feet tall and 1 to 2 feet in diameter. On mature trees, the light-brown bark is broken up into long scales.

BITTERNUT HICKORY *(Carya cordiformis)* leaves are 6 to 9 inches long, with 7 to 11 lanceolate leaflets, bright green above and paler below. Bitter, ovoid, thin-shelled, 4-ribbed nut, about 1 inch long, is enclosed in a thin, yellow-scaly husk, 4-winged above middle. Buds yellow, with valvate scales. Bark gray and smooth, except on large trunks. Bitternut Hickory grows 40 to 60 feet tall and 1 to 3 feet in diameter; usually in moist soils.

BLACK HICKORY *(Carya texana)* leaves are 8 to 12 inches long, with slender stems and usually 7 leaflets (occasionally 5). Leaflets dark green above, hairy below in axils of veins. Round to oblong, 4-ribbed, dark reddish-brown nut has a thin shell; enclosed in a thin, slightly 4-winged husk that splits to base. Buds have valvate scales. Bark black, deeply furrowed. To 50 feet tall and 2 feet in diameter.

NUTMEG HICKORY *(Carya myristicaeformis)* leaves are 7 to 14 inches long, with hairy stems and 7 to 9 leaflets, dark green above and silvery-hairy below. Bony nuts have a very thin, 4-winged husk, 1.5 inches long, covered with yellowish-brown hairs; splits nearly to base when ripe. The buds have valvate scales. Nutmeg Hickory's bark is scaly and reddish brown. The tree grows 100 feet tall and 2 feet in diameter.

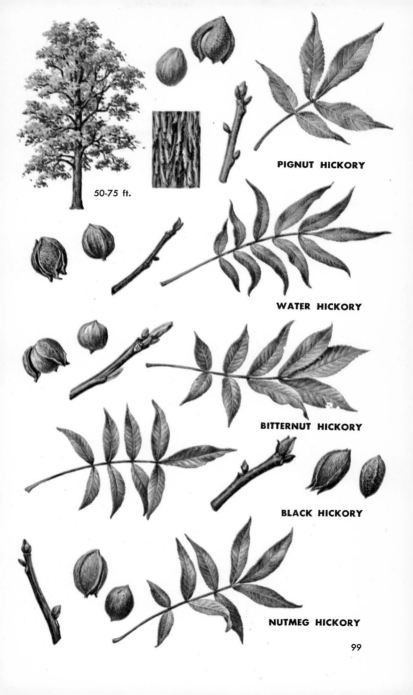

50-75 ft.

PIGNUT HICKORY

WATER HICKORY

BITTERNUT HICKORY

BLACK HICKORY

NUTMEG HICKORY

99

PECAN *(Carya illinoensis)* leaves are 12 to 20 inches long, with 9 to 17 narrow leaflets that are somewhat curved at their narrow, pointed ends. The oblong, reddish-brown nuts are 4-ribbed and 1 to 2.5 inches long, with a rather thin shell. The thin, dark-brown, prominently 4-winged husk splits to the base when the nut is ripe. The sharp-pointed buds have valvate scales with yellow hairs, and the twigs are somewhat hairy. On mature trees, the bark is light brown to gray and broken into narrow, vertical, scaly ridges. Largest of the hickories, the Pecan attains a height of 100 to 140 feet and a trunk diameter of 2 to 4 feet. It is most common and grows most rapidly on bottomlands in southeastern U.S. Not an important timber tree but valued commercially for nuts.

SWAMP HICKORY *(Carya leiodermis)* leaves are 12 to 14 inches long with slender, hairy stems. The 7 (occasionally 5) leaflets are smooth and dark green above; hairy below, especially along the midrib. The reddish-brown nut is enclosed in a thick, 4-ribbed husk, 1.5 to 1.8 inches long and 1.3 inches in diameter. It splits to the base when ripe. The pale, gray-brown bark is only slightly ridged. Swamp Hickory, most common in moist soils, may grow 50 to 70 feet tall, 1 to 2 feet in diameter. It has a round-topped crown, somewhat pendant branches, and reddish-brown branchlets.

OTHER NATIVE HICKORIES

SCRUB HICKORY *(Carya floridana)* **AND SAND HICKORY** *(C. pallida)* both grow to 75 feet tall, 2 feet in diameter. In early spring, leaf stems and underside of Scrub Hickory's 5 to 7 leaflets are brown, hairy. Nuts small, husks narrowed at base and depressed at apex. Sand Hickory has 7 to 9 long-pointed leaflets, silvery on underside; round nuts in oval husks. Both species are native to southeastern United States.

CORKWOOD FAMILY (Leitneriaceae)

CORKWOOD *(Leitneria floridana)*, the only species in its family, has extremely light wood. Leaves are deciduous, short-stemmed, smooth-margined. They are bright green above and somewhat hairy below, elliptic-lanceolate, and may be 4 to 6 inches long and 1.5 to 2.5 inches wide. Staminate and pistillate flowers on different trees; the leathery, brown, pointed-oval fruit, 0.8 of an inch long and 0.3 of an inch thick, is conspicuously net-veined. Corkwood grows about 20 feet tall and 5 inches in diameter.

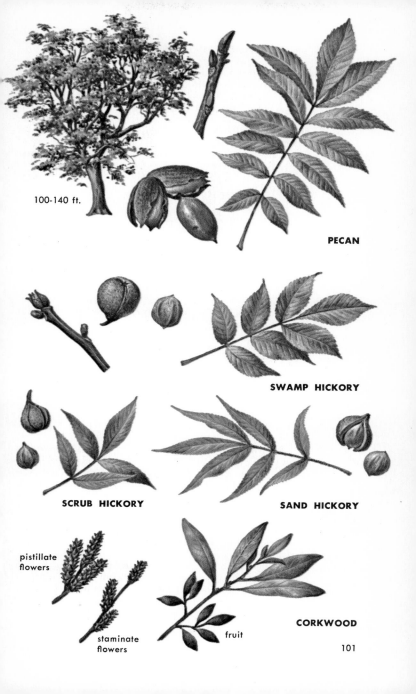

100-140 ft.

PECAN

SWAMP HICKORY

SCRUB HICKORY

SAND HICKORY

pistillate
flowers

staminate
flowers

fruit

CORKWOOD

BIRCH FAMILY (Betulaceae)

The birch family comprises about 100 species of trees and shrubs, found primarily in cooler parts of the Northern Hemisphere. The birches *(Betula)*, alders *(Alnus)*, hornbeams *(Carpinus)*, hophornbeams *(Ostrya)*, and hazels, or filberts *(Corylus)*, are represented by native species in North America. A sixth genus *(Ostryopsis)* occurs in eastern Asia. All members of the birch family have alternate, deciduous leaves. Staminate and pistillate flowers are in different inflorescences on the same tree. Staminate catkins are developed the previous season (preformed) in all except hornbeams.

BIRCHES *(Betula)*

In early spring the preformed staminate catkins of birches become distinctively tassel-like, 1 to 4 inches long. Their conelike strobiles, about 1 to 1.5 inches long, disintegrate when ripe, scattering their numerous scales and tiny seeds. The leaves, which vary in shape, have prominent veins, noticeably toothed margins, and short stems. The bark, marked by conspicuous, horizontal lenticels, peels in some species into long, curled, horizontal strips.

Most of the some 40 species of birches are small to medium-sized trees. They grow rapidly, often forming extensive forests in the North, but are relatively short-lived. The hard, beautiful wood of some birches is used for veneers, cabinet work, and interior finish. Birches are also used for paper pulp, woodenware, and novelties. The twigs of some are distilled to get oil of wintergreen. Because of their beauty of form, foliage, and bark, several species of birches are grown as ornamentals; in addition, several horticultural varieties have been developed for this purpose. Ground Birch *(Betula rotundifolia)* is a low-growing Alaskan shrub important as a summer food for reindeer.

PAPER BIRCH *(Betula papyrifera)* leaves are oval to ovate, 2 to 3 inches long and 1.5 to 2 inches wide, with a rounded base, pointed tip, and doubly toothed margins. On branches or on the trunks of young trees, the bark is brown to bronze. On the trunks of mature trees, the bark is white, peeling into long, narrow, horizontal strips that are curled at the ends. The bark at the base of the trunk of older trees is black and fissured. Paper Birch grows to 80 feet tall and 2 feet in diameter, with a central trunk and an irregular, pyramidal to rounded crown. Areas destroyed by fire are quickly reseeded by the Paper Birch, which is found in several varieties throughout northern North America. The use of Paper Birch bark by Indians of the North Country in making canoes is legendary.

COMPARISONS OF FRUITS OF VARIOUS MEMBERS OF BIRCH FAMILY

Birch (*Betula*) "cone," or strobile, disintegrates when mature.

Alder (*Alnus*) "cone," or strobile, thick and woody; does not disintegrate.

Hornbeam (*Carpinus*) seed is attached to a 3-lobed leafy bract. The bracts hang in clusters.

Hophornbeam (*Ostrya*) produces a cluster of leafy bladders, each containing a single seed.

Hazelnut, or filbert (*Corylus*), is oval and enclosed in a leathery, leafy cluster, or husk.

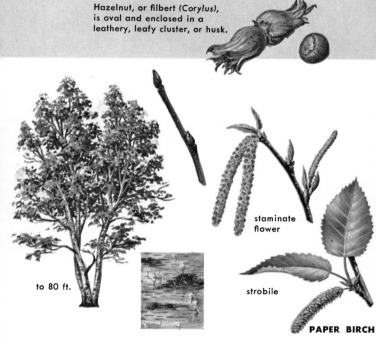

to 80 ft.

staminate flower

strobile

PAPER BIRCH

103

YELLOW BIRCH *(Betula alleghaniensis)* leaves resemble those of the Paper Birch but are longer and narrower—3 to 4.5 inches long, 1.5 to 2 inches wide. They have a rounded to heart-shaped base, somewhat hairy stems, and tufts of fine hairs in axils of veins on underside. Strobiles are ovoid, erect, and shed scales slowly. (Paper Birch strobiles are cylindrical, pendant, and shed scales quickly.) Yellow Birch bark is yellowish to bronze and peels into narrow, curled strips; on large trees, occurs in reddish-brown plates. Bark flammable even when wet, hence useful in starting campfires; slender twigs have a wintergreen flavor. Resembles Paper Birch in size and form; also reseeds burned areas quickly.

WATER BIRCH *(Betula occidentalis)* has leaves similar to those of Paper Birch but smaller, 1 to 2 inches long and 0.8 to 1 inch wide. The dark-brown, lustrous bark does not readily separate into thin layers. Water Birch is a small, often shrubby tree, growing 20 to 25 feet tall and 1 foot in diameter, with a broad, open crown of somewhat slender, drooping branches. It commonly forms impenetrable thickets, especially along streams.

SWEET BIRCH *(Betula lenta)* leaves are ovate to oblong-ovate, 2.5 to 5 inches long and 1.5 to 3 inches wide, with a tapered apex, often heart-shaped base, singly toothed margin, and hairy stem. Tufts of fine hairs occur in axils of veins on underside. The strobiles are ovoid and erect, resembling those of Yellow Birch but with smooth rather than hairy scales. Bark of young trees is black or dark reddish brown, marked with horizontal lenticels; does not peel. Bark in scaly plates on old trunks. Twigs have a strong wintergreen flavor. Grows 60 feet tall and 2 feet in diameter; has a round-topped, spreading crown. Prefers good soil.

GRAY BIRCH *(Betula populifolia)* leaves are triangular, 2.5 to 3.5 inches long, with coarse, doubly toothed margins. On trunks of young trees or on branches of older trees, the bark is brownish; on trunks of mature trees, it is chalky white, with prominent horizontal lenticels and triangular black patches below branch insertions. Bark resembles that of the Paper Birch but does not peel readily. Grows to 30 feet tall and 1 foot in diameter, with an irregular, open crown. Gray Birch is able to establish itself quickly in poor soils and invades abandoned farms and cutover lands.

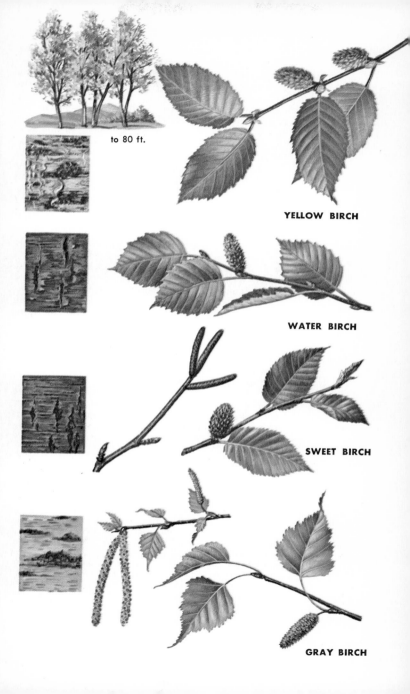

to 80 ft.

YELLOW BIRCH

WATER BIRCH

SWEET BIRCH

GRAY BIRCH

RIVER BIRCH *(Betula nigra)* leaves are irregularly oval, 1.5 to 3 inches long and 1 to 2 inches wide, with coarse, doubly toothed margins. They are hairy on the stems and on the underside of the stout midrib. Bark on young trees thin and pinkish to reddish brown; on older trunks, gray to black and scaly. A medium-sized tree, to 80 feet tall and 3 feet in diameter, the River Birch's trunk is commonly divided into several arching limbs, forming an irregular crown. Seeds mature in late spring when banks are exposed by receding flood waters, providing places for germination. River Birch is the only native birch at low elevations in southeastern United States; common along streams.

BLUELEAF BIRCH *(Betula caerulea-grandis)* is most commonly a shrub but sometimes a tree, growing to 30 feet tall and 10 inches in diameter, with a crown of slender, ascending branches. The bark, which does not peel, is white with a rosy hue. The bluish-green leaves, paler below, are 2 to 2.5 inches long and 1 to 1.5 inches wide, with a long-pointed tip and a wedge-shaped base. The margins are sharply double-toothed, and the veins and midrib on the underside are somewhat hairy. The cylindric strobiles, also hairy, are about 1 inch long, 0.3 of an inch in diameter.

YUKON BIRCH *(Betula eastwoodiae)* is a natural hybrid that grows to 20 feet tall and 6 inches in diameter. Bark chestnut brown, with white lenticels. Its elliptical to ovate leaves are 1 to 1.5 inches long and 0.8 to 1.5 inches wide, with an abruptly pointed apex and coarsely toothed margins, except along wedge-shaped base. The pendant strobiles are 0.8 of an inch long and less than 0.3 of an inch in diameter, their scales not hairy.

AN INTRODUCED BIRCH

EUROPEAN WHITE BIRCH *(Betula pendula)* leaves are ovate to somewhat diamond-shaped, 1 to 2.5 inches long and to 1.5 inches wide, with a rounded to wedge-shaped base and coarse, irregularly toothed margins. The white bark, marked with conspicuous horizontal lenticels and with black triangular patches below the branch insertions, is somewhat similar to Gray Birch bark but rougher and thicker. European White Birch grows to 60 feet tall and 2 feet in diameter, with either a central or a divided trunk. Its branches are spreading and ascending or pendant. In northern Europe, the European White Birch is an important commercial hardwood tree. Several varieties are planted as ornamentals in the United States. Among these are the Weeping Birch, which has a crown of slender, gracefully drooping branches; and the even more attractive Cut-leaved Birch, with deeply cut, lobed leaf margins in which the margins of the lobes are coarsely toothed.

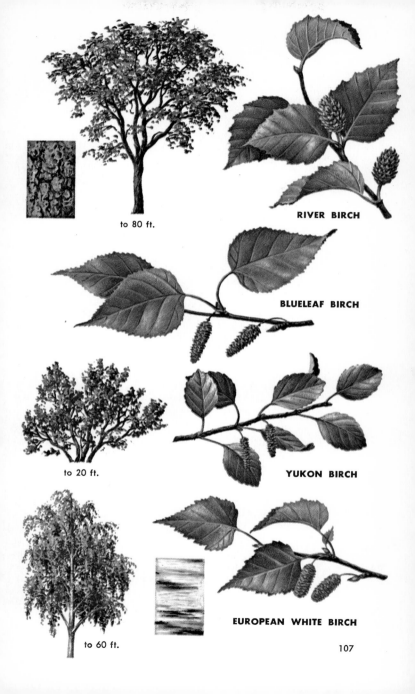

to 80 ft.

RIVER BIRCH

BLUELEAF BIRCH

to 20 ft.

YUKON BIRCH

to 60 ft.

EUROPEAN WHITE BIRCH

107

ALDERS *(Alnus)*

Alders have irregularly toothed, often shallowly lobed, oval to elliptical or oblong leaves, prominently veined. In spring, preformed staminate catkins (p. 102), 4- to 6-inches long, become tassel-like. Conelike strobiles, 0.5 to 1.3 inches long, do not disintegrate as do those of birches (p. 103). Stalked, reddish-brown buds are usually covered with several valvate scales. Alders grow rapidly and often form thickets in moist soils. They are relatively short-lived. Eight species native to the U.S. and Canada reach tree size. In addition to those described here, Speckled Alder *(A. rugosa)* and Hazel Alder *(A. serrulata)* are usually shrubs occasionally reaching tree size, along streams in eastern U.S. and Canada.

RED ALDER *(Alnus rubra)* leaves are ovate to elliptical, 3 to 6 inches long and 2 to 3 inches wide, dark green above and lighter with rusty-brown hairs below. Their coarsely doubly toothed margins are slightly curled under. Staminate catkins lengthen before leaves develop in spring, giving thickets a distinctive greenish-brown cast. Bark of young trees is smooth and blue-gray, with whitish blotches; on older trunks, darker and broken into flat plates. Inner bark is reddish brown. Usually grows 30 to 60 feet tall and 1 to 2 feet in diameter, with a central trunk and a domelike crown. On burned or logged-off land, becomes established quickly and adds humus and nitrogen to soil, preparing the way for the more valuable conifers. Favored for fireplace fuel, since it does not scatter sparks; also increasing in importance for furniture, veneers, and paper pulp.

WHITE ALDER *(Alnus rhombifolia)* resembles Red Alder but is smaller. Ovate leaves are small, light green, 2 to 4 inches long and 1.5 to 2.5 inches wide, and usually have single-toothed margins, which are not turned under. Pith chamber of twigs is distinctly triangular in cross section; Red Alder's is only roughly triangular.

SITKA ALDER *(Alnus sinuata)* has ovate leaves, 2 to 5 inches long and 1.5 to 4 inches wide, with sharply doubly toothed margins. The staminate catkins lengthen as the leaves develop in early spring, and the gray-green bark is smooth, except for warty lenticels. Though usually a sprawling shrub, it may grow to 30 feet tall and 6 inches in diameter.

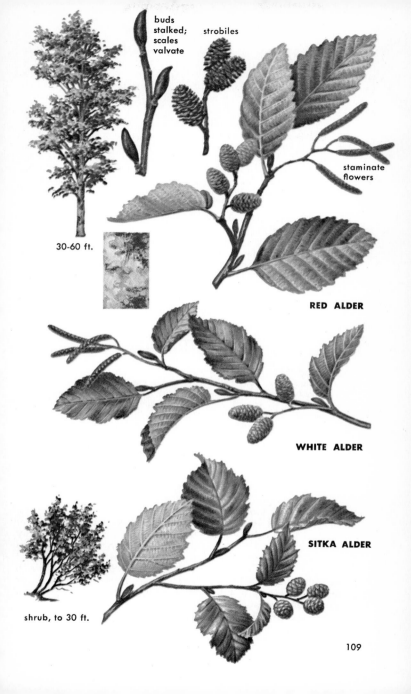

buds stalked; scales valvate

strobiles

staminate flowers

30-60 ft.

RED ALDER

WHITE ALDER

SITKA ALDER

shrub, to 30 ft.

THINLEAF ALDER *(Alnus tenuifolia)*, similar in size to Sitka Alder, has ovate to oblong leaves, 2 to 4 inches long and 1.5 to 2.5 inches wide, with shallowly lobed, doubly toothed margins. Leaves have a stout, orange-brown midrib and rusty-brown hairs below.

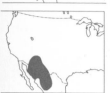

ARIZONA ALDER *(Alnus oblongifolia)*, about the same size as Sitka Alder, has elliptical leaves, 2 to 3 inches long and 1.5 to 2 inches wide, usually with doubly toothed margins. They are dark green above, paler and slightly hairy on yellow midrib and veins below. Staminate catkins lengthen in winter, dropping before leaves unfold. Bark smooth, gray to brown.

SEASIDE ALDER *(Alnus maritima)* has broadly elliptical leaves with small, incurved marginal teeth. They are lustrous green above, with stout, yellow midrib and stem. The flowers open in the fall, staminate catkins to 2.5 inches long and bulky pistillate strobiles to 1 inch long. Seeds ripen the following year. Bark smooth, gray to light brown. Seaside Alder has a narrow, round-topped crown of zigzag branches; grows to about 30 feet tall, 6 inches in diameter.

AN INTRODUCED ALDER

EUROPEAN ALDER *(Alnus glutinosa)* is a medium-sized tree, 50 to 70 feet tall and 1 to 2 feet in diameter. Most common of several foreign alders planted as ornamentals. Bark is dark and has many warty stripes. Leaves, broadly ovate or widest above middle and with coarse marginal teeth, are dark green above and paler below, with fine hairs especially along veins. Young leaves and twigs are gummy.

HAZELS, OR FILBERTS *(Corylus)*

Hazels, or Filberts, are shrubs and small trees with hairy, ovate to elliptical leaves, 3 to 5 inches long and 2 to 4 inches wide, with heart-shaped base and coarse, doubly toothed margins. Preformed staminate catkins resemble those of birches, but the buds are oval and the fruit is a nut surrounded by leafy bracts or enclosed by a leafy husk (p. 103). American Hazel *(C. americana)* and Beaked Hazel *(C. rostrata)* are native shrubs of eastern United States and Canada. California Hazel *(C. cornuta* var. *californica)*, a tall shrub with fruit resembling Beaked Hazel, occurs in the West. The Giant Filbert *(C. maxima)*, a small tree (to 25 feet) native to southeastern Europe, is occasionally planted in the United States as an ornamental. Varieties are grown commercially for edible nuts.

THINLEAF ALDER

ARIZONA ALDER

SEASIDE ALDER

to 70 ft.

EUROPEAN ALDER

BEAKED HAZEL

GIANT FILBERT

111

HOPHORNBEAMS *(Ostrya)*

Hophornbeams are small trees with birchlike leaves and preformed staminate catkins that become about 2 inches long. Hophornbeams are most distinctive for their pendant clusters of flattened, leafy, hoplike bladders, each with a small, nutlike seed attached inside at base. Two species are native to North America; other species occur in Europe and in Asia.

EASTERN HOPHORNBEAM *(Ostrya virginiana)* is often called Ironwood because of its very hard, heavy wood. Its oblong, lanceolate leaves, 3 to 5 inches long and 1.5 to 2 inches wide, are narrowed to a slender point and have doubly toothed margins. Leaves are dull yellow-green above and lighter below, with tufts of hairs in the axils of veins. The clusters of bladder-like, seed-bearing pods are 1.5 to 2 inches long. Reddish-brown bark is broken into thick, narrow scales that are loose at ends; giving trunk a shaggy appearance. A round-topped tree, 20 to 30 feet tall (rarely to 50 feet) and 1 to 1.5 feet in diameter. Usually grows in dry soils.

KNOWLTON HOPHORNBEAM *(Ostrya knowltonii)* is generally smaller than the above and may have several stems. Leaves elliptical. Knowlton Hophornbeam is often found in moist canyons.

HORNBEAMS *(Carpinus)*

Hornbeams are small trees with birchlike leaves. Staminate catkins, to 1.5 inches long in spring, are not preformed (p. 102). Recognized by their many pendant clusters of loose, leafy, 3-pointed bracts, each bearing a small, nutlike seed attached to the base. Of about 26 species, all found in the Northern Hemisphere, only one is native to North America. European Hornbeam *(C. betulus)* is occasionally planted in the United States as an ornamental or shade tree.

AMERICAN HORNBEAM *(Carpinus caroliniana)*, also called Blue Beech or Water Beech, has elliptical leaves, 2 to 4 inches long and 1 to 2 inches wide. They are dull green above and yellow-green below, with tufts of hairs in axils of the veins and doubly toothed margins. The light-green, leafy clusters of seed-bearing bracts are 3 to 6 inches long and conspicuous in late spring. A small tree with a round-topped crown, American Hornbeam has a short, fluted, or "muscular," trunk, and smooth, blue-gray bark. It grows to 40 feet tall and 1 to 2 feet in diameter. Most common in moist, rich soil bordering streams or swamps.

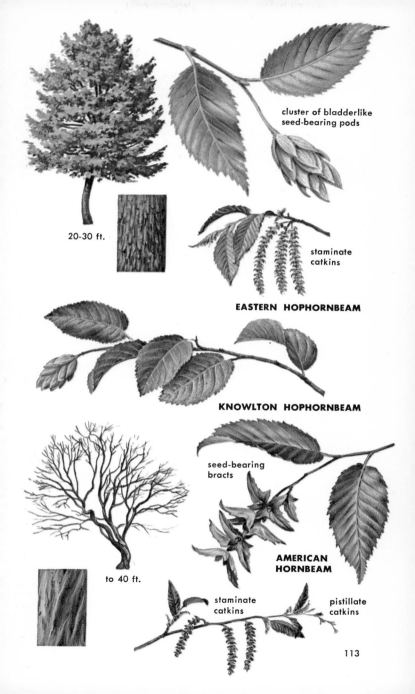

cluster of bladderlike
seed-bearing pods

20-30 ft.

staminate
catkins

EASTERN HOPHORNBEAM

KNOWLTON HOPHORNBEAM

seed-bearing
bracts

**AMERICAN
HORNBEAM**

to 40 ft.

staminate
catkins

pistillate
catkins

113

BEECH FAMILY (Fagaceae)

One of the most important of families of trees, both commercially and aesthetically, the beech family is widespread in both the Northern and Southern hemispheres. Of the 600 species, nearly 100 are native to North America. Familiar members are the beeches, oaks, and chestnuts, prized for the quality of their wood and admired for their regal beauty. Less familiar are the chinkapins and tanoaks, most typical of southeastern Asia and adjacent islands but each including one tree species native to the Pacific Coast states. The beechlike, deciduous or evergreen trees of the genus *Nothofagus* occur in South America, Australia, and New Zealand. All members of the beech family have alternate leaves.

BEECHES *(Fagus)*

Beeches are handsome deciduous trees with short-stemmed, prominently veined elliptical leaves that have wide-spaced marginal teeth. Monoecious, the flowers appearing with the leaves—the staminate yellowish green, in long-stemmed heads; pistillate, in 2- to 4-flowered spikes. Triangular, edible nuts are borne in 2's or 3's in a husk covered by weak, unbranched spines. Bark is smooth and gray, even on large trunks. Long, spindle-shaped, scaly buds extend at sharp angle from slender twigs. Of 10 species in this genus, one is native to U.S. and Canada; others grow in Europe.

AMERICAN BEECH *(Fagus grandifolia)* leaves are 2 to 6 inches long and 1 to 2.5 inches wide, with small but prominent, incurved marginal teeth. They are smooth on both surfaces, except for hairy tufts in axils of veins on underside, and taper to a pointed apex. The smooth bark is blue-gray and commonly blotched. A medium-sized to large tree, 60 to 100 feet tall and 2 to 3 feet in diameter, with a short trunk and a broad, rounded crown. Grows best in soils with ample surface moisture, as the wide-spreading root system is shallow.

AN INTRODUCED BEECH

EUROPEAN BEECH *(Fagus sylvatica)*, a common and important European timber tree, is widely planted in the United States as an ornamental. Resembles American Beech but is smaller, has darker bark, and smaller, more elliptical leaves, 2 to 4 inches long and 1 to 2 inches wide, with smaller, rounded marginal teeth. Leaf margins and veins on underside are noticeably hairy, especially on young leaves. Purple Beech *(F. sylvatica* var. *atropunica)* has purplish-bronze or copper-colored foliage. Other varieties include one with pendant branches (var. *pendula)* and a cut-leaved form (var. *laciniata).*

Beech
Fagus

angled nuts in bur with weak spines; mature 1st season

Chinkapin
Castanopsis

rounded nuts in prickly bur; mature 2nd season

Chestnut
Castanea

rounded nuts in prickly bur; mature 1st season

Tanoak
Lithocarpus

acorn, matures in 2nd season

Oak
Quercus

acorn; matures in 1st or 2nd season

COMPARISON OF NUTS IN THE BEECH FAMILY

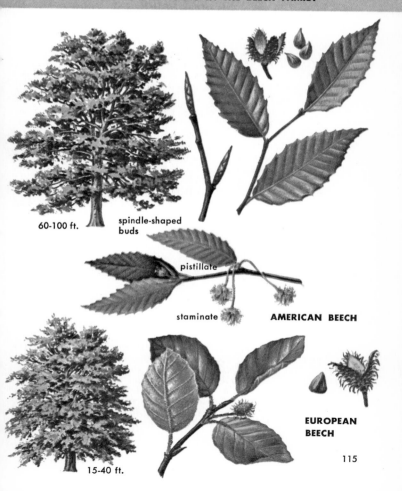

60-100 ft.

spindle-shaped buds

pistillate

staminate

AMERICAN BEECH

EUROPEAN BEECH

15-40 ft.

115

CHESTNUTS *(Castanea)*

Chestnuts are deciduous trees with short-stemmed, prominently veined leaves that have coarse, bristly marginal teeth. Small flowers, in slender, erect, unisexual or bisexual catkins (aments), appear after the leaves. Staminate catkins are long and drooping; bisexual catkins shorter, with pistillate flowers at base. Rounded, edible nuts are in husks (burs) covered with stiff, branched, prickly spines; husks split open when nuts mature. About 10 species occur in southern Europe, northern Africa, eastern Asia, and eastern North America.

AMERICAN CHESTNUT *(Castanea dentata)* leaves are oblong-lanceolate, 5 to 8 inches long and 2 inches wide, dull dark green above, paler below, and smooth on both surfaces. Slender, arching, staminate catkins, 6 to 8 inches long, are conspicuous near ends of the branches in spring; bisexual flowers are shorter. Prickly husks, about 2.5 inches in diameter, contain two or three somewhat flattened nuts, about 1 inch in diameter. Bark dark brown; smooth on young trees and broken into broad, flattened, scaly ridges on large trunks. Once one of the most valuable of American hardwoods, this species has been virtually destroyed by chestnut blight, an introduced fungus disease affecting the bark. Few uninfected trees exist, though stump sprouts persist. Grew nearly 100 feet tall and 4 feet in diameter, with a broad, rounded crown.

ALLEGHENY CHINKAPIN *(Castanea pumila)* resembles the American Chestnut but is smaller and usually occurs in dry soils. A shrub or a small tree, rarely to 50 feet tall and 2 feet in diameter. Its leaves, not as sharply tapered, are 3 to 5 inches long and 1.5 inches wide, covered with gray hairs on underside and on stem. Smaller nuts, 0.8 of an inch in diameter, are borne singly in husks 1 to 1.5 inches in diameter. Other similar southern trees include Ashe Chinkapin *(C. pumila* var. *ashei),* Ozark Chinkapin *(C. ozarkensis),* and Florida Chinkapin *(C. alnifolia* var. *floridana),* a treelike variety of a shrubby species.

INTRODUCED CHESTNUTS

SPANISH CHESTNUT *(Castanea sativa),* native to southern Europe, Asia, and northern Africa, is grown in North America as an ornamental. It grows 75 feet tall and 2 feet in diameter. Leaves are 6 to 9 inches long and about 2 inches wide, and the nuts are over 1 inch in diameter. Two Oriental species of chestnuts have also been introduced; both produce large nuts. Chinese Chestnut *(C. mollissima)* becomes 60 feet tall. Japanese Chestnut *(C. crenata)* is rarely more than 30 feet tall.

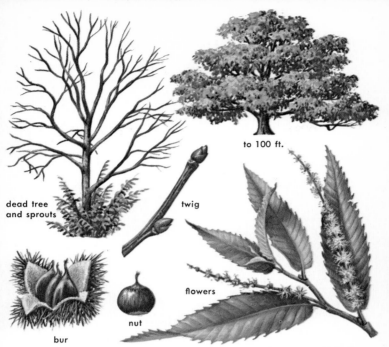

to 100 ft.

dead tree and sprouts

twig

bur

nut

flowers

AMERICAN CHESTNUT

ALLEGHENY CHINKAPIN

SPANISH CHESTNUT

117

CHINKAPINS *(Castanopsis)*

This group of about 30 species of evergreen trees and shrubs is found primarily in southeastern Asia, but two species grow in western United States. One *(C. sempervirens)* is a shrub of coastal ranges and Sierra Nevada in California and southern Oregon.

GOLDEN CHINKAPIN *(Castanopsis chrysophylla)* has leathery, lanceolate or oblong-lanceolate, evergreen leaves, with smooth, curled margins. Dark glossy green above and golden yellow on underside, they are 2 to 5 inches long and 0.5 to 1.5 inches wide. Flowers, similar to those of chestnuts, are in erect, 2- to 2.5-inch aments. Staminate flowers are creamy white. The burs resemble chestnuts but are smaller and mature in two years; they contain either one or two edible, rounded nuts. On young trees, bark is smooth; on older trees, it is broken into reddish-brown plates. In northern California and southern Oregon, grows 50 to 100 feet tall and 1 to 3 feet in diameter, with a dense, conical crown.

TANOAKS *(Lithocarpus)*

Except for the one species native to California and southern Oregon, this group of about 100 species is confined to southeastern Asia. Tanoak flowers resemble those of the chestnuts, while the fruits are like those of the oaks.

TANOAK *(Lithocarpus densiflorus)* has leathery, evergreen leaves that are elliptical to oblong-lanceolate, 2 to 5 inches long and 1 to 2.5 inches wide, with wide-spaced marginal teeth and short, hairy stems. They are smooth and dark green above; the underside is at first covered with rusty-brown hairs, later becoming blue-gray and only slightly hairy. Young twigs are also hairy. Catkins are similar to those of the chestnut, though 3 to 4 inches long. The fruit, an acorn about 0.8 of an inch long, has a shallow cup covered by many hairy, linear scales. The acorns are bitter and require two years to mature. Bark of large trees is ridged and fissured. Formerly the bark was used for tanning, and because the tree was once considered to be an oak, the name Tanoak was applied. Under best conditions, Tanoak grows 60 to 100 feet tall and 1 to 3 feet in diameter, with a narrow, pyramidal crown of ascending branches.

50-100 ft.

flowers

nut

bur

GOLDEN CHINKAPIN

60-100 ft.

TANOAK

119

OAKS *(Quercus)*

Oaks are widely distributed in North America. Of about 60 species native to the area covered by this book (p. 3), 41 are described. (Varieties, hybrids, shrubs, and rare or localized species are omitted.) Some oaks are deciduous, others evergreen; some are either, depending on local conditions. Monoecious—the staminate flowers in pendant, clustered aments near ends of twigs; pistillate, solitary or in several-flowered spikes in new-leaf axils. Fruit an acorn. Buds clustered at tips of twigs. Leaves alternate.

North American oaks are divided into two groups: white oaks and red oaks. Most white oaks have leaves with rounded lobes or marginal teeth not tipped with bristles. Their acorns mature in one season, and the shells are hairless inside. Their meat is not bitter. Red oaks have pointed bristle-tipped lobes; bristle-tipped or spiny marginal teeth; or smooth margins, often with a spiny or bristle-tipped apex. Usually their acorns mature in two years, the shells are hairy inside, and the meat is bitter. Chestnut oaks form a subsection of the white oak group; the willow oaks and live oaks are subsections of the red oak group.

WHITE OAK GROUP

WHITE OAK *(Quercus alba)* leaves are deciduous, 5 to 9 inches long and 2 to 4 inches wide, with 7 to 9 rounded lobes divided by narrow, variable sinuses often extending nearly to the midrib. The oblong acorns, 0.5 to 0.8 of an inch long, are set in a bowl-like cup covered with warty scales. The gray bark is in narrow, vertical blocks of scaly plates. Grows 80 to 100 feet tall and 3 to 4 feet in diameter, with a wide-spreading crown.

BUR OAK *(Quercus macrocarpa)* has deciduous leaves, 6 to 12 inches long and 3 to 6 inches wide, with 5 to 9 rounded lobes; only central sinuses extend nearly to midrib. The broadly ovoid acorn, 0.8 to 1.5 inches long, has a fringed cup covering lower half. Twigs often have corky "wings." Bark resembles White Oak's. Bur Oak prefers bottomland soils. Grows 70 to 80 feet tall, 2 to 3 feet in diameter.

OVERCUP OAK *(Quercus lyrata)* has deciduous leaves, 6 to 10 inches long and 1 to 4 inches wide, with 5 to 9 rounded lobes separated by broad, irregular sinuses. The broad, nearly round acorn, 0.5 to 1 inch long, is covered almost completely with a scaly cup. The bark is similar to White Oak's. Typical of wet bottomlands, Overcup Oak may grow 60 to 100 feet tall and 3 to 4 feet in diameter, usually smaller.

most with rounded lobes

acorns sweet, mature in 1st season

WHITE OAKS

most with spiny, pointed lobes

acorns mostly bitter; mature in 2nd season

RED OAKS

80-100 ft.

pistillate flowers in axils of new leaves

staminate flowers

WHITE OAK

BUR OAK

OVERCUP OAK

POST OAK *(Quercus stellata)* has leathery, deciduous leaves, 4 to 6 inches long and 3 to 4 inches wide, usually deeply 5-lobed, with center lobes squarish. Leaf margins are somewhat curled under, surfaces slightly hairy. A bowl-like, scaly cup covers lower third of the ovoid-oblong acorns, 0.5 to 0.8 of an inch long. Bark similar to White Oak's. Often found in dry soils. Grows 40 to 50 feet tall and 1 to 2 feet in diameter, usually with a crown of gnarled, twisted branches.

OREGON WHITE OAK *(Quercus garryana)* leaves are deciduous, 4 to 6 inches long and 2 to 5 inches wide. Sinuses separating the 5 to 7 (occasionally 9) rounded lobes extend about halfway to the midrib. The lower surface and petioles somewhat hairy, the margin slightly curled under. The ovoid to obovoid acorn, about 1 inch long, has a shallow cup with hairy scales loose at tip. Bark resembles White Oak's. Grows 50 to 70 feet tall and 2 to 3 feet in diameter, with rounded crown.

CALIFORNIA WHITE OAK *(Quercus lobata)* has deciduous leaves, 2 to 4 inches long and 1 to 2 inches wide, with 7 to 11 rounded lobes. The slim, conical acorn, 1 to 2.5 inches long, has a deep cup covering the lower third. At first green, acorns later turn brown; cup scales are knobby, with free tips. Largest of western oaks, it grows 80 to 120 feet tall and 3 to 5 feet in diameter, with a short trunk and a broad crown.

GAMBEL OAK *(Quercus gambelii)* leaves are deciduous, 2 to 7 inches long and 1.5 to 3.5 inches wide, with 7 to 11 deep lobes. They are smooth on upper surface, hairy below. Broadly oval acorns, 1 inch long, are nearly half enclosed by a bowl-like cup with hairy scales. Bark similar to White Oak's. Grows 15 to 30 feet tall and 5 to 10 inches in diameter, with rounded crown.

CHAPMAN OAK *(Quercus chapmanii)* leaves, 2 to 3 inches long and 1 inch wide, are obovate or oblong, with smooth or undulating margins. They are leathery, dark green above and silvery below, sometimes remaining until new foliage forms. Oval acorns, about 0.8 of an inch long, are half enclosed by a cup with pointed scales. Bark usually in dark-gray plates. A shrub or small tree of sandy soils, to 50 feet tall, 1 foot in diameter.

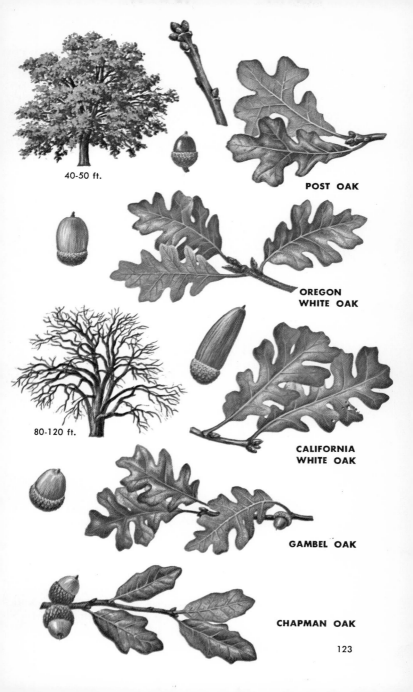

40-50 ft.

POST OAK

OREGON WHITE OAK

80-120 ft.

CALIFORNIA WHITE OAK

GAMBEL OAK

CHAPMAN OAK

123

CHESTNUT OAK *(Quercus prinus)* has obovate to nearly lanceolate, deciduous leaves, 4 to 8 inches long, 1.5 to 3 inches wide; margins with large, rounded teeth; undersurface often hairy. Oval acorns, 1 to 1.5 inches long, are lustrous and short-stemmed, their lower third covered with a thin cup with fused scales. Bark dark brown to black, deeply ridged, furrowed. Chestnut Oak grows 50 to 60 feet tall and 1 to 2 feet in diameter, preferring drier soils. Also called Rock Oak, as it is common in drier, often rocky soils.

SWAMP CHESTNUT OAK *(Quercus michauxii)* leaves are deciduous, obovate, 5 to 8 inches long, 3 to 4 inches wide; silvery or somewhat hairy on underside; marginal teeth coarse, rounded. Lower third of oblong acorns, 1 to 1.5 inches long, covered by a bowl-like cup with coarse, wedge-shaped scales. Bark gray to reddish, irregularly furrowed. Prefers moist bottomland soils, growing 60 to 80 feet tall, 2 to 3 feet in diameter, usually with its trunk clear of branches for some distance above the ground. Swamp Chestnut Oak is known also as Cow Oak, since cattle eat the acorns.

SWAMP WHITE OAK *(Quercus bicolor)* has obovate, deciduous leaves, 5 to 6 inches long and 2 to 4 inches wide. The margin is irregularly and shallowly lobed or has bluntly pointed teeth; lower surface is hairy. Long-stemmed (1-4 inches), oval acorns are usually in pairs. Each acorn is about 1 inch long and has a scaly, somewhat fringed cup enclosing lower third. Dark-brown to black bark is coarsely ridged, furrowed, or scaly on upper branches. Swamp White Oak generally grows in moist to swampy soils; it may be 50 to 70 feet tall and 1 to 3 feet in diameter.

CHINKAPIN OAK *(Quercus muehlenbergii)* leaves are deciduous, oblong-lanceolate, 4 to 7 inches long and 1 to 4 inches wide, with coarse, bluntly pointed marginal teeth and fine white hairs below. Acorns sessile, brown to black, ovoid, 0.5 to 0.8 of an inch long, the lower half in a bowl-shaped, scaly cup. Bark ash gray, rough and flaky. Grows 50 to 80 feet tall and 1 to 3 feet in diameter, usually in dry rocky soils. Dwarf Chinkapin Oak *(Q. prinoides)* grows in same area, has smaller obovate leaves, and is rarely tree size.

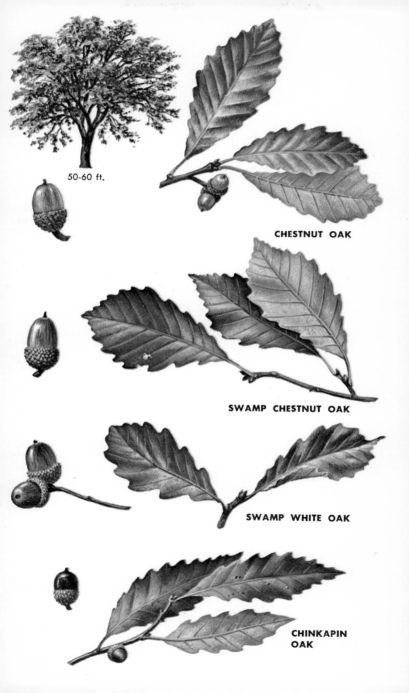

50-60 ft.

CHESTNUT OAK

SWAMP CHESTNUT OAK

SWAMP WHITE OAK

CHINKAPIN OAK

RED OAK GROUP
(see pp. 120-121)

NORTHERN RED OAK *(Quercus rubra)* has deciduous leaves, 5 to 8 inches long and 4 to 5 inches wide, with 7 to 11 pointed, toothed lobes separated by regular sinuses that extend halfway to the midrib. The leaves turn red in the fall. The oblong-ovoid acorns are 0.8 to 1 inch long, with a flat, saucer-like cup at their base. The dark-brown to black bark is ridged and furrowed. Grows 50 to 70 feet tall and 1 to 3 feet in diameter, with a rounded crown.

BLACK OAK *(Quercus velutina)* leaves resemble those of Northern Red Oak but have 5 to 7 lobes separated by variable sinuses and are coppery with axillary tufts of hair below. Ovoid acorns, 0.5 to 0.8 of an inch long, have deep, bowl-like, scaly cups. Bark is black, ridged, and furrowed. Grows 50 to 70 feet tall and 1 to 3 feet in diameter, with rounded crown.

SCARLET OAK *(Quercus coccinea)* has deciduous leaves about the same size as those of Northern Red Oak, but the 5 to 9 narrow, toothed, and pointed lobes are separated by deep, rounded sinuses that extend nearly to the midrib. In fall, the leaves turn red or scarlet. The oval acorns, 0.5 to 1 inch long, have a deep, bowl-like, scaly cup, and the apex is often marked with circular lines. Grows 50 to 75 feet tall and 1 to 3 feet in diameter, with an irregular, spreading crown.

PIN OAK *(Quercus palustris)* leaves are deciduous, 3 to 5 inches long and 2 to 5 inches wide. The 5 (occasionally 7 to 9) lobes are toothed and pointed, with deep, irregular sinuses extending nearly to the midrib. The leaves turn red in fall. The nearly round, brownish, and hairless acorns are 0.5 of an inch long, have a thin, scaly, shallow cup; the branches have short, stubby twigs. Prefers bottomland soils. Grows 50 to 75 feet tall and 1 to 3 feet in diameter, with smooth to ridged, gray-brown bark.

NORTHERN PIN OAK *(Quercus ellipsoidalis)* is similar to Pin Oak, except the slim, tapered acorns, about 1 inch long, are in a deep, scaly cup. Also, Northern Pin Oak grows on dry and higher ground.

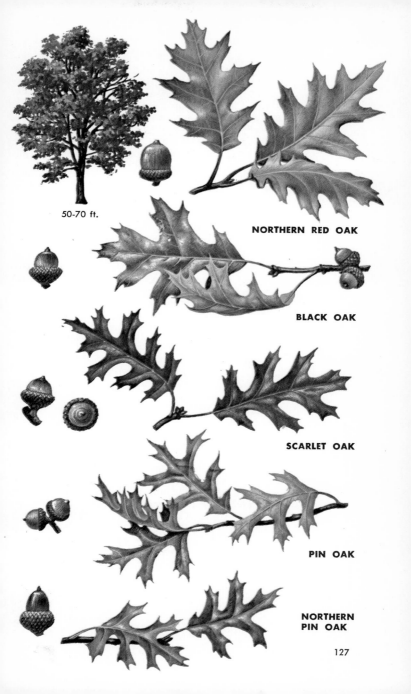

50-70 ft.

NORTHERN RED OAK

BLACK OAK

SCARLET OAK

PIN OAK

NORTHERN PIN OAK

127

SOUTHERN RED OAK *(Quercus falcata)* has deciduous leaves, 5 to 9 inches long and 4 to 5 inches wide, with a rusty or hairy underside. They are deeply 3- to 7-lobed, the terminal lobe much longer and narrower than the others. Rounded acorns, 0.5 of an inch long, have a scaly cup over lower third. Grows 60 to 80 feet tall and 1 to 3 feet in diameter, with a large, rounded crown and dark-brown to black, roughly ridged bark. Usually found in poor upland soils.

SHUMARD OAK *(Quercus shumardii)* has deciduous leaves, 6 to 8 inches long and 4 to 5 inches wide, with 7 to 9 toothed lobes. Acorns are oblong-ovoid and 0.8 to 1.3 inches long, with a thick, shallow, saucer-like, scaly cup. Attaining a height of more than 100 feet and a trunk diameter of 2 to 5 feet, this is one of the largest of the "red oaks." Bark on the usually clear trunk is gray, ridged, and furrowed, the crown wide-spreading. Grows commonly in moist bottomland soils.

NUTTALL OAK *(Quercus nuttallii)* has deciduous leaves, 4 to 8 inches long and 2 to 5 inches wide, with 5 to 7 broad lobes separated by deep sinuses. Oblong-ovoid acorns, 0.8 to 1 inch long, have a thick, deep, scaly cup. Grows 60 to 80 feet tall and 1 to 3 feet in diameter, most commonly in moist bottomland soils.

BLACKJACK OAK *(Quercus marilandica)* has leathery, deciduous leaves, 3 to 7 inches long, variable in shape but widest and shallowly 3-lobed at the apex. Their undersurface is brown and hairy. The small, oblong acorns, 0.8 of an inch long, are about half covered with a thick, scaly, bowl-shaped cup, and the black bark is in thick, rough plates. Blackjack Oak grows 20 to 30 feet tall and 1 foot in diameter. It is a ragged tree of poorer soils.

TURKEY OAK *(Quercus laevis)* has deciduous leaves, 3 to 12 inches long and 1 to 6 inches wide, with 3 to 7 narrow, curved, and often toothed lobes. Lower third of the ovoid acorns, about 1 inch long, are in a thin, bowl-shaped cup. Turkey Oak has gray to black, scaly and ridged bark. Grows 20 to 30 feet tall and 1 to 2 feet in diameter, with stout branches and an irregular, rounded crown. Common in sandy soils.

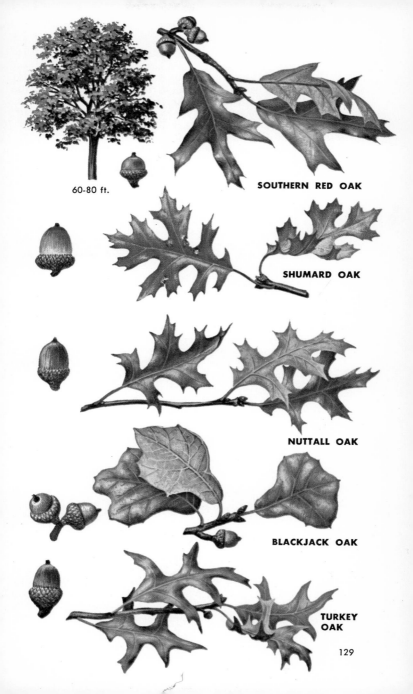

60-80 ft.

SOUTHERN RED OAK

SHUMARD OAK

NUTTALL OAK

BLACKJACK OAK

TURKEY OAK

129

CALIFORNIA BLACK OAK *(Quercus kelloggii)* has deciduous leaves, 3 to 6 inches long and 2 to 3 inches wide, with 5 to 7 toothed lobes. The ellipsoidal, inch-long acorn, once a staple food of California Indians, has a deep, bowl-like, roughly scaly cup covering lower third. Usually with a short trunk and rounded crown, California Black Oak has black, heavily ridged bark. Grows 50 to 100 feet tall, 1 to 3 feet in diameter; most common on drier soils.

BLUE OAK *(Quercus douglasii)* has oblong to oval, deciduous leaves, 3 inches long, the margins smooth or with 4 or 5 lobes. The ellipsoidal acorn, about 1 inch long, has a shallow cup. Unlike many "red oaks," the meat of the Blue Oak's acorn is not bitter, the shell is hairless inside, and it matures in one season. The gray-brown bark is scaly. Blue Oak grows 50 to 75 feet tall and 1 to 3 feet in diameter, with a rounded to irregular crown.

BEAR OAK *(Quercus ilicifolia)* leaves are deciduous, 2 to 5 inches long and 1 to 3 inches wide, with wide, shallow sinuses and 3 to 7 (usually 5) toothed lobes. The underside of the leaves is silvery-haired. A scaly cup surrounds lower half of broadly ovoid acorn, 0.5 of an inch long. Grows 15 to 20 feet tall, 6 inches in diameter, with slender branches and round-topped crown; usually in dry, sandy soil.

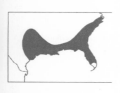

BLUEJACK OAK *(Quercus incana)* leaves are blue-green, oblong-lanceolate, 2 to 5 inches long and 0.5 to 1.5 inches wide, with smooth margins (occasionally 3-lobed at apex), and white-hairy below. They are tardily deciduous; very young leaves pink and pubescent. Acorns variable, ovoid to globose, sometimes flattened, 0.5 of an inch long, hairy at apex, striated, with thin, scaly cup. Bark reddish-brown to black, broken into small blocks. A shrub or small tree of dry soils; to 20 feet tall and 6 inches in diameter.

MYRTLE OAK *(Quercus myrtifolia)* leaves are ever-green, 0.5 to 2 inches long and 0.3 to 1 inch wide, widest above the middle; tips sharp or rounded, base gradually narrowed. The margins are smooth and turned under. Acorns are dark lustrous brown, nearly round, 0.3 to 0.5 inch long, striated, with a scaly cup on the lower third. A shrub or small tree of sandy coastal soils, to 40 feet tall and 5 inches in diameter.

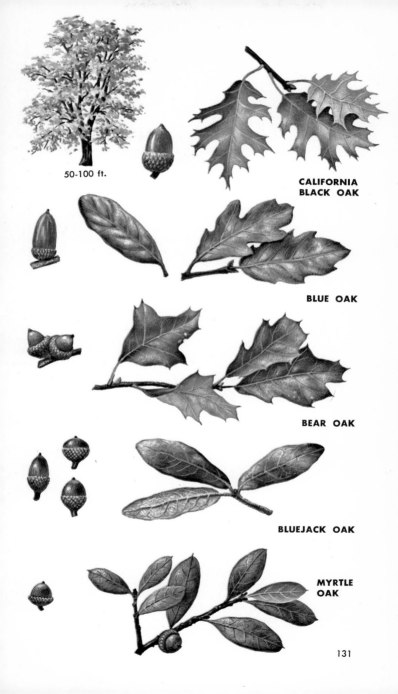

50-100 ft.

CALIFORNIA BLACK OAK

BLUE OAK

BEAR OAK

BLUEJACK OAK

MYRTLE OAK

131

WILLOW OAK (*Quercus phellos*) has willow-like, deciduous leaves, 2 to 5 inches long and 0.5 to 1 inch wide, with smooth margins and a bristle-tipped apex. They are light green above, dull and paler below. The small, roundish acorns, 0.5 inch long, have a thin, scaly, saucer-like cup. Typical of bottomland soils, Willow Oak grows 80 to 100 feet tall and 2 to 4 feet in diameter, with gray to black, irregularly furrowed bark, a short trunk, and a broad, rounded crown. It may also be nearly evergreen in the South.

WATER OAK (*Quercus nigra*) has deciduous leaves, 2 to 4 inches long and 1 to 2 inches wide, which remain on tree well into winter. They are variable in shape but usually taper from a broad, shallowly 3-lobed apex, and have smooth to shallowly lobed margins. Small, ovoid, black acorns, 0.5 inch long, are set in a shallow, scaly cup. Bark mottled gray-black, broken into scaly ridges. A bottomland species; grows 60 to 70 feet tall and 2 to 3 feet in diameter, usually with a rounded crown.

SHINGLE OAK (*Quercus imbricaria*) has laurel-like, oblong-lanceolate to oblong-obovate, deciduous leaves, with smooth, wavy, and slightly curled margins. They are 4 to 6 inches long and 1 to 2 inches wide, brown-hairy below. The acorns, 0.5 to 0.8 of an inch long, are oval, the lower third enclosed in a thin, scaly cup. Common in moist soils near streams, Shingle Oak has gray-brown, broadly ridged bark. It grows 40 to 60 feet tall and 1 to 3 feet in diameter. The common name was applied during pioneer days, when its wood was widely used for split shingles. It is known also as Northern Laurel Oak.

LAUREL OAK (*Quercus laurifolia*) is semi-evergreen, the leaves of the current year remaining on the tree through the winter. Elliptical and occasionally irregularly lobed, they are 2 to 4 inches long and 0.5 to 1 inch wide, with a pointed apex, smooth margin, and a prominent yellow midrib. The ovoid, dark-brown to black acorn, 0.5 of an inch long, has a saucer-like cup with hairy scales. The bark is brown to black, smooth or broadly ridged. Usually in moist soils bordering streams, Laurel Oak grows 80 to 100 feet tall and 3 to 4 feet in diameter. It has a broad, rounded crown.

WILLOW OAK

80-100 ft.

WATER OAK

SHINGLE OAK

LAUREL OAK

133

LIVE OAK *(Quercus virginiana)* has elliptical to ob-ovate, evergreen leaves, 2 to 5 inches long and 1 to 2.5 inches wide. They usually have smooth margins, a rounded apex, and often are hairy below. The 0.8-inch-long acorn is brown to black and ellipsoidal, its lower third enclosed in a deep, tapering, scaly cup. Unlike many "red oaks," acorns of the Live Oak mature in one season and the meat is not bitter. Bark is dark reddish brown, scaly, and fissured. Grows 40 to 50 feet tall and 3 to 4 feet in diameter, with a short trunk and huge, wide-spreading crown. It is one of the more majestic trees of the coastal region of the Deep South, and its branches are often heavily festooned with Spanish Moss.

CANYON LIVE OAK *(Quercus chrysolepis)* has ever-green leaves, 1 to 4 inches long and 0.5 to 2 inches wide. Oblong to elliptical, some of the leaves have smooth margins and a rounded apex; others are holly-like. The ovoid acorn, 1.5 inches long, has a thick, scaly cup covered with a golden-yellow "wool." Bark is black, ridged, and scaly. Typical of rocky canyon sites, it is medium-sized to large, with a short, crooked trunk and massive limbs that form a broad, irregular crown. Canyon Live Oak grows 60 to 80 feet tall, 1 to 5 feet in diameter. Because of its striking acorns, it is also known as Golden Cup Oak.

INTERIOR LIVE OAK *(Quercus wislizenii)* leaves are evergreen, 1 to 1.5 inches long and 0.5 to 0.8 of an inch wide. Elliptical to broadly lanceolate and with smooth or holly-like margins, they remain on the tree through the second season. Acorns, about half en-closed in a deep, bowl-like, scaly cup, are an inch long. Bark black and furrowed. Grows 50 to 80 feet tall and 2 to 3 feet in diameter, with short trunk and large branches forming a broad, rounded crown.

CALIFORNIA LIVE OAK *(Quercus agrifolia)* resem-bles Interior Live Oak, but its evergreen leaves are often somewhat larger and remain on the tree only through one year. Acorns are chestnut brown, conical, 0.8 to 1.5 inches long, with a bowl-like cup having thin, somewhat hairy scales covering the lower third; mature in one season. California Live Oak grows 60 to 90 feet tall and 2 to 3 feet in diameter, with a short trunk and large branches forming a broad, rounded, wide-spreading crown.

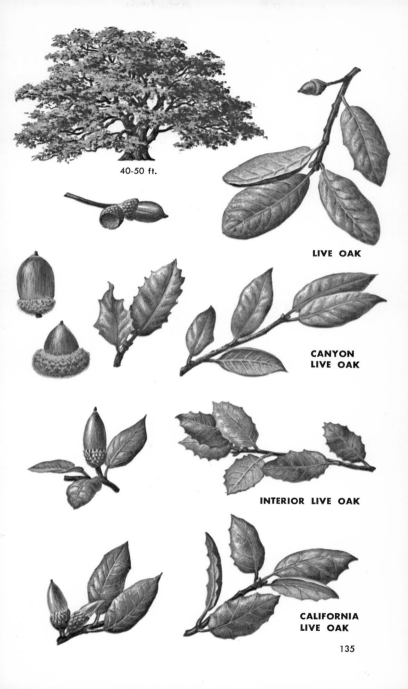

40-50 ft.

LIVE OAK

CANYON
LIVE OAK

INTERIOR LIVE OAK

CALIFORNIA
LIVE OAK

135

EMORY OAK *(Quercus emoryi)* leaves are evergreen, 2.5 inches long and oblong-lanceolate, with smooth or spiny-toothed margins. The oblong acorns, 0.8 of an inch long, mature in one season. The base is set in a deep cup covered with hairy scales. The inner shell is hairy. The meat is not bitter. Bark is black, in rectangular blocks like an alligator's hide. A shrub or small tree, 20 to 60 feet tall and 1 to 3 feet in diameter.

ARIZONA WHITE OAK *(Quercus arizonica)* has broadly oval leaves, 2.5 inches long, with smooth or spiny-toothed margins. The acorns, 1 inch long, have lower half enclosed in a hairy-scaled, bowl-like cup; they mature in one season and inner shell is hairless. Grows 20 to 60 feet tall, 1 to 3 feet in diameter, with rounded crown and plated bark. In spite of its common name this evergreen tree is classed with "red oaks."

ENGELMANN OAK *(Quercus engelmannii)* leaves are evergreen, 1 to 3 inches long and 2 inches wide, with smooth, shallowly lobed or toothed margins. The oblong acorns are 0.8 of an inch long, the lower half covered by a tapering cup with hairy scales. Bark gray-brown, in scaly ridges, its thick branches forming a broad, irregular crown. Engelmann Oak grows 20 to 50 feet tall and 1 to 3 feet in diameter.

MEXICAN BLUE OAK *(Quercus oblongifolia)* leaves are evergreen, 2 inches long, their margins curled and either smooth or with small teeth. The lower third of the ovoid acorns, 0.5 of an inch long, is enclosed in a bowl-like, scaly cup fringed on margin. Ash-gray bark is in scaly plates. A shrub or small tree, grows 10 to 30 feet tall and 1 foot in diameter.

SILVERLEAF OAK *(Quercus hypoleucoides)* has lance-shaped, evergreen leaves, 2 to 4 inches long and 0.5 to 1 inch wide, which are white-hairy on the underside. A few coarse teeth occur near the tapered apex, otherwise the rolled-under margin is smooth. Acorns are conical, 0.5 to 0.8 of an inch long, dark green to chestnut brown; a deep cup covering the lower third has thick, often silvery-haired scales. The bark is black, deeply ridged, and furrowed. Silverleaf Oak is a shrub or small tree, to 60 feet tall, usually found in moist, shaded canyons.

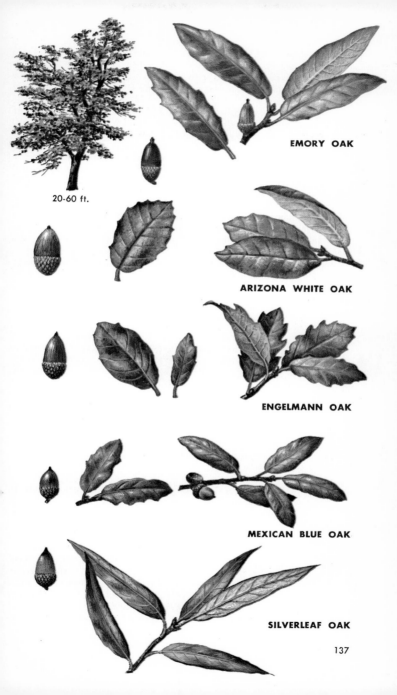

20-60 ft.

EMORY OAK

ARIZONA WHITE OAK

ENGELMANN OAK

MEXICAN BLUE OAK

SILVERLEAF OAK

137

ELM FAMILY (Ulmaceae)

Over 150 species of trees and shrubs, all with simple, alternate leaves, comprise the elm family, worldwide in distribution but mainly in temperate regions.

Elms *(Ulmus)* have distinctive wafer-like fruits (samaras). Leaves of native species are deciduous, pinnately veined, and short-stemmed, with doubly toothed margins; usually rough-textured and lopsided at base. Small, perfect flowers lack petals; borne on slender, jointed stems in several types of clusters. Flowers of some species develop in early spring before leaves unfold; others flower in autumn. Several introduced species (p. 140) are planted in various parts of the United States as ornamentals and in windbreaks.

Hackberries *(Celtis),* with five native species and several varieties, have deciduous, usually long-pointed leaves, with singly toothed or smooth margins. Small clusters of perfect or imperfect flowers develop with the leaves, and small fruits consist of a hard seed in a thin leathery covering (drupe).

Other members of the elm family in North America are the Planertree *(Planera aquatica)* of southeastern United States and several species of the tropical genus *Trema* occurring in southern Florida.

AMERICAN ELM *(Ulmus americana)* has elliptical to oblong-ovate leaves, 4 to 6 inches long and 1 to 3 inches wide. Greenish, wafer-like fruits, 0.5 inch long, usually mature as the leaves unfold; papery wing surrounding the flat seed is oblong, the tip deeply notched and the edges hairy. On mature trees, bark is dark gray, in flat-topped ridges separated by roughly diamond-shaped areas. Grows 80 to 120 feet tall and 2 to 4 feet in diameter, its vase-shaped form recognizable even at a distance. Unfortunately many American Elms have been destroyed by the Dutch elm disease, an introduced fungus spread by a bark beetle.

SLIPPERY ELM *(Ulmus rubra)* leaves are similar to American Elm's but are rougher and also somewhat larger, 5 to 7 inches long and 2 to 3 inches wide. The greenish fruits, 0.8 of an inch long, are only slightly notched at the apex; the surface of the wing is smooth but the seed cavity is hairy. On mature trees, the gray to reddish-brown bark is in flat-topped, nearly vertical ridges, and the inner bark, especially on twigs, contains a sticky, aromatic substance that once was chewed for relief of throat ailments. Slippery Elm grows 60 to 80 feet tall and 1 to 3 feet in diameter, resembling the American Elm's vase-shaped form.

leaf margin
doubly toothed

fruit a samara

ELMS *Ulmus*

leaf more pointed;
margin singly toothed
or smooth

fruit a drupe

HACKBERRIES *Celtis*

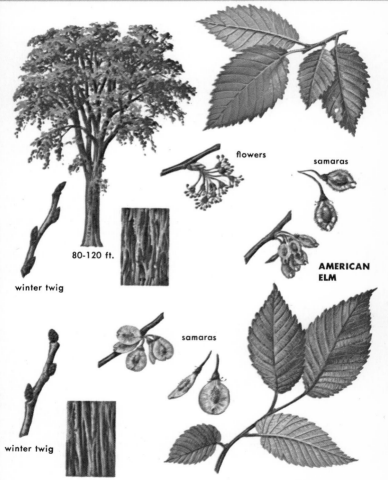

flowers

samaras

80-120 ft.

winter twig

AMERICAN ELM

samaras

winter twig

SLIPPERY ELM

ROCK ELM *(Ulmus thomasii)* leaves resemble those of American Elm but are smaller, 2.5 to 4.5 inches long and 1.5 to 2.5 inches wide. The fruits, 0.8 to 1 inch long, have an indistinct seed cavity and are irregularly oval, with a rounded rather than notched apex and with a hairy margin. Twigs often have corky wings. Bark of mature trees is similar to American Elm's. Grows 60 to 80 feet tall and 1 to 3 feet in diameter, with a central trunk and oval crown.

WINGED ELM *(Ulmus alata)* leaves are oblong, 1.5 to 3 inches long and 1 to 1.5 inches wide, with base wedge-shaped or unequally rounded. Hairy, reddish fruits, 0.3 of an inch long, have narrow wings and a distinctive 2-pronged apex. Twigs have corky wings, often 0.5 of an inch wide. Bark is reddish brown, in flat-topped, vertical ridges. A small tree, 40 to 50 feet tall and 3 feet in diameter, with a narrow, oblong crown. Most common in dry soils.

CEDAR ELM *(Ulmus crassifolia)* leaves are 1 to 2 inches long and 0.5 to 1 inch wide. Flowers develop in late summer. The fruits are 0.5 of an inch long, deeply notched, and white-hairy; they mature in fall. Bark is gray to reddish brown and scaly; the twigs often have two narrow, corky wings. Grows 60 to 80 feet tall and 2 to 3 feet in diameter. September Elm *(U. serotina)*, also a southern species, flowers in late summer. Fruits white-haired, notched; twigs with corky wings. Leaves 3 to 4 inches long and 1 to 2 inches wide.

SOME INTRODUCED ELMS

ENGLISH ELM *(Ulmus campestris)* grows 40 to 100 feet tall and 1 to 3 feet in diameter. Crown is wide-spreading. Branches have corky wings. Leaves, unequal at base, are 2 to 3.5 inches long and 1 to 2.5 inches wide. Oval fruit deeply notched at apex.

WYCH ELM *(Ulmus glabra)* resembles English Elm but has smoother bark, leaves 3 to 6 inches long and 2 to 4 inches wide. Fruit slightly notched. Camperdown Elm *(U. glabra camperdownii)*, a variety also called Umbrella Elm, has pendant branches and larger, more lopsided leaves.

CHINESE ELM *(Ulmus parviflora)* is 20 to 60 feet tall, with a rounded crown. Bark smooth. Flowers in fall. Elliptical, singly toothed leaves, 0.8 to 2.5 inches long and to 1 inch wide, slightly unequal at base. May be evergreen in warm regions. Native to Orient; commonly planted in U.S.

SIBERIAN ELM *(Ulmus pumila)*, often confused with Chinese Elm, has rough bark. Flowers in spring; leaves usually more equal at base. Planted in central and western U.S. for windbreaks. Native to Siberia and northern China. Grows 15 to 40 feet tall; occasionally shrublike.

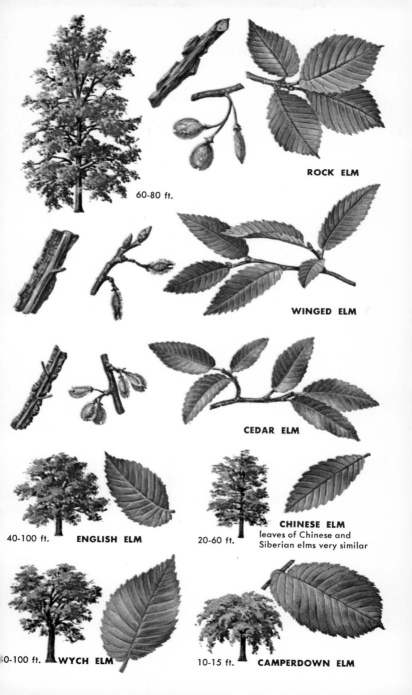

60-80 ft.

ROCK ELM

WINGED ELM

CEDAR ELM

40-100 ft. **ENGLISH ELM**

20-60 ft. **CHINESE ELM**
leaves of Chinese and
Siberian elms very similar

0-100 ft. **WYCH ELM**

10-15 ft. **CAMPERDOWN ELM**

HACKBERRY *(Celtis occidentalis)* has ovate to ovate-lanceolate leaves, 2.3 to 4 inches long and 1.5 to 2 inches wide. The margins are singly toothed and the tapering apex slightly curved; the base is obliquely rounded. Dark-red to purple fruits, 0.3 of an inch in diameter, are borne on slender stems, 0.5 of an inch long. The warty, gray to brown bark is an excellent identification feature. Usually grows 30 to 40 feet tall and 1 to 2 feet in diameter; occasionally much larger. It has a narrow, round-topped crown.

SUGARBERRY *(Celtis laevigata)* and 3 other species resemble Common Hackberry. Sugarberry has oblong-lanceolate, smooth-margined leaves, 2 to 5 inches long; fruit orange or yellow. Georgia Hackberry *(C. tenuifolia)* leaves are ovate, about 2 inches long, with smooth or toothed margins; fruit orange-red. Lindheimer Hackberry *(C. lindheimeri)* has oblong-ovate leaves, 1 to 3 inches long, with smooth or toothed margins; fruit reddish brown. Netleaf Hackberry *(C. reticulata)* has ovate leaves, 1 to 3 inches long, the margins smooth or occasionally toothed; fruit red.

PLANERTREE *(Planera aquatica)* has ovate-oblong, deciduous leaves, 2 to 2.5 inches long and 0.5 to 1 inch wide, with single-toothed margins, a pointed apex, and wedge-shaped base. Clusters of small, greenish, perfect, and unisexual flowers appear in spring. The brown, nutlike fruit, 0.5 of an inch long, is covered by soft, irregular projections. The outer bark is gray-brown and scaly; inner bark, exposed when scales peel, is reddish brown. Planertree grows 30 to 40 feet tall and 10 to 20 inches in diameter, forming a broad, low crown. Common in swamps and along streams.

FLORIDA TREMA *(Trema micrantha)* leaves are ever-green, 3 to 4 inches long and 1 to 2.5 inches wide, with a short, hairy stem, fine, singly toothed margins, a rounded, heart-shaped, or oblique base, and abruptly pointed apex. Dark green and finely haired above; white-woolly below. Clusters of small, unisexual flowers appear in spring. Fruit is a yellowish-orange drupe, 0.3 of an inch in diameter. The dark-brown bark is warty. Usually a shrub, occasionally grows 20 to 30 feet tall and 1 to 2 feet in diameter, with a single trunk and rounded crown.

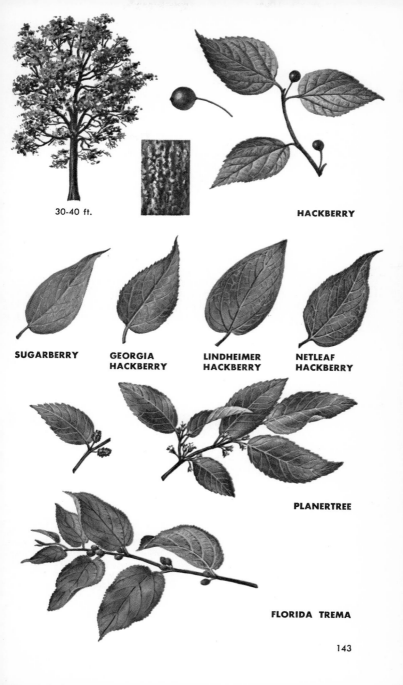

30-40 ft.

HACKBERRY

SUGARBERRY

GEORGIA
HACKBERRY

LINDHEIMER
HACKBERRY

NETLEAF
HACKBERRY

PLANERTREE

FLORIDA TREMA

143

MULBERRY FAMILY (Moraceae)

About 1,000 species of deciduous and evergreen trees, shrubs, and herbs form the mulberry family. All have simple, alternate leaves. Some, like the mulberries (Morus), certain figs (Ficus), and Breadfruit (Artocarpus), bear valuable fruits. Commercial figs grown in warmer parts of the United States are varieties of a deciduous species (Ficus carica) native to the Mediterranean region. The India rubber-plant (Ficus elastica) and the rubber tree of the American tropics (Castilla elastica) yield a latex that has been a minor source of rubber. In Japan, mulberry leaves are food for silkworms. Hop (Humulus) and Hemp (Cannabis), both herbs, are the only members of the family that do not produce a milky sap, or latex.

MULBERRIES (Morus)

RED MULBERRY (Morus rubra) leaves are deciduous, 3 to 5 inches long and 2 to 3 inches wide, hairy below, and with coarse marginal teeth. Though usually broadly ovate, they often have 2 or 3 lobes. The leaves turn yellow in the fall. Staminate and pistillate flowers commonly occur on different trees in pendant, greenish spikes. Staminate spikes are narrow, 2 to 2.5 inches long; pistillate are oblong, about 1 inch long. Juicy, edible, multiple fruit, 1 to 1.3 inches long, resembles an elongated blackberry; red at first, purple when ripe. Bark on mature trees is in dark reddish-brown, scaly plates. In fertile, moist soils, grows 50 to 70 feet tall and 2 to 3 feet in diameter, with a dense, round-topped crown.

TEXAS MULBERRY (Morus microphylla) is similar to Red Mulberry but smaller (10 to 20 feet tall, 1 foot in diameter). The leaves are 1.5 inches long and 0.8 of an inch wide, and the fruit is black and subglobose, about 0.5 of an inch long when ripe.

SOME INTRODUCED MULBERRIES

WHITE MULBERRY (Morus alba) leaves are smooth on the underside, and the fruit is white. An introduced native of the Orient, it is now common in eastern U.S.

BLACK MULBERRY (Morus nigra) leaves are rarely lobed. Cultivated for the large fruit, which are black when ripe. Native of Asia.

PAPER MULBERRY (Broussonetia papyrifera) leaves resemble Red Mulberry's. Dioecious—staminate flowers in greenish aments 2 to 3 inches long, the pistillate in globose heads 0.8 of an inch in diameter. Fruit red, in globose heads. Native of Orient where bark is used in papermaking. An ornamental in eastern U.S.; also grows wild.

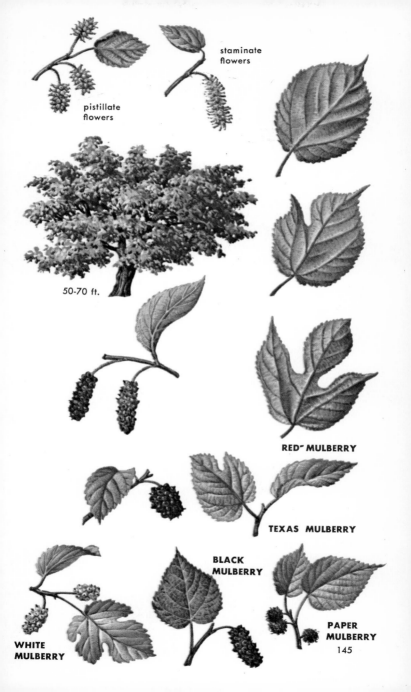

pistillate flowers

staminate flowers

50-70 ft.

RED MULBERRY

TEXAS MULBERRY

BLACK MULBERRY

WHITE MULBERRY

PAPER MULBERRY

145

FIGS *(Ficus)*

FLORIDA STRANGLER FIG *(Ficus aurea)* leaves are evergreen, smooth-margined, leathery, and elliptical to oblong. They are 2 to 5 inches long and 1 to 3 inches wide. The small flowers, separated by reddish-purple, chaffy scales, are borne in nearly closed receptacles, either attached directly to the branch or on very short stems; they are yellow at first, later turning red. The fruit consists of small drupelets embedded in a fleshy, yellow to reddish-purple receptacle, about 0.5 to 0.8 of an inch in diameter. On young trees, the bark is smooth and ash-gray, sometimes becoming scaly on large trunks. Florida Strangler Fig grows 40 to 50 feet tall and 1 to 3 feet in diameter. Usually the seeds germinate in bark crevices of other trees. They send out aerial roots that eventually reach the ground and develop an independent root system. Commonly several aerial roots may wrap around or "strangle" the host tree. Branches that touch the ground may also take root, forming a compound tree of many trunks much like the Banyan of India. The less common Shortleaf Fig *(F. laevigata)* of the Florida Keys, Bahamas, and Cuba is similar in growth habits but has broader leaves with heart-shaped bases, larger fruit (to 1 inch), and longer stems on flowers and fruit.

SOME INTRODUCED FIGS

COMMON FIG *(Ficus carica)* is a deciduous shrub or small tree, to 30 feet tall, with a low, wide, rounded crown. The leaves, 4 to 8 inches long and nearly as broad, are palmately 3- to 5-lobed. Margins of lobes are wavy. There are many varieties, grown commercially in warmer parts of the U.S. for fruit. Also planted as an ornamental in areas of moderate climate.

FIDDLE-LEAF FIG *(Ficus lyrata)* is also a house plant but is not as popular as the India Rubber-plant. Grown outdoors in warmer parts of the U.S., it may reach a height of 30 feet. Differs from other common species of *Ficus* in having irregular, violin-shaped leaves with conspicuous whitish veins. In its native West Africa, the Fiddle-leaf Fig grows 70 feet tall.

INDIA RUBBER-PLANT *(Ficus elastica)* is a popular house plant. When grown outdoors in warmer parts of the U.S. it may become 100 feet tall. The dark, glossy, evergreen leaves are pinnately veined and to 12 inches long, with smooth margins and an abruptly pointed apex. The fruits of the India Rubber-plant are greenish yellow when ripe. The tree is native to tropical Asia.

BENJAMIN FIG *(Ficus benjamina)*, also known as Weeping Laurel, has slender, drooping branches. Grows to 30 feet tall. The thin, shiny-green, prominently veined, ovate-elliptical leaves are 2 to 4.5 inches long, with smooth margins and an abruptly pointed apex. Globose fruit is yellowish to reddish. Native to tropical Asia. Grown as a potted plant, or outdoors in warm parts of U.S.

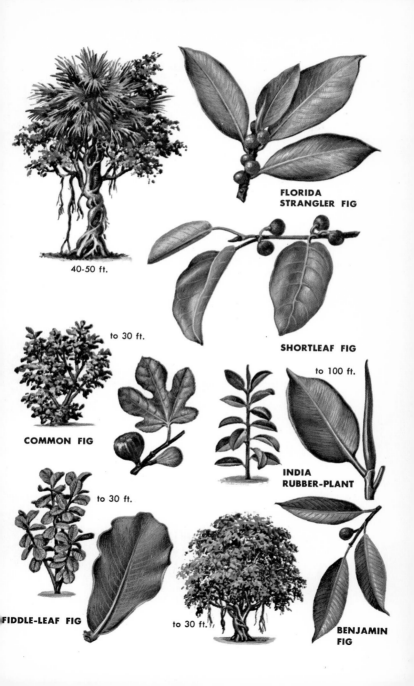

FLORIDA
STRANGLER FIG

40-50 ft.

SHORTLEAF FIG

to 30 ft.

COMMON FIG

to 100 ft.

INDIA
RUBBER-PLANT

to 30 ft.

FIDDLE-LEAF FIG

to 30 ft.

BENJAMIN
FIG

OSAGE-ORANGE *(Maclura pomifera)* has ovate to ovate-lanceolate, deciduous leaves, 3 to 5 inches long and 2 to 3 inches wide, with smooth margins. Leaves turn bright yellow in fall. Flowers, staminate (in racemes) and pistillate (in heads), are borne in leaf axils on separate trees after leaves appear. Inedible, rough, multiple fruit, 3 to 5 inches in diameter, exudes milky juice when bruised. Bark breaks into broad, rounded, scaly ridges; twigs often thorny. Grows 10 to 50 feet tall, 1 to 2 feet in diameter. Hedge plantings have extended range over much of U.S.

OLAX (TALLOWWOOD) FAMILY (Olacaceae)

TALLOWWOOD *(Ximenia americana)* leaves are evergreen, alternate, leathery, oblong to elliptical, 1 to 2.5 inches long and 0.5 to 1 inch wide. Apex spiny or notched, margin curled under. Short-stalked clusters of two to four fragrant, yellowish-white flowers, each with four curled, hairy petals, occur in leaf axils. Yellowish-red, plumlike fruits, about 1.3 inches long, have thin, astringent flesh. Bark smooth and dark reddish brown, twigs spiny, wood fragrant. Grows 30 feet tall, 1.5 feet in diameter.

BUCKWHEAT FAMILY (Polygonaceae)

SEAGRAPE *(Coccoloba uvifera)* has leathery, evergreen leaves, 4 to 5 inches long and 5 to 6 inches wide, smaller at growing tip. Flowers white, produced singly or in fascicles and in racemes 5 to 15 inches long. Grapelike fruits greenish white to purple. To 25 feet tall and 1.5 feet in diameter; bark smooth, gray to mottled brown. On sandy shores.

DOVEPLUM *(Coccoloba diversifolia),* or Pigeon Seagrape, has leathery, evergreen leaves, 3 to 4 inches long and 1.5 to 2.5 inches wide. Fascicles of white flowers in racemes 2 to 3 inches long; fruit dark red. Reddish-brown bark smooth, occasionally scaly. Grows 70 feet tall, 2 feet in diameter; rounded crown. In sandy soils.

FOUR-O'CLOCK FAMILY (Nyctaginaceae)

LONGLEAF BLOLLY *(Torrubia longifolia)* has evergreen leaves, 1 to 2 inches long, 0.5 to 1 inch wide. Small, greenish-yellow flowers, in loose clusters; fruits red, ribbed, 0.8 of an inch long. Bark reddish brown, scaly. A shrub or small tree, to 40 feet tall, 1.5 feet in diameter. Two similar shrubby species in same area.

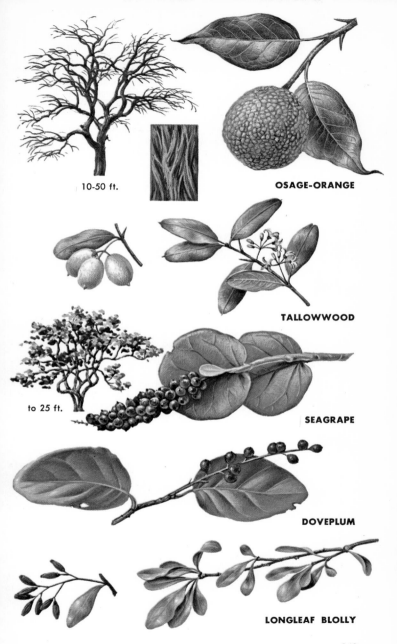

10-50 ft.

OSAGE-ORANGE

TALLOWWOOD

to 25 ft.

SEAGRAPE

DOVEPLUM

LONGLEAF BLOLLY

149

MAGNOLIA FAMILY (Magnoliaceae)

This is a family of about 100 species of trees and shrubs that grow in the warmer parts of North America and eastern Asia. Trees in two of the 10 genera, *Magnolia and Liriodendron,* grow in the United States. Two species of Anis-trees *(Illicium),* usually shrubs but rarely trees, grow in northern Florida and on Gulf Coast.

Magnolias have unique scarlet to rust-brown aggregate fruit composed of numerous podlike follicles, each containing 1 or 2 crimson seeds that hang by slender threads when ripe. The alternate leaves, deciduous or evergreen, have short stems and smooth, usually wavy margins. A single scale covers each bud, and stipule scars encircle the twigs. Asiatic magnolias grown as ornamentals include Star Magnolia *(M. stellata),* Kobus Magnolia *(M. kobus),* and Saucer Magnolia *(M. soulangeana).*

SOUTHERN MAGNOLIA *(Magnolia grandiflora)* leaves are evergreen, leathery, oval to ovate, 5 to 10 inches long, 2 to 3 inches wide; dark, glossy green above, lighter and brown-hairy below, with short, pointed apex. Fragrant flowers, 6 to 9 inches in diameter, have 3 sepals and 6 to 12 showy white petals. Aggregate fruit, 3 to 4 inches long and about 2 inches in diameter, red to rust-brown, hairy. Bark is brownish gray and scaly. Grows 25 to 80 feet tall, 2 to 3 feet in diameter, with a pyramidal or a round-topped crown.

SWEETBAY *(Magnolia virginiana)* leaves are deciduous in the North, but in the South remain on tree until new foliage forms. They are 4 to 6 inches long and 1 to 3 inches wide, with a blunt-pointed apex; shiny green above, whitish below. Fragrant, cup-shaped flowers are 2 to 3 inches in diameter, with 3 sepals and 9 to 12 creamy-white, concave petals. Dark red aggregate fruit is 2 inches long and about 0.5 of an inch in diameter; not hairy. Bark light brown, scaly. Usually 10 to 30 feet tall, 1 to 1.5 feet in diameter.

CUCUMBERTREE *(Magnolia acuminata)* leaves are deciduous, 6 to 10 inches long and 3 to 5 inches wide, with a pointed apex; yellow-green above, paler below. Flowers, about 2 inches long, have 3 sepals and 6 greenish-yellow petals (canary yellow or orange in rare variety). Red to brown, hairless, aggregate fruit is 2 to 3 inches long, 1 inch in diameter. Bark of mature trees gray-brown, scaly. Cucumbertree grows 40 to 90 feet tall and 3 to 4 feet in diameter, with straight trunk and pyramidal crown.

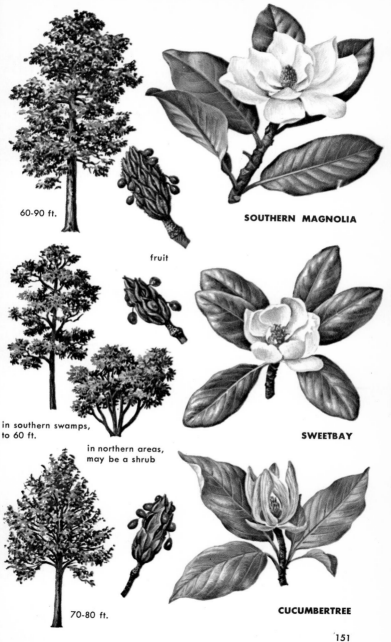

60-90 ft.

fruit

SOUTHERN MAGNOLIA

in southern swamps,
to 60 ft.

in northern areas,
may be a shrub

SWEETBAY

70-80 ft.

CUCUMBERTREE

151

UMBRELLA MAGNOLIA *(Magnolia tripetala)* has deciduous, broadly elliptical leaves, 18 to 20 inches long and 8 to 10 inches wide, clustered near the ends of the branches. The flowers, 6 to 10 inches in diameter, with 3 sepals and 6 or 9 narrow, concave, creamy-white petals, have an unpleasant odor. Rose-colored, hairless, aggregate fruit is 2.5 to 4 inches long. A large shrub or small tree, 10 to 35 feet tall and 1 to 1.5 feet in diameter, Umbrella Magnolia is typical of moist places.

BIGLEAF MAGNOLIA *(Magnolia macrophylla)* has huge, deciduous leaves, 20 to 30 inches long and 8 to 10 inches wide, often widest above the middle; apex rounded or bluntly pointed, the narrowed base shallowly lobed. Fragrant, cup-shaped flowers are 10 to 12 inches in diameter, with 3 sepals, which later turn dull yellow, and 6 creamy-white petals, with rose at base. Ovoid, aggregate fruit, 2.5 to 3 inches long, is rose-colored and hairy. Grows 30 to 50 feet tall and 1 to 1.5 feet in diameter, with a round-topped crown of wide-spreading branches. The bark is gray and often scaly on older trees.

ASHE MAGNOLIA *(Magnolia ashei)* resembles Bigleaf Magnolia but has shorter, broader leaves, smaller flowers, and longer (to 5 inches), more cylindrical fruit. Rarely grows to small tree size.

FRASER MAGNOLIA *(Magnolia fraseri)* leaves are deciduous, 10 to 12 inches long, 6 to 7 inches wide; widest above the middle, with bluntly pointed apex and conspicuous, earlike lobes at the narrowed base. Fragrant flowers, 8 to 10 inches in diameter, have 3 sepals (falling soon after opening of flower) and 6 or 9 pale-yellow petals. Rose-red, hairless, oblong, aggregate fruit is 4 to 5 inches long and 1.5 to 2 inches in diameter. Grows 30 to 40 feet tall and 1 to 1.5 feet in diameter. Bark brown, scaly, or warty.

PYRAMID MAGNOLIA *(Magnolia pyramidata)* leaves are similar to Fraser Magnolia's but smaller, 5 to 9 inches long and 3 to 5 inches wide. Flowers, 3 to 4 inches in diameter, have 3 sepals and 6 or 9 creamy-white petals. Rose-colored, oblong, aggregate fruit is 2 to 2.5 inches long and 1 to 1.5 inches in diameter. Grows 20 to 30 feet tall, 1 to 2 feet in diameter.

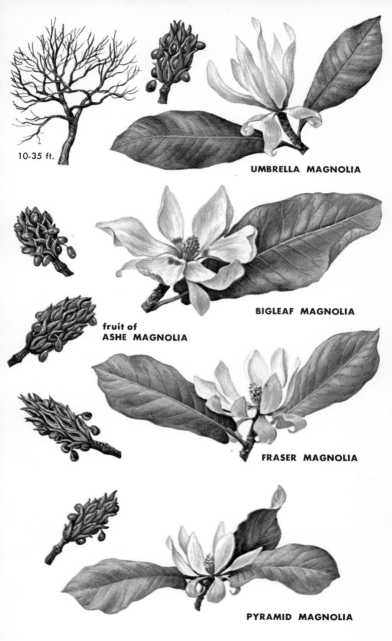

10-35 ft.

UMBRELLA MAGNOLIA

BIGLEAF MAGNOLIA

**fruit of
ASHE MAGNOLIA**

FRASER MAGNOLIA

PYRAMID MAGNOLIA

YELLOW-POPLAR *(Liriodendron tulipifera)*, also called Tuliptree, has long-stemmed, 4-lobed, deciduous leaves, with a tulip-like outline. They are 4 to 6 inches long, bright green above and paler below. The tulip-shaped flowers, 1.5 to 2 inches in diameter, have 6 greenish-yellow petals with orange at base. They do not appear until well after the leaves develop. Fruit is a conelike aggregate of single-winged samaras, which fall apart when mature. Buds have two valvate scales, and stipule scars encircle the twigs. Mature trees have gray-brown, ridged, and furrowed bark. One of the largest of eastern hardwoods, grows 80 to 150 feet tall and 4 to 6 feet in diameter, usually with a straight, clear trunk and pyramidal crown.

CUSTARD-APPLE (ANNONA) FAMILY
(Annonaceae)

This is a large (70 genera and about 600 species), primarily tropical family of deciduous and evergreen trees and shrubs with two representatives in United States. Leaves simple, alternate.

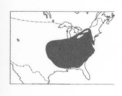

PAWPAW *(Asimina triloba)* leaves are deciduous, 10 to 12 inches long and 4 to 6 inches wide, widest above the middle. The apex is pointed, the margins smooth. Flowers, about 2 inches in diameter, have 3 green sepals and 6 heavily veined, purple petals in two ranks. Fruit irregularly oblong, to 5 inches long and 1.5 inches thick, with a yellow to dark-brown rind enclosing the white to yellow flesh and flat, dark-brown seeds. Edible when ripe. Blotched, gray-brown bark is thin and smooth to warty. A large shrub or small tree, 20 to 30 feet tall and 6 to 15 inches in diameter.

POND-APPLE *(Annona glabra)* leaves are leathery, oblong to elliptical, 3 to 5 inches long and 1.5 to 2 inches wide, with smooth margins and a pointed apex. They are bright green above, paler below, and are shed late in the fall. The flowers, about an inch in diameter, have 6 dull yellowish-white petals. The fleshy, aromatic, yellowish-brown, compound fruit is somewhat heart-shaped, 3 to 5 inches long and 2 to 3.5 inches in diameter with light-green, insipid flesh. Bark is thin, reddish brown, sometimes scaly. Small to medium-sized, 40 to 50 feet tall and 1 to 2 feet in diameter. Trunk short, usually buttressed base, and a spreading crown of somewhat twisted branches.

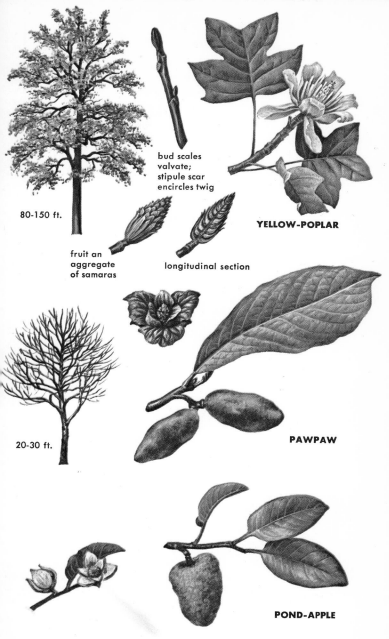

80-150 ft.

bud scales
valvate;
stipule scar
encircles twig

YELLOW-POPLAR

fruit an
aggregate
of samaras

longitudinal section

20-30 ft.

PAWPAW

POND-APPLE

155

LAUREL FAMILY (Lauraceae)

Deciduous and evergreen trees and shrubs, usually with alternate leaves, are included in the more than 1,000 species of this primarily tropical family. Many have aromatic leaves, bark, twigs, and roots, providing cinnamon, camphor, and various oils used in drugs, soaps, and perfumes. Also included are the Avocado (Persea americana) and several important timber trees. Stinkwood (Ocotea bullata), of South Africa, and the Walnut Bean (Endriandra palmerstonii), of eastern Australia, furnish beautiful cabinet woods. Camphor-tree (Cinnamomum camphora), a source of commercial camphor, is grown as an ornamental in California and in southern United States, where it has escaped cultivation and grows wild. Greenheart (Nectandra rodioei) is used in marine construction; a related, native species, Jamaica Nectandra or Lancewood (N. coriacea), is common along the Florida coast.

SASSAFRAS (Sassafras albidum) has deciduous leaves, 4 to 6 inches long and 2 to 4 inches wide. Both elliptical or 2- to 3-lobed leaves may occur on same tree; turn yellow to red in fall. Dioecious; the small, yellow-green flowers in loose racemes appear with leaves in spring. Stalked, ovoid fruits, about 0.3 of an inch long, are blue with a hard seed enclosed in thin flesh. Aromatic leaves, bark, twigs, and roots yield oils used in soaps. Sassafras tea, a "spring tonic" of bygone years, is made by boiling roots or bark. Commonly grows 20 feet tall, rarely to 50 feet, with a diameter of nearly 3 feet. Often forms dense, shrubby thickets.

CALIFORNIA-LAUREL (Umbellularia californica) leaves are evergreen, lanceolate to elliptical, 2 to 5 inches long and 0.5 to 1.5 inches wide; aromatic when crushed. Loose axillary clusters of small, yellowish-green flowers appear in winter or early spring. Fruit greenish to purple, about 1 inch long. Bark greenish brown, smooth to scaly. Usually a shrub or small tree, rarely to 80 feet tall. Also called Oregon-myrtle.

REDBAY (Persea borbonia) has aromatic, evergreen leaves, 3 to 4 inches long and 1 to 1.5 inches wide. These are the bay leaves used as herbs. The creamy-white, bell-shaped flowers lack petals but have hairy sepals; they occur in loose axillary clusters. Blue to violet-black, ovoid fruit is 0.5 of an inch in diameter. Usually in moist soils near streams or swamps. To 60 feet tall.

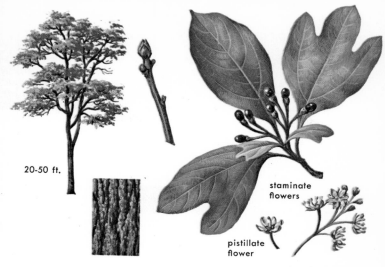

20-50 ft.

staminate
flowers

pistillate
flower

SASSAFRAS

to 80 ft. (rare)

CALIFORNIA-LAUREL

REDBAY

157

WITCH-HAZEL FAMILY (Hamamelidaceae)

About 100 species of deciduous trees and shrubs make up the witch-hazel family. Species are found in North America, South Africa, Madagascar, Australia, and Asia. One tree-sized species and a half dozen shrubs, several of which occasionally reach tree height, are native to eastern United States and southeastern Canada.

SWEETGUM *(Liquidambar styraciflua)* has distinctive star-shaped leaves, alternate, 5 to 7 inches wide and with 5 to 7 pointed lobes, with toothed margins. They are bright green, turning a brilliant red-and-gold in fall. Staminate and pistillate flowers are in separate, headlike clusters on same tree—the staminate in racemes, pistillate solitary. Fruit is a long-stemmed, woody, burlike head of capsules, 1.5 inches in diameter; each capsule contains two small seeds. Twigs often have corky wings. Grows 80 to 120 feet tall and 3 to 5 feet in diameter, with gray to brown, ridged and furrowed bark. Wood used for furniture, veneer, interior trim, and novelties.

WITCH-HAZEL *(Hamamelis virginiana)* leaves are alternate, 4 to 6 inches long and 2 to 3 inches wide, their greatest width above the middle. Leaves have deep, widely spaced, rounded marginal teeth and a lopsided base; dull green above and lighter below, with hairs along midrib and veins; turn delicate yellow in autumn. Flowers with 4 narrow, yellow petals appear in fall or winter. They produce a 2-beaked, woody capsule, 0.5 of an inch long, which splits open when mature and forcefully ejects lustrous black seeds. A shrub or a small tree, to 30 feet tall and 12 inches in diameter, usually in moist soils near streams.

CAPER FAMILY (Capparidaceae)

JAMAICA CAPER *(Capparis cynophallophora)* leaves are evergreen, alternate, 2 to 3 inches long and 1 to 1.5 inches wide, with smooth margins and a rounded or notched apex. They are yellow-green above, with fine brownish scales below. Flowers, 1.3 inches across, have 4 scaly sepals, 4 petals (at first white, becoming purple), and a tuft of purple stamens 1 to 2 inches long with yellowish-orange anthers. Podlike fruit, 9 to 10 inches long, is constricted between seeds. To 20 feet tall, usually in sandy tidewater soils. Limber Caper *(C. flexuosa)* is similar, with lighter leaves; less commonly tree size.

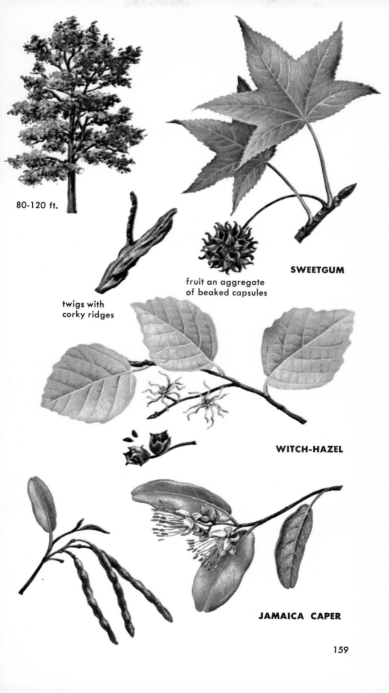

80-120 ft.

twigs with
corky ridges

fruit an aggregate
of beaked capsules

SWEETGUM

WITCH-HAZEL

JAMAICA CAPER

159

SYCAMORE FAMILY (Platanaceae)

This is a family of only one genus containing about six species, the sycamores, or planetrees. Three species are native to the United States. The other three are found in Mexico, Central America, southwestern Asia, and southeastern Europe. All have deciduous, alternate, palmately lobed leaves, usually with a hairy undersurface. Under the hollow, enlarged base of each leaf stem is a shiny-brown, conical bud covered by a single caplike scale. When the leaves fall, the buds are exposed, completely encircled by the leaf scar. Staminate and pistillate flowers are in separate globular heads on the same tree. The unique multiple fruit, commonly called buttonballs, consists of many tiny, elongated seeds with upright hairs at the base. The fruit breaks apart when ripe. Sycamore bark peels in thin, irregular patches giving the trunks a whitish-brown appearance. The twigs, encircled by stipule scars, have a distinctive zigzag form. Sycamores are typical of moist soils and are common along streams. They grow well in a variety of conditions, however, and are used as shade and street trees.

AMERICAN SYCAMORE *(Platanus occidentalis)* leaves are broadly ovate, 4 to 8 inches wide, and shallowly 3- to 5-lobed, the lobes with large marginal teeth. Globular heads of seeds, 1 to 1.5 inches in diameter, hang singly on slender stems 3 to 6 inches long. American Sycamore is a massive tree, frequently attaining a height of 100 feet and a diameter of 3 to 10 feet, with a wide-spreading crown.

CALIFORNIA SYCAMORE *(Platanus racemosa)* leaves are 6 to 10 inches wide, with 3 to 5 lobes that are longer than broad; margins toothed (occasionally smooth). Globular seed heads, to 1 inch in diameter, are in racemes of 3 to 7. California Sycamore grows 40 to 90 feet tall and 1 to 3 feet in diameter.

ARIZONA SYCAMORE *(Platanus wrightii)* is similar to California Sycamore, but its leaves are often 7-lobed and the globular seed heads are in racemes of 2 to 4.

INTRODUCED SYCAMORES

ORIENTAL PLANETREE *(Platanus orientalis)* resembles American Sycamore but has smaller, more deeply lobed leaves. Seed heads are in strings of 2 to 4. London Planetree *(P. acerifolia)*, a hybrid between American Sycamore and Oriental Planetree, has leaves like American Sycamore; seed heads like Oriental Planetree's. Bark greenish brown.

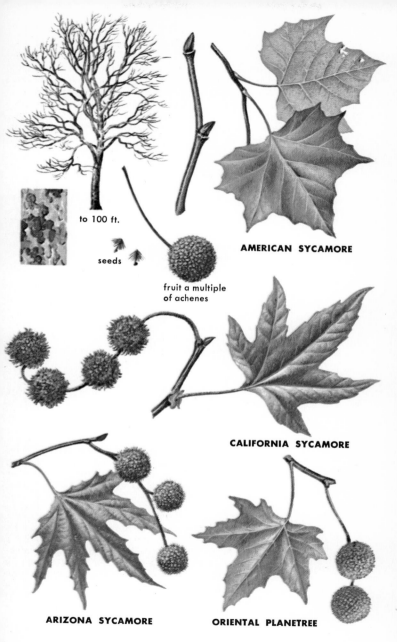

to 100 ft.

seeds

fruit a multiple
of achenes

AMERICAN SYCAMORE

CALIFORNIA SYCAMORE

ARIZONA SYCAMORE

ORIENTAL PLANETREE

ROSE FAMILY (Rosaceae)

This large, diversified family contains more than 3,000 species of trees, shrubs, and herbaceous plants, most abundant in temperate regions. Their perfect flowers typically have 5 sepals and 5 petals. Among familiar members are apples, cherries, plums, peaches, pears, apricots, almonds, strawberries, raspberries, and blackberries. Important ornamentals include the roses, spireas, hawthorns, firethorns, and mountain-ashes.

APPLES *(Malus)*

About 25 species of apples are native to temperate regions of the Northern Hemisphere; five native North American species are included here. All are small trees or occasionally shrubs, their leaves deciduous, alternate, and toothed or less commonly lobed. Apple blossoms, usually fragrant, are white to pink and 1 to 1.5 inches in diameter. They are clustered in racemes on short, spurlike branches. The fruit (a pome) of native species is much smaller than the fruit of commercially grown varieties.

Numerous varieties of apples have been developed from *Malus pumila,* the common native apple of southeastern Europe and central Asia. This species was introduced into North America by early settlers and is now naturalized in many parts of the United States and Canada. Its toothed, ovate to elliptical leaves have white hairs on the underside and on the stems. Other species with showy flowers or attractive fruits are planted as ornamentals.

SOUTHERN CRAB APPLE *(Malus angustifolia)* leaves are elliptical to ovate, 1 to 3 inches long and 0.5 to 2 inches wide. They have toothed margins, a wedge-shaped base, and blunt to pointed apex. Fragrant, pinkish flowers, about 1 inch in diameter, are in clusters of 3 to 5. The apples are pale yellow-green, broader than long, and about 1 inch in diameter. A shrub or small tree, to 30 feet tall and 10 inches in diameter, with a broad, open crown of stiff branches.

SWEET CRAB APPLE *(Malus coronaria)* leaves are 2 to 3 inches long and 1.5 inches wide. Oval to ovate, with a rounded to abruptly pointed apex, usually a rounded base, and toothed margins. The fragrant, pinkish-white flowers, to 1.5 inches in diameter, are in clusters of 3 to 6. The yellow-green fruit is about an inch in diameter and broader than long. Grows as a shrub or small tree, often forming thickets in moist soils. The twigs are armed with sharp spines.

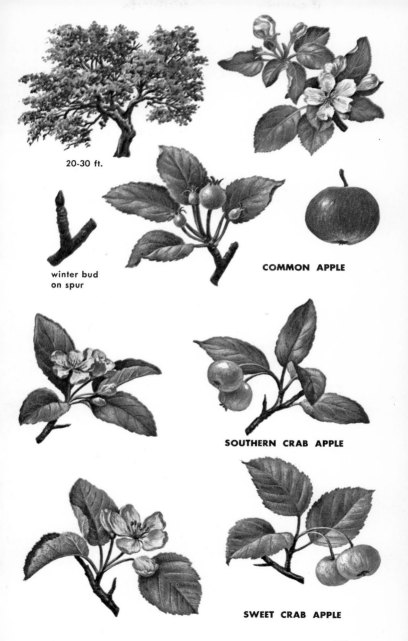

20-30 ft.

winter bud
on spur

COMMON APPLE

SOUTHERN CRAB APPLE

SWEET CRAB APPLE

163

BILTMORE CRAB APPLE (*Malus glabrata*) leaves are roughly triangular, 2.5 to 3.5 inches long, 2 to 2.5 inches wide, with 3 to 5 coarsely toothed, pointed lobes. Pink flowers, about 1.3 inches in diameter, are in clusters of 4 to 7. The fruit, about 1.5 inches in diameter, is ribbed at the apex. The twigs often have stout spines up to 1.5 inches long. A shrub or small tree to 25 feet tall, most common in mountain valleys.

PRAIRIE CRAB APPLE (*Malus ioensis*) leaves, usually hairy below, are 2 to 4 inches long, 1 to 1.5 inches wide. The rosy-white flowers, 1.5 to 2 inches in diameter, occur in clusters of 3 to 6 and the greenish-yellow fruit is about 1.3 inches in diameter. Grows as a shrub or a small bushy tree, to 30 feet tall.

OREGON CRAB APPLE (*Malus diversifolia*) leaves are ovate to elliptical, 1 to 4 inches long, 0.5 to 1.5 inches wide, occasionally 3-lobed; base wedge-shaped or rounded. White flowers, about 0.8 of an inch in diameter, occur in clusters of 4 to 10. Oblong, yellow-green to reddish-purple apples are 0.5 to 0.8 of an inch long. Oregon Crab Apple may form thickets in moist soil; it grows to 40 feet tall.

MOUNTAIN-ASHES (*Sorbus*)

About 80 species of small, deciduous trees and shrubs of cooler parts of the Northern Hemisphere are known as mountain-ashes; not related to ashes (p. 254). Mountain-ashes have pinnately compound, alternate leaves, flat-topped clusters (cymes) of small, white flowers that develop after leaves appear, and small, apple-like, red or orange fruits. In North America, only eastern species reach tree size.

AMERICAN MOUNTAIN-ASH (*Sorbus americana*) leaves are 6 to 8 inches long, with 13- to 17-toothed, lanceolate leaflets 2 to 4 inches long, 0.3 to 1 inch wide, toothed above middle; turn yellow in fall. To 30 feet tall; bark light gray-brown, smooth to scaly. The smaller Showy Mountain-ash (*S. decora*), in the same area, has 7 to 13 broader leaflets, with larger flowers and fruits. Sitka Mountain-ash (*S. sitchensis*), of northwestern North America, rarely reaches tree size.

EUROPEAN MOUNTAIN-ASH (*Sorbus aucuparia*) is similar to American Mountain-ash but has smaller, bluntly pointed leaflets, 0.8 to 2 inches long and 0.5 to 0.8 of an inch wide, often somewhat hairy below. Also called Rowan Tree, it occurs in several varieties and is planted widely as an ornamental in North America.

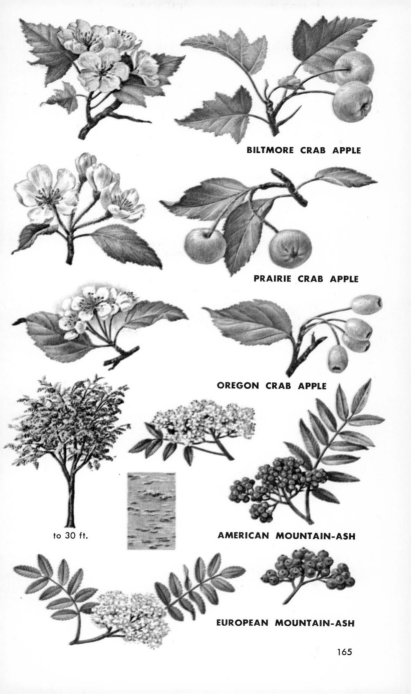

BILTMORE CRAB APPLE

PRAIRIE CRAB APPLE

OREGON CRAB APPLE

to 30 ft.

AMERICAN MOUNTAIN-ASH

EUROPEAN MOUNTAIN-ASH

165

CHERRIES AND PLUMS *(Prunus)*

Widely distributed in cool parts of the Northern Hemisphere, cherries and plums produce delicious fruits, are prized as ornamentals and, in some cases, are valuable for their beautiful wood. All have simple, alternate leaves, usually with serrate margins. The fruit is a drupe. Most cultivated cherries and plums came originally from Europe; ornamental flowering species from Asia. Several introduced species have escaped cultivation and are now naturalized in eastern North America. These include Mazzard Cherry *(P. avium)*, Sour Cherry *(P. cerasus)*, Garden Plum *(P. domestica)*, Bullace Plum *(P. insititia)*, Mahaleb Cherry *(P. mahaleb)*, Peach *(P. persica)*, and Sloe, or Blackthorn *(P. spinosa)*. Apricots and almonds also belong to this genus. Desert Apricot *(P. fremontii)*, of southern California, is a native apricot that is most commonly a shrub, rarely a tree.

BLACK CHERRY *(Prunus serotina)* has narrowly oval to oblong-lanceolate, deciduous leaves, 2 to 6 inches long and 1 to 1.5 inches wide, with fine marginal teeth. White flowers, about 0.3 of an inch in diameter, in racemes 4 to 6 inches long. Fruit 0.5 of an inch in diameter, black with dark-purple flesh. Satiny, reddish-brown wood prized for fine furniture. Grows 50 to 60 feet tall, 1 to 3 feet in diameter. Bark of young trees smooth, dark reddish brown to black, and marked with horizontal lenticels (raised, warty patches); scaly on large trees.

PIN CHERRY *(Prunus pensylvanica)* has oblong-lanceolate leaves, 3 to 4 inches long and 0.8 to 1.3 inches wide, with small marginal teeth. Creamy-white flowers, about 0.5 of an inch in diameter and 4 to 5 per cluster (umbels or corymbs), appear with or after leaves. Bright-red cherries, 0.3 of an inch in diameter, have acid taste. Bark smooth, reddish brown, with horizontal lenticels; later in broad plates. Grows 15 to 25 feet tall, 18 to 20 inches in diameter.

COMMON CHOKECHERRY *(Prunus virginiana)* has broadly obovate leaves, 2 to 4 inches long and 1 to 2 inches wide; apex pointed; margins often doubly toothed. White flowers, 0.5 of an inch in diameter, in racemes 3 to 6 inches long. Astringent, dark-red cherries are 0.3 of an inch in diameter. Lustrous-brown bark, with pale lenticels, is ill-smelling; later becomes scaly. A bushy tree, Common Chokecherry grows to 25 feet tall and 8 inches in diameter.

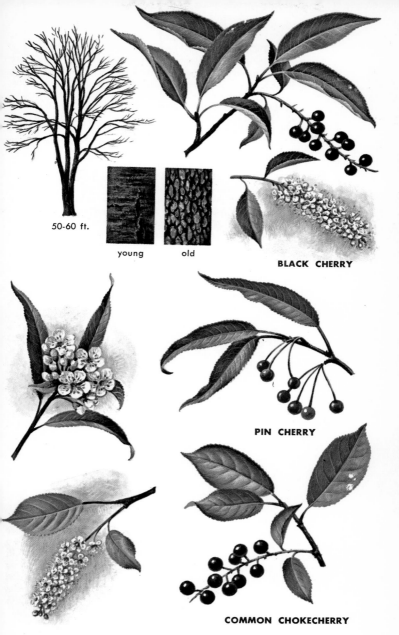

50-60 ft.

young   old

BLACK CHERRY

PIN CHERRY

COMMON CHOKECHERRY

BITTER CHERRY *(Prunus emarginata)* has elliptical or oblong-obovate leaves, 1 to 3 inches long and 0.5 to 1.5 inches wide, with toothed margins. White flowers, 0.5 of an inch across, are in 6- to 12-flowered corymbs; appear when leaves are about half grown. Red to black cherries, about 0.5 of an inch in diameter, have thin, astringent flesh. Bark brownish, with horizontal, orange lenticels. Bitter Cherry grows 30 to 40 feet tall and 1 to 1.5 feet in diameter, forming an oblong crown.

CATALINA CHERRY *(Prunus lyonii)* leaves are evergreen, ovate to lanceolate, 2 to 4 inches long and 0.5 to 2.5 inches wide; margins are smooth, thickened and wavy, occasionally sparingly toothed. White flowers, about 0.3 of an inch across, are in racemes 3 to 4 inches long. Dark-purple to black cherries, about 1 inch in diameter, have thick, delicious flesh. A bushy tree, 25 to 30 feet tall and 1 to 3 feet in diameter, with a compact crown and reddish-brown bark.

MYRTLE LAURELCHERRY *(Prunus myrtifolia)* leaves are evergreen, elliptical to oblong-ovate, 2 to 4.5 inches long and 1 to 1.5 inches wide, with smooth margins. White flowers with yellow at base of the petals are 0.1 of an inch in diameter. They appear late in fall, in short racemes. Fruit is orange-brown, nearly round, 0.3 to 0.5 of an inch in diameter, with thin, dry flesh. Myrtle Laurelcherry grows to 30 feet tall and 6 inches in diameter.

CAROLINA LAURELCHERRY *(Prunus caroliniana)* leaves are evergreen, oblong-lanceolate, 2 to 5 inches long and 0.8 to 1.5 inches wide; smooth or sparingly toothed margins. Short racemes of cream-white flowers appear in late winter or early spring. Oblong fruit, about 0.5 of an inch in diameter, is nearly black, with thin, dry flesh. Gray bark is at first smooth, later roughened. Carolina Laurelcherry grows to 40 feet tall and 10 inches in diameter.

HOLLYLEAF CHERRY *(Prunus ilicifolia)* has ovate to ovate-lanceolate, evergreen leaves, 1 to 2 inches long and 1 to 1.5 inches wide, with coarsely toothed margins. White flowers, 0.3 of an inch in diameter, are in short racemes. Thin-fleshed fruit is nearly black and about 0.5 of an inch in diameter when they are ripe. Hollyleaf Cherry grows to 25 feet tall, with dark reddish-brown, fissured bark.

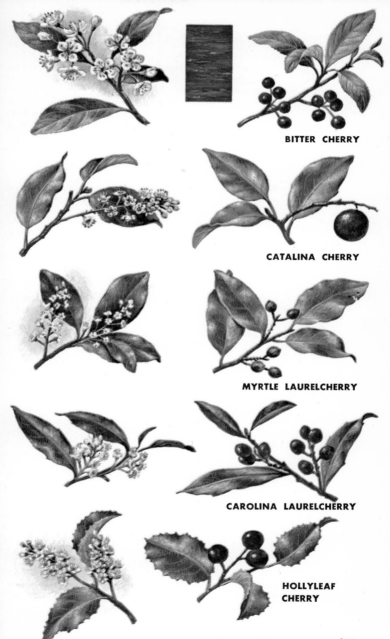

BITTER CHERRY

CATALINA CHERRY

MYRTLE LAURELCHERRY

CAROLINA LAURELCHERRY

HOLLYLEAF
CHERRY

AMERICAN PLUM *(Prunus americana)* has oblong-ovate leaves, 3 to 4 inches long and 1.5 to 2 inches wide, with a long, tapering apex and toothed margins. The ill-smelling flowers, about 1 inch in diameter, are white with red sepals and occur in 2- to 5-flowered umbels; they appear before the leaves. The round, red fruit is about 1 inch in diameter and has tart, yellow flesh. On young trees the bark is thin, smooth, and brown; on mature trees, scaly. Grows 20 to 30 feet tall and 1 foot in diameter with a broad, spreading crown; commonly forms thickets in moist soil.

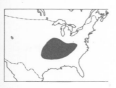

ALLEGHENY PLUM *(Prunus alleghaniensis)* leaves are narrowly lanceolate, 2 to 3.5 inches long and 0.8 to 1.3 inches wide, with small marginal teeth. The white flowers, 0.5 of an inch in diameter, are in 2- to 4-flowered umbels; they appear with the leaves. Globular plums, about 0.5 of an inch in diameter, are dark reddish purple with yellow flesh. A small tree to 20 feet tall, it has scaly, dark-brown bark.

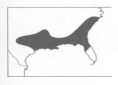

FLATWOODS PLUM *(Prunus umbellata)* resembles Allegheny Plum, but slightly smaller leaves are oblong-lanceolate. Flowers, 1 inch in diameter, appear before leaves. The tart plums are usually purplish black, though sometimes yellow.

HORTULAN PLUM *(Prunus hortulana)* leaves are oblong-lanceolate, 4 to 6 inches long, with slender, orange stems. Flowers, to 1 inch across, have white petals with orange at the base; they appear after the leaves. Plums are red, occasionally yellowish, with thin flesh. Hortulan Plum is a small tree to 30 feet tall, with dark-brown bark.

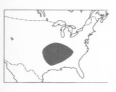

WILDGOOSE PLUM *(Prunus munsoniana)* has elliptical to lanceolate leaves, 2 to 4 inches long. Flowers are white, 0.5 to 0.8 of an inch across; the red plums, with yellow flesh, are about 0.8 of an inch long. To 20 feet tall and 6 inches in diameter, usually with smooth, brown bark; twigs occasionally thorny.

CHICKASAW PLUM *(Prunus angustifolia)* has lanceolate leaves, 1 to 2 inches long. White flowers, 0.3 of an inch across, appear before the leaves; the red to yellow plums are 0.5 of an inch in diameter. To 25 feet tall, often with spurlike, lateral twigs on branches.

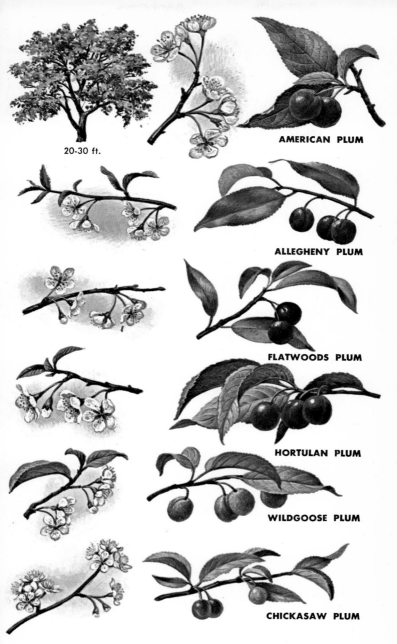

20-30 ft.

AMERICAN PLUM

ALLEGHENY PLUM

FLATWOODS PLUM

HORTULAN PLUM

WILDGOOSE PLUM

CHICKASAW PLUM

KLAMATH PLUM *(Prunus subcordata)* has elliptical to broadly ovate leaves, 1 to 3 inches long and 0.5 to 2 inches wide, with finely toothed margins. White flowers, 0.7 of an inch in diameter, are in 2- to 4-flowered umbels; bloom before leaves appear. The tart, dark-red or occasionally yellow plums are 0.8 to 1.3 inches long. Klamath Plum grows to 25 feet tall, with a rounded crown, gray-brown, scaly, and fissured bark. Branches are often spiny.

CANADA PLUM *(Prunus nigra)* leaves are oblong-ovate to obovate, 3 to 5 inches long and 1.5 to 3 inches wide, with an abrupt, narrow apex and marginal teeth. White flowers, about 1.3 inches in diameter, appear in 3- to 4-flowered umbels before or with the leaves. The yellow-fleshed, orange-red plums are 1 to 1.3 inches long. Grows 30 feet tall. Has a short trunk with gray-brown bark that peels off in layers.

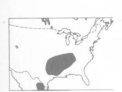

MEXICAN PLUM *(Prunus mexicana)* has ovate to elliptical leaves, 1.8 to 3.3 inches long. White flowers, about 1 inch in diameter and in 3- to 4-flowered umbels, bloom before leaves appear. Dark purple-red plums, to 1.5 inches long, have thick, sweet flesh. To 30 feet tall, with dark-gray, scaly to fissured bark.

SERVICEBERRIES *(Amelanchier)*

Widely distributed throughout temperate regions, these shrubs or small trees have deciduous, simple, alternate leaves, with either toothed or smooth margins; white flowers in racemes; the nearly round, usually succulent fruit is dark blue to black.

ALLEGHENY SERVICEBERRY *(Amelanchier laevis)* leaves are elliptical to ovate, 2 to 2.5 inches long and 1 to 1.5 inches wide, with apex abruptly pointed and toothed margins. Flowers, 0.5 to 0.8 of an inch long, appear when leaves are about half grown. Edible fruit, 0.3 inch in diameter. To 40 feet tall, 1 to 1.5 feet in diameter, with rounded crown; bark dark reddish brown. Downy Serviceberry *(A. arborea)*, more southern, has larger leaves, woolly below, and fruit is dry and tasteless. Pacific Serviceberry *(A. florida)* has oval to oblong-ovate leaves; juicy fruit. Similar species that may become small trees are Saskatoon Serviceberry *(A. alnifolia)*, Roundleaf Serviceberry *(A. sanguinea)*, Utah Serviceberry *(A. utahensis)*, and Inland Serviceberry *(A. interior)*.

KLAMATH PLUM

CANADA PLUM

MEXICAN PLUM

to 40 ft.

ALLEGHENY SERVICEBERRY

DOWNY SERVICEBERRY

PACIFIC SERVICEBERRY

HAWTHORNS (*Crataegus*)

This very complex genus includes many species of shrubs or small, round-topped, usually thorny trees. They are most abundant in eastern North America, but nearly 100 species are found in the cooler parts of Europe and Asia. Hawthorns are easy to recognize as a group, but the species are difficult to identify. All have alternate, conspicuously toothed, sharply incised, or lobed leaves. They bear clusters of showy white, pink, or red flowers, each from 0.3 to 1 inch in diameter. The attractive, though dry and mealy, apple-like fruits, 0.3 to 0.8 of an inch in diameter, are usually red or orange but in some species are dark blue, black, or yellow. The smooth, greenish-brown bark of the branches and smaller trunks breaks up into thin, scaly plates with age. Trunks of mature trees are often fluted, or "muscular." The wood is hard and heavy but not commercially important. Hawthorns are popular as ornamentals, and a number of horticultural varieties have been developed. Twelve of the more than 100 native North American species of hawthorns are described and illustrated here.

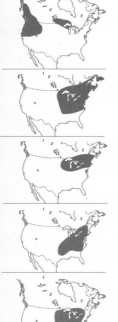

BLACK HAWTHORN (*Crataegus douglasii*) leaves are ovate to obovate, about 1 to 2 inches long and 0.5 to 1.5 inches wide, and coarsely toothed near apex. Flowers are in broad clusters. Fruits shiny black.

FROSTED HAWTHORN (*Crataegus pruinosa*) leaves, 1 to 1.5 inches long and 1 inch wide, have either deeply cut margins or 3 to 4 pairs of shallow lobes. Few flowers in a cluster. Dark purple-red fruit, about 0.5 of an inch in diameter, is covered with small, dull dots.

SCARLET HAWTHORN (*Crataegus pedicellata*) leaves are broadly ovate to diamond-shaped, 3 to 4 inches long, and shallowly lobed. Many flowers per cluster. Fruits red with dark dots. Spines are 1 to 2 inches long.

COCKSPUR HAWTHORN (*Crataegus crus-galli*) leaves are 1 to 4 inches long and 0.3 to 1 inch wide, widest and toothed above the middle. Each of the many-flowered clusters produces oval, scarlet fruits about 0.5 of an inch long. The spines of Cockspur Hawthorn are 3 to 4 inches long.

DOWNY HAWTHORN (*Crataegus mollis*) leaves are 3 to 4 inches long and about as wide, broadest near their base. The margins are either sharply cut or shallowly lobed. Many flowers in each cluster. Fruits scarlet; spines may be 2 inches long.

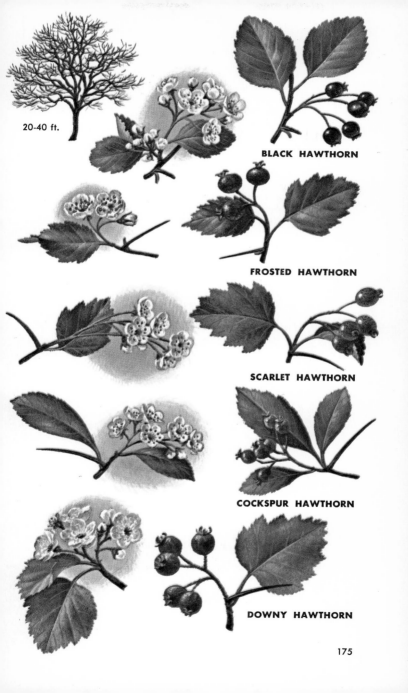

20-40 ft.

BLACK HAWTHORN

FROSTED HAWTHORN

SCARLET HAWTHORN

COCKSPUR HAWTHORN

DOWNY HAWTHORN

175

LITTLEHIP HAWTHORN *(Crataegus spathulata)* leaves are spatula-shaped, often 3-lobed near apex. Many flowers in each cluster. Small, scarlet fruits are about 0.1 of an inch in diameter. Spines 1 to 1.5 inches long.

BLUEBERRY HAWTHORN *(Crataegus brachycantha)* leaves, 1 to 2 inches long, are usually widest near the rounded apex, with rounded marginal teeth. Flowers white, fading to orange. Fruit bright blue. Spines less than 1 inch long. Usually small but may grow to 50 feet tall.

BOYNTON HAWTHORN *(Crataegus boyntonii)* leaves are broadly ovate, toothed, and occasionally lobed near the apex. Flowers, in clusters of 4 to 10, produce yellowish-red fruits about 0.5 of an inch in diameter. The spines are 1.5 to 2 inches long.

TURKEY HAWTHORN *(Crataegus induta)* leaves are oblong-ovate, 3 to 4 inches long, with coarsely toothed to shallowly lobed margins. Flowers many per cluster. Oblong fruit, 0.8 to 2 inches in diameter, is red to reddish yellow with pale dots. Spines 2.5 inches long.

BARBERRYLEAF HAWTHORN *(Crataegus berberifolia)* leaves are oblong-obovate, to 2 inches long, hairy below. Flowers 4 to 5 in a cluster; fruits orange, about 0.5 of an inch in diameter. Spines 1 to 1.5 inches long.

PARSLEY HAWTHORN *(Crataegus marshallii)* leaves are broadly ovate to orbicular, with 5- to 7-toothed lobes. The many-flowered clusters produce oblong, scarlet fruits 0.3 of an inch long. The spines are 1 to 1.5 inches long.

WILLOW HAWTHORN *(Crataegus saligna)* leaves are narrowly oval, 1.5 to 2 inches long, and toothed toward apex; turn red in fall. Globose fruit, 0.8 of an inch in diameter, is first red, later turning black.

SOME INTRODUCED HAWTHORNS

ENGLISH HAWTHORN *(Crataegus oxyacantha)* leaves are broadly ovate, with 3 to 5 shallow lobes. Flowers red or white. Bright-red fruit contains two seeds. Native to Europe and northern Africa.

ONE-SEED HAWTHORN *(Crataegus monogyna)* resembles English Hawthorn, but leaves have 3 to 7 lobes, often with smooth margins. Fruits have one seed. Native to Europe, northern Africa, western Asia.

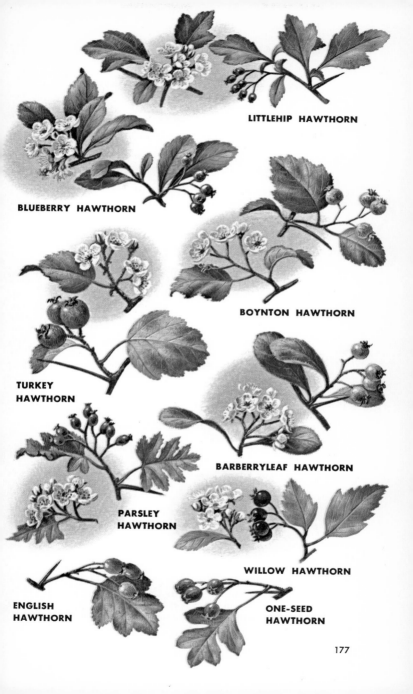

LITTLEHIP HAWTHORN

BLUEBERRY HAWTHORN

BOYNTON HAWTHORN

TURKEY HAWTHORN

BARBERRYLEAF HAWTHORN

PARSLEY HAWTHORN

WILLOW HAWTHORN

ENGLISH HAWTHORN

ONE-SEED HAWTHORN

177

CERCOCARPUS OR MOUNTAIN-MAHOGANY
(*Cercocarpus* spp.)

These shrubs or small trees are found in the dry, mountainous regions of western North America. Their leaves are simple, alternate, leathery, and either deciduous or evergreen, with either smooth or toothed margins. Flowers are solitary or clustered on short, lateral branchlets. They lack petals, and the greenish-white sepals form an elongated tube, expanded into a 5-lobed cup at the apex. Each flower produces a dry, leathery fruit that has a twisted, feathery plume at its apex. All have scaly bark and stiff branches.

BIRCHLEAF CERCOCARPUS (*Cercocarpus betuloides*) has obovate to oval leaves, 1 to 1.3 inches long and 0.3 to 0.5 of an inch wide, with rounded, toothed apex and wedge-shaped base. Dark green above; paler, often hairy below. Flowers 1 to 3 per cluster. A shrub or small tree to 25 feet tall; several varieties.

HAIRY CERCOCARPUS (*Cercocarpus breviflorus*) leaves are oblong to nearly elliptical, 0.5 to 1 inch long and 0.3 to 0.5 of an inch wide. They are gray-green, with rounded teeth near the apex, and hairy below. Flowers 1 to 3 per cluster. A shrub or small tree, to 15 feet tall and 5 inches in diameter, with erect branches forming an irregular, spreading crown.

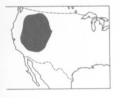

CURLLEAF CERCOCARPUS (*Cercocarpus ledifolius*) has narrow, lanceolate leaves, 0.5 to 1 inch long and 0.3 to 0.8 of an inch wide, with smooth, curled-under margins. They are dark green above and hairy below. Flowers usually solitary. A shrub or small tree, to 25 feet tall and to 2 feet in diameter; branches stout, spreading.

MEMBERS OF MISCELLANEOUS GENERA IN THE ROSE FAMILY

CHRISTMASBERRY (*Photinia arbutifolia*) has alternate, oblong to elliptical, evergreen leaves, 3 to 4 inches long and 1 to 1.5 inches wide, with prominent marginal teeth. The white flowers occur in terminal clusters, 4 to 6 inches across. They develop somewhat pear-shaped, scarlet (rarely yellow) fruit, about 0.3 of an inch long. They ripen from October to December. Christmasberry grows as a shrub or small tree, to 30 feet tall and 1.5 feet in diameter, with gray bark and a narrow, round-topped crown of erect branches.

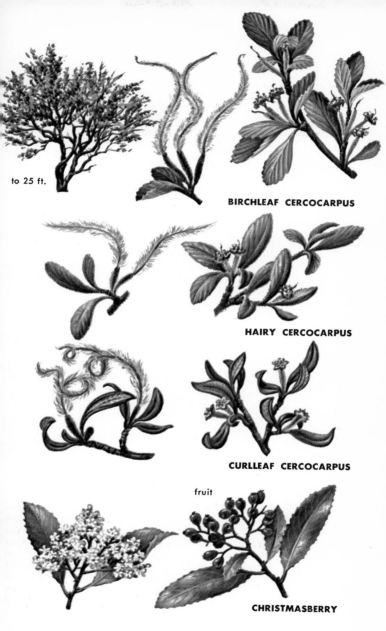

to 25 ft.

BIRCHLEAF CERCOCARPUS

HAIRY CERCOCARPUS

CURLLEAF CERCOCARPUS

fruit

CHRISTMASBERRY

ICACO COCO-PLUM (*Chrysobalanus icaco*) leaves, 1 to 3.5 inches long and 1 to 2.3 inches wide, are alternate, broadly elliptical to obovate leathery, evergreen, and smooth-margined. White flowers are in clusters 1 to 2 inches long. Fruit, 1.5 to 1.8 inches in diameter, is pink, yellow, or creamy, with thick, white, juicy flesh. The reddish-brown bark is scaly. Usually a shrub, often forming thickets in moist soils, but may grow to small-tree size (10 to 12 feet), with erect branches. The similar Smallfruit Coco-plum (*C. icaco* var. *pellocarpus*) occurs farther south.

LYONTREE (*Lyonothamnus floribundus*) has opposite, evergreen leaves, often of two types: simple and lanceolate, 4 to 8 inches long and 0.5 of an inch wide, with smooth or toothed margins; or pinnately compound, 3 to 6 inches long, with 3 to 7 leaflets. White flowers, 0.3 of an inch across, are in terminal clusters 4 to 8 inches broad, each flower producing a conical, woody carpel about 0.3 of an inch long. The dark reddish-brown bark peels into thin, papery strips. A small tree, often with several stems, but occasionally with a single trunk; to 40 feet tall and 10 inches in diameter. Grows in dry soils.

TORREY VAUQUELINIA (*Vauquelinia californica*) has leathery, usually alternate, lanceolate leaves, 1.5 to 3 inches long and 0.3 to 0.5 of an inch wide, with toothed margins and hairy below. Remain on the tree through the first winter after they form. White flowers, about 0.3 of an inch in diameter, occur in terminal clusters 2 to 3 inches across. Each produces a hairy, woody, ovoid capsule about 0.3 of an inch long. Grows in dry or rocky soils, as a shrub or a small tree, with scaly, reddish-brown bark. To 20 feet tall, 6 inches in diameter.

CLIFFROSE (*Cowania mexicana*) has wedge-shaped leaves less than 1 inch long, divided into 3 to 5 narrow lobes. Leathery, hairy below, and covered with resinous specks, they usually persist through the first winter. The white to pale-yellow flowers, about 1 inch in diameter, develop into a dry fruit with feathery plumes about 2 inches long. Usually a shrub but occasionally a small tree, to 25 feet tall and 8 inches in diameter, with stiff, erect branches. It has gray, scaly bark and grows in dry, rocky soils.

ICACO COCO-PLUM

LYONTREE

TORREY VAUQUELINIA

leaves

CLIFFROSE

LEGUME FAMILY (Leguminosae)

This family contains more than 500 genera and about 13,000 species of herbs, vines, shrubs, and trees found throughout the world. Many species have thorny branches. Leaves are alternate, compound in most. Some shed their leaves; others are evergreen. All produce a legume, or pod. Clover, alfalfa, peas, and beans are important legume crops. Other species are well-known ornamentals. Some, especially tropical trees, yield wood, dyes, and similar products. Nitrogen-fixing bacteria in root nodules of legumes aid in enriching the soil.

Silktree *(Albizia julibrissin)*, a native of southern Asia, is grown as an ornamental in California and southeastern United States where it now also grows wild. Lebbek or Woman's Tongue *(A. lebbek)*, a similar tree, is common in southern Florida, as are Flamboyant-tree, or Royal Poinciana *(Delonix regia)*, a native of Madagascar; Flower-fence, or Dwarf Poinciana *(Poinciana pulcherrima)*, of unknown origin; and Tamarind *(Tamarindus indica)*, of the Old World tropics. Paradise Poinciana *(P. gilliesii)*, of South America, is naturalized in parts of the Southwest.

BLACKBEADS *(Pithecellobium spp.)* are shrubs or small trees, to 30 feet tall. Bipinnately compound leaves are evergreen or tardily deciduous; twigs spiny. Catclaw Blackbead *(P. unguis-cati)* has one pair of leaflets on its two pinnae; flowers in globular heads; pods contorted. Huajillo *(P. pallens)* has many small leaflets on 8 to 10 pinnae; flowers in globular heads, pods straight and flat. Ebony Blackbead *(P. flexicaule)* has several leaflets on 4 to 6 pinnae, light-yellow flowers in spikes; pods thick and hairy.

BAHAMA LYSILOMA *(Lysiloma bahamensis)* leaves are evergreen, with 2 to 6 pairs of pinnae having numerous oblong leaflets 0.3 to 0.5 of an inch long. Small, greenish-white flowers, in globose heads, produce reddish-brown, pointed pods, 4 to 5 inches long, with dark-brown, oval seeds about 0.5 of an inch long. Branches not spiny. Bahama Lysiloma grows to 60 feet tall, 3 feet in diameter.

LEADTREES *(Leucaena spp.)*, shrubs or small trees, have bipinnate, evergreen leaves with numerous small leaflets; white flowers in globose heads and many-seeded pods; twigs not spiny. Native species include Littleleaf Leadtree *(L. retusa)*, Gregg Leadtree *(L. greggii)*, and Great Leadtree *(L. pulverulenta)*. Leadtree *(L. glauca)* is an introduced species in Florida.

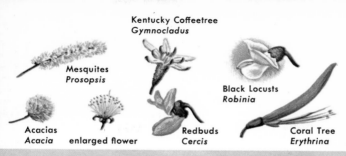

Mesquites
Prosopis

Kentucky Coffeetree
Gymnocladus

Black Locusts
Robinia

Acacias
Acacia

enlarged flower

Redbuds
Cercis

Coral Tree
Erythrina

DIFFERENCES IN FLOWERS OF SOME NATIVE LEGUMES

CATCLAW BLACKBEAD

HUAJILLO

EBONY BLACKBEAD

BAHAMA LYSILOMA

LITTLELEAF LEADTREE

183

CATCLAW ACACIA (*Acacia greggii*) leaves are gray-green, with 1 to 3 pairs of pinnae, each with 4 to 6 pairs of oval leaflets to 0.3 of an inch long. Cylindrical spikes of small, creamy-yellow, fragrant flowers are 1 to 2.5 inches long. Fruit a flattened pod, 1 to 6 inches long, 0.8 of an inch wide, often curled and constricted between seeds. Branches bear short, curved spines, 0.3 of an inch long; bark brown and scaly. A shrub or small tree, to 18 feet tall.

SWEET ACACIA (*Acacia farnesiana*) has bright-green, deciduous leaves with 2 to 8 pairs of pinnae, each having 10 to 25 pairs of pointed leaflets about 0.2 of an inch long. Small, yellow, fragrant flowers are in globular heads about 0.8 of an inch in diameter. Thickened, lustrous reddish-purple pods, 2 to 3 inches long and 0.5 to 0.8 of an inch in diameter, contain ovoid seeds embedded in pulp. Grows to 30 feet tall and 1.5 feet in diameter, with a round, wide-spreading crown, reddish-brown bark, and straight, stiff spines about 1.5 inches long.

TWISTED ACACIA (*Acacia tortuosa*) has light-green leaves divided into 3 to 4 pairs of pinnae, with 10 to 15 pairs of small, linear, pointed leaflets. Small, bright-yellow, fragrant flowers in globular heads, 0.5 to 0.8 of an inch in diameter. Fruit a reddish-brown, slightly compressed pod, 3 to 5 inches long and 0.3 of an inch wide, constricted between seeds. Branches bear slender spines, 0.8 of an inch long. Grows to 20 feet tall, 6 inches in diameter; round, widespread crown and dark-brown to black, furrowed bark. Emory Acacia (*A. emoryana*), found in the same region, has flowers in short spikes and has larger pods.

WRIGHT ACACIA (*Acacia wrightii*) leaves are bright green and somewhat hairy. They are divided into 1 to 3 pairs of pinnae, each with 2 to 5 pairs of leaflets 0.3 to 0.8 of an inch long. Small, light-yellow, fragrant flowers are borne in cylindrical spikes about 1.5 inches long. Fruit is a compressed pod, 2 to 4 inches long and 1 to 1.5 inches wide, with narrow, oval seeds about 0.3 of an inch long. A few stout, curved, chestnut-brown spines, 0.3 of an inch long, occur on the branches. Grows to 30 feet tall and 1 foot in diameter with a wide crown and scaly, furrowed bark.

to 18 ft.

CATCLAW ACACIA

SWEET ACACIA

TWISTED ACACIA

WRIGHT ACACIA

185

MESQUITE *(Prosopis juliflora)* and its three varieties have deciduous leaves divided into 2, or occasionally 4, pinnae, each with many small leaflets. Greenish-white, fragrant flowers are in slender, cylindrical spikes 1.5 to 4 inches long. Narrow pods, 4 to 9 inches long and 0.3 to 0.5 of an inch in diameter, are constricted between seeds. Spines 0.5 to 2 inches long. Grows 20 to 50 feet tall, 1 to 3 feet in diameter.

SCREWBEAN MESQUITE *(Prosopis pubescens)* has hairy, deciduous leaves divided into 2, or occasionally 4, pinnae, each with 10 to 16 small leaflets. Small, greenish-white flowers in cylindrical spikes 2 to 3 inches long. The distinctive spiraled pod is 1 to 2 inches long. This mesquite grows to 20 feet tall, 1 foot in diameter; branches twisted, spiny.

EASTERN REDBUD *(Cercis canadensis)* leaves are deciduous, broadly ovate to heart-shaped, 3 to 5 inches wide, with a pointed tip and smooth margins. Turn yellow in fall. Flowers pinkish to lavender, 0.5 of an inch long, in loose clusters of 4 to 8; appear before leaves. Pinkish, flattened pods, 2.5 to 3.5 inches long, have several seeds about 0.3 of an inch long. Bark reddish brown, scaly. Usually small, occasionally to 50 feet, with a broad, rounded crown.

CALIFORNIA REDBUD *(Cercis occidentalis)* leaves are round or notched at apex, 2 to 4 inches broad, with a heart-shaped base and smooth margins. Lavender flowers, 0.5 of an inch long, appear before leaves. Pods are dull red, 1.5 to 3 inches long and 0.5 to 0.8 of an inch wide. Though usually a shrub, California Redbud is sometimes a small tree, to 20 feet tall.

KENTUCKY COFFEETREE *(Gymnocladus dioicus)* has bipinnately compound leaves, 1 to 3 feet long, with 5 to 9 pinnae, each bearing 6 to 14 pointed, oval leaflets 2 to 2.5 inches long and about 1 inch wide. Terminal racemose clusters of staminate and pistillate flowers are on separate trees; the former 3 to 4 inches long, the latter 10 to 12 inches long. Purplish-brown pods, 4 to 10 inches long and 1 to 2 inches wide, have 6 to 8 round, flattened, reddish-brown seeds, about 0.8 of an inch in diameter, embedded in pulp. Grows 75 to 100 feet tall and 2 to 3 feet in diameter. Furrowed bark is dark gray to brown; branches lack spines.

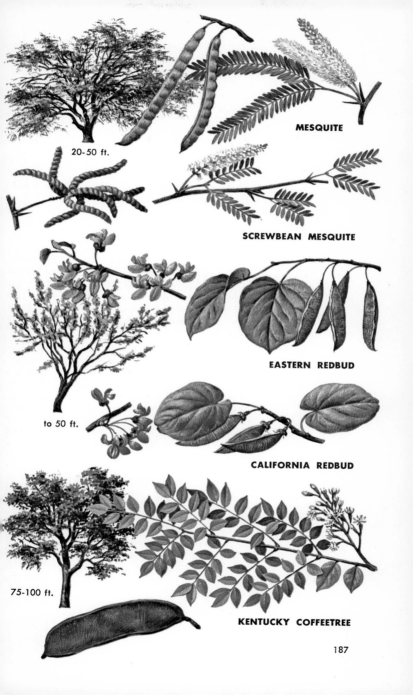

MESQUITE

20-50 ft.

SCREWBEAN MESQUITE

EASTERN REDBUD

to 50 ft.

CALIFORNIA REDBUD

75-100 ft.

KENTUCKY COFFEETREE

187

HONEYLOCUST *(Gleditsia triacanthos)* has pinnately or bipinnately compound leaves, 7 to 8 inches long. Elliptical to ovate leaflets, about 1 to 2 inches long and 0.3 to 0.5 of an inch wide, with smooth or remotely round-toothed margins; bipinnate leaflets smaller. Flowers greenish white, in racemes. Pods dark reddish brown, twisted, flattened, 7 to 18 inches long and 1 inch wide, with dark-brown, oval seeds, 0.3 of an inch long, in succulent pulp. Branches, and often trunk, armed with simple to 3-branched spines 2 to 3 inches long. Bark dark gray-brown, in narrow, flat-topped plates. In moist, fertile soils, Honeylocust grows 75 to 80 feet tall and 2 to 3 feet in diameter. It has a broad, flat-topped crown.

TEXAS HONEYLOCUST *(Gleditsia texana)* is considered to be a natural hybrid between Honeylocust and Waterlocust. Leaves and leaflets are smaller than Honeylocust's. Racemes of staminate flowers, 3 to 4 inches long, are orange-yellow; the shorter, many-seeded pods (4 to 5 inches long, 1 inch wide) lack pulp; twigs not spiny. Bark resembles Honeylocust's. Grows 100 to 120 feet tall and 2.5 feet in diameter. The crown is narrow and spreading.

WATERLOCUST *(Gleditsia aquatica)* leaves are 5 to 8 inches long and pinnate or bipinnately compound. The ovate-oblong leaflets are 1 inch long and to 0.5 of an inch wide. Flowers, in racemes 3 to 4 inches long, have greenish petals and sepals with soft, orange-brown hairs. Pods are oval, pointed at the apex, chestnut brown, 1 to 2 inches long and 1 inch wide. They lack pulp and contain 1 to 3 flat, nearly round seeds about 0.5 of an inch across. Twigs spiny; bark gray to reddish brown, in small, platelike scales. Waterlocust grows to 60 feet tall and 2.5 feet in diameter, with an irregular, flat-topped crown. It is most common in swampy places.

JERUSALEM-THORN *(Parkinsonia aculeata)* leaves are short-stemmed, bipinnately compound, with 1 to 3 pairs of wiry, flattened, evergreen pinnae 8 to 20 inches long, and many narrowly oblong, gray-green, deciduous leaflets about 0.1 of an inch long. Flowers golden yellow, in 3- to 6-inch racemes. Pods linear-cylindric, 2 to 6 inches long, constricted between seeds. Both the twigs and the base of the leaves are spiny. Jerusalem-thorn grows 15 to 20 feet tall.

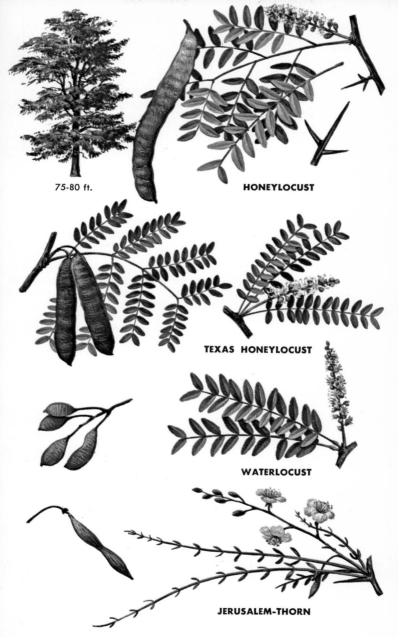

75-80 ft.

HONEYLOCUST

TEXAS HONEYLOCUST

WATERLOCUST

JERUSALEM-THORN

189

YELLOWWOOD *(Cladrastis lutea)* has pinnately compound leaves, 8 to 12 inches long, with 5 to 11 obovate leaflets 3 to 4 inches long and 1 to 2 inches wide. They turn yellow in fall. White flowers are in terminal panicles, 12 to 14 inches long. Pods are flat, 2 to 4 inches long, with 4 to 6 seeds. Smooth bark is dark gray to brown. Grows to 60 feet tall, 2 feet in diameter.

TEXAS SOPHORA *(Sophora affinis)* leaves are deciduous, 6 to 9 inches long, and pinnately compound. Each of the 13 to 19 elliptical leaflets is 1 to 1.5 inches long and about 0.5 of an inch wide. Flowers, white tinged with pink, are in racemes 3 to 5 inches long. Black pods are cylindrical, often hairy, 0.5 to 3 inches long and constricted between oval seeds. Grows to 20 feet tall and 10 inches in diameter, with spreading, round-topped crown and dark-brown, scaly bark.

MESCALBEAN *(Sophora secundiflora)* leaves are evergreen, hairy, pinnately compound, and 4 to 6 inches long. The 7 to 9 elliptical leaflets are 1 to 2.5 inches long and 0.5 to 1.5 inches wide. Fragrant, violet, pea-like flowers, about 1 inch long, occur in racemes 2 to 3 inches long. Cylindrical, hairy pods, 1 to 7 inches long and 0.5 of an inch in diameter, are constricted between scarlet seeds that contain poisonous alkaloid (sophrium). A shrub or small tree, to 30 feet tall, with a narrow crown.

BLUE PALOVERDE *(Cercidium floridum)* has scattered, bipinnately compound leaves, 1 to 1.5 inches long, with 2 pinnae, each with 2 to 3 pairs of dull-green, oblong leaflets 0.3 of an inch long. Yellow flowers, 0.8 of an inch across, are in racemes to 2 inches long. Flat, yellowish-brown pods are 3 to 4 inches long. The twigs are spiny. Smooth bark is bluish gray, becoming scaly and brown. Grows to 25 feet tall.

YELLOW PALOVERDE *(Cercidium microphyllum)* branches end in sharp spines. Leaves, to 1 inch long, have 2 pinnae, each with 4 to 7 pairs of tiny, elliptical leaflets, which are shed early. Small, yellow flowers are in racemes. Cylindrical pods, 2 to 3 inches long, are constricted between seeds. Bark is yellow-green to gray. A shrub or small tree, to 25 feet tall.

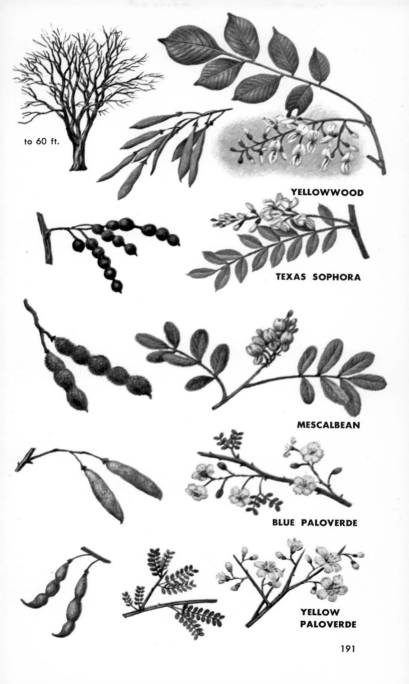

to 60 ft.

YELLOWWOOD

TEXAS SOPHORA

MESCALBEAN

BLUE PALOVERDE

YELLOW PALOVERDE

BLACK LOCUST *(Robinia pseudoacacia)* has pinnately compound leaves, 8 to 14 inches long; 7 to 19 smooth-margined leaflets 1 to 2 inches long, 0.5 to 0.8 of an inch wide. Fragrant, white flowers in drooping racemes. Flat, brown to black pods, 2 to 4 inches long, 0.5 of an inch wide; the 4 to 8 seeds are kidney-shaped, orange-brown. Spines, 0.5 to 0.8 inch, on twigs. Bark nearly black, in "corded" ridges. To 80 feet tall, 2 to 4 feet in diameter.

CLAMMY LOCUST *(Robinia viscosa)* leaves are 7 to 12 inches long, pinnately compound; 13 to 21 oval leaflets, 1.5 to 2 inches long, 0.8 of an inch wide, hairy below. Rose-colored, odorless flowers in drooping racemes. Pods, 2 to 3.5 inches long, contain several reddish-brown, mottled seeds. Twigs sparingly thorny. Pods, leaf stems, and branchlets covered with sticky, clammy hairs. Shrubby to 40 feet tall; bark reddish brown, generally smooth. New-Mexican Locust *(R. neomexicana)* is a common, generally shrubby species of the Southwest.

SMOKETHORN *(Dalea spinosa)* has simple, wedge-shaped leaves, 0.8 to 1 inch long, 0.1 to 0.5 of an inch wide, densely hairy, early deciduous. Leaves, twigs, flowers, and pods dotted with glands. Spiny twigs gray with dense hairs when young. Purple flowers, 0.5 of an inch long, in racemes 1 to 1.5 inches long. Ovoid pod contains 1 or 2 seeds. Bark gray-brown, scaly. Smokethorn grows to 20 feet tall.

FLORIDA FISHPOISON-TREE *(Piscidia piscipula)* has pinnately compound leaves, 4 to 9 inches long, the 5 to 11 leaflets 1.5 to 3 inches long, hairy below and along stems. Flowers white, tinged with red, in panicles; appear in spring before leaves. Winged pods, 3 to 4 inches long and constricted. The bark is olive-gray and scaly. This tree grows to 50 feet tall.

EASTERN CORALBEAN *(Erythrina herbacea)* has ever-green leaves 6 to 8 inches long, with three shallowly lobed leaflets 2.5 to 3.5 inches long, 1.5 to 2.3 inches wide. Elongated, scarlet flowers, 2 to 2.5 inches long, in racemes 8 to 13 inches long. Pods are 4 to 6 inches long, constricted between scarlet seeds. Branchlets have stout, curved spines. A shrub or small tree, to 25 feet tall. Southwestern Coralbean *(E. flabelliformis)*, ranging from Mexico into southwestern U.S., is occasionally tree size.

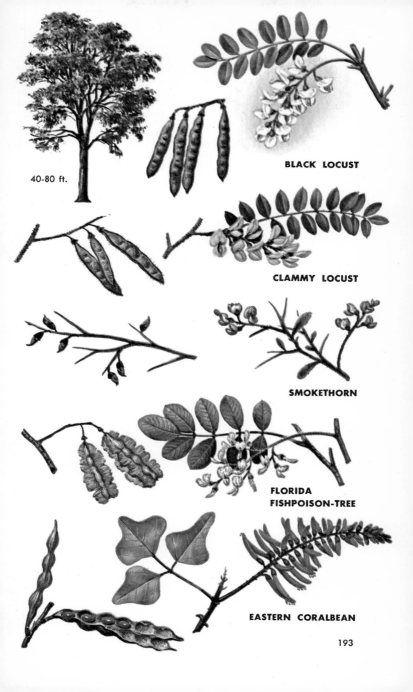

40-80 ft.

BLACK LOCUST

CLAMMY LOCUST

SMOKETHORN

FLORIDA FISHPOISON-TREE

EASTERN CORALBEAN

193

RUE FAMILY (Rutaceae)

More than 1,000 species of trees, shrubs, and herbs native to the tropics and warm temperate zones belong to this family. It is best represented in Australia and South Africa, but a number of small trees of this family grow in North America. Several species of *Citrus* have escaped cultivation and are naturalized in Florida.

HERCULES-CLUB *(Zanthoxylum clava-herculis)*, also called Toothache-tree, has alternate, odd-pinnately compound, tardily deciduous leaves, 5 to 8 inches long. The 7 to 19 leaflets, 1 to 2.5 inches long, are bright green above, paler and somewhat hairy below; margins toothed; stems spiny. Greenish staminate and pistillate flowers on separate trees clustered (in cymes) at ends of branches. Brown, wrinkled capsule, 0.8 of an inch long, splits open to release a black seed on a slender thread. Spines, 0.5 of an inch long, arm stout, gray to brown twigs. A small tree, rarely to 40 feet, with a short trunk; light-gray bark often studded with stout spines.

YELLOWHEART *(Zanthoxylum flavum)* has alternate, odd-pinnately compound, evergreen leaves, 6 to 9 inches long. The 5 to 11 leathery, ovate to lanceolate to elliptical leaflets are 1.5 to 2 inches long, with smooth or finely toothed margins and dotted with translucent glands. Both flowers and fruits are similar to those of Hercules-club, but twigs are not spiny. Smooth, light-gray bark becomes fissured with age. Grows to 20 feet tall.

LIME PRICKLY-ASH *(Zanthoxylum fagara)* leaves are evergreen, alternate, odd-pinnately compound, 3 to 4 inches long, with 7 to 9 glandular-dotted leaflets finely toothed above middle. Leaf stems are winged; brownish twigs spiny. Yellow-green staminate and pistillate flowers in axillary clusters (cymes) on separate trees. Warty, brown capsule contains one black seed. A shrub or small tree, to 30 feet tall, with thin, gray, "warty" bark.

COMMON PRICKLY-ASH *(Zanthoxylum americanum)* foliage resembles Hercules-club, but margins of leaflets (5-11) are smooth or have only small, rounded teeth. Small, greenish flowers are in sessile, axillary clusters. Bark gray to bluish. It is usually a spiny shrub but occasionally is a small tree, to 25 feet tall.

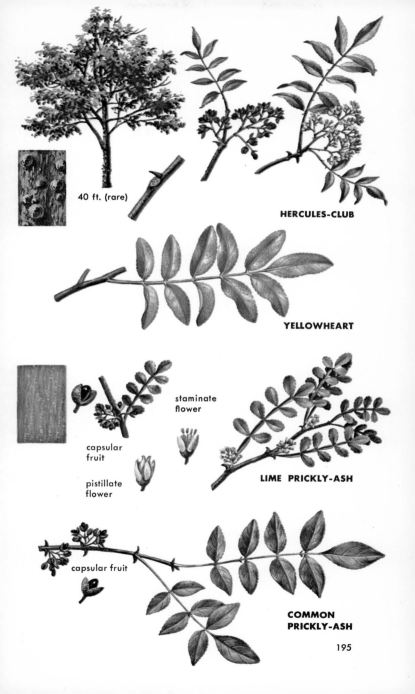

40 ft. (rare)

HERCULES-CLUB

YELLOWHEART

capsular
fruit

staminate
flower

pistillate
flower

LIME PRICKLY-ASH

capsular fruit

**COMMON
PRICKLY-ASH**

COMMON HOPTREE *(Ptelea trifoliata)* has alternate, usually 3-foliate, deciduous leaves, 4 to 6 inches long; leaflets, 2 to 4 inches long, have smooth to finely toothed margins. Polygamous, greenish-white flowers in terminal clusters (cymes). Buff-colored, wafer-like fruit (samara), about 1 inch in diameter, has a broad, veined wing. Twigs slender, giving off rank odor when broken. Bark thin, gray, warty. Crown broad, rounded; to 25 feet tall, 1 foot in diameter. Pale Hoptree *(P. pallida)* and Narrowleaf Hoptree *(P. angustifolia)*, most commonly shrubs, grow in southwestern United States and also in Mexico.

SEA AMYRIS *(Amyris elemifera)* has opposite, evergreen leaves, with 3 broadly lance-shaped leaflets, each 1 to 2.5 inches long; margins smooth or with small, rounded teeth. Flowers white, in terminal clusters (panicles). Fruit black, cherry-like, palatable, about 0.5 of an inch in diameter. Bark thin, gray-brown, becoming furrowed. To 50 feet tall, 1 foot in diameter. Balsam Amyris *(A. balsamifera)* ranges from Florida southward.

BURSERA FAMILY (Burseraceae)

GUMBO-LIMBO *(Bursera simaruba)* has alternate, odd-pinnately compound leaves, 6 to 8 inches long, clustered at ends of branches. The 3 to 9 leathery leaflets are 2 to 3 inches long. Small, greenish-white flowers in racemes 2 to 5 inches long. Red, leathery, 3-angled fruits, about 0.3 of an inch long, split into 3 parts, releasing single seed. Bark thin, smooth, reddish brown; light wood sometimes used for fishing floats. To 60 feet tall, 3 feet in diameter. Elephanttree *(B. microphylla)* and the smaller Fragrant Bursera *(B. fagaroides)* are shrubs or small trees of southwestern U.S. Flowers and fruits are similar to Gumbo-limbo's; leaves have winged petioles and 5 to 30 leaflets about 0.8 to 1.5 inches long.

CALTROP FAMILY (Zygophyllaceae)

HOLYWOOD LIGNUMVITAE *(Guaiacum sanctum)* has opposite, even-pinnately compound, evergreen leaves, with 3 to 4 pairs of opposite, leathery, smooth-margined leaflets about 1 inch long. Blue flowers, about 0.8 of an inch across, in 2- to 4-flowered, terminal clusters. Orange, obovoid, fleshy capsule, about 0.8 of an inch long, contains scarlet-coated black seeds. Bark chalky; wood heavy. To 30 feet tall.

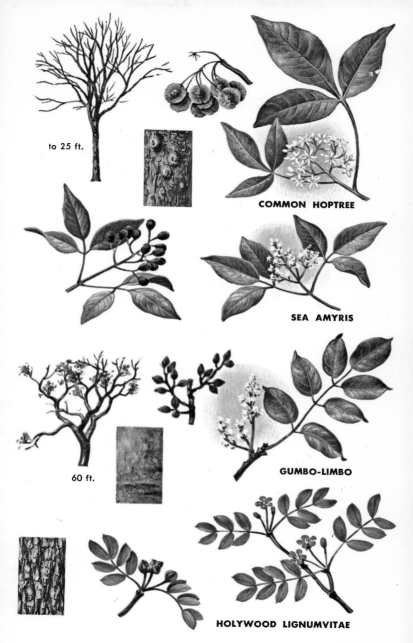

to 25 ft.

COMMON HOPTREE

SEA AMYRIS

60 ft.

GUMBO-LIMBO

HOLYWOOD LIGNUMVITAE

197

AILANTHUS (QUASSIA) FAMILY
(Simaroubaceae)

PARADISE-TREE *(Simarouba glauca)* leaves are evergreen, pinnately compound, alternate, and to 10 inches long. Their 10 to 14 leathery, oblong to obovate leaflets are 2 to 3 inches long and either alternate or opposite; dark green above, lighter below. Yellow staminate and pistillate flowers, on separate trees, are in axillary or terminal clusters (panicles). Fruit, about 1 inch long, is red, becoming purple as it ripens. A small tree, to 50 feet tall and 2 feet in diameter, with brown, scaly bark.

BITTERBUSH *(Picramnia pentandra)* leaves are evergreen, alternate, odd-pinnately compound and 8 to 12 inches long, with 5 to 9 leathery, pointed leaflets 1 to 3 inches long. Greenish staminate and pistillate flowers on separate trees, in slender racemes, 6 to 8 inches long. Oval fruit is 1- to 2-seeded and about 0.5 of an inch long, lustrous black when ripe. Slender twigs are hairy. A shrub or small tree, Bitterbush grows to 20 feet tall and 6 inches in diameter. It has smooth, yellowish-brown bark.

MEXICAN ALVARADOA *(Alvaradoa amorphoides)* has alternate, pinnately compound, evergreen leaves, 4 to 12 inches long. The 21 to 41 leaflets, 0.5 to 0.8 of an inch long, taper from a broad, rounded apex. Staminate and pistillate flowers, on separate trees, are in slender racemes 3 to 8 inches long. Reddish fruit is lance-shaped and 2-winged with fringed margins, about 0.8 of an inch long. A shrub or small tree of dry soils, to 30 feet tall and 8 inches in diameter, with gray or reddish-tinged bark.

AN INTRODUCED MEMBER OF AILANTHUS FAMILY

AILANTHUS *(Ailanthus altissima),* also called Tree-of-Heaven, has alternate, odd-pinnately compound, deciduous leaves, 1 to 3 feet long. The 11 to 41 ovate to ovate-lanceolate leaflets are 3 to 5 inches long and 1 to 2 inches wide. They are toothed at the base and have a disagreeable odor when crushed. Staminate and pistillate flowers are on different trees; they are small, greenish, and in dense, terminal panicles. Staminate flowers also have an unpleasant odor. The fruit is an oblong, twisted samara, about 1.5 inches long, with a seed in the center of the wing. They are in large, dense clusters that hang on the tree through the winter. Bark is thin, dark gray, and somewhat roughened. A rapidly growing tree with stout, hairy twigs and a flat-topped crown of stout branches, Ailanthus thrives even in poor soils and may grow to 100 feet tall and 3 feet in diameter. Produces many suckers; often a weed tree. Native to eastern Asia but grown widely as an ornamental.

PARADISE-TREE

BITTERBUSH

MEXICAN ALVARADOA

to 100 ft.

AILANTHUS

199

MAHOGANY FAMILY (Meliaceae)

WEST INDIES MAHOGANY (*Swietenia mahogoni*) leaves are evergreen, alternate, even-pinnately compound, 4 to 7 inches long, the 6 to 8 leathery, ovate to lanceolate, opposite leaflets 3 to 4 inches long. Flowers cup-shaped, 0.1 of an inch long, the 5 petals greenish or white; in long, axillary panicles. Reddish-brown capsular fruit, 3 to 4 inches long, splits from base along 5 valves, releasing squarish, winged seeds about 0.8 of an inch long. Bark dark brown, scaly. To 60 feet tall, 2 feet in diameter; rare in U.S.

AN INTRODUCED MEMBER OF MAHOGANY FAMILY

CHINABERRY (*Melia azedarach*) has alternate, bipinnately compound, deciduous leaves, 1 to 2 feet long. The numerous bright-green, pointed leaflets 1 to 3 inches long, with toothed (or slightly lobed) margins. Purplish, showy, fragrant flowers, about 0.8 of an inch in diameter; in loose panicles, 4 to 8 inches long. Fleshy fruits, 0.5 to 0.8 of an inch in diameter, yellow when mature. Rapid-growing, short-lived tree native of Asia, grown as an ornamental in southern U.S.

SPURGE FAMILY (Euphorbiaceae)

The more than 7,000 species of herbs, shrubs, and trees in this family include the Para or Brazilian Rubber Tree (*Hevea brasiliensis*), Tapioca (*Manihot esculenta*), and other commercially valuable tropical plants, plus poinsettia, crotons, snow-on-the-mountain, and other ornamentals. Castor-bean Plant (*Ricinus communis*) plus Brazil Sapium (*Sapium glandulosum*) and the Chinese Tallowtree (*S. sebiferum*), both related to Mexican Jumping-bean (*S. biloculare*), have escaped cultivation and now grow in warm parts of North America. Many members of the family have a milky juice, poisonous in some.

GUIANAPLUM (*Drypetes lateriflora*) leaves are evergreen, alternate, smooth-margined, broadly elliptical, 2 to 4 inches long. Small, greenish, staminate and pistillate flowers in leaf axils on separate trees, the staminate clustered. Fruit a scarlet, nearly globose drupe about 0.3 of an inch in diameter. Bark light brown, smooth; usually scaly. A shrub or small tree, to 25 feet tall, 6 inches in diameter. Milkbark (*D. diversifolia*), found only in southern Florida, has white fruit.

OYSTERWOOD (*Gymnanthes lucida*) has leathery, alternate, evergreen leaves, 2 to 3 inches long; margins usually smooth. Staminate (clustered) and pistillate (usually solitary) flowers on adjoining axillary stalks. Fruit a dark, 3-lobed capsule, 0.3 of an inch in diameter. To 35 feet tall. Bark thin, scaly.

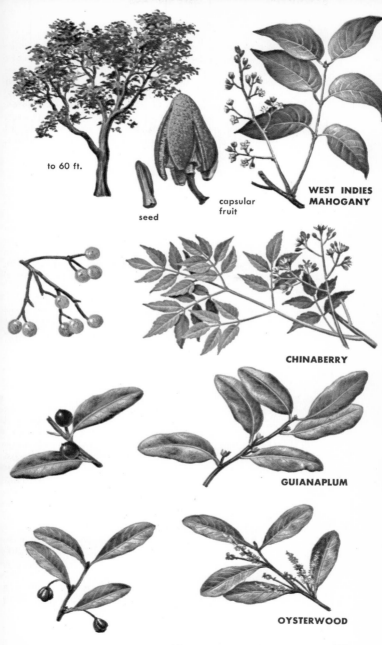

to 60 ft.

seed

capsular fruit

WEST INDIES MAHOGANY

CHINABERRY

GUIANAPLUM

OYSTERWOOD

MANCHINEEL *(Hippomane mancinella)* has alternate, broadly ovate leaves, 3 to 4 inches long, 1 to 2 inches wide; tips pointed, margins finely round-toothed. Flowers in terminal stalks 4 to 6 inches long; yellow-green staminate above, pistillate below. Fruits drupaceous, yellow-green with red cheeks, 1.5 inches in diameter, with milky flesh. Bark white to dark brown, smooth; scaly on large trunks. A shrub or small tree, to 20 feet tall, 6 inches in diameter. Sap highly poisonous.

CASHEW (SUMAC) FAMILY (Anacardiaceae)

This family, represented in temperate and tropical regions, comprises about 600 species of trees, shrubs, and vines, with resinous, acrid, or caustic juice. In addition to the species listed here, the Mango *(Mangifera indica)* is grown in Florida and throughout the tropics and subtropics for its fruit. Peppertree *(Schinus molle)*, from South America, is grown as an ornamental in California and in southern Florida, where it is now naturalized and grows wild. Cashew *(Anacardium occidentale)* and Pistachio *(Pistachia vera)* are grown mainly in the tropics for nuts.

AMERICAN SMOKETREE *(Cotinus obovatus)* has alternate, simple, oval to obovate, deciduous leaves, 4 to 6 inches long, 2 to 3 inches wide; margins smooth, curled under; hair on veins below. Leaves turn orange or red. Dioecious; sparsely flowered terminal clusters, 5 to 6 inches long. Fruit a dry, oblong, compressed, brown drupe, 0.3 of an inch long. Shrubby, to 35 feet tall.

FLORIDA POISONTREE *(Metopium toxiferum)* leaves are evergreen, alternate, odd-pinnately compound, 6 to 10 inches long, the 5 (occ. 3) to 7 leaflets 3 to 4 inches long, 2 to 3 inches wide, with slightly curled margins. Dioecious; the yellow-green flowers in loose clusters 6 to 12 inches long in leaf axils near tips of branches. Orange fruits (drupes) 0.8 of an inch long, resinous. Bark thin, reddish brown, mottled with dark gummy secretions; scaly on older trees. A shrub or small tree, to 35 feet tall. Poisonous to touch.

TEXAS PISTACHE *(Pistacia texana)* leaves are evergreen, alternate, pinnately compound, with slightly winged stems. The 9 to 19 leaflets, 0.8 of an inch long, widest above middle. Dioecious; small flowers without sepals or petals, in panicles to 2.5 inches long. Fruit a dark reddish-brown drupe, 0.2 of an inch long. A shrub or small tree, to 30 feet tall.

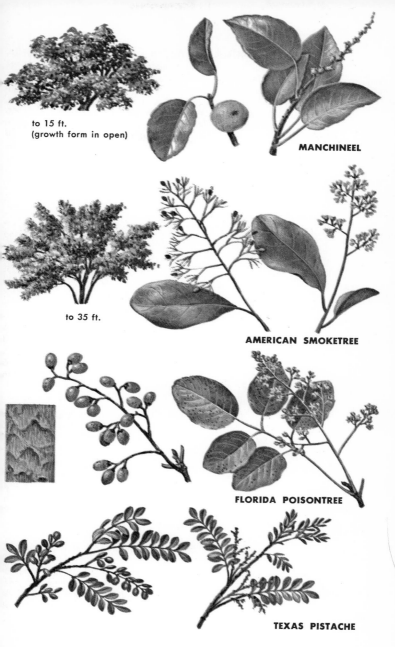

to 15 ft.
(growth form in open)

MANCHINEEL

to 35 ft.

AMERICAN SMOKETREE

FLORIDA POISONTREE

TEXAS PISTACHE

STAGHORN SUMAC *(Rhus typhina)* leaves are deciduous, alternate, odd-pinnately compound, and 12 to 24 inches long, with stout, hairy stems. The 11 to 31 lance-shaped leaflets are 2 to 5 inches long, with toothed margins; dull green above, paler and hairy on midrib below; scarlet in fall. Greenish staminate and pistillate flowers in dense panicles at ends of branches on separate trees. Fruits dry, red-hairy drupes, 0.1 of an inch in diameter. Stout, densely hairy twigs exude milky fluid when crushed. Bark of young trees thin, dark brown; on older trees, scaly. Shrub or small tree, to 35 feet tall. Smooth Sumac *(R. glabra)*, similar but smaller, has smooth twigs. Lemonade Sumac *(R. integrifolia)* and Kearney Sumac *(R. kearneyi)* are among western species occasionally tree size.

SHINING SUMAC *(Rhus copallina)* leaves are similar to Staghorn Sumac's but have winged stems and fewer leaflets (9 to 21), usually not toothed. Flower clusters less dense, fruits smaller. Bark thin, reddish brown.

POISON-SUMAC *(Toxicodendron vernix)* leaves are 7 to 15 inches long, similar to those of *Rhus* but smaller and with fewer leaflets. Leaflets 3 to 4 inches long, with smooth margins. Clusters of greenish-yellow flowers produce ivory-white drupes about 0.3 of an inch in diameter. Thin, gray-brown bark smooth except for lenticels. Usually a shrub, rarely to 30 feet. Contains poisonous oil, like Poison Ivy of same genus.

CYRILLA FAMILY (Cyrillaceae)

SWAMP CYRILLA *(Cyrilla racemiflora)* leaves are simple, alternate, 2 to 3 inches long and 0.5 to 1 inch wide; tardily deciduous. Fragrant, white to pinkish flowers in racemes 4 to 6 inches long, near end of twigs. Dry, conical fruit about 0.1 of an inch long. Bark lustrous reddish brown. To 25 feet tall. Florida Cyrilla *(C. arida)* and Littleleaf Cyrilla *(C. parvifolia)* are two small, tree-size species found only in Florida.

BUCKWHEAT-TREE *(Cliftonia monophylla)* has simple, alternate, smooth-margined, evergreen leaves, 1 to 2 inches long and to 1 inch wide. Flowers white to pink, in slender, erect racemes. Fruit 4-winged, about 0.3 of an inch long. Bark reddish brown. A shrub or small tree, Buckwheat-tree grows to 35 feet tall and may form thickets in moist soils.

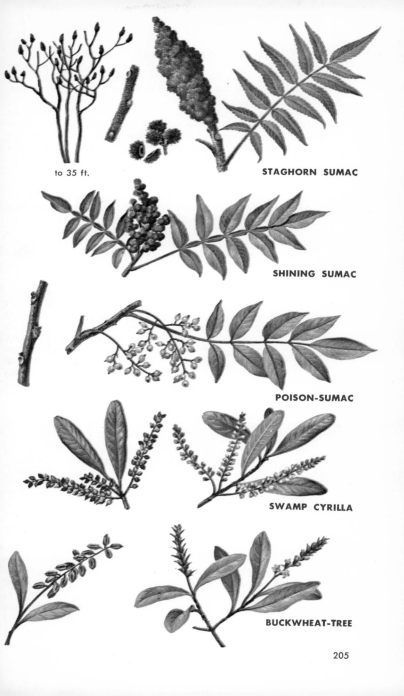

to 35 ft.

STAGHORN SUMAC

SHINING SUMAC

POISON-SUMAC

SWAMP CYRILLA

BUCKWHEAT-TREE

HOLLY FAMILY (Aquifoliaceae)

Hollies (*Ilex*) are the most familiar of three genera of trees and shrubs in this family, with nearly 300 species in temperate and tropical areas of both hemispheres. In addition to the species described here, six others that are most commonly shrubs are native to eastern United States. Those with leathery, spiny-toothed, evergreen leaves, and bright-red fruits are used in Christmas decorations. Others are deciduous, with smooth-margined leaves and fruits of a different color. In all hollies the leaves are alternate.

AMERICAN HOLLY (*Ilex opaca*) has leathery, evergreen leaves, 2 to 4 inches long and 1 to 2 inches wide, with a sharp-pointed tip and spiny-toothed (occasionally smooth) margins. Greenish-white staminate and pistillate flowers borne on separate trees. Fleshy, berry-like, bright-red fruits, 0.3 of an inch in diameter, contain several ribbed nutlets. Bark thin, gray, often warty. Grows to 50 feet tall, with short branches forming a narrow, pyramidal crown.

TAWNYBERRY HOLLY (*Ilex krugiana*) leaves are evergreen, 2.5 to 4 inches long and 1 to 1.5 inches wide. They have a long-pointed apex and smooth margins. Flowers are similar to American Holly's, and fruits, about 0.1 of an inch long, are purple-brown. Grows as a shrub or a small tree, to 30 feet tall and 6 inches in diameter. On twigs or trunks of young trees, bark is smooth and whitish; on mature trees, scaly and brown.

DAHOON (*Ilex cassine*) leaves are evergreen, oblanceolate to oblong-ovate, 1.5 to 3 inches long and 0.5 to 1 inch wide, with margins smooth or slightly toothed above the middle. Flowers, similar to American Holly's, produce bright-red, occasionally yellowish fruits, 0.3 of an inch in diameter. The gray bark is marked with numerous lenticels. Dahoon grows to 30 feet tall and 1.5 feet in diameter. It is often common in moist soils.

YAUPON (*Ilex vomitoria*) resembles Dahoon, but has smaller, elliptical, toothed leaves. The scarlet fruits are produced in greater abundance. Bark scaly and brown. Yaupon grows as a shrub or small tree, to 20 feet tall and 6 inches in diameter, often forming dense thickets. The leaves of Yaupon have been used in preparing a purgative.

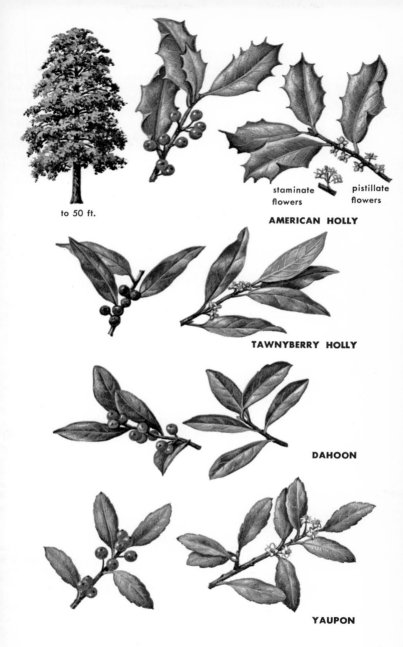

to 50 ft.

staminate flowers   pistillate flowers

AMERICAN HOLLY

TAWNYBERRY HOLLY

DAHOON

YAUPON

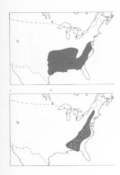

POSSUMHAW *(Ilex decidua)* has ovate-lanceolate, deciduous leaves, 2 to 3 inches long and 0.5 to 1 inch wide, with finely toothed margins. Flowers are similar to American Holly's, and the fruits, 0.3 of an inch in diameter, are reddish orange. Thin, smooth bark is greenish gray to brown. Usually a shrub but occasionally grows to 25 feet tall; common in moist soils.

MOUNTAIN WINTERBERRY *(Ilex montana)* resembles Possumhaw, but the leaves are 2 to 5 inches long and 0.5 to 2.5 inches wide, with larger, glandular, marginal teeth. Red fruits 0.5 of an inch in diameter.

AN INTRODUCED HOLLY

ENGLISH HOLLY *(Ilex aquifolium),* of Europe and Asia, is widely planted as an ornamental. Resembles American Holly, but English Holly has smaller leaves and a greater abundance of fruit.

BITTERSWEET FAMILY (Celastraceae)

EASTERN WAHOO *(Euonymus atropurpureus)* has opposite, ovate to elliptical, deciduous leaves, 2 to 5 inches long and 1 to 2 inches wide, with finely toothed margins. Perfect flowers are 0.5 of an inch wide, with 4 dark-purple petals, in 7- to 15-flowered, axillary clusters. Fruit, 0.5 of an inch in diameter, a deeply 4-lobed purplish-red capsule with red seeds. Bark thin, gray, scaly. To 25 feet. The similar Western Wahoo *(E. occidentalis)* is most commonly a shrub.

WEST INDIES FALSEBOX *(Gyminda latifolia)* leaves are leathery, evergreen, 1 to 2 inches long and 0.8 to 1 inch wide, opposite, obovate, with smooth or finely toothed margins. Staminate and pistillate flowers, in short-stalked, axillary clusters (cymes) on separate trees, have 4 white petals. Black to dark-blue, oval, drupaceous fruits are about 0.3 of an inch long. Bark thin, scaly, light brown, often mottled with red. A shrub or small tree, to 25 feet tall.

CANOTIA *(Canotia holacantha)* is a leafless shrub or small tree, to 18 feet tall and 1 foot in diameter, with rough, gray-brown bark and many upright, yellowish-green branches and twigs ending in spiny tips. Greenish-white flowers, 0.3 of an inch across, are in clusters of 3 to 7 along the twigs. The fruit is a woody, ovoid, pointed capsule to 1 inch long. Typical of dry slopes and mesas.

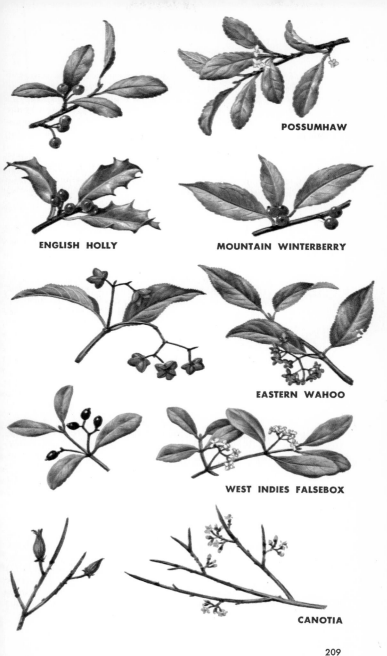

POSSUMHAW

ENGLISH HOLLY

MOUNTAIN WINTERBERRY

EASTERN WAHOO

WEST INDIES FALSEBOX

CANOTIA

209

MAPLE FAMILY (Aceraceae)

Maples (Acer) are among the most distinctive trees and shrubs in North America. Their winged seeds are in pairs (rarely in 3's) and their deciduous leaves are opposite on the branches. In most species the leaves are simple and palmately lobed. An exception is the Boxelder (Acer negundo), which has odd-pinnately compound foliage. Boxelder also differs from other native maples in having staminate and pistillate flowers on separate trees.

Maples, with nearly 150 species, are most abundant in eastern Asia. About a dozen species are native to the United States and Canada, but a number of foreign species have been introduced as ornamentals. The maple family has one other genus (Dipteronia), native to China.

SUGAR MAPLE (Acer saccharum) leaves are 3 to 5 inches in diameter and usually 5-lobed, their margins with several large, pointed teeth and the sides of the center lobe roughly parallel. Clusters of yellow, long-stemmed polygamous flowers develop with leaves. Inch-long, U-shaped pair of winged seeds ripen in fall. On young trees the bark is smooth and gray-brown, becoming scaly and furrowed with maturity. Sugar Maple grows 75 to 100 feet tall and 2 to 4 feet in diameter. In crowded woods, it has a long, branchless trunk; in the open a shorter trunk and a large, rounded crown. Its hard wood is used for furniture, in cabinet work, for interior trim, and flooring. The sap is the source of maple sugar and syrup. Sugar Maples are popular for shade and ornamental plantings because of their colorful red-and-yellow fall foliage.

BLACK MAPLE (Acer nigrum) is similar to the Sugar Maple, but the leaves are usually 3-lobed. In addition, the sides of the leaves tend to bend downward, and the underside, especially along the yellow veins, is somewhat hairy. Like the Sugar Maple, it is tapped in early spring for its sugary sap, and its hard wood is commercially valued.

FLORIDA MAPLE (Acer barbatum) resembles Sugar Maple but is smaller, growing to 60 feet tall and 3 feet in diameter. Its blue-green, 3- to 5-lobed leaves are 1.5 to 3 inches in diameter and usually hairy below. The lobes have wavy margins and rounded rather than pointed tips. In Florida Maple, the base of the leaf stem is noticeably enlarged.

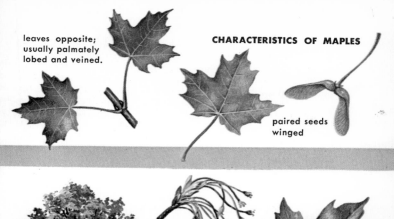

leaves opposite; usually palmately lobed and veined.

CHARACTERISTICS OF MAPLES

paired seeds winged

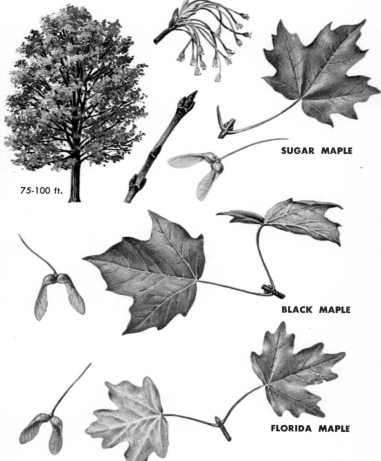

75-100 ft.

SUGAR MAPLE

BLACK MAPLE

FLORIDA MAPLE

211

RED MAPLE *(Acer rubrum)* leaves are 2 to 6 inches across, with 3, or occasionally 5, roughly triangular, coarsely toothed lobes; turn scarlet in autumn. Leaf stems usually reddish. Red to yellow polygamous flowers, in short-stemmed clusters, appear before the leaves. The paired seeds have slightly divergent wings, 0.8 of an inch long; they ripen in late spring. The twigs are reddish, with blunt reddish buds. The smooth, light-gray bark of young trees develops narrow, scaly plates with age. Red Maple reaches 75 to 80 feet in height and 1 to 2 feet in diameter. This tree grows rapidly, especially in moist to swampy soils. It is commonly planted as an ornamental.

SILVER MAPLE *(Acer saccharinum)* leaves are 6 to 7 inches across and deeply 5-lobed, with large marginal teeth; silvery below. Clusters of short-stemmed, greenish-yellow polygamous flowers appear before the leaves in early spring and produce paired seeds with widely spread wings, 1.5 to 2 inches long. The seeds ripen in spring. The bark of young trees is smooth and silver-gray; bark of old trees is characterized by long, narrow scales loose at their ends, giving the trunk a "shaggy" appearance. Silver Maple, typical of moist soils, grows rapidly. It reaches a height of 60 to 80 feet and a diameter of 2 to 4 feet, with a widespread crown of brittle branches. Although this maple is planted as an ornamental, its leaves do not become highly colored in fall.

BIGTOOTH MAPLE *(Acer grandidentatum)* leaves are 2 to 5 inches in diameter and 3-lobed, with blunt teeth on their margins. Leaves turn red or yellow in fall. The flowers, appearing with the leaves, resemble Sugar Maple's. The U-shaped, paired, winged seeds of Bigtooth Maple are about an inch long. The thin, gray to brown bark may be smooth or scaly. This tree grows to 50 feet tall and 1 foot in diameter, with a spreading, rounded crown. It is usually found in moist soils along canyon streams.

CHALK MAPLE *(Acer leucoderme)* leaves are 2 to 3.5 inches in diameter with 3 (occasionally 5) blunt lobes, their margins wavy or with widely spaced, blunt teeth. The leaves are hairy below and often turn red in fall. The flowers resemble those of Sugar Maple, but the paired seeds have widely spread wings, 0.5 to 1 inch long. Chalk Maple's bark is smooth and chalky white. This maple grows to 25 feet tall.

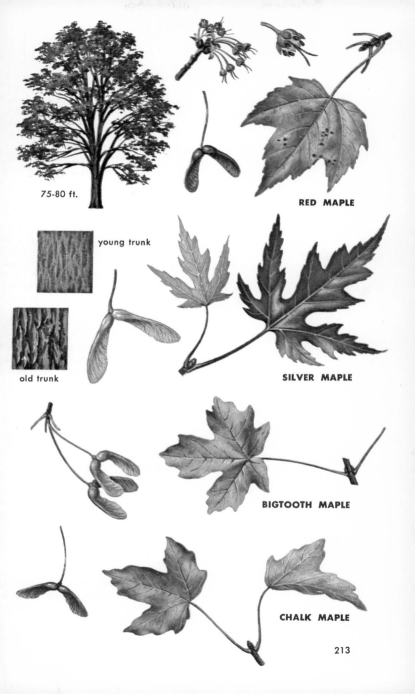

75-80 ft.

RED MAPLE

young trunk

old trunk

SILVER MAPLE

BIGTOOTH MAPLE

CHALK MAPLE

213

STRIPED MAPLE (*Acer pensylvanicum*) leaves are 5 to 6 inches long and 4 to 5 inches wide, with a rounded to heart-shaped base, and 3-lobed with doubly toothed margins. Turn yellow in fall. Bright-yellow flowers are borne in slender, drooping racemes 4 to 6 inches long, appearing when leaves are nearly grown; staminate and pistillate flowers are separate but on the same tree. Paired seeds have widely spread wings, about 0.8 to 1 inch long. Twigs and buds smooth. Bark smooth and green, with longitudinal, whitish stripes; later darker and warty. A shrub or small tree, to 40 or more feet tall; common in cool, moist places.

MOUNTAIN MAPLE (*Acer spicatum*) leaves have 3 (occasionally 5) lobes with coarsely toothed margins. The yellow flowers are in erect racemes, with staminate above and pistillate below; they appear after the leaves and produce paired seeds with somewhat divergent wings, about 0.5 of an inch long; they are red in midsummer. Twigs and buds covered with fine "hairs." The thin bark is reddish brown. A shrub or small tree, to 30 feet tall. Mountain Maple is common in cool, moist places.

BIGLEAF MAPLE (*Acer macrophyllum*) leaves may be 12 inches in diameter, largest of any maple. The 5 deeply cut lobes have smooth margins, except for a few large, blunt teeth. In autumn, leaves turn yellow-brown. Pendant racemes of yellow, somewhat fragrant polygamous flowers appear with leaves. Paired seeds have slightly divergent wings, 1.5 to 2 inches long, with a densely brown-haired seed cavity; mature in fall. On young trees, bark is smooth, greenish brown; on old trees, black and deeply ridged. Grows to 100 feet tall, 4 feet in diameter. In open situations, trunk usually short, crown broad.

VINE MAPLE (*Acer circinatum*) leaves are 2 to 6 inches in diameter, with 7 to 9 pointed lobes having toothed margins. The leaves are usually tinged with red when they unfold; turn scarlet in fall. Loose clusters of purple-red polygamous flowers appear when leaves are about half grown. The paired, red seeds have widely divergent wings, 0.8 of an inch long. Ripen in fall. Usually a tall shrub with many supple stems; occasionally a small tree—to 40 feet tall and 1 foot in diameter. Bark smooth, greenish to reddish brown. Commonly forms dense thickets on logged-off land in Pacific Northwest. A favored browse food of deer.

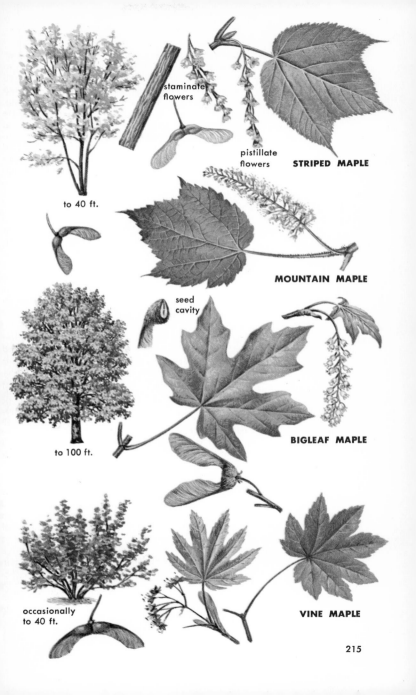

staminate flowers

pistillate flowers

STRIPED MAPLE

to 40 ft.

MOUNTAIN MAPLE

seed cavity

to 100 ft.

BIGLEAF MAPLE

occasionally to 40 ft.

VINE MAPLE

215

BOXELDER (*Acer negundo*) with its several varieties, has pinnately compound leaves, 6 to 15 inches long, with 3 to 7 coarsely toothed or shallowly lobed leaflets. Greenish-yellow staminate and pistillate flowers are on separate trees, the staminate in drooping clusters and the pistillate in drooping racemes. V-shaped, winged seeds are 1.5 to 2 inches long, the clusters hanging on the branches through winter. On young trees, bark is gray-brown and slightly ridged; on old trees, heavily furrowed. Rapid-growing but short-lived, Boxelder reaches a height of 50 to 75 feet and a diameter of 2 to 4 feet. It prefers moist soils along streams, ponds, and lakes but is hardy on poor sites.

ROCKY MOUNTAIN MAPLE (*Acer glabrum*) resembles Vine Maple but has smaller leaves, 3 to 5 inches in diameter, with 3 to 5 lobes. The wings of its seeds are spread only slightly. Douglas Maple (*A. glabrum* var. *douglasii*) often grows with the more common Vine Maple in the Pacific Northwest.

SOME INTRODUCED MAPLES

NORWAY MAPLE (*Acer platanoides*) leaves resemble Sugar Maple's, but the stems exude a milky fluid when squeezed. Also, the clustered, long-stemmed, greenish-white flowers appear after the leaves, and the winged seeds, 1.5 to 2 inches long, are widely spread.

PLANETREE (SYCAMORE) MAPLE (*Acer pseudoplatanus*) grows to 90 feet tall, with a wide-spreading crown and scaly bark. Leaves are 3 to 7 inches in diameter, 5-lobed, and coarsely toothed. Greenish-yellow flowers, in pendant panicles 3 to 6 inches long, appear after leaves. Paired seeds have wings 1.3 to 2 inches long, spread widely to form a right angle.

FULLMOON MAPLE (*Acer japonicum*) has 7- to 11-lobed leaves, 2 to 5 inches in diameter, with sharply toothed margins and drooping clusters of purple flowers. Winged seeds spread in wide "V", 1.8 to 2 inches long. To 25 feet tall.

ENGLISH FIELD MAPLE (*Acer campestre*) is a small tree, to 30 feet tall, with a rounded crown. Its small leaves, 1 to 4 inches in diameter, have 3 to 5 blunt lobes with smooth margins or rounded marginal teeth. The greenish-white flowers are in clusters, and the winged seeds, 1 to 1.3 inches long, are spread wide, sometimes forming almost a straight line.

JAPANESE MAPLE (*Acer palmatum*) has deeply cleft leaves, 2 to 4 inches in diameter, with 5 to 9 narrow, pointed, toothed leaves. It bears erect clusters of purple flowers, producing widely spread winged seeds about 0.8 of an inch long. A shrub or small tree, to 25 feet tall.

AMUR MAPLE (*Acer ginnala*) has narrow, 3-lobed, toothed leaves. They are 1.5 to 3.5 inches long and 1.3 to 2.5 inches wide. Clusters of yellow flowers produce V-shaped, winged seeds about 1 inch long. A shrub or small tree, to 20 feet tall.

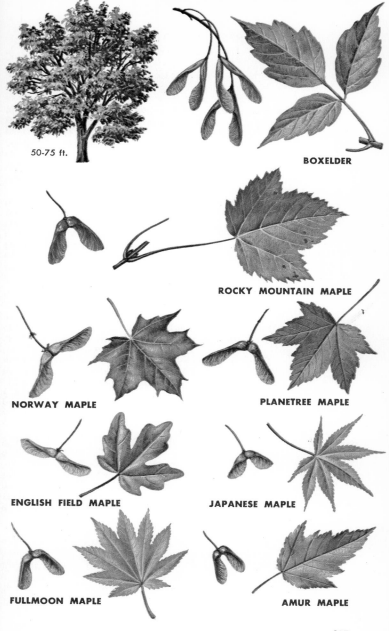

50-75 ft.

BOXELDER

ROCKY MOUNTAIN MAPLE

NORWAY MAPLE

PLANETREE MAPLE

ENGLISH FIELD MAPLE

JAPANESE MAPLE

FULLMOON MAPLE

AMUR MAPLE

217

HORSECHESTNUT (BUCKEYE) FAMILY
(Hippocastanaceae)

This family has but two genera, most important being the horse-chestnuts, or buckeyes, including about 30 species of trees and shrubs of North America, southeastern Europe, and Asia. Approximately one-third are native to the United States. All have opposite, palmately compound, deciduous leaves, the margins of the leaflets coarsely toothed. Large, showy, erect panicles of tubular or bell-shaped flowers develop after the leaves in the spring. Large, leathery capsules, 1 to 3 inches in diameter, are formed by fall. They split open when ripe and release the round, inedible seeds, 1 to 2 inches in diameter. Except for a large, lighter spot (hilum), they are a polished, dark chestnut brown.

The other genus in this family (Billia) includes two species of ever-green trees native to the area from Colombia north into Mexico.

YELLOW BUCKEYE (Aesculus octandra) leaves have 5 to 7 short-stemmed, obovate, pointed leaflets, each 4 to 6 inches long and 1.5 to 2.5 inches wide. The yellow flowers, hairy below and with stamens shorter than the petals, are borne in erect panicles, 5 to 7 inches long. The capsules, about 2 inches in diameter, are smooth on the surface and usually enclose two seeds, each about 1 to 1.5 inches in diameter. Brown bark is fissured and scaly. Grows 50 to 90 feet tall and 2 to 3 feet in diameter; crown oblong, rounded.

OHIO BUCKEYE (Aesculus glabra) resembles Yellow Buckeye but has narrower leaflets, stamens are longer than the petals, and surface of capsules is spiny. Also, leaves and twigs have an unpleasant odor when bruised. Texas Buckeye (A. arguta), once considered a variety, is similar to Ohio Buckeye.

PAINTED BUCKEYE (Aesculus sylvatica) leaves have 5 short-stemmed, oblong-obovate, pointed leaflets, each 4.5 to 6 inches long and 1.5 to 2.5 inches wide, with an orange midrib. Flowers are yellow, occasionally tinged with red, and hairless. Smooth-surfaced capsules usually contain only one seed. Painted Buckeye grows to 30 feet tall, 10 inches in diameter. It has brown, scaly bark.

RED BUCKEYE (Aesculus pavia) leaves have 5 short-stemmed, oblong-obovate leaflets, 4 to 5 inches long and 1.5 to 2 inches wide. Dark-red flowers produce smooth-surfaced capsules containing 1 to 2 seeds. A shrub or small tree, Red Buckeye grows to 25 feet tall; bark smooth, pale brown.

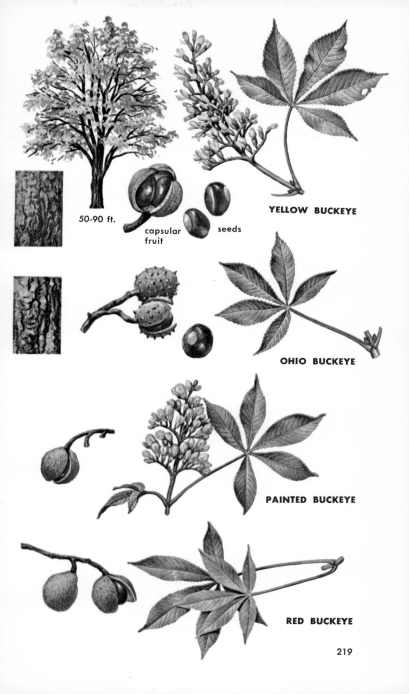

50-90 ft.

capsular
fruit

seeds

YELLOW BUCKEYE

OHIO BUCKEYE

PAINTED BUCKEYE

RED BUCKEYE

CALIFORNIA BUCKEYE *(Aesculus californica)* leaves have 4 to 7 (usually 5) distinctly stemmed, oblong-lanceolate leaflets. Each is 4 to 6 inches long and 1.5 to 2 inches wide. Trees growing in drier foothill regions usually lose their leaves early. White to pale-rose flowers are produced in panicles 5 to 10 inches long, and the pear-shaped, usually one-seeded capsules are 1.5 to 2 inches long and smooth-surfaced. California Buckeye may be a shrub or a small tree, to 40 feet tall and 8 inches in diameter. Its bark is smooth and light gray to brown.

AN INTRODUCED MEMBER OF BUCKEYE FAMILY

HORSECHESTNUT *(Aesculus hippocastanum)* leaves have 5 to 7 leaflets, each 4 to 10 inches long and 2 to 3.5 inches wide, distinctly widest near abruptly pointed apex. Creamy-white flowers are marked with red or yellow and are borne in erect panicles 8 to 12 inches long. Spiny capsules are 2.5 inches in diameter and contain 1 to 2 large seeds. Terminal bud large and sticky. Dark-brown bark is smooth or broken into irregular plates. A medium-sized to large tree, 25 to 60 feet tall, with rounded crown of wide-spreading branches. Horsechestnut is native to Asia and southeastern Europe; it is planted as a shade and street tree throughout central North America.

PAPAYA FAMILY (Caricaceae)

This is a small family of tropical and subtropical shrubs and trees. Best-known member is the Papaya, native from southern Florida southward into the tropics. Horticultural varieties are now widely planted in subtropical and tropical regions. The fruit is eaten raw or is processed to make juice. Papain, from the milky sap of stems and young fruit, is used as a meat tenderizer.

PAPAYA *(Carica papaya)* leaves are evergreen, 12 to 24 inches in diameter, palmately lobed, with pointed tips. The base is deeply heart-shaped, and the stout stems are 1 to 3 feet long, hollow, and enlarged at base. Staminate and pistillate flowers are borne in different clusters on separate trees or, less commonly, on the same tree. Staminate flowers are fragrant, with 5 spreading lobes at apex of narrow tube, clustered on long, many-flowered stalks; pistillate flowers tubular with separate petals, 1 to 3 on short stalks. Fruits melon-like, yellowish green to orange, about 4 inches long and 3 inches in diameter (much larger in horticultural forms), with a thick skin and sweet, whitish to orange flesh enclosing many dark seeds. Bruised twigs exude milky sap. Bark smooth, greenish gray. Papaya grows to 20 feet tall and 6 inches in diameter.

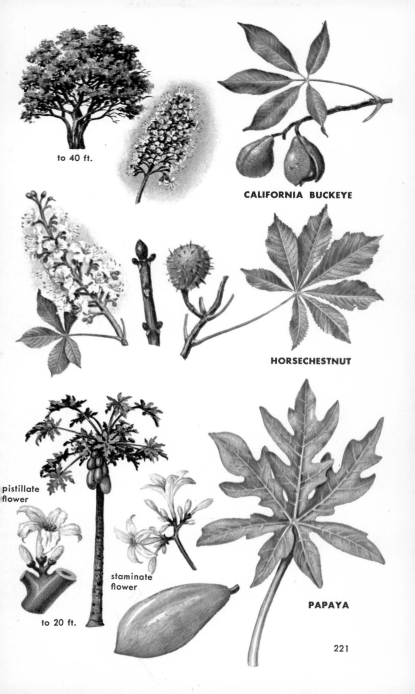

to 40 ft.

CALIFORNIA BUCKEYE

HORSECHESTNUT

pistillate
flower

staminate
flower

to 20 ft.

PAPAYA

221

BUCKTHORN FAMILY (Rhamnaceae)

Includes some 600 species of shrubs and small trees, largely tropical and subtropical. About 100 species in United States. In addition to the native species described here, Common Jujube *(Ziziphus jujube),* from Asia, Africa, and Australia, is grown as an ornamental in California and is naturalized in parts of the South.

CASCARA BUCKTHORN *(Rhamnus purshiana)* has usually alternate, broadly elliptical, deciduous leaves, 2 to 6 inches long and 1 to 2 inches wide; apex rounded or bluntly pointed, margins finely toothed and slightly curled under. Small clusters of tiny yellowish-green flowers occur in leaf axils. Black, globose, fleshy fruits, about 0.3 of an inch in diameter, contain several seeds. The bark is smooth and dark gray, often with cream-colored stripes; contains a drug used in laxatives. A small tree, to 40 feet tall. Birchleaf Buckthorn *(R. betulaefolia)* and the evergreen California Buckthorn *(R. californica* var. *ursina),* usually shrubs, grow in the Southwest.

CAROLINA BUCKTHORN *(Rhamnus caroliniana)* resembles Cascara Buckthorn but has tapered leaves and greenish-white flowers. The fruit has a drier flesh. The ash-gray bark is smooth to slightly furrowed, sometimes with dark markings. Carolina Buckthorn is a shrub or a small tree, growing to 30 feet tall.

LEADWOOD *(Krugiodendron ferreum)* has leathery, usually opposite, evergreen leaves, with smooth to wavy margins. They are broadly oval, notched at apex, and somewhat hairy above, 1 to 1.8 inches long and 0.5 to 1.5 inches wide. Clusters of 3 to 5 greenish-yellow flowers are in leaf axils. Fruit ovoid, black, about 0.3 of an inch long. Gray bark scaly, ridged. A shrub or small tree, to 30 feet tall, 10 inches in diameter. The wood of this species is the heaviest of any native tree.

DARLING-PLUM *(Reynosia septentrionalis)* leaves are evergreen, leathery, opposite, 1 to 1.5 inches long and 0.5 to 0.8 of an inch wide, usually oblong, with a notched or round, bristle-tipped apex. Greenish-yellow flowers, in small axillary clusters, produce dark-purple fruits, 0.5 of an inch long, with a pointed tip. Bark reddish brown and scaly; wood heavy. A shrub or small tree, to 25 feet tall and 9 inches in diameter.

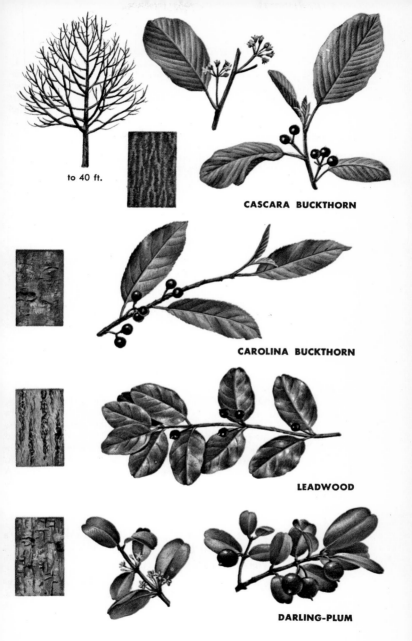

to 40 ft.

CASCARA BUCKTHORN

CAROLINA BUCKTHORN

LEADWOOD

DARLING-PLUM

223

SPINY CEANOTHUS *(Ceanothus spinosus)* has alternate, elliptical to oblong, evergreen leaves, about 1 inch long and 0.5 of an inch wide, with a stout midrib and pinnate venation. On young shoots, leaves are generally larger and have three palmate veins. Blue, fragrant flowers, resembling lilacs, are borne in dense clusters 5 to 6 inches long. Bark greenish on branches and trunks of small trees; reddish brown on older trunks. A shrub or small tree, to 20 feet tall and about 6 inches in diameter, with a narrow, open crown of slender, angled branches, often with spiny tips.

BLUEBLOSSOM *(Ceanothus thyrsiflorus)* has alternate, oblong to oblong-ovate, evergreen leaves, 1 to 1.5 inches long, 0.5 to 1 inch wide, slightly hairy on underside; fine marginal teeth, 3 prominent palmate veins. Flowers, blue or occasionally white, in 2- to 3-inch axillary clusters. Fruits black, 3-lobed. A shrub or small tree, to 20 feet tall, 8 inches in diameter. Bark greenish on young trunks and branches; reddish brown on larger, older trunks.

FELTLEAF CEANOTHUS *(Ceanothus arboreus)* leaves are alternate, elliptical to broadly ovate, with rounded marginal teeth; dark green above, lighter and densely hairy below, prominently 3-veined; 2.3 to 4 inches long, 1 to 2.5 inches wide. Flowers pale blue, in dense axillary clusters 3 to 4 inches long, 1.5 to 2 inches wide. Black fruit, 0.3 of an inch in diameter. To 25 feet tall, 10 inches in diameter, with stout branches. Greenish bark becomes gray on older trunks.

SOLDIERWOOD *(Colubrina reclinata)* leaves are alternate, 2.5 to 3 inches long, 1.5 to 2 inches wide; elliptical to lanceolate; yellow-green with stout midrib; persist until second season. Yellow flowers in small axillary clusters. Capsules oval, dark orange-red, 3-valved, 0.3 of an inch in diameter. Thin, orange-brown bark peels off in large, papery scales, leaving light patches on trunk. To 60 feet tall, 4 inches in diameter. Coffee Colubrina *(C. arborescens)*, found in same area, has leathery leaves hairy below.

SOME INTRODUCED BUCKTHORNS

GLOSSY BUCKTHORN *(Rhamnus frangula)*, also from Europe, is generally a shrub. Twigs lack thorns but are somewhat hairy.

EUROPEAN BUCKTHORN *(Rhamnus cathartica)* is a shrub or small tree, resembling Cascara and Carolina buckthorns. Twigs often spiny.

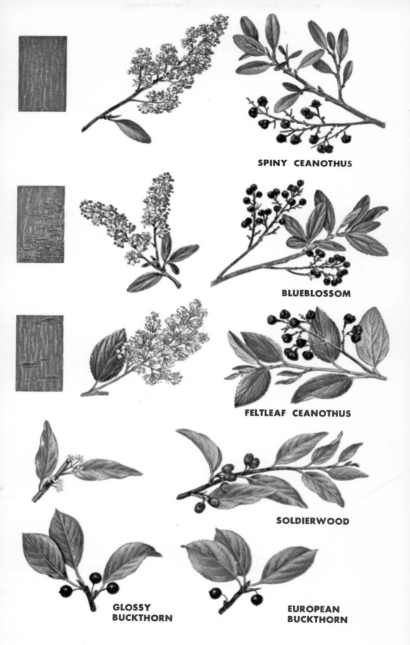

SPINY CEANOTHUS

BLUEBLOSSOM

FELTLEAF CEANOTHUS

SOLDIERWOOD

GLOSSY
BUCKTHORN

EUROPEAN
BUCKTHORN

CANELLA FAMILY (Canellaceae)

CANELLA *(Canella winterana)* leaves are evergreen, leathery, alternate, 3 to 5 inches long, 1 to 2 inches wide; apex rounded, margins smooth. White to purplish flowers, 0.1 of an inch in diameter, produce fleshy, bright-red berries, 0.5 of an inch in diameter, each with 2 to 4 seeds. Outer bark gray; yellow inner bark is source of commercial cinnamon. To 25 feet tall, 10 inches in diameter.

SOAPBERRY FAMILY (Sapindaceae)

This large family of trees and shrubs is primarily tropical. Chinese Lychee *(Litchi chinensis),* from which lychee nuts are obtained, is a well-known foreign member of the family. Mexican-buckeye *(Ungnadia speciosa)* is a shrub or small tree ranging into Mexico.

WINGLEAF SOAPBERRY *(Sapindus saponaria)* leaves are evergreen, alternate, pinnately compound, 6 to 7 inches long. The 5 to 9 leathery leaflets (terminal leaflet sometimes lacking) are smooth-margined. Leaf stem winged between leaflets. Small, white flowers in panicles, to 12 inches long, appear in fall. Globular, orange-brown berries, 0.8 of an inch in diameter, have thin, juicy several-seeded flesh; when crushed, serves as a soap substitute. Bark gray, roughened, scaly. To 30 feet tall, 12 inches in diameter.

FLORIDA SOAPBERRY *(Sapindus marginatus)* resembles Wingleaf Soapberry but lacks winged leaf stems and has 7 to 13 leaflets, curved at pointed tips. Fruit keeled, yellow; bark ash gray. To 25 feet tall.

WESTERN SOAPBERRY *(Sapindus drummondii)* leaves are deciduous, even-pinnately compund; 8 to 18 leaflets 2 to 3 inches long, 0.3 to 0.8 of an inch wide, hairy below. Flower panicles 6 to 9 inches long. Yellow berries, 0.5 of an inch in diameter, turn black, may hang through winter. To 50 feet tall, 2 feet in diameter; bark scaly, reddish brown.

BUTTERBOUGH *(Exothea paniculata)* leaves are evergreen, alternate, pinnately compound, the 2 to 6 wavy-margined leaflets 4 to 6 inches long, 1.5 to 2 inches wide. Flowers white. Fleshy berry purple (occasionally orange), 0.5 of an inch long. Bark reddish brown, scaly. To 50 feet tall, 1 foot in diameter.

CANELLA

WINGLEAF SOAPBERRY

FLORIDA SOAPBERRY

WESTERN SOAPBERRY

BUTTERBOUGH

227

LINDEN FAMILY (Tiliaceae)

This family, consisting of over 40 genera with several hundred species of herbs, shrubs, and trees, is best represented in the tropics and regions south of the equator. One genus of trees—linden, or basswood *(Tilia)*—is widely distributed over parts of the Northern Hemisphere and includes four species native to eastern North America. They are distinctive for their simple, alternate, broadly ovate, deciduous leaves with coarsely toothed margins and unequally heart-shaped bases. The small clusters of creamy-white flowers develop later into nutlike fruits that hang on slender stalks attached to a narrow, leafy bract. Cordage was made from the tough inner bark by American Indians. An herbaceous Asiatic genus *(Corchorus)* is a source of jute, a widely used fiber.

AMERICAN BASSWOOD *(Tilia americana)* has the largest leaves, 5 to 6 inches long and 3 to 4 inches wide, of the native American lindens, or basswoods. The few-flowered clusters, each flower, 0.5 of an inch long, and the nutlike fruits, 0.3 of an inch in diameter, are attached to a leafy bract 4 to 5 inches long and 0.5 to 0.8 of an inch wide. On large trees the dark-gray bark is ridged and furrowed. American Basswood grows 60 to 80 feet tall and 2 to 3 feet in diameter. Its wood is light and strong. The tree is valued most as a shade and ornamental tree and for the flavor of honey from its flowers.

CAROLINA BASSWOOD *(Tilia caroliniana)* leaves are 3 to 4 inches long and 2.5 to 5 inches wide, often hairy-brown on the underside. The flower clusters contain 8 to 15 blossoms. The nutlike fruits, also covered with rust-colored hairs, are 0.1 of an inch long, smaller than American Basswood's.

FLORIDA BASSWOOD *(Tilia floridana)* is smaller than American Basswood, growing 50 feet tall and 15 inches in diameter. The leaves of Florida Basswood are 3 to 5 inches long and 2.5 to 3.5 inches wide, and silvery on their underside, especially in spring. They are not hairy when mature.

WHITE BASSWOOD *(Tilia heterophylla)* grows to 80 feet tall and 2.5 feet in diameter. The finely toothed leaves are 3.5 to 5 inches long and 2 to 3 inches wide; they are densely covered with white to brownish hairs on lower surfaces. Numerous (10-24) flowers are borne in each cluster. White Basswood's nutlike fruits are somewhat hairy.

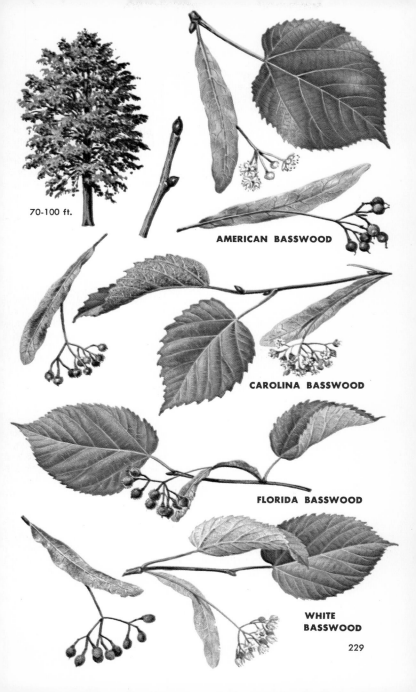

70-100 ft.

AMERICAN BASSWOOD

CAROLINA BASSWOOD

FLORIDA BASSWOOD

WHITE BASSWOOD

229

TEA FAMILY (Theaceae)

This family of several hundred species of largely evergreen trees includes the commercial tea plant *(Thea sinensis)* and also the camellias, prized ornamentals. The family is primarily Asiatic, but includes several small trees in southeastern United States, all with simple, alternate leaves. The rare Franklinia *(Franklinia alatamaha)* has not been recorded in nature since 1790, when it was found along the Georgia coast. It is believed to exist now only in cultivation.

LOBLOLLY-BAY *(Gordonia lasianthus)* has leathery, oblong to lanceolate, evergreen leaves, 4 to 6 inches long and 1.5 to 2 inches wide, with finely toothed margins; turn scarlet before falling. Long-stemmed, fragrant, white flowers, 2 to 2.5 inches in diameter, produce a hairy, ovoid, woody capsule, 0.8 of an inch long. Reddish-brown bark is broken into scaly ridges. Short-lived; to 70 feet tall, 20 inches in diameter.

MOUNTAIN STEWARTIA *(Stewartia ovata)* has elliptical to oblong, deciduous leaves, 2 to 5 inches long and 1 to 2.5 inches wide, with pointed tips and toothed, hairy margins. Flowers 4 inches in diameter; hairy capsule splits along 5 sutures. A shrub or small tree, to 25 feet tall. Virginia Stewartia *(S. malacodendron)* is less widely distributed, has smaller leaves.

CACTUS FAMILY (Cactaceae)

Cacti of more than 1,000 species grow largely in arid lands of the Western Hemisphere; a few range northward to British Columbia and southern New England. Most have leaves reduced to spines, photosynthesis occurring in the green, fleshy stems. Large, colorful flowers produced singly; fruit is a fleshy berry, edible in many species. Of native cacti in western North America, Saguaro and a few Mexican species are tree-sized with a single trunk. Organpipe Cactus, Senita, and others are tall but many-stemmed. Key West Cephalocereus *(Cephalocereus keyensis)* grows to tree size in the Florida Keys.

SAGUARO *(Cereus giganteus)* has clusters of gray spines, 0.5 to 2 inches long, on 12 to 30 prominent ridges around stout trunk. Funnel-shaped flowers, 4 to 4.5 inches long and 2 to 3 inches in diameter, occur at top of branches; open at night in May and June and have a melon-like odor. Red fruits, 2 to 3.5 inches long, are sweet, edible. Grows 25 to 50 feet tall, 1 to 3 feet in diameter.

FRANKLINIA

LOBLOLLY-BAY

MOUNTAIN STEWARTIA

fruit

25-50 ft.

SAGUARO

MYRTLE FAMILY (Myrtaceae)

This family contains about 3,000 shrubs and trees native principally to the tropics and Australasia. Many are aromatic. A few species are native to Florida.

Eugenias spp.

EUGENIAS (*Eugenia* spp.) have simple, opposite, usually black-dotted, evergreen leaves; white flowers in axillary clusters and juicy, berry-like fruits. White-stopper Eugenia (*E. axillaris*) has leaves 1 to 3 inches long and 0.5 to 1 inch wide. The sweet, black fruits are 0.5 of an inch in diameter, and the tree's bark is light brown, ridged, and scaly. Grows to 30 feet tall and 1 foot in diameter, in sandy soil near tidewater. Redberry Eugenia (*E. confusa*) is similar but larger, to 60 feet tall and 2 feet in diameter, with red fruits. Simpson Eugenia (*E. simpsonii*), also with red fruit, may grow 50 feet tall and 1 foot in diameter. Twinberry Eugenia (*E. dicrana*) grows 25 feet tall and 8 inches in diameter and has reddish-brown, aromatic fruits. There are four other native species. Spiceberry Eugenia (*E. rhombea*), common in the West Indies, and Bahama Eugenia (*E. bahamensis*) are rare, small trees. Smalls Eugenia (*E. anthera*) and Boxleaf Eugenia (*E. myrtoides*) are usually shrubs.

Lidflowers spp.

LIDFLOWERS (*Calyptranthes* spp.) have simple, opposite, evergreen leaves and clusters of small flowers lacking petals. Sepals capped in bud by a lidlike cover, which is shed later. Fruits dry, berry-like, reddish brown. Bark pale white, smooth to scaly. Pale Lidflower or Spicewood (*C. pallens*) is a shrub or small tree, to 25 feet tall, with leaves 2 to 3 inches long and 0.8 of an inch wide; fruits oblong. Myrtle-of-the-river (*C. zuzygium*) has smaller, elliptical leaves, nipple-like apex on floral lid, and globular fruits.

SOME INTRODUCED MEMBERS OF MYRTLE FAMILY

EUCALYPTUS (*Eucalyptus* spp.) is the most important genus in the myrtle family, with more than 500 species native to Australia. Many are grown in other parts of the world either for wood or as ornamentals. About 75 species have been introduced to California, including Red Ironbark (*E. sideroxylong*), Manna Gum (*E. viminalis*), and Bluegum (*E. globulus*).

CAJEPUT-TREE (*Melaleuca quinquenervia*), an Australian species, is grown in California and Florida, where it has become naturalized. Bark thick, spongy.

COMMON GUAVA (*Psidium guajava*), native to Central America, is widely planted in warm regions for its fruit but also grows as an escape. Bark is smooth.

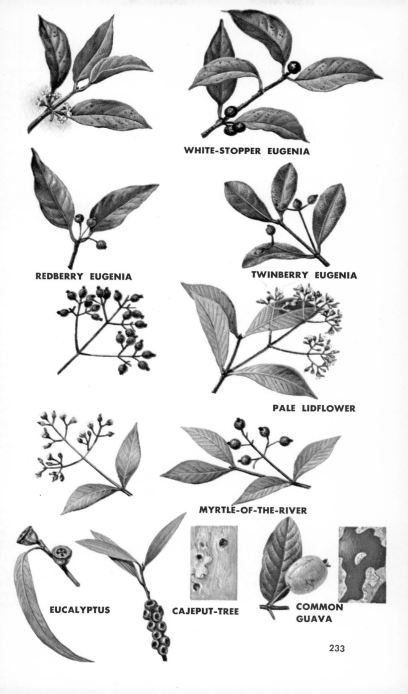

WHITE-STOPPER EUGENIA

REDBERRY EUGENIA

TWINBERRY EUGENIA

PALE LIDFLOWER

MYRTLE-OF-THE-RIVER

EUCALYPTUS

CAJEPUT-TREE

COMMON GUAVA

MANGROVE FAMILY (Rhizophoraceae)

This tropical family includes about 60 species of evergreen trees and shrubs that form dense thickets in tidal creeks and estuaries. Soil and debris carried by the tides is washed into the network of stiltlike roots and becomes caught there. Over many years this process slowly extends the shoreline. Mangrove seeds germinate while still attached to the tree. Upon dropping, they float until contacting mud, then begin growth immediately. Bark yields tannin; the wood, charcoal. Commonly associated with Black-Mangrove (p. 262.)

RED MANGROVE *(Rhizophora mangle)* leaves are leathery, simple, opposite, ovate to elliptical, 3 to 5 inches long and 1 to 2 inches wide. Flowers are pale yellow, 1 inch in diameter and clustered. Fruit is a roughened, conical, rusty-brown berry about 1 inch long, with a short apical tube through which the dart-like radicle of the developing embryo protrudes, becoming 6 to 12 inches long. Bark gray to gray-brown, thick, scaly, and furrowed. Rarely over 20 feet tall in Florida; to 80 feet tall and 2 feet in diameter in tropics.

COMBRETUM (WHITE-MANGROVE) FAMILY (Combretaceae)

Species in this primarily tropical family have leathery, evergreen leaves. Many grow in tidewater flats. Oxhorn Bucida *(Bucida buceras)* has limited distribution in the Florida Keys. Indian-Almond *(Terminalia catappa)* is naturalized in southern Florida.

BUTTON-MANGROVE *(Conocarpus erectus)* leaves are simple, alternate, 2 to 4 inches long and 0.5 to 1.5 inches wide, with smooth margins and a pointed apex. Flowers in dense, globular heads, about 0.3 of an inch in diameter, on panicles 3 to 10 inches long. Tiny, leathery, reddish fruits in conelike heads about 1 inch in diameter. Bark brown to black, in scaly ridges. A shrub or tree, Button-mangrove grows to 60 feet tall and 2 feet in diameter.

WHITE-MANGROVE *(Laguncularia racemosa)* has simple, opposite leaves, 1 to 3 inches long and 1 to 1.5 inches wide, with a rounded or notched apex, red petioles, and glandular swellings along margin. Greenish-white flowers borne in 1.5- to 2-inch spikes. Fruit about 0.5 inch long, 10-ribbed, obovoid, leathery, reddish brown. Bark reddish brown, ridged, and scaly. A sprawling shrub in Florida, but may grow 60 feet tall in parts of the tropics.

to 20 ft.

RED MANGROVE

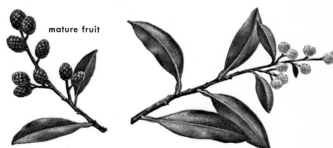

mature fruit

BUTTON-MANGROVE

WHITE-MANGROVE

235

DOGWOOD FAMILY (Cornaceae)

About 100 species, found primarily in the temperate regions, constitute the dogwood family. Two genera represented in the United States and Canada. Dogwoods (*Cornus*), the most familiar, include the diminutive Bunchberry (*C. canadensis*), a small herbaceous plant of spongy forest soils, and three species that are usually shrubs but sometimes reach tree size—two western species, Western Dogwood (*C. occidentalis*) and Blackfruit Dogwood (*C. sessilis*); and one eastern, Stiffcornel Dogwood (*C. stricta*). Wavyleaf Silktassel (*Garrya elliptica*) is a shrub or rarely a small tree on the Pacific coast.

FLOWERING DOGWOOD (*Cornus florida*) has simple, opposite, deciduous leaves, 3 to 6 inches long and 1.5 to 2 inches wide, usually oval with a pointed apex and with primary veins curving upward along smooth, wavy margins. Scarlet in fall. Small, greenish-white flowers are in compact heads, surrounded by four large, white (occasionally pink or rose), petal-like bracts, notched at apex. Clusters often erroneously considered to be single flowers. Bright-red, ovoid fruits, about 0.5 of an inch long and 0.3 of an inch in diameter, also clustered. Smooth, dark-brown to black bark of young trees breaks up into small, scaly blocks at maturity. Flowering Dogwood, often cultivated as an ornamental, grows 15 to 40 feet tall, 6 to 18 inches in diameter. It has a rounded, rather bushy crown and hard, heavy wood. Prefers moist, rich soils.

ALTERNATE-LEAF DOGWOOD (*Cornus alternifolia*) leaves resemble those of other dogwoods but are alternate. White flowers, in loose, flat-topped clusters (cymes), rather than heads. Fruits deep blue to black, 0.3 of an inch in diameter. Bark of young trees is dark reddish brown, smooth; on older trees, fissured. Alternate-leaf Dogwood is a shrub or small tree, growing to 30 feet tall and 8 inches in diameter. It has a broad, flattened crown.

ROUGHLEAF DOGWOOD (*Cornus drummondii*) has opposite leaves, rough above and woolly below. Flowers and fruit white, in open clusters. A shrub or small tree.

RED-OSIER DOGWOOD (*Cornus stolonifera*) resembles Roughleaf Dogwood but has reddish twigs. Usually a shrub, rarely growing to small-tree size. It commonly occurs along watercourses and in similar moist locations.

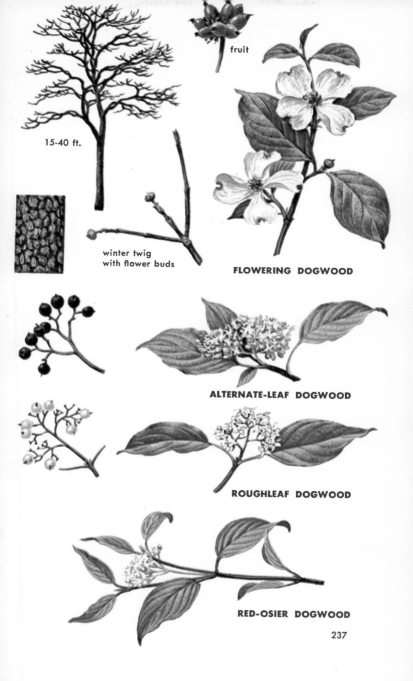

15-40 ft.

fruit

winter twig
with flower buds

FLOWERING DOGWOOD

ALTERNATE-LEAF DOGWOOD

ROUGHLEAF DOGWOOD

RED-OSIER DOGWOOD

237

PACIFIC DOGWOOD (*Cornus nuttallii*) leaves resemble Flowering Dogwood's but are larger and more ovate, 4 to 6 inches long and 1.5 to 3 inches wide. Greenish-white flowers, in larger heads, are surrounded by 4 to 6 bracts, not notched at apex; bright-red, ellipsoidal fruits in larger clusters. Dark-brown to black bark normally smooth, but breaks into scaly plates at base of large trees. Medium-sized to 60 feet tall and 2 feet in diameter, with a narrow, pyramidal crown. Pacific Dogwood grows at low elevations in shaded, coniferous forests. It is a popular ornamental.

TUPELO FAMILY (Nyssaceae)

Ten species in three genera make up this small family, closely related to dogwood family. Represented in North America only by tupelos, or black gums (*Nyssa*). The two other genera in the tupelo family occur in eastern Asia.

BLACK TUPELO (*Nyssa sylvatica*) has simple, alternate, usually obovate, deciduous leaves, 2 to 5 inches long and 1 to 3 inches wide, with smooth margins. Leaves are often clustered near ends of lateral branches; turn scarlet in fall. Small, greenish flowers are on separate stalks—the staminate in dense clusters and the pistillate few-flowered. Dark-blue, ovoid fruit, about 0.5 of an inch long, has thin flesh surrounding indistinctly ribbed seed. Bark is gray-brown and commonly in small, rectangular blocks. Young twigs greenish yellow, becoming gray to reddish brown. Grows 60 to 90 feet tall, 2 to 3 feet in diameter, mainly in moist soils.

WATER TUPELO (*Nyssa aquatica*) is similar to Black Tupelo but has larger leaves, 5 to 7 inches long and 2 to 4 inches wide, margins occasionally toothed. Fruit 1 inch long, the seed more prominently ribbed. Grows best in swampy situations, usually standing in water several feet deep during wet season. Base of trunk is usually swollen or buttressed, similar to Baldcypress (p. 52).

OGEECHEE TUPELO (*Nyssa ogeche*) resembles Water Tupelo but differs in having less sharply pointed leaves and short-stalked, red fruits, 1 to 1.5 inches long. Seed has winglike ribs. Usually a shrub, occasionally a small tree. Bear Tupelo (*Nyssa ursina*), also most commonly a shrub, grows in northwestern Florida.

winter twig
with flower bud

fruit

PACIFIC DOGWOOD

60-90 ft.

BLACK TUPELO

WATER TUPELO

OGEECHEE TUPELO

239

HEATH FAMILY (Ericaceae)

Members of the heath family, more than 1,500 species, grow in acid soils in temperate regions throughout the world. All have simple and, in most, alternate leaves. Most are shrubs. Blueberries, cranberries, rhododendrons, and heathers are among the great variety of familiar plants in this family.

PACIFIC MADRONE *(Arbutus menziesii)* leaves are evergreen, leathery, oval to oblong, 3 to 6 inches long and 2 to 3 inches wide. The white, urn-shaped flowers, 0.3 of an inch long, are in drooping panicles 5 to 6 inches long. Fruits are orange or red, mealy, and berry-like, about 0.5 of an inch in diameter. Reddish-brown bark peels into thin, irregular sections exposing greenish-brown inner bark; scaly at base of large trees. To 100 feet tall and 4 feet in diameter, with varied form.

TEXAS MADRONE *(Arbutus texana)* leaves are evergreen, oval to lanceolate, 1 to 3 inches long and 0.8 to 1.5 inches wide. The flower clusters are 2.5 inches long, and the dark-red fruits are 0.3 of an inch in diameter. The bark is reddish brown. A rare tree with a crooked trunk, Texas Madrone grows about 20 feet tall and 10 inches in diameter, in dry soils.

ARIZONA MADRONE *(Arbutus arizonica)* resembles Texas Madrone in form, size, habitat, and size of flower and orange-red fruit clusters. But the evergreen leaves are lanceolate, 1.5 to 3 inches long and 0.5 to 1 inch wide. On trunks of older trees the bark is ash gray and scaly.

SOURWOOD *(Oxydendrum arboreum)* leaves are simple, alternate, elliptical, 5 to 7 inches long and 1 to 3 inches wide, margins finely toothed; turn scarlet. White, urn-shaped flowers, about 0.3 of an inch long, are in 1-sided, clustered racemes. Fruits are 5-angled, gray capsules. Bark gray, tinged with red; scaly and furrowed at base. Sourwood occasionally grows to 60 feet tall but is usually smaller.

TREE LYONIA *(Lyonia ferruginea)* has leathery, evergreen leaves, 1 to 3 inches long and about 1 inch wide, usually tipped with a stiff point. White, globular flowers, 0.1 of an inch in diameter, are in small, axillary clusters. The fruit is a light-brown capsule about 0.5 of an inch long. Bark on twisted trunk reddish brown, scaly, and ridged. A shrub or small tree, to 30 feet tall and 10 inches in diameter.

to 100 ft.

PACIFIC MADRONE

TEXAS MADRONE

ARIZONA MADRONE

SOURWOOD

TREE LYONIA

241

PACIFIC RHODODENDRON *(Rhododendron macrophyllum)* has oblong, leathery, evergreen leaves, 3 to 10 inches long, 1.5 to 2.5 inches wide, with smooth margins that are characteristically turned under. The flowers, 1.5 inches long, are white to pink, trumpet-shaped, and in compact clusters about 5 inches in diameter at ends of branches. The fruits are reddish-brown capsules about 0.5 of an inch long. Bark reddish brown. Usually a shrub, rarely to 25 feet.

ROSEBAY RHODODENDRON *(Rhododendron maximum)* resembles Pacific Rhododendron but has oval to obovate leaves, 4 to 12 inches long, 1.5 to 2.5 inches wide, often whitish below. Fruits slim, sticky. Usually a sprawling, twisted shrub, forming dense thickets. Rarely to 40 feet tall, 1 foot in diameter. Catawba Rhododendron *(R. catawbiense)*, more southern and not as tall, has broader leaves and light-purple flowers.

ELLIOTTIA *(Elliottia racemosa)* leaves are deciduous, ovate to oblong, 3 to 4 inches long, 1 to 2 inches wide, with smooth margins, hairy below. White flowers, with 4 narrow petals, are in erect, terminal panicles. Fruit is a dry, 4-celled (rarely 3 or 5), globular capsule, about 0.3 of an inch in diameter. Bark smooth, gray-brown. A rare shrub or small tree, to 20 feet tall, 6 inches in diameter.

MOUNTAIN-LAUREL *(Kalmia latifolia)* has leathery, elliptical to lanceolate, evergreen leaves, 3 to 4 inches long and 1 to 1.5 inches wide, alternate or in whorls. Deep pink to white, starlike flowers nearly 1 inch in diameter occur in compact clusters at ends of branches. Each produces a 5-celled capsule about 0.5 of an inch in diameter and ending in a slender style. Grows in moist soils, commonly forming thickets. Usually a shrub; rarely reaches a height of 30 feet and a diameter of 1 foot. Bark reddish brown and scaly.

TREE SPARKLEBERRY *(Vaccinium arboreum)* leaves are deciduous in North but persistent in South, oval to oblong, 1 to 3 inches long, 1 inch wide. Bell-shaped white flowers in axillary racemes produce tart, shiny-black, globular berries about 0.3 of an inch in diameter. Bark dark brown, ridged, and shreddy. Tree Sparkleberry is a sprawling shrub or small, crooked tree, growing to 30 feet tall and 10 inches in diameter.

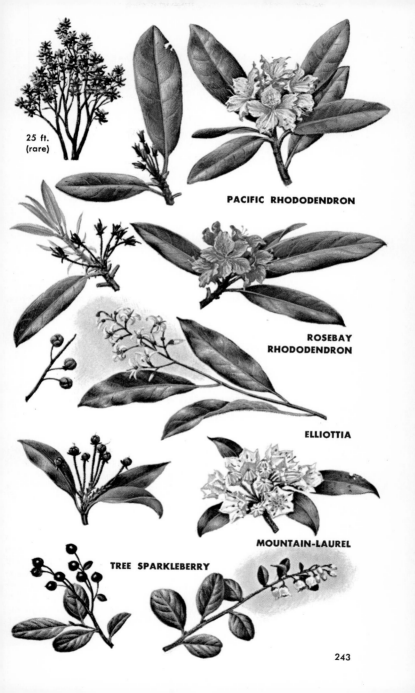

25 ft.
(rare)

PACIFIC RHODODENDRON

**ROSEBAY
RHODODENDRON**

ELLIOTTIA

MOUNTAIN-LAUREL

TREE SPARKLEBERRY

GINSENG FAMILY (Araliaceae)

DEVILS-WALKINGSTICK *(Aralia spinosa)* has alternate, odd-bipinnately compound, deciduous leaves, 2 to 4 feet long and 2 to 3 feet wide, with spiny stalks. Each leaflet has a terminal and several pairs of opposite, ovate subleaflets, with a tapered apex and toothed margins, 2 to 4 inches long and 1.5 inches wide; midvein often spiny below. Small, white flowers in compound, terminal clusters, to 4 feet long, with yellowish stems. Fruit black, berry-like, and juicy, 0.3 of an inch in diameter. Coarse twigs bear stout spines. Bark brown, ridged, furrowed; inner bark yellow. Grows rapidly, to 30 feet tall and 10 inches in diameter, usually in moist soils.

MELASTOME (MEADOW BEAUTY) FAMILY (Melastomataceae)

FLORIDA TETRAZYGIA *(Tetrazygia bicolor)* has simple, opposite, lanceolate, evergreen leaves, 3 to 5 inches long, 1 to 2 inches wide. Dark green above, paler below, with 3 main veins and smooth, thickened, rolled-under margin. White flowers, 0.8 of an inch in diameter, in loose, terminal panicles. Ovoid, purplish fruits, 0.3 of an inch long, constricted at apex. Usually a shrub, Florida Tetrazygia occasionally grows to 30 feet tall and 4 inches in diameter.

MYRSINE FAMILY (Myrsinaceae)

MARBLEBERRY *(Ardisia escallonioides)* is a shrub or small tree, to 25 feet tall, with gray to pinkish bark. Leathery, evergreen leaves are simple, alternate, ovate to obovate, 3 to 6 inches long, 1 to 2 inches wide, with many dark dots on undersurface. Fragrant, starlike flowers have 5 petals dotted with red on inner surface; in rusty-haired panicles, to 5 inches long. Shiny-black fruit is round, 0.3 of an inch in diameter, with a sharp point and dotted with resin. Flesh thin and dry.

GUIANA RAPANEA *(Rapanea guianensis)* has leathery, simple, alternate, oblong to obovate, evergreen leaves, 2 to 4 inches long and 1 to 2 inches wide, notched at apex. Usually crowded near ends of branches. Small axillary clusters of white flowers, about 0.1 of an inch in diameter, are marked with purple; produce globular, dark-blue or black fruit, about 0.2 of an inch in diameter, with pointed apex. A shrub or small tree, to 25 feet tall, with smooth, gray bark.

DEVILS-WALKINGSTICK

FLORIDA TETRAZYGIA

MARBLEBERRY

**GUIANA
RAPANEA**

SAPOTE (SAPODILLA) FAMILY (Sapotaceae)

This family of about 500 species of tropical trees and shrubs includes the Central American Sapota, or Sapodilla *(Achras zapota)*, from which chicle for chewing gum is obtained. The fruit is also delicious. Sapodillas grow wild in extreme southern Florida and on the Keys. Gutta percha, a gum, is derived from sap of species from southeastern Asia; other members of the family provide cabinet woods, oils, and other useful products. Only a few species, none of commercial importance, occur in temperate North America.

Gum Bumelia

Tough Bumelia

Saffron-plum Bumelia

Buckthorn Bumelia

False-mastic

Willow Bustic

BUMELIAS *(Bumelia* spp.) of four tree-sized species are native to southeastern United States.

Gum Bumelia *(B. lanuginosa)* is a small, narrow-crowned tree, to 40 feet tall and 2 feet in diameter. Simple, ovate to oblong, evergreen leaves are alternate, appearing whorled; 1 to 3 inches long, 1 inch wide, with silvery or rust-brown hairs below. Most have blunt or rounded tips, some pointed. Small white flowers, clustered in leaf axils, produce black fruits about 0.5 of an inch long. Bark dark gray to black, scaly, and fissured.

Tough Bumelia *(B. tenax)*, similar but smaller, has shiny, reddish-yellow hairs under leaves and on twigs, which often bear inch-long spines.

Saffron-plum *(B. celastrina)* leaves are 1 to 1.5 inches long and 0.3 to 1 inch wide. The black fruits are nearly an inch long.

Buckthorn Bumelia *(B. lycioides)* has deciduous leaves, 3 to 6 inches long and 0.5 to 2 inches wide. Black fruit about 0.8 of an inch long; twigs have curved spines.

FALSE-MASTIC *(Sideroxylon foetidissimum),* a medium-sized tree with an irregular crown, has simple, alternate, oval, evergreen leaves, 3 to 5 inches long and 1 to 2 inches wide. Tiny, yellow flowers in small, axillary clusters; inch-long, yellow, berry-like fruit has a thick, juicy flesh. Bark reddish brown and scaly.

WILLOW BUSTIC *(Dipholis salicifolia)* has simple, alternate, oblong to lanceolate, evergreen leaves, 3 to 5 inches long, 1 to 2 inches wide. Tiny, white flowers borne in small clusters, usually in leaf axils, have sepals covered with rusty-brown, silky hairs. Globular, leathery, black fruits are 0.3 of an inch in diameter. Bark reddish brown, scaly. Grows 50 feet tall and 18 inches in diameter, with a narrow, graceful crown.

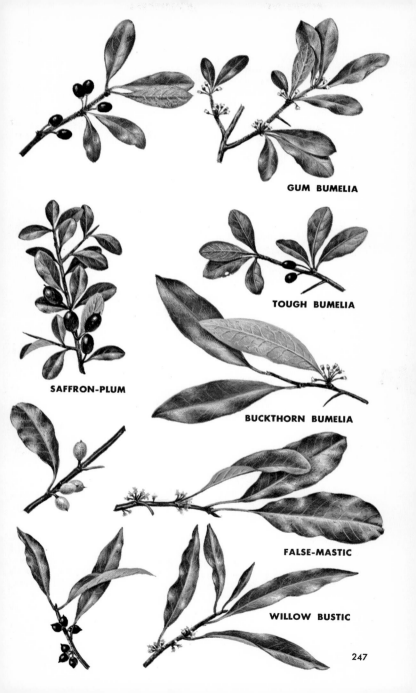

GUM BUMELIA

TOUGH BUMELIA

SAFFRON-PLUM

BUCKTHORN BUMELIA

FALSE-MASTIC

WILLOW BUSTIC

247

SATINLEAF *(Chrysophyllum oliviforme)* has simple, alternate, oval, leathery, evergreen leaves, 2 to 3 inches long and 1 to 2 inches wide; shiny, coppery hairs make undersurface like suede. The small, white flowers in axillary clusters produce dark-purple, juicy berries 0.8 of an inch long. Reddish-brown bark is scaly. A shrub or small tree, Satinleaf grows to 30 feet tall, 1 foot in diameter.

WILD-DILLY *(Achras emarginata)* has simple, alternate, oblong to obovate, leathery, evergreen leaves, clustered at ends of twigs. They are 3 to 4 inches long and 1 to 2 inches wide, waxy above and covered with brown hairs below. Light-yellow flowers, clustered in leaf axils on slender, reddish, hairy stems. Fleshy fruit (berries), 1.5 inches in diameter, have a thick, brown, scaly skin. Each contains one seed surrounded by soft flesh with milky juice. Bark gray to reddish brown, scaly, fissured. To 40 feet tall, 18 inches in diameter, with a short, gnarled trunk.

THEOPHRASTA (JOEWOOD) FAMILY
(Theophrastaceae)

JOEWOOD *(Jaquinia keyensis)* has simple, leathery, evergreen leaves, usually alternate but crowded near ends of twigs. They are 1 to 3 inches long and 0.5 to 1 inch wide, with greatest width above middle and with a rounded, notched, or spined apex. Fragrant, pale-yellow, trumpet-shaped flowers, 0.3 of an inch in diameter, occur in loose racemes, to 3 inches long, at ends of branches. Fruit, 0.3 of an inch in diameter, is an orange-red berry with many seeds. To 15 feet tall and 7 inches in diameter, with smooth, blue-gray bark, commonly mottled.

SWEETLEAF FAMILY (Symplocaceae)

The one genus in this family contains about 300 species of shrubs and small trees, one of them native to southeastern United States. Others occur in the West Indies, Asia, and Australia.

COMMON SWEETLEAF *(Symplocos tinctoria)* has simple, alternate, oblong, leathery leaves, 5 to 6 inches long and 1 to 2 inches wide, with wavy margins. Leaves remain on tree most of year. White, fragrant flowers, 0.3 to 0.5 of an inch long, occur in clusters on silky stalks. Dry, brown, ovoid fruit is 0.5 of an inch long. Bark ash gray, with corky tubercles. A shrub or small tree, to 35 feet tall, 6 inches in diameter.

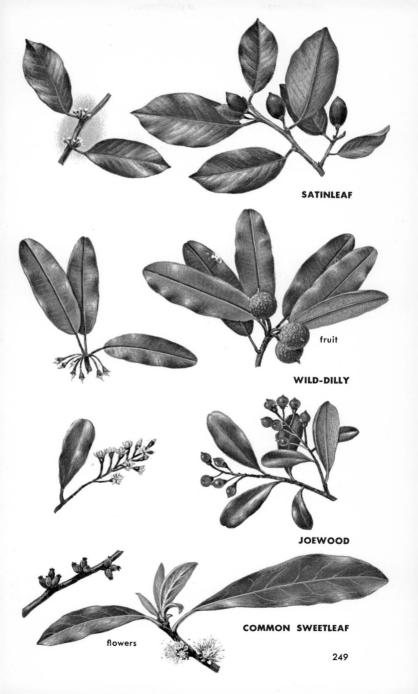

SATINLEAF

WILD-DILLY

fruit

JOEWOOD

COMMON SWEETLEAF

flowers

249

EBONY FAMILY (Ebenaceae)

Most of the more than 300 species in this family grow in the tropics and subtropics. The most famous is Ebony (*Diospyros ebenum*), a native of southeastern Asia; it provides the hard black wood used for piano keys and fine furniture.

COMMON PERSIMMON (*Diospyros virginiana*) has simple, alternate, ovate-oblong, deciduous leaves, 4 to 6 inches long and 2 to 3 inches wide and with smooth margins. Small staminate and pistillate flowers are on twigs of the current year on separate trees; the staminate in few-flowered clusters, the pistillate solitary. The fruit is orange to reddish purple and several-seeded, about 1.5 inches in diameter; astringent when green but sweet and edible when ripe. Bark is almost black, broken into small, rectangular blocks. The Common Persimmon grows to 60 feet tall and 2 feet in diameter, with a divided trunk and broad, rounded crown. It attains its best growth in moist, rich soils.

TEXAS PERSIMMON (*Diospyros texana*) resembles the Common Persimmon in form but has smaller, obovate leaves, with a rounded apex, hairy below. The flowers are on twigs of the previous season, the smaller fruit is black, and the bark is gray and scaly.

SNOWBELL (STORAX) FAMILY (Styracaceae)

Includes over 100 species of trees and shrubs native to North and South America, eastern Asia, the Malay Archipelago, and the Mediterranean region. Many have attractive flowers.

BIGLEAF SNOWBELL (*Styrax grandifolia*) has simple, alternate, obovate, deciduous leaves, 2.5 to 5 inches long, 1 to 3 inches wide; margins finely toothed or smooth; veins hairy below. White, 5-lobed, bell-shaped flowers, to 1 inch long, in axillary racemes to 6 inches long. The fruit is dry, oval, and 0.3 of an inch long. Bigleaf Snowbell grows to 40 feet tall and 8 inches in diameter.

SILVERBELLS (*Halesia* spp.) are three species of deciduous shrubs or small trees. Leaves alternate, oblong to elliptical, hairy below, with toothed margins. Flowers showy, white, bell-shaped, to 2 inches long. Carolina Silverbell (*H. carolina*) has 4-winged, nutlike fruit; Two-wing Silverbell (*H. diptera*), 2-winged. Little Silverbell (*H. parviflora*), usually a shrub, has small flowers. The 4-winged fruit is club-shaped.

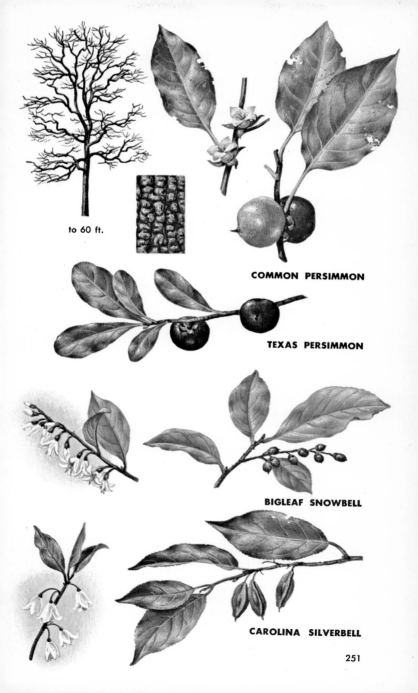

to 60 ft.

COMMON PERSIMMON

TEXAS PERSIMMON

BIGLEAF SNOWBELL

CAROLINA SILVERBELL

251

OLIVE FAMILY (Oleaceae)

This family, mainly of the Northern Hemisphere includes about 500 species of shrubs and trees. Olives and olive oil are provided by *Olea europa*, native to the Mediterranean Basin but now cultivated widely. Ashes *(Fraxinus)* and others are the source of timber. Lilac *(Syringa)*, forsythia *(Forsythia)*, jasmine *(Jasminum)*, and privet *(Ligustrum)*, well-known shrubs of the olive family, are widely used as ornamentals.

FRINGETREE *(Chionanthus virginicus)* leaves are deciduous, simple, opposite, ovate-oblong, 4 to 8 inches long and 0.5 to 4 inches wide; margins smooth to wavy, veins hairy beneath. Fragrant flowers, with 4 to 6 narrow, white petals, about 1 inch long, borne in clusters, 4 to 6 inches long; flowers dioecious or, rarely, perfect. Dark-purple, oval fruits, about 1 inch long, have thin, dry flesh enclosing one seed (occasionally 2 or 3). The fruit is sometimes covered with a white, powdery wax. Bark brown, scaly. A shrub or small tree, Fringetree grows to 30 feet tall and 1 foot in diameter, with a narrow, oblong crown. Planted as an ornamental.

DEVILWOOD *(Osmanthus americanus)* has simple, opposite, oblong-lanceolate, leathery, evergreen leaves, 4 to 5 inches long and 1 to 1.5 inches wide, with smooth, somewhat curled margins. Small, creamy-white flowers (perfect and unisexual on different plants) in axillary clusters. Fruit oval, dark blue, about 1 inch long, with a thin, fleshy covering over single seed. Bark gray-brown, scaly. A shrub or small, narrow-crowned tree, to 70 feet tall, 1 foot in diameter. Bigfruit Osmanthus *(O. megacarpus)*, also a southern species, has plumper, greenish-yellow fruit, larger leaves, and hairy flower stems.

SWAMP-PRIVET *(Forestiera acuminata)* leaves are deciduous, simple, opposite, elliptical, 2 to 4 inches long and 1 to 1.5 inches wide, with small, widely spaced teeth above middle. Dioecious; small clusters of pistillate and yellowish-green staminate flowers, lacking petals, appear before leaves. Fruit is dark purple, narrowly oblong, 1 to 1.3 inches long, with thin, dry flesh enclosing one seed. Bark dark brown, ridged. Swamp-privet is a shrub or small tree, to 25 feet tall, usually in moist soils. Texas Forestiera *(F. texana)*, Florida-privet *(F. segregata)*, and Desert-olive Forestiera *(F. phillyreoides)*, also shrubs, occur in southern United States.

FRINGETREE

DEVILWOOD

SWAMP-PRIVET

253

ASHES *(Fraxinus)*

Approximately 65 species of trees and shrubs belong to the genus *Fraxinus* in the olive family. Largely confined to temperate regions of Northern Hemisphere, but a few occur in the tropics. In addition to trees described here, four small trees, usually shrubby, grow in southwestern U.S. southward into Mexico—Berlandier Ash *(F. berlandieriana)*, Two-petal Ash *(F. dipetala)*, Goodding Ash *(F. gooddingii)*, and Chihuahua Ash *(F. papillosa)*.

Ashes are easily recognized as a group, but species are difficult to distinguish. Leaves are deciduous, opposite, and, with few exceptions, odd-pinnately compound. Some species are dioecious; others have polygamous or perfect flowers in clusters (panicles), appearing before or with the leaves. Flowers of most North American species lack petals; one has flowers with showy white petals. Fruit is a samara, with single terminal wing. In winter, naked twigs have blunt buds (terminal larger than lateral) with 1 to 3 pairs of exposed scales. In most species, the leaf scars are notched and half-round, with an elliptical line of tiny, vascular bundle scars.

WHITE ASH *(Fraxinus americana)* leaves are 8 to 12 inches long, usually with 7 (sometimes 5 to 13) oval to oblong-lanceolate leaflets, 3 to 5 inches long and 1.5 to 3 inches wide; margins smooth or finely toothed, essentially glabrous below. Stems of leaflets are very long and slender. Dioecious, flowers appearing before leaves. Samaras 1 to 2 inches long, with wing extending only part way along seed. Twigs round, usually not hairy, with half-round, notched leaf scars. White Ash has gray bark, with diamond-shaped ridges appearing on the trunks of older trees. To 80 feet tall, 3 feet in diameter.

GREEN ASH *(Fraxinus pennsylvanica)* resembles White Ash but has slightly smaller leaves, 6 to 9 inches long, with leaflets 3 to 4 inches long and 1 to 1.5 inches wide. Margins of the leaflets are toothed above the middle. The underside of the leaflets may be smooth to hairy. In addition, the dioecious flowers of Green Ash appear after the leaves have begun to unfold.

PUMPKIN ASH *(Fraxinus profunda)* has leaves 9 to 18 inches long. The lanceolate to elliptical, usually smooth-margined leaflets are 5 to 8 inches long and 1.5 to 4 inches wide; they are hairy below, especially on midribs and veins. Leaf stems and twigs also hairy. Pumpkin Ash samaras are 2 to 3 inches long and 0.5 of an inch wide, with the wing extending below the middle of the seed.

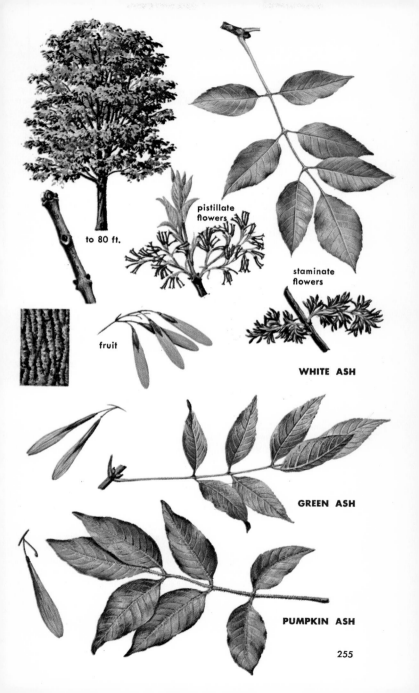

to 80 ft.

pistillate
flowers

staminate
flowers

fruit

WHITE ASH

GREEN ASH

PUMPKIN ASH

255

BLACK ASH *(Fraxinus nigra)* leaves are 12 to 16 inches long. They have 9 (sometimes 7 to 13) stemless, oblong to oblong-lanceolate leaflets, 4 to 5 inches long and 1.5 inches wide, with finely toothed margins; essentially glabrous below. Polygamous flowers appear before the leaves. Samaras are oblong to elliptical, 1 to 1.8 inches long, with a thin wing extending below the center of the indistinct seed cavity. Grows to 90 feet tall, 2 feet in diameter.

BLUE ASH *(Fraxinus quadrangulata)* twigs are distinctly 4-angled. The leaves, 8 to 12 inches long, have 5 to 11 stalked lanceolate to oblong-lanceolate leaflets, 3 to 5 inches long and 1 to 2 inches wide; margins toothed. Flowers are perfect. Samaras are oblong-ovate, 1 to 2 inches long with a thin wing extending to the base of the seed. Blue Ash grows to 60 feet tall and 2 feet in diameter. During pioneer days, a blue dye was obtained from the inner bark.

SINGLELEAF ASH *(Fraxinus anomala)* has simple (occasionally with 2 to 3 leaflets), long-stalked, broadly oval leaves, 1.5 to 2 inches long and 1 to 2 inches wide, with margins entire or toothed above middle. Polygamous flowers appear when leaves are nearly grown. Samaras, to 0.8 of an inch long, have a broad wing extending around seed. The twigs are 4-angled. Singleleaf Ash is a shrub or small tree, growing to 20 feet tall and 6 inches in diameter. Often occurs in dry or rocky soils.

TEXAS ASH *(Fraxinus texensis)* leaves are 5 to 8 inches long. The 5 (occasionally 7) long-stalked, oval to obovate leaflets are 1 to 3 inches long and 1 to 2 inches wide, with toothed margins and tufts of white hair in axils of veins below. Dioecious flowers appear as leaves unfold. Spatulate samara, to 1 inch long, has a seed nearly round in cross section. To 50 feet tall and 3 feet in diameter.

CAROLINA ASH *(Fraxinus caroliniana)* leaves are 7 to 12 inches long. The 5 to 7 long-stalked, oblong-ovate leaflets are 3 to 6 inches long and 2 to 3 inches wide, with coarsely toothed margins. Glabrous below. Dioecious flowers appear before leaves. Samaras are to 3 inches long, the thin, broad wing surrounding seed sometimes 3-winged. Bark scaly, light gray. To 40 feet tall, 1 foot in diameter.

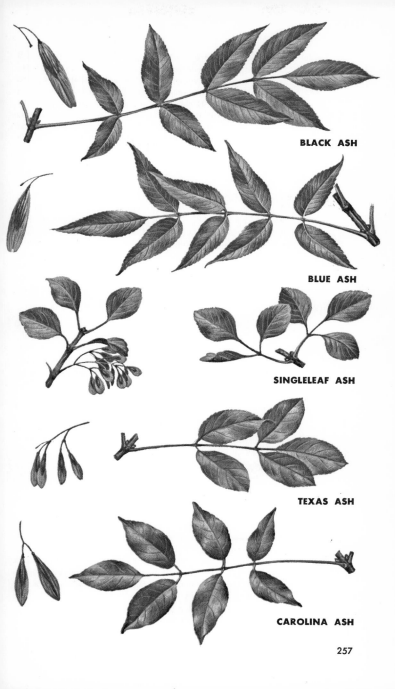

BLACK ASH

BLUE ASH

SINGLELEAF ASH

TEXAS ASH

CAROLINA ASH

257

GREGG ASH *(Fraxinus greggii)* leaves are 1.5 to 3 inches long, with winged main stem; they remain on the tree through the winter, until flowering time. The 3 to 7 leathery, obovate leaflets are 0.5 to 1 inch long and 0.3 of an inch wide; margins are smooth or inconspicuously toothed and the pale-green underside is marked with black dots. Polygamous flowers appear before the leaves. Samara is spatulate, to 0.8 of an inch long, with a broad wing extending to about the middle of the seed. A shrub or small tree, to 20 feet tall and 8 inches in diameter.

VELVET ASH *(Fraxinus velutina)* leaves are 3 to 6 inches long, with 5 (sometimes 3 to 9) elliptical to lanceolate leaflets, 1 to 2 inches long and to 1 inch wide; margins entire or finely toothed above the middle and often hairy below. Dioecious, the flowers appearing in spring before or with the leaves. The samara is obovate to elliptical, to 1 inch long, with wing extending only part way along the seed. Velvet Ash attains a height of 30 feet and a diameter of 1 foot. Its gray bark is ridged and furrowed.

OREGON ASH *(Fraxinus latifolia)* leaves are 5 to 14 inches long, with 5 to 7 (occasionally 9) ovate to obovate leaflets, 3 to 6 inches long and 1 to 1.5 inches wide, with smooth or finely toothed margins; usually slightly hairy below and lateral leaflets often stemless. Dioecious flowers appear with leaves. Samara elliptical to oblanceolate, to 1.5 inches long, with wing extending to middle of seed. Oregon Ash grows to 75 feet tall and 3 feet in diameter. In moist, fertile soils, it has a long, clear trunk, but on poorer soils, its form is often crooked and ragged.

FRAGRANT ASH *(Fraxinus cuspidata)* leaves are 3 to 7 inches long, with 3 to 7 long-stalked, lanceolate to ovate leaflets, 1.5 to 2.5 inches long and to 0.8 of an inch wide; margins entire or with widely spaced teeth above the middle. Perfect flowers appear with leaves; they differ from most ashes in being fragrant and having showy white petals. Samaras are elliptical to oblong-ovate, to 1 inch long, with wing extending nearly to the base of the seed. Scattered lenticels mark the reddish-brown twigs; bark of larger trunks is gray. A shrub or small tree, to 20 feet tall and 8 inches in diameter. A variety *(F. cuspidata* var. *macropetala)* has broader leaflets with entire margins, and occasionally its leaves are simple.

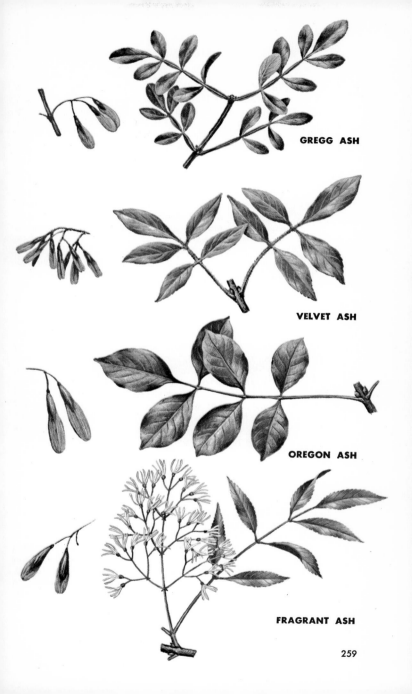

GREGG ASH

VELVET ASH

OREGON ASH

FRAGRANT ASH

259

BORAGE FAMILY (Boraginaceae)

The 90 genera and some 1,500 species of trees, shrubs, and herbs in this family are found primarily in warm regions. The family is represented most abundantly in the Mediterranean area and in Central Asia. Several species attaining the size of small trees are native to southeastern United States, southern Texas, and southward into Mexico and Central America. Heliotropes and forget-me-nots are familiar flowers of the borage family.

BAHAMA STRONGBARK (*Bourreria ovata*) has alternate, ovate to obovate, smooth, evergreen leaves, 2 to 3 inches long and 1 to 2 inches wide; margins smooth and apex rounded, notched, or pointed. Leaves hairy when young. White, bell-shaped flowers, 0.8 of an inch in diameter, in terminal clusters. Calyx of flower remains attached to orange-red fruit, 0.5 of an inch in diameter. Bark brownish gray, with thin scales. Bahama Strongbark grows in moist soils, to 50 feet tall and 1 foot in diameter, with a fluted trunk and an irregular, rounded crown. Rough Strongbark (*B. revoluta*), usually a shrub, is similar to Bahama Strongbark, but its leaves are rough.

GEIGER-TREE (*Cordia sebestena*) has simple, alternate, ovate, evergreen leaves, 5 to 6 inches long and 3 to 4 inches wide, with margins smooth or coarsely toothed above middle. Apex usually pointed; stout stem and underside of principal veins hairy. Trumpet-shaped, bright-orange flowers, 0.7 of an inch long and 1 to 1.5 inches across, in terminal clusters; hairy exterior. Fruit ivory, 1.3 inches long and 0.8 of an inch in diameter, with tail-like appendage at apex. Bark dark brown to black, ridged, scaly. Geiger-tree is a shrub or small tree, to 30 feet tall and 6 inches in diameter. Anacahuita (*C. boissieri*), a rare tree of southern Texas and Mexico, has white flowers, and calyx enclosing fruit is ribbed.

ANAQUA (*Ehretia anacua*) almost evergreen, has tardily deciduous, simple, alternate, oval to oblong leaves, 3 to 4 inches long and 2 to 3 inches wide. The apex is pointed, and the margins are toothed above the middle. Small, white flowers occur in loose terminal clusters about 2 inches long; blooms in late winter and spring. Fruit, 0.3 of an inch in diameter, is light yellow to red, fleshy, and edible. Brownish-gray bark is scaly. Anaqua grows to 50 feet tall and 3 feet in diameter, with stout branches forming round-topped crown.

BAHAMA STRONGBARK

GEIGER-TREE

ANAQUA

261

VERBENA FAMILY (Verbenaceae)

Shrubs and trees are included in the 80 genera and 1,200 species of largely herbaceous plants. Teak *(Tectona grandis)* is one of several valuable timber trees in this family.

BLACK-MANGROVE *(Avicennia nitida)* has opposite, oblong to elliptical, evergreen leaves, 2 to 3 inches long and 0.8 to 1.5 inches wide, with smooth, slightly curled margins; they are hairy below. White, 4-lobed flowers, 0.3 to 0.5 of an inch across, are in terminal clusters to 1.5 inches long. Fruit is a compressed, 2-valved and 1-seeded capsule, to 1.5 inches long and 1 inch wide. Bark of larger trees is dark reddish brown and scaly, with orange-red inner bark sometimes exposed between the scales. Forms dense thickets just inshore of Red Mangrove (p. 234). In Florida and adjacent Gulf Coast areas, a shrub or small tree, to 30 feet tall and 6 inches in diameter. To 70 feet tall in parts of wide range.

FLORIDA FIDDLEWOOD *(Citharexylum fruticosum)* leaves are evergreen, simple, opposite, oblong to obovate, 3 to 4 inches long and 1 to 1.3 inches wide, with curled margin. Small, white, fragrant flowers are tubular, with small, rounded petals; in axillary racemes 2 to 4 inches long. Blooms throughout year. Lustrous reddish-brown to black fruit, 0.3 of an inch in diameter, has thin, sweet, juicy flesh. Bark reddish brown, scaly. A shrub or small tree, to 30 feet tall, 6 inches in diameter.

NIGHTSHADE FAMILY (Solanaceae)

This is a family of some 85 genera and more than 1,800 species of herbs, vines, shrubs, and trees of temperate and tropical regions. Includes such valuable plants as potato, tomato, eggplant, tobacco, and petunia. Tree Tobacco *(Nicotiana glauca)* is a South American shrub or small tree naturalized in extreme southern United States.

MULLEIN NIGHTSHADE *(Solanum verbascifolium)* leaves are evergreen, simple, alternate, ovate to elliptical, hairy, and with wavy margins. Lower leaves are 5 to 7 inches long, 1 to 3 inches wide; smaller near growing tip. White, starlike flowers in axillary clusters 2 to 4 inches long; fruit yellow, round, 0.5 to 0.8 of an inch in diameter. Greenish to yellowish-gray, warty bark. A shrub or small tree, to 20 feet tall, usually in rich, moist soils. May be a naturalized species.

30-70 ft.

BLACK-MANGROVE

FLORIDA FIDDLEWOOD

MULLEIN NIGHTSHADE

263

BIGNONIA (TRUMPET CREEPER) FAMILY
(Bignoniaceae)

Some 700 species of trees and shrubs belong to this family. Most common in the tropics; a few species occur in temperate regions.

NORTHERN CATALPA *(Catalpa speciosa)* leaves are deciduous, long-stemmed, heart-shaped; 10 to 12 inches long and 7 to 8 inches wide, whorled or opposite. Tubular, white flowers, marked with purple and yellow, bloom after leaves develop; they are 2 inches long and 2.5 inches wide, in showy, 5- to 6-inch panicles. Each produces a brown capsule, 9 to 20 inches long and 0.5 to 0.8 of an inch in diameter, containing many fringed seeds about 1 inch long. Brown bark often scaly. To 100 feet tall and 4 feet in diameter, usually with a short trunk, stout branches, and a broad, rounded crown.

SOUTHERN CATALPA *(Catalpa bignonioides)* is smaller (60 feet tall; 3 feet in diameter). Flowers in denser clusters and with more yellow and purple. Capsules have thinner walls.

BLACK-CALABASH *(Enallagma latifolia)* leaves are evergreen, leathery, and alternate, widest above middle, 6 to 8 inches long and 1 to 4 inches wide. Creamy-white to dull-purple flowers, 2 inches long, in spring and fall; usually have a disagreeable odor. Oval fruit, 3 to 4 inches long and 1.5 to 2 inches in diameter, has a shiny-green, hard, 4-ridged, and somewhat roughened husk. Contains many seeds about 0.5 of an inch long. Bark reddish brown, scaly. Grows to 20 feet tall.

DESERTWILLOW *(Chilopsis linearis)* leaves are 6 to 12 inches long and 0.3 of an inch wide; deciduous. Tubular, white flowers, tinged with purple and yellow, are 0.8 to 1.5 inches long and in clusters 3 to 4 inches long. Narrow fruit capsule is 7 to 12 inches long. Bark dark brown, ridged, and scaly. To 30 feet tall, 1 foot in diameter, with narrow crown.

AN INTRODUCED SPECIES

ROYAL PAULOWNIA *(Paulownia tomentosa)* resembles a catalpa, but fragrant, deep-purple flowers appear before leaves. Twigs at first hairy, later smooth. Ovoid, woody capsules, 1 to 1.5 inches long. To 40 feet tall and 1.5 feet in diameter. Native to China; widely planted in the U.S., mainly in southeastern states.

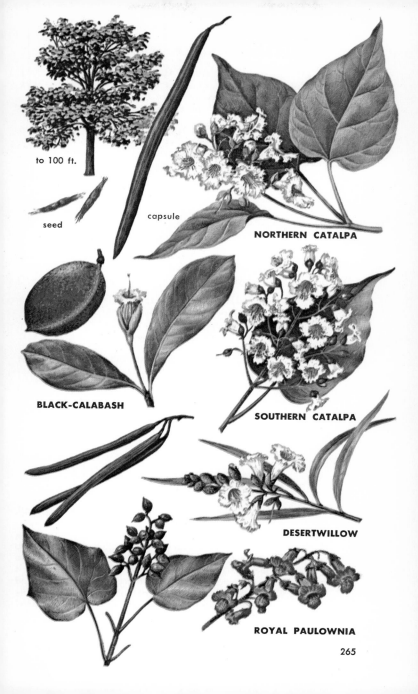

to 100 ft.

seed

capsule

NORTHERN CATALPA

BLACK-CALABASH

SOUTHERN CATALPA

DESERTWILLOW

ROYAL PAULOWNIA

265

HONEYSUCKLE FAMILY (Caprifoliaceae)

Most of the 275 species in about 10 genera are shrubs; a few attain small-tree size. Some of the shrubs are grown as ornamentals for their fragrant, showy flowers or for their colorful fruit. Represented most abundantly in temperate regions of the world.

ELDERS *(Sambucus* spp.) of more than 12 species grow in North America. All have opposite, odd-pinnately compound, deciduous leaves, with 5- to 7-toothed leaflets. Pith of twigs is large, spongy. Small, usually white flowers are in elongated or flat-topped clusters, and fruits are about 0.5 of an inch in diameter. Common native species that occasionally attain tree size include Pacific Red Elder *(S. callicarpa),* with red fruit; Blueberry Elder *(S. glauca)* and American Elder *(S. canadensis),* with blue fruit; Blackbead Elder *(S. melanocarpa),* Mexican Elder *(S. mexicana),* and Florida Elder *(S. simpsonii),* which have black fruit. Velvet Elder *(S. velutina)* has black fruit, hairy leaflets, and yellow flowers.

VIBURNUMS *(Viburnum* spp.) of some 20 species occur in North America. Their leaves are simple, opposite, and usually with toothed margins; in some species turn red in fall. Creamy-white flowers are in flat-topped clusters, 3 to 5 inches across. Fruits, about 0.3 of an inch in diameter, are black or blue. Native species that may attain tree size are Walter Viburnum *(V. obovatum),* which has scented, stemless leaves; Nannyberry *(V. lentago),* with sharply toothed leaf margins; Blackhaw *(V. prunifolium),* which has finely toothed leaf margins; and Possumhaw Viburnum *(V. nudum),* which usually has smooth leaf margins and long-stalked flower clusters.

COMPOSITE (SUNFLOWER) FAMILY (Compositae)

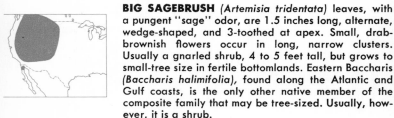

BIG SAGEBRUSH *(Artemisia tridentata)* leaves, with a pungent "sage" odor, are 1.5 inches long, alternate, wedge-shaped, and 3-toothed at apex. Small, drab-brownish flowers occur in long, narrow clusters. Usually a gnarled shrub, 4 to 5 feet tall, but grows to small-tree size in fertile bottomlands. Eastern Baccharis *(Baccharis halimifolia),* found along the Atlantic and Gulf coasts, is the only other native member of the composite family that may be tree-sized. Usually, however, it is a shrub.

to 25 ft.

PACIFIC
RED ELDER

AMERICAN
ELDER

FLORIDA ELDER

VELVET
ELDER

NANNYBERRY

BLACKHAW

WALTER VIBURNUM

POSSUMHAW VIBURNUM

15-20 ft. (rare)

BIG SAGEBRUSH

267

MADDER FAMILY (Rubiaceae)

These are mainly tropical trees, shrubs, and herbs forming 350 genera and nearly 6,000 species. Coffee, the South American cinchonas (the bark of which yields quinine), and such ornamentals as Cape Jasmine and gardenias belong to this family. Seven-year Apple *(Genipa clusiaefolia)*, Scarletbush *(Hamelia patens)*, Bahama Balsamo, or Wild Coffee *(Psychotria ligustrifolia)*, and Seminole Balsamo *(P. undata)* are small trees or shrubs of southern Florida and the Keys.

COMMON BUTTONBUSH *(Cephalanthus occidentalis)* leaves are deciduous, opposite or whorled, 4 to 7 inches long, 2 to 3.5 inches wide, hairy along midvein below. Fragrant flowers in globular heads, 1 to 1.5 inches in diameter, on slender stems 1 to 2 inches long. Seeds in greenish to reddish-brown balls. Bark gray-brown (black on older trees), ridged, scaly. Shrub or small tree, to 30 feet tall, 8 inches in diameter; swampy ground.

CARIBBEAN PRINCEWOOD *(Exostema caribaeum)* has opposite, orange-stemmed, leathery, evergreen leaves, 1.5 to 3 inches long, 0.5 to 0.8 inches wide. Fragrant, solitary, axillary flowers 3 inches long with 5 narrow petals at apex of a thin tube. Capsule 2-celled, many-seeded, 0.7 of an inch long; black when mature. Bark thin, gray. A shrub or small tree, to 25 feet tall.

ROUGHLEAF VELVETSEED *(Guettarda scabra)* leaves are leathery, evergreen and opposite, 2 to 5 inches long and 1.5 to 3 inches wide, rusty-hairy below. Flowers white, tubular, about 1 inch long, on slender, few-flowered, axillary stalks. Fruit fuzzy, red at first but purple when ripe; 0.3 of an inch in diameter. To 30 feet tall and 15 inches in diameter; in sandy soil near salt water.

EVERGLADES VELVETSEED *(Guettarda elliptica)* resembles above species but has silky-haired leaves, 1.0 to 2.5 inches long and 0.5 to 1 inch wide. Creamy-white flowers. To 20 feet tall, 6 inches in diameter.

PINCKNEYA *(Pinckneya pubens)* leaves are deciduous, simple, opposite, 5 to 8 inches long, 3 to 4 inches wide. Tubular flowers, 2.5 inches long, in few-flowered clusters. Globular capsule 2-celled, about 1 inch long. Bark brown, scaly. Pinckneya grows to 30 feet tall and 10 inches in diameter.

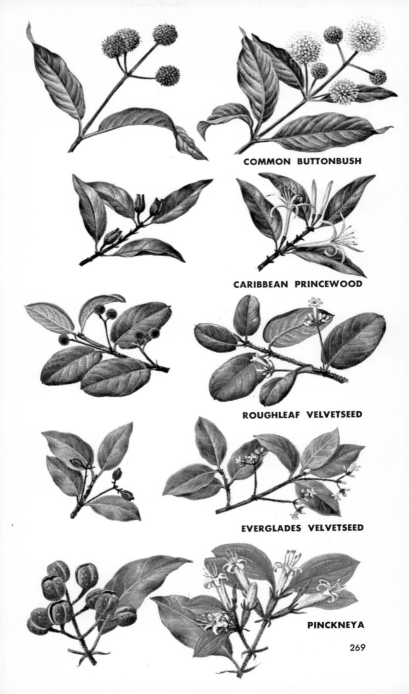

COMMON BUTTONBUSH

CARIBBEAN PRINCEWOOD

ROUGHLEAF VELVETSEED

EVERGLADES VELVETSEED

PINCKNEYA

269

ADDITIONAL EXOTIC SPECIES IN MISCELLANEOUS FAMILIES

HORSETAIL CASUARINA *(Casuarina equisetifolia),* one of 25 species of the family Casuarinaceae, is native to Australia and nearby lands. Evergreen leaves are tiny, toothlike scales, whorled at joints on the wiry, pale-green, drooping branches. Fruit conelike. Also called Australian-pine, Ironwood, and Beefwood. Naturalized in Florida and California. Grows 100 to 150 feet tall. Similar C. *glauca* used as a windbreak.

CHINESE PARASOLTREE *(Firmiana platanifolia),* of the chocolate family, Sterculiaceae, has 3- to 5-lobed, heart-shaped, deciduous leaves, 6 to 12 inches across. Crown rounded. Bark smooth, greenish. Grown in warm parts of North America and now naturalized in Southeast. Native to China and Japan. To 40 feet tall.

SILK-OAK *(Grevillea robusta),* in the family Proteaceae, is a native of Australia grown as an ornamental in California, Texas, and northern Florida. May grow 30 to 70 feet tall. Leaves evergreen, fernlike, bipinnately compound, 4 to 12 inches long, silvery below. Flowers yellow to reddish, in clusters 3 to 5 inches long. Wood lustrous, silky.

RUSSIAN OLIVE *(Elaeagnus angustifolia),* in the family Elaeagnaceae and native to Europe and Asia, is widely planted in the United States. Leaves are deciduous, willowlike, 1.5 to 3 inches long, gray-green above and silvery below. Flowers are small, yellowish, fragrant. Fruit is olivelike, 0.4 of an inch long, yellowish-white. To 20 feet tall.

HORSERADISH-TREE *(Moringa oleifera),* in the family Moringaceae, is an East Indian species grown as an ornamental in southern Florida. Leaves deciduous, alternate, bipinnately (sometimes tripinnately) compound, to 2 feet long. Fragrant, white flowers about 0.8 of an inch across, in clusters 4 to 8 inches long. Capsules 7 to 14 inches long; cooked and eaten when young. Roots have horseradish odor and taste. To 30 feet tall.

SMALLFLOWER TAMARISK *(Tamarix parviflora)* and the smaller Five-stamen Tamarisk *(T. pentandra),* in the family Tamaricaceae, are native to the Mediterranean region. Branches graceful, slender; foliage small, scalelike; pink flowers in clusters 1 to 1.5 inches long. Shrubs or small trees, to 15 feet tall.

BIBLIOGRAPHY

Bailey, L. H. *The Cultivated Conifers.* N. Y., Macmillan, 1933

Benson, Lyman, and Robert A. Darrow. *The Trees and Shrubs of the Southwestern Deserts.* Tucson, Univ. of Arizona Press, 1954

Blakeslee, A. F., and Charles D. Jarvis. *Trees in Winter.* N. Y., Macmillan, 1931

Bonhard, Miriam L. *Palm Trees in the United States.* U.S.D.A., Forest Service, Agric. Inf. Bull. No. 22, Wash., D. C., Gov. Printing Office, 1950

Brown, H. P. *Trees of Northeastern United States, Native and Naturalized.* N. Y., Christopher, 1964

Collingwood, G. H., and Warren D. Brush (revised and edited by Devereux Butcher). *Knowing Your Trees.* Wash., D. C., Amer. Forestry Assoc., 1964

Dallimore, W., and Bruce Jackson (4th ed., revised by S. G. Harrison). *A Handbook of Coniferae, including Ginkgoaceae.* London, Edward Arnold, 1966

Harlow, W. H., and E. S. Harrar. *Textbook of Dendrology.* N. Y., McGraw-Hill, 1968

Harlow, W. M. *Trees of the Eastern and Central United States and Canada.* N. Y., Dover, 1957

Harrar, E. S., and J. G. Harrar. *Guide to Southern Trees.* N. Y., McGraw-Hill, 1946

Hosie, R. C. *Native Trees of Canada.* Canadian Forestry Service, Department of Fisheries and Forestry, Ottawa, Queen's Printer, 1969

Hough, R. B. *Handbook of the Trees of the Northeastern States and Canada (east of the Rocky Mountains).* N. Y., Macmillan, 1947

Lawrence, G. H. *Taxonomy of Vascular Plants.* N. Y., Macmillan, 1951

Ledin, R. Bruce (ed.). *Cultivated Palms.* Amer. Hort. Mag. (special issue), Vol. 40, No. 1, January 1961

Little, Elbert L., Jr. *Check List of Native and Naturalized Trees of the United States (inc. Alaska).* Forest Service Tree and Range Plant Committee, Agric. Handbook No. 41, Wash., D. C., Gov. Printing Office, 1953

Little, Elbert L., Jr.. *Southwestern Trees, A Guide to the Native Species of New Mexico and Arizona.* Agric. Handbook No. 9, Wash., D. C., Gov. Printing Office, 1950

Little, Elbert L., Jr. and Frank H. Wadsworth. *Common Trees of Puerto Rico and the Virgin Islands.* Agric. Handbook No. 249, U.S.D.A., Forest Service, Wash., D. C., Gov. Printing Office, 1964

McMinn, H. E., and E. Maino. *Illustrated Manual of Pacific Coast Trees.* Berkeley, Calif., Univ. of Calif. Press, 1947

Muirhead, Desmond. *Palms.* Globe, Ariz., D. S. King, 1961

Peattie, Donald Culross. *Natural History of Trees of Eastern and Central North America.* Boston, Houghton Mifflin, 1950

Peattie, Donald Culross. *A Natural History of Western Trees.* Boston, Houghton Mifflin, 1953

Preston, R. J. *North American Trees (exclusive of Mexico and Tropical United States).* Cambridge, Mass., M.I.T. Press, 1961

Sargent, C. S. *Manual of the Trees of North America (exclusive of Mexico).* Boston, Houghton Mifflin, 1923

Sudworth, George B. *Forest Trees of the Pacific Slope.* Wash., D. C., U. S. Gov. Printing Office, 1908

Trelease, William. *Winter Botany,* N. Y., Dover (paperback), 1967

U.S.D.A. *Trees—The Yearbook of Agriculture.* Wash., D. C., Gov. Printing Office, 1949

U.S.D.A., Forest Service (compiled and revised by H. A. Fowells). *Silvics of Forest Trees of the United States.* Agric. Handbook No. 271, Wash., D. C., Gov. Printing Office, 1965

Vines, R. H. *Trees, Shrubs and Woody Vines of the Southwest.* Austin, Univ. of Texas Press, 1960

West, Erdman, and Lillian E. Arnold. *The Native Trees of Florida.* Gainseville, Univ. of Fla. Press, 1956

In addition, many regional books and pamphlets are available locally in forestry offices, educational institutions, and libraries.

INDEX

Common names are indicated by two text page numbers for species that are illustrated —the even page number for the text, the odd for the illustration. Single text page numbers (even) are for scientific names and also for species not illustrated. Inclusive page numbers are given for families and for some genera or groups in which a number of species are listed. For explanation of names used in this book, see p. 4.

275

277

279

The Gawgon
and the BOY

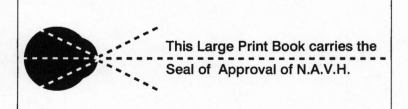

This Large Print Book carries the Seal of Approval of N.A.V.H.

The Gawgon and the BOY

Lloyd Alexander

Thorndike Press • Waterville, Maine

Published in 2003 by arrangement with Puffin Books, a member of Penguin Group, (USA) Inc.

Thorndike Press® Large Print Juvenile Series.

The tree indicium is a trademark of Thorndike Press.

The text of this Large Print edition is unabridged.
Other aspects of the book may vary from the original edition.

Set in 16 pt. Plantin by Minnie B. Raven.

Printed in the United States on permanent paper.

Library of Congress Cataloging-in-Publication Data

Alexander, Lloyd.
    The Gawgon and The Boy / by Lloyd Alexander.
      p. cm.
    Summary: In Depression-era Philadelphia, when eleven-year-old David is too ill to attend school, he is tutored by the unique and adventurous Aunt Annie, whose teaching combines with his imagination to greatly enrich his life.
    ISBN 0-7862-5433-5 (lg. print : hc : alk. paper)
    1. Imagination — Fiction. 2. Teacher–student relationships — Fiction. 3. Depressions — 1929 — Fiction. 4. Philadelphia (Pa.) — Fiction. I. Title.
PZ7.A3774 Gaw 2003
  [Fic]—dc21   2003048394

For those with a Gawgon of their own,
and those who wish for one

Contents

The Gawgon
and the BOY

Family Tree (Our Irish Shillelly)

🦎 **Mother's Side** 🦎

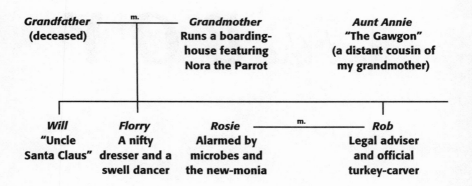

Grandfather —— m. —— **Grandmother**   **Aunt Annie**
(deceased)   Runs a boarding-   **"The Gawgon"**
                  house featuring   (a distant cousin of
                  Nora the Parrot   my grandmother)

Will   **Florry**   **Rosie** —— m. —— **Rob**
"Uncle   A nifty   **Alarmed by**   Legal adviser
Santa Claus"   dresser and a   microbes and   and official
            swell dancer   the new-monia   turkey-carver

m. = married

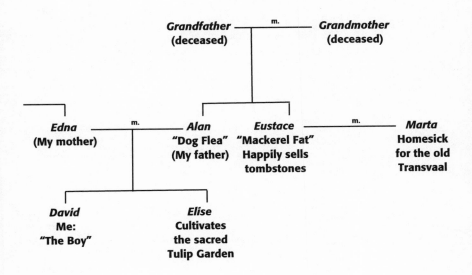

❧ Father's Side ❧

Grandfather
(deceased) —— m. —— Grandmother
(deceased)

Edna
(My mother) —— m. —— Alan
"Dog Flea"
(My father)

Eustace
"Mackerel Fat"
Happily sells
tombstones —— m. —— Marta
Homesick
for the old
Transvaal

David
Me:
"The Boy"

Elise
Cultivates
the sacred
Tulip Garden

1

The Sea-Fox

When I first met The Gawgon, I never suspected who she was: climber of icy mountains, rescuer of King Tut's treasure, challenger of master criminals, and a dozen other things. But that came later, after I died — nearly died, anyhow.

"They really thought you were a goner," my sister said cheerfully. She had come to stand at my bedroom door. "What a nuisance you are."

In April of that year — one of those sour-tempered Philadelphia Aprils — I had the good luck to fall sick. I was delighted. Not that I enjoyed the worst part of it, but the best part was: It kept me out of school. Aside from a beehive buzzing in my head and a herd of weasels romping through my insides, I was beginning to feel pretty chipper.

No one told me straight out what ailed me. I was eleven and had not reached complete visibility. My relatives, talking among

13

themselves, tended to look through me — the Amazing Invisible Boy — or change the subject. I did overhear my mother and my aunt Rosie whispering in the hall about something Aunt Rosie called the New Monia. "Thank heaven it wasn't the Spanish Influenzo," she said to my mother. "Spaniards! What else will they send us?" Aunt Rosie lived in a state of eternal indignation and distrusted anything foreign.

"That's right, you nearly croaked," my sister happily went on. "Uncle Eustace was ready to sell us a tombstone."

Uncle Eustace, my father's brother, indeed sold tombstones for a living. As a result of sinus operations, deep scars crisscrossed his face. It made him look grim and somber, an advantage in his line of work.

"If I croaked" — I made frog noises — "it wouldn't bother me. I'd come back as a duppy and haunt you."

Duppy was the West Indian word for "ghost." I learned it from my father, born in Kingston, Jamaica. The prospect of meeting a duppy scared the wits out of him. Otherwise, he was completely fearless.

"There aren't any duppies in Philadelphia," my sister said. "So shut up about them. Just be glad you weren't quarantined."

I was not glad. I was disappointed. I would have liked one of those red or yellow stickers plastered on the front door, a badge of distinction. We still lived in the house on Lorimer Street then, and I had seen a few go up in the neighborhood, usually for measles, chicken pox, diphtheria (the Dip Theory, Aunt Rosie called it). Every so often a boy suddenly vanished as if the goblins had got him. The black-lettered warning would appear, then a few days later, the boy himself, grinning behind the windowpane, his face magnificently blotched — almost as good as being tattooed. What was done with girls, I had no idea. They were a tribe apart.

I knew my sister was frantic over the possibility of a quarantine. No one could have gone in or out except the adults and our family physician, Dr. McKelvie. She would have been confined to quarters along with me. She was seventeen, and it would have devastated her Tulip Garden.

The Tulip Garden was the name I gave her circle of girlfriends, all looking much alike with their bobbed hairdos of chestnut, auburn, blond on slender necks. Their meetings were forbidden to me. I could only lurk in the hall while, behind her bedroom door, the Tulip Garden whispered and giggled. Separated, they would have withered; or their hair might have fallen out in despair. When no quarantine was needed, my sister grew more kindly disposed toward me.

"You're going to be all right, blighter," she said. She held her nose and stepped away from the door. "Pee-you. What do you do in here?"

She hurried to her room as if legions of my germs might attack her.

As for what I did: Apart from reading everything I could lay hands on, my favorite occupation was making up stories and drawing pictures to go with them. Before coming down sick, I had taken a fancy to piracy, gorging myself on *Treasure Island*, *Captain Blood*, and *The Sea-Hawk*. Now sitting up again, I went back to the high seas.

My mind began drifting. The Spanish Influenza got mixed up with the Spanish Main, with quarantines, duppies, Uncle Eustace, and my grandmother's green parrot, Nora. The best pirates had beautiful ladies to worship from afar. I did not. I had only begun to suspect that girls were

16

interesting beings. But I remembered my Jamaican cousin Allegra — we had, the year before, taken a trip to Kingston. Golden-skinned, with a peach and turpentine fragrance of mangoes, she would, I thought, be just fine.

THE SEA-FOX

The Sea-Fox stood at the railing of the quarterdeck, his trusty parrot, Nora, on his shoulder, a spyglass to his eye. Who would have guessed this slim, steel-sinewed youth, captain of the most dreaded pirate ship to sail the Spanish Main, was the son of Lord Aldine, England's grandest nobleman?

A curious fate had set him on this course. Stricken by a terrible case of the New Monia, he had been sent on a sea voyage to regain his health.

"No member of this family has had a sick day since the Norman Conquest," declared his father. "Off you go, you puny blighter. Never set foot in this manor again till you're fit to wrestle a bear."

Months later, sailing homeward strong and vigorous, he was sorry to end the happy life he had found on the open sea. But then, nearly in sight of England's bleak and rainy shore, pirates attacked — "Avast! Belay!" — boarded his vessel, and swarmed over the deck.

Now lithe and muscular as a tiger, and handsomely suntanned, the lad fought so ferociously, to the wonder and admiration of friend and foe alike, that he was unanimously acclaimed — "Hip-hip hooray!" — captain of the buccaneers. All hands turned pirate, eager to serve under his command. From that day, he and his loyal crew became the terror of the sea-lanes; his good ship *Allegra* could overtake any sluggish merchantman — "Surrender, you lubbers! Join us or walk the plank."

Lord Aldine assumed the boy had either died at sea — proving a flaw in his son's character; or the ship had sunk — proving incompetence on the part of the shipmaster. Had the noble lord the slightest inkling of his son's profession, he would have exploded with purple rage.

The Sea-Fox narrowed his gaze on Kingston harbor: the green hills under a cloudless blue sky; the coconut palms and mango trees swaying in the warm breeze; taverns and storehouses clustering at the waterfront; the governor's gleaming white mansion rising above the town.

He smiled with satisfaction and called for the bosun, a grizzled old sea dog, brow and cheekbones crisscrossed by cutlass scars and a bad sinus condition.

"Mr. Eustace," ordered the Sea-Fox, "strike the Jolly Roger."

"Haul down the skull and bones? Aarr, Cap'n, what's afoot?"

"Then run up the yellow flag. Quarantine. Pestilence aboard."

"But, Cap'n" — the puzzled bosun frowned — "there's not even a case of measles. Except for Dr. McKelvie, the ship's surgeon, seasick as usual, we're hale and hearty, all the rest."

"Exactly."

When the Sea-Fox explained his plan, Mr. Eustace grinned and tugged a forelock: "Aye, a sweet little scheme. Aarr, Cap'n, they don't call ye Sea-Fox for nowt. And so we take the town, is it?"

"Kingston?" The Sea-Fox laughed. "Mr. Eustace, we shall take the whole island."

The bosun's face lit up. "Aarr, then we loot, sack, rifle, pillage —"

"Whatever amuses you. Seize the jewels, gold, ginger ale, and all the mangoes. Spare only the governor's mansion."

The Sea-Fox again turned his spyglass landward to focus on the upper floor of the building where Allegra, the governor's golden-skinned niece, had stepped onto the balcony.

"As for plunder, Mr. Eustace, divide it equally among the crew. But," the Sea-Fox murmured, "one priceless gem is mine."

2

The Cupped Boy

Next morning, I felt a lot less chipper. My eyelids seemed to be glued shut; I spent some time and effort getting them open. I had thrashed around during the night, the bedclothes were in a tangled mess on the floor; even without them I sweltered. My mother, meantime, must have called Dr. McKelvie; for here he was, big, cheerful, and smelling like Listerine.

"Well, now, laddie-buck, let's have a look at you." Dr. McKelvie dressed always in a black suit; a broad expanse of vest supported a gold watch and chain. His beard wreathed the bottom half of his face; it made me think of a bird's nest and I would not have been too surprised to see a cuckoo, like the one in my grandmother's clock, pop out of it.

While my mother hovered, Dr. McKelvie went about his ritual of sticking a thermometer under my tongue, thumping my chest, listening through his stethoscope as if he were getting radio messages.

After that, there was talk about something to do with a hospital.

"Certainly not," my mother said. "Put him in with a crowd of sick people? To catch who knows what else?"

"Dear lady, in my considered opinion —"

"In *my* considered opinion," my mother said, "I know how to look after my own child."

Most people would have been overawed by Dr. McKelvie, for he took up a lot of space. My mother was overawed by no one. She went on in a pleasant tone but one not to be contradicted.

"Out of the question. A hospital will do more harm than good. No, he is in the best of hands." Under her breath, she added, "Mine."

My mother, alarmed, must have telephoned my father, for he came home much earlier than usual. He had no difficulty getting time off, since he ran his own business in center city: a store that sold Oriental goods. He took me there on the occasional Saturday and I loved it: a treasure house smelling of joss sticks and incense, crowded with paper lanterns, screens, lamps, vases, and jewelry. He once had been a stockbroker. Why he quit and chose this exotic profession, I never knew; unless it simply amused him.

He came to bend over me. He wore elegant pince-nez glasses which I expected to fall off at any moment, but they always stayed clamped to the bridge of his nose. "How are you, Bax old sport?"

"Bax" was his latest nickname for me. I had no idea where or why he came up with it. Names in our family were flexible. While my sister Elise and I addressed our parents as "Mother" and "Father," other titles came up on the spur of the moment and stuck until new ones replaced them. Some stayed permanent. Though my mother always called my father by his proper name, Alan, he called her "Ed" or "Eddie." He still called his brother Eustace by his Jamaican boyhood nickname, "Mackerel Fat" and was, in turn, addressed as "Dog Flea."

Of names, I enjoyed more than my share. To Dr. McKelvie, I was "laddie-buck." To my sister, "blighter." To my various relatives, I was at one time or another "Skeezix," "Skinamalink," or "Snickle-fritz." Only my mother called me by my given name, David.

To his question, I insisted I was fine.

"Of course you are," my father said.

My mother motioned with her head, and they went out into the hall.

For the next couple of days, I was too foggy to be interested in much of anything. But I did perk up enough to try drawing pictures, imitating the cartoon panels I saw in the comic strips, and went back to Kingston, where I had left the Sea-Fox.

THE SEA-FOX CLAIMS
HIS PRIZE

Mr. Eustace, as ordered, had run up the yellow flag to signal pestilence aboard. The *Allegra* drifted closer to the harbor. Consternation reigned along the waterfront. The townsfolk crowded the wharves, shaking their fists and warning the plague-ridden vessel to stand away. A boat was launched and rowed within a safe distance from the ship. The harbormaster, standing in the bow, commanded the *Allegra* to turn about and sail as far as possible out to sea.

"Aarr, it can't be done," Mr. Eustace

called through a speaking trumpet.

"It demmed well better be," flung back the harbormaster, "else we open fire on you."

The *Allegra*'s crew, meantime, had hidden themselves well out of sight. Mr. Eustace repeated, "Can't be done, no matter."

Silently watchful on the quarterdeck, the Sea-Fox — who never told a lie — had assigned the bosun — who never told the truth — this deceptive but necessary task:

"No hands to work the ship," declared Mr. Eustace. "They're dead, all but me and the cap'n. Died of the Spanish Influenzo; bloated bellies, running sores, that kind of thing."

"Dead! Awk, awk!" Nora bounced up and down on the shoulder of the Sea-Fox. "Every man jack, dead as doorknobs."

"No business of mine." The harbormaster held a handkerchief to his nose. "Don't come near. Can't work the ship? Then drift out to sea on the night tide. Drift to the devil, for all I care."

"Aye, aye," replied the bosun, "so we'll do."

At midnight, following his plan, the

Sea-Fox ordered the jolly boats lowered over the side. The *Allegra* carried a number of these small, light craft for just such occasions. With muffled oars, the Sea-Fox leading, the jolly boats skimmed swiftly to the sleeping harbor.

The crew, also according to plan, had draped themselves in lengths of sail-cloth. Reaching the docks, they clambered ashore and gave voice to blood-curdling shrieks. The drowsy watchman, rousing, gaped in terror.

"Duppies!" he bawled. "Hundreds! Duppies everywhere!"

Seeing the white-shrouded figures, convinced the town had been invaded by the ghosts of diseased sailors, the entire population raced for the hills. Adding to the panic, the crew smashed many huge barrels of ginger ale, and the amber liquid gushed in rivers down the streets. Warehouses were broken into, thousands of mangoes rolled in all directions.

The Sea-Fox, discarding his ghostly disguise, strode to the governor's mansion. Unchallenged, he climbed the marble staircase and halted at a bedchamber door. With one mighty kick from his booted foot, he shattered it from its hinges.

Allegra turned toward him. Months before, the Sea-Fox had boarded a vessel carrying her, the governor, and his lady to Jamaica. Ordinarily, the Sea-Fox would have set the passengers adrift. However, the sparkle in Allegra's eyes betokened more than passing interest and held a promise for the future.

"We shall meet again," he whispered in her shell-like ear.

Now here she was, her face aglow with the same illumination he had seen at their first encounter.

"You idiot," she said, "why did you kick down my door? It was unlatched; I was waiting for you. At least," she added, "you could have knocked."

The Sea-Fox nodded acceptance of this gentle reproof. He pointed at the town below, where his loyal crew were guzzling ginger ale and stuffing themselves with mangoes.

"Kingston is mine. And yours," he said. "I mean to declare Jamaican independence. The grateful population will acclaim us president and first lady. Or king and queen, if you prefer. We shall occupy this splendid residence —"

"Have you lost your mind?" Allegra

burst out. "Gone stark raving bonkers? Why do you suppose I waited for you? To stay on some boring island? Besides, I hate mangoes. I say we haul out of here, back to the high seas, plundering merchantmen, sinking frigates."

"Then so we shall!" happily exclaimed the Sea-Fox, who had not really looked forward to life ashore. "Yes, the two of us will terrify the Spanish Main to-gether."

"My Sea-Fox!" cried Allegra.

"My pirate bride!" he answered.

"Your Sea-Vixen," said Allegra.

⊱❧C ⊱❧C ⊱❧C

Later, my sister came to announce confidentially: "You're going to be cupped."

I had no idea what she meant. Put into a cup? It would have to be a large one.

"Grandmother phoned. She told Mother it would be a good idea. They did it to me once," she added. "It was disgusting and weird. Just the kind of thing you like. They're calling Mrs. Jossbegger."

This puzzled me. I knew Mrs. Jossbegger, a woman of some bulk who wheezed a lot. She had, so far as I could tell, nothing to do with cups. She made her living from feet: cutting ladies' toenails and paring their corns.

Mrs. Jossbegger made regular visits to Larchmont Street, where my grandmother kept a boardinghouse. On those occasions, my mother and my various aunts gathered in the parlor. We all lived within a few blocks of each other, so it was an easy walk.

I was always glad to be taken along. At the boardinghouse, something was always going on: lodgers coming in and out, meals being cooked, a cluttered cellar I was allowed to explore. And, above all, Nora the parrot.

Nora had been left behind when one of the lodgers furtively departed still owing a good amount of back rent. Now she lived in the parlor, free to perch on her T-shaped pole or do acrobatics on top of her cage.

I never missed a chance to talk with her, though what she said was mainly gibberish, with a lot of squawking and whistling. Sometimes she did come out with understandable sentences:

"We're all drunk but Nora," she warbled, adding noises like breaking glass. Then she whooped and giggled. "Naughty boy, get your hand off my leg. Hoorah, hoorah!"

I could only guess at the life she had led before settling into the boardinghouse.

The corn-cutting sessions were social events as much as they were podiatric treatments. Awaiting Mrs. Jossbegger, the ladies gathered in a circle, a grown-up Tulip Garden, drinking tea and gossiping.

Also attending was one of the two permanent residents: Aunt Annie (an honorary title, she was my grandmother's distant cousin), thin as a stick, always in floor-length black skirts, her white hair twisted into a bun. Although she hobbled downstairs for meals and other important happenings, she had never to my knowledge set foot outside the boardinghouse. The other permanent resident was Captain Jack — not a real captain, we called him that because it pleased him. Shell-shocked in the Great War, he never left his room at all; except, from time to time, when he went sleepwalking.

I admired Captain Jack as a great hero. His sleepwalking also fascinated me, and I wished I, too, could be a sleepwalker. I liked visiting with him and listening to his gramophone records. To him, I was "First Sergeant," and we were fond friends.

Aunt Annie, however, seemed a grim and forbidding presence. Not that she treated me with anything less than kindness. To her credit, at Christmas and my birthdays, when my relatives usually gave me handkerchiefs and underwear, she gave me books. Still, she made me uneasy. Invisibility has its advantages; but when she turned her sharp glances on me, watching me closely, I was no longer the Amazing Invisible Boy. On the contrary, I felt she could see me very clearly indeed and quite possibly could read my mind. For that reason, she frightened me a little. Or perhaps it was simply because she was very old.

Nevertheless, I saw no connection between corn cutting and being cupped. So, that evening, when Mrs. Jossbegger came wheezing into my room, I was curious, eager to know what she intended to do, and maybe a touch apprehensive. My sister holed up in her own quarters; my father preferred staying downstairs. My mother stripped off my pajama top while Mrs. Jossbegger set half a dozen globes like small fishbowls on the night table.

Flat on my stomach, my mother more or less squashing down my head, I could not see precisely what was going on. From the corner of my eye, I glimpsed Mrs. Jossbegger setting fire to a cotton ball on a stick. I braced myself, suspecting she planned on setting me alight as well. Instead, heating the inside of the globes, she planted them in rows along my back, where they stuck as if glued there. I was commanded not to move. After a time, Mrs. Jossbegger pulled off the globes; they came away with a pop like the rubber suction cups on toy arrows.

"Would you look at that?" she whispered to my mother. "Black as ink. There's all the bad blood coming out."

I was allowed, with a hand mirror, to admire the result. Dark bumps like giant mosquito bites covered my back; a spectacular effect. I was as proud as if I had received tribal initiation marks like those I had seen in *National Geographic*.

Mrs. Jossbegger nodded professional satisfaction. My mother gave me a drink of something that smelled like mothballs. Of course, blessedly, I had no hint then of what would catch us all up and shatter us. Without a thought even for the Sea-Fox, I slept happily, dreamlessly.

3

The Back-Alley Gang

Mrs. Jossbegger's cups and Dr. McKelvie's foul-tasting concoctions must have combined to good effect. Despite a couple of setbacks, when I felt as if I were going down the wrong end of a telescope, by the end of May I was out of bed some of the time, ready to receive visiting aunts and uncles.

An outsider would have been bewildered by the array of relatives and lost in the tangled branches of the family tree. But I had known them all my life, knew them as I knew the fingers of my hand, and had no trouble sorting them out. They were, in sum, the family.

I saw little of my father's brother Eustace — my tombstone uncle. He was busy reading the death notices in the morning papers and hurrying out to drum up customers. But his wife, Marta, came by. Stout, ruddy-cheeked, she was born in South Africa and had been homesick ever since. I thought of her as my singing aunt, for she had a clear, beautiful voice. I begged her to sing her favorite, "Sari Marais," and joined in the yearning refrain:

Oh, take me back to the old Transvaal,
That's where I long to be.
Down among the mealies
And the green thorn trees . . .

Mealies, she explained as she tried to teach me the words in Afrikaans, were ears of corn. I had never seen a mealie or a green thorn tree, but the melody brought tears to my eyes each time I heard it. However, it vexed Uncle Eustace.

"Transvaal?" he would burst out, putting his hands to his shattered forehead. "Transvaal? What's wrong with Philadelphia?"

My grandmother came as often as she could leave the boardinghouse to itself. I thought she looked a little like George Washington in the portrait on my classroom wall, except she smiled more and her wrinkled cheeks turned pale pink when she threw back her head and laughed, which was frequently. She moistened her fingertips in her mouth and rubbed away smudges on my face, confident that grandmotherly saliva cured everything.

Aunt Rosie, of course, was always there, spreading alarm about microbes drifting in through open windows; and warning my mother I could poke my eye out with a pencil when I bent over my sketch pad. Her husband, Rob, my mother's eldest brother, was the distinguished uncle. He had a job with the Pennsylvania Railroad.

So, I felt highly honored when Uncle Rob came in person to visit me.

"Here's a little something for you, Snicklefritz." Uncle Rob slipped me a quarter. He always and unfailingly slipped me a quarter each time we met. "I hear you're doing fine. You'll be back to school in no time."

In our family, Uncle Rob was the one who handled wills, last testaments, codicils, and all such grim and stifling business. Naturally, he would bring up the subject of school.

The mere mention of the word sent me into a sudden choking fit, and he had to go away. I had forgotten about school. It was the distant past, long out of my thoughts. Now that Uncle Rob had reminded me, I would have begged to be flogged, disemboweled, and forced to drink molten lead rather than returned to classes. I had some reluctance about being educated.

35

My sister did not seem to mind, which made me doubt her sanity. We both went to Rittenhouse Academy: she in Upper School, I in Middle School. The headmaster, Dr. Legg, a solemn figure in black academic robes, believed in plain living and high thinking, a sound mind in a sound body, those goals to be attained through cold showers and scratchy toilet paper.

The soundness of our bodies was enhanced by endless games of soccer. We turned out, rain or shine, in baggy white shorts and drooping athletic supporters, or exercised in the gymnasium, which smelled as if foxes lived there. To strengthen our minds, we plodded through our classes grimly fixated on each subject, never venturing on any exciting side trips. It felt like trudging down a rutted road. Yawning mentally, hypnotically bored, I paid barely enough attention to squeak by. Mainly, I drew pictures or penciled stick figures — "Skinny Pinnies" — on the margins of my textbooks.

Dr. Legg assured us, whenever he addressed the assembled school, that Rittenhouse Academy was preparing us for the great battle of life. We would be ready to conquer empires or run for Congress.

My father had more modest expectations. If I studied hard and seriously applied myself, he told me, I might, like Uncle Rob, get an office job with the Pennsylvania Railroad.

Whether Uncle Rob put the question into my mother's head or whether it occurred to her on her own, I did not know. But the next time Dr. McKelvie came, she asked him when I could go back to Rittenhouse Academy.

"My dear madam" — Dr. McKelvie chewed his beard for a moment — "you surely understand the boy has been gravely ill. Return to school? For what little remains of the term? No, surely not. Possibly not the fall term either. That remains to be seen. A lengthy convalescence, absolutely essential —"

"I won't have him turned into a shut-in," my mother said. "That simply won't do at all."

"I agree," Dr. McKelvie said. "School can wait, no rush about it. What I recommend is some fresh air, mild exercise." He turned to me. "How does that suit you, laddie-buck?"

I could have kissed his stethoscope.

Dr. McKelvie snatched me from the gallows. Had I known the consequences, I might have been more wary; but I cared only to be set loose for my "mild exercise" in the world. That is, the back-alley world of Lorimer Street; canyons of green-painted board fences, trash bins, garbage cans, tiny courtyards and areaways — "airy ways," Aunt Rosie called them. Hucksters pushed carts through the alleys, hawking berries, melons, vegetables. The passages were barely wide enough for the iceman's horse and wagon. When he reined up to chop out the glittering blocks, grappling them with iron tongs, to shoulder them into kitchen iceboxes, he was ambushed by knickered bandits seizing the frozen splinters, crunching them loudly or sucking them until they melted.

By the middle of June, I had gained a couple of henchmen who lived nearby: Deveraux, whose arms had grown faster than the rest of him and, as a result, did convincing imitations of a chimpanzee, hooting, grinning, scratching himself, scuffing his knuckles along the pavement; Barnick, spiky-haired, wearing knee-length boots, which I coveted, all the more since one boot had a sheath for a jackknife. We had, until then, seen little of each other; we became cronies nonetheless. They knew I went to private school, but good-natured fellows, they never held it against me.

I supplied them with cootie-catchers. Producing those items was one of my major skills, perfected while wool-gathering in class. Like Japanese origami, the cootie-catcher began with a square of paper folded in on itself a couple of times. Its construction let a boy (I never saw a girl use a cootie-catcher) hold it so that one inside surface was blank.

Passing the cootie-catcher through a victim's hair, then changing finger position, it appeared filled with lice and fleas (drawn there beforehand). By unspoken agreement, the one whose cooties had thus been caught was required to yell in disgust at the vermin found on his person. The joke had limitations. After a few times, the effect wore off, by the law of diminishing cootie returns. The only solution: to draw the creatures larger, more grotesque. After a time, nevertheless, the most nauseating roaches and giant bedbugs ceased to shock. Even Deveraux had to force himself, out of politeness, to hoot in mock terror.

I pondered improvements. My downfall began, as with so many artists, with a grand vision, a new conception. I was inspired to paint the cooties in vivid colors.

Uncle Rob, when last we met, had slipped me the ritual quarter. I intended buying paints. Where the back alleys ended, a miniature city included a barber-shop, shoeshine parlor, drugstore with a marble soda fountain, and a movie house. A penny-candy store also offered small toys and art supplies. There, in artistic frenzy, I sacrificed all of Uncle Rob's quarter and bought a tin box of water-colors and a scraggy brush.

I was eager to take my purchases home, but Barnick and Deveraux wanted to see a movie; the neighborhood theater was showing one of the new films that actually talked. Deveraux produced a dime. Barnick dredged up three cents. I was already totally bankrupt. Much as I would have loved an afternoon movie, it was not possible. Pooling our resources came far short of the admission price for all of us. I saw no way around that hard financial fact.

Deveraux and Barnick looked at me with the tolerant amusement shown to puppies and idiots. They had a plan, simple and elegant. Deveraux would pay to get in. Barnick and I were to wait outside the fire exit, which Deveraux would open for us: a scheme worthy of the Sea-Fox.

Deveraux, winking and making chimpanzee faces, headed for the box office. Barnick and I crouched amid the trash barrels by the fire exit. Moments later, the door swung open just wide enough for us to squeeze through.

4

A Hardened Criminal

Sudden darkness blinded me, the bright silver screen dazzled me. I had taken no more than two steps into the half-empty theater when a figure loomed up. Barnick yelled, I tried to dodge aside. A hand clamped the scruff of my neck. Collared likewise, Barnick was thrashing around beside me. The usher, triumphant in a pillbox hat and brass buttons, hustled us through the movie house. The flickering figures on the screen kept on talking, laughing, and tap-dancing heedless of our fate.

Deveraux had streaked away into the shadows of the aisles. We thought no less of him for his desertion; he could do nothing but save himself. Hopeless prisoners, we were marched up a flight of iron steps into a tiny office.

The windowless room stank of cigar smoke and celluloid film. At a cluttered table, arm garters on his sleeves, hair slicked down with Vaseline and parted in the middle, the manager congratulated our captor, dismissed him, and turned a fish eye on us.

"What's this, eh? I'd say we've got a couple of fine young hoodlums here." Mr. Kardon — I later learned this was his despicable name — got up to strut back and forth like a bantam rooster. "Now, you little thugs, what's to be done with you? Want to guess? No? I'll tell you, then. Make an example of you. Hooligans like you sneaking in here — I'm fed up with it. Barefaced thievery, money out of my pocket. Next, you'll rob me at gunpoint. So, it's police business now. Oh, yes, the station house for you. In handcuffs. Behind bars, where you belong."

Barnick started blubbering. I tried to assume a scornful attitude — the Sea-Fox in the clutches of the enemy — but I was blubbering as well, no doubt louder than Barnick.

Mr. Kardon blustered and browbeat us awhile, then demanded our telephone numbers. He did not call the police. Worse, he called our mothers.

We stood waiting, sniffling, not daring to wipe our eyes and noses. Mr. Kardon had caught sight of the jackknife in Barnick's boot and confiscated it. When Mrs.

Barnick arrived, he went through the sorry tale of our crime.

"And this? What's this?" Mr. Kardon pried open the evidence to reveal a broken-tipped blade. "A lethal weapon."

My mother, meantime, had come into the office and the whole business started up again.

"Call them children?" Mr. Kardon folded his arms. "I'll tell you what they are. A disgrace to their families. Bad to worse if they keep on like this. Hardened criminals."

Mr. Kardon ranted on about a life of crime, jailbirds, a road to the penitentiary, a strong likelihood of the electric chair — at this, he eyed me directly, as if seeing me (as I saw myself) strapped into that particular item of furniture. He finally got tired and decided to grant clemency.

We were paroled into the custody of our mothers. Mrs. Barnick hustled her son from the office. Beyond the door, I could hear Barnick having his head smacked.

I was fidgeting to be gone. Mr. Kardon sat down at his table and shuffled papers. My mother did not budge. She bent forward and said, almost in a whisper: "You miserable little man, how dare you? How dare you call my son a criminal? Jailbird?

44

Prison? This is outrageous. You, sir, should be the one behind bars for your atrocious behavior."

The Vaseline on Mr. Kardon's hair seemed to melt. My mother dipped into her purse and took out a quarter.

"This" — she set the coin on the table — "will more than pay his admission. You may keep the change."

As we walked home, I steeled myself to be scolded. My mother said not a word, as if the shameful event had never happened. When my father came home and we all sat down to dinner, she still mentioned nothing about it. We were all in a good mood. Relieved, I sped to my room.

Later, my sister poked her head in. "You got caught, didn't you? That's what happens to sneaky little blighters."

Surprised, I asked how she knew.

"Oh, I know," she said. "The whole thing. They were talking after you went upstairs."

I had no reason to doubt her. Unlike myself, the Amazing Invisible Boy, she was totally visible at all times, counted as a young lady, and thus privy, if not specifically invited, to adult conversations. She was always glad to pass along disagreeable information.

"They're going to do something to you," she said.

I asked what it was.

"They aren't sure." She shrugged. "They're thinking about it. You're not getting off, you know. Whatever it is, you're not going to like it."

She wished me a cheery good night.

I tried to imagine what punishments would be inflicted. Confinement, hard labor, exile — none of them absolutely unbearable. Besides, I judged myself relatively blameless. Uncle Rob was at the root of it. If he hadn't given me the quarter, I wouldn't have spent it. If I hadn't spent it, I'd have had money for legal admission. If I'd paid to get in, I wouldn't have been grabbed by a pimply-faced usher decked out like an organ grinder's monkey and threatened with electrocution by a cock-of-the-walk with Vaseline on his head. Still, the nameless, shapeless "something" hung over me. The Sea-Fox, meantime, was having his own troubles.

THE SEA-FOX IN CHAINS

Shackled hand and foot, the Sea-Fox lay on the damp straw of his cell in Portsmouth Prison. Through the grated window trickled the busy clatter of the waterfront and the stench of bodies hanging in chains at Execution Dock. For all that, he kept a calm spirit. When last seen, Mr. Eustace the bosun, Dr. McKelvie the ship's surgeon, and the rest of the crew, urged on by Nora the parrot, were in the jolly boats rowing away as fast as their arms could work the oars.

Treachery and deception had led him to this dismal cell. A week before, he had sighted a lazy merchantman ripe for plucking. Sea-Vixen at the helm, the *Allegra* closed rapidly with the vessel.

"All hands on deck! Prepare to board!" the Sea-Fox commanded.

"Sink the lubbers!" Nora crowed gleefully. "Yo-ho! Awk, awk!"

No sooner did the *Allegra* come alongside than the merchantman hoisted the white flag of surrender. With the ships hull to hull, the Sea-Fox sprang lightly over the railing to the deck of the captured prize. The captain, a puffed-up little man, hair slick with Vaseline, approached to offer his sword in submission. As the Sea-Fox reached for it, a company of seagoing constables, pimply-faced, in pillbox hats and brass-buttoned uniforms, burst up from the hatches. Royal Navy gunners ran out cannon disguised as innocent pieces of hardware and fired point-blank at the helpless *Allegra*.

"Shameful treachery!" the Sea-Fox indignantly exclaimed. "Is this conduct worthy of an officer and gentleman?"

"Heh-heh-heh," sneered the captain. "You plundered Kingston, made off with every mango on the island, and stole the governor's niece. We've been on your trail ever since."

"Save yourselves!" the Sea-Fox shouted to the crew. "Into the jolly boats!"

The struggling Allegra was taken in hand by the constables and led to a cabin. The Sea-Fox was immediately clapped in irons.

"You'll swing for this," declared the gloating captain. "I'll see you dance on the gallows, you hardened criminal!"

When the First Lord of the Admiralty

learned Allegra's true identity as the governor's niece, he instantly pardoned and set her free. The Sea-Fox, never breathing a word of his noble parentage, languished in a cell until hauled into court to stand in the prisoners' dock.

"You have no possible defense, not the slightest mitigating circumstance that will save you from condemnation," declared the white-wigged, red-robed judge while the Sea-Fox maintained a dignified silence. "The jury" — he gestured at the grim faces in the box — "will hardly need to withdraw to determine a verdict." He reached for his black velvet cap, signifying a sentence of death.

"Milord!" a familiar voice rang out. "I submit overriding evidence!"

Allegra, now charmingly gowned, swept her way to the bar of justice.

"I have consulted with the directors of the Bank of England." A hush fell over the spectators at the mention of this sacred institution; Allegra held up a sheaf of papers.

"The figures are indisputable. The depredations of this gallant Sea-Fox have devastated the whole Spanish economy. Spain has become too impoverished to threaten anyone, least of all Great Britain."

"Commendable that may be," replied the judge, "but the Sea-Fox has also plundered English merchantmen."

"Yes, from time to time," admitted Allegra. "Not enough to matter. Without competition from Spain, Britannia rules the waves, and prosperity reigns throughout the British Isles.

"Until now, England faced financial ruin," Allegra went on. "No longer. The Sea-Fox has saved the British Empire from bankruptcy."

"Good heavens, I had no idea this was the state of affairs." The judge flung away his black cap and turned to the Sea-Fox. "This case, I am happy to declare, is dismissed. You are free to go, accompanied by the thanks of a grateful nation."

The spectators burst into cheers and threw their hats in the air. The jurymen streamed from the box to hoist Allegra and the Sea-Fox onto their shoulders and bear them from the courtroom.

"Brilliantly argued," remarked the Sea-Fox to Allegra. "You saved my life — but what if the judge had not accepted your defense? What if the case had gone to the jury and they chose to convict me?"

"I took that remote possibility into account," said Allegra, "and used my considerable influence as the governor's niece to guard against it. The Lord Chief Justice himself allowed me to pick the jury; and the jury — *this* jury would have never found you guilty."

The jurymen began pulling off false beards and mustaches, green spectacles, and cardboard noses, revealing themselves as Mr. Eustace, Dr. McKelvie, and others of the Sea-Fox's loyal crew, including Nora the parrot.

"Justice has prevailed," said the Sea-Fox.

"With a little help," said the Sea-Vixen.

The *Allegra* had gone into dry dock for repairs; the crew waited eagerly to set sail again as soon as the vessel was shipshape. One duty remained.

Once more in England, the Sea-Fox thought it only correct to present Allegra to his noble father. The happy couple rode to Aldine Manor in a golden coach and four, a gift from the grateful Board of Trade, and entered the baronial hall. Lord Aldine, surrounded by suits of armor and ancestral portraits, sat drinking a glass of vintage root beer.

"My dear father," said the Sea-Fox, "I have returned home."

"Gadzooks! So you have." Lord Aldine blinked. "Not drowned after all? Bit of a surprise, wot? Didn't you used to be a puny sort of blighter?"

"Allegra and I seek your blessing," said the Sea-Fox, "which we pray you will grant."

"Zounds! Nothing would please me more, haw, haw! Handsome pair you make, new branch on the old family tree —" Lord Aldine stopped and raised a hand. "Here, now, just a minute. I distinctly recall telling you never to set foot in this manor until you were fit to wrestle a bear."

The Sea-Fox bowed gracefully. "I stand ready to fulfill that condition."

Lord Aldine ordered a footman to lead in a huge bear from his private zoo. Allegra gasped at the sight of the gigantic animal, but the face of the Sea-Fox brightened.

"Bruno!" he cried. "How you've grown!"

The eyes of the bear also lit up, recognizing his old playmate. Since he was a cub, Bruno and the young Sea-Fox had romped over the meadows of the estate.

The Sea-Fox and the bear held out their arms to each other. Instead of wrestling, however, the two began dancing happily, whirling around the great hall.

"Good enough!" exclaimed Lord Aldine. "Right-o! I give you my blessings and welcome to them."

Allegra stepped to the side of the smiling bear.

"May I have the next waltz?" she said.

⊷⊷ ⊷⊷ ⊷⊷ Thuh End ⊷⊷ ⊷⊷ ⊷⊷

As for the "something" my sister warned lay in store for me, I was present when it was revealed.

My mother had taken me to my grandmother's boardinghouse for Mrs. Jossbegger's corn-cutting session. I fed Nora grapes; the ladies chatted as usual, though in a different, more earnest tone. I had gone totally invisible and was probably considered deaf as well. I heard Aunt

Rosie, paying no attention to whether I was there or not, say: "Of course, he can't be allowed to run the streets like a savitch. You see the mischief he got into. Bad company. Rotten apples."

"A childish prank," my mother said. "I wouldn't call Mrs. Deveraux's son a rotten apple; Mrs. Barnick's, either."

"With a knife in his boot?" Aunt Rosie countered.

"I don't want things to get out of hand," my mother admitted. "He's missed too much school already, and likely to miss more. Dr. McKelvie was very uncertain about that."

Aunt Rosie clicked her tongue. "He could turn out to be some kind of ignoramiss."

"Alan and I thought the vicar could help," my mother said. "He might suggest someone to give private lessons."

"A tooter?" said Aunt Rosie.

"Something like that," said my mother, and my grandmother nodded agreement. "Maybe Mr. Milliken, the Sunday-school teacher. He seems to be a pleasant sort of fellow. Or a university student in his spare time. I suppose, if we had to, we could put a classified advertisement in the paper."

Aunt Rosie snorted. "The public press?

You never know what you'll fish up."

My heart chilled as they went on calmly discussing my fate. One way or another, I was doomed to be removed from the back alley. A private teacher? One person, face-to-face, with a constant eye on me? Worse than Rittenhouse Academy, where I could hide unnoticed among my classmates.

Aunt Annie, silent until now, put down her cup. In a tone that made me think of the Almighty commanding Abraham to sacrifice young Isaac, she said:

"Give me the boy."

5

The Gawgon

"Why, Annie, that's a fine idea," my mother said. "It never occurred to me. If you feel up to it —"

"I've dealt with harder cases." Aunt Annie gave me a glance which included me in that category.

"I'll talk to Alan," my mother said. "We'll work out the details."

No one asked the Amazing Invisible Boy's opinion. I would have told them that if I was doomed to be educated, I preferred a total stranger, one I could shirk, dodge, and bamboozle. Aunt Annie saw me all too clearly. My animal instinct warned me that she was not to be bamboozled.

I expected the plan would go into immediate effect. But for the next several days, no one said anything more. I hoped it had been forgotten or, when consulted, my father had rejected it.

Meanwhile, I had no heart for the

charms of the back alley. Barnick and Deveraux had been banished to summer camp in the Poconos. Their punishment: to play baseball, swim in lakes, ride horses, and toast marshmallows.

I hoped Aunt Rosie, indignant about everything else, would come up with overpowering objections. She did not, though I heard her remark, later, to my mother:

"She was a hellion in her younger days, you know. Oh, I'll bet she can still be a real gawgon."

Whatever a hellion was did not sound promising. Gawgon — by that I understood Aunt Rosie meant "gorgon." I knew about gorgons, and Medusa, a horrible monster with snakes for hair, the sight of whom turned everybody to stone. The hero Perseus slew her, cleverly looking only at her reflection in his polished shield. This I gleaned from a book of Greek mythology The Gawgon herself had given me as a birthday gift. ("The Gawgon" was now my secret name for Aunt Annie. It had a ring more sinister than "gorgon.")

Desperate, I prayed the government would step in and save me when I heard my father say something about approval from the Board of Education. But it turned out The Gawgon had a certificate that made everything legal.

My mother outlined the schedule: classes on Monday, Wednesday, and Friday afternoons. Then, a special treat: Saturdays, I could sleep overnight at the boardinghouse.

That, in itself, was worth a few miserable hours with The Gawgon. I could visit Captain Jack, talk to Nora, explore the cellar, wind up the cuckoo clock, and eat pancakes on Sunday morning.

As I told my sister, I looked forward to the weekend holidays.

"You really are a stupid blighter," said my sister, who claimed to understand the twisted minds of adults. "It's a chance for Mother and Father to get you out of the house. Holiday? Yes. For them."

The Monday following, my mother deposited me at the boardinghouse. I had been outfitted with composition books, paper, pens, and pencils. Thus heavily armed, I cautiously made my way upstairs to The Gawgon's lair.

I ran into Dr. McKelvie coming down the hall. He clapped me on the shoulder, addressed me as "laddie-buck," and said he was glad to see me on the mend. I supposed he had been visiting Captain Jack, but the door was shut and Captain Jack was playing his gramophone.

I went on to The Gawgon's den. The room was crowded, but neatly crowded, with a rolltop desk and cluttered pigeon-holes, a dresser and oval mirror, bookcases, a narrow bed, an electric lamp on the night table. For a den, it was fairly sunny, with pale light from the window that overlooked the street. A card table had been unfolded, waiting. The Gawgon sat in a rocking chair. She motioned with her head.

"Doctors is all swabs," she remarked as I entered. Until now, I had never noticed her eyes were a bright, frosty blue. "Who said that?"

"Why — you did, Aunt." I had not expected such a comment or question. "Just now."

"No, no, boy. Who else? In a book I gave you at Christmas."

Things were not beginning well. I thought hard for a while. Something stirred; it came to me.

"Billy Bones? In *Treasure Island?*"

The Gawgon nodded. "Who wrote it? A Scotsman," she went on as I shrugged, having forgotten. "Robert Louis Stevenson. You should always remember authors' names. Out of courtesy; poor devils, they haven't much else to hang on to.

"He wrote it for a boy about your age," she added. "To amuse him. Did it amuse you?"

"Yes," I cautiously admitted, suspecting some kind of Gawgon-ish trap.

"Stevenson wrote a good many of his books in bed, did you know that? He was very sick. Oh, a lot sicker than you were. He went to live in Samoa, at the end. They called him *Tusitala* — 'storyteller.' When he died, they buried him in the mountains. He wrote this — it's on his gravestone:

Under the wide and starry sky,
Dig the grave and let me lie.
Glad did I live and gladly die,
   And I laid me down with a will.

This be the verse you grave for me:
Here he lies where he longed to be;
Home is the sailor, home from the sea,
And the hunter home from the hill.

The Gawgon had been looking beyond the window. She glanced back at me:

"Do you understand any of that?"

I had to confess I did not. (Also, at the edge of my mind a picture briefly took shape: Uncle Eustace scrambling up the

60

mountains of Samoa to sell Robert Louis Stevenson a tombstone.) I said I couldn't see why anybody would be glad to die.

"Nor should you." The Gawgon brushed away an invisible gnat. "Not yet. Not yet," she said as much to herself as to me. "Pay me no mind," she added. "It's McKelvie, that cheerful undertaker. He puts morbid notions into people's heads."

She gestured for me to sit at the card table. "Let's see your hand . . . No, boy, your hand*writing*." I had raised a palm. "Use a new pen point."

I took a fresh steel nib from my box. Before fitting it into the wooden penholder, I put it into my mouth to suck away the coating film of oil, common practice at school.

"Are you trying to skewer your tongue?" said The Gawgon, when I explained what I was doing. "Next time, burn the tip with a match. Now, copy down that poem as I read it out."

The glass inkwell — a pleasant surprise — held nothing but ink, unlike those set into the desks of Rittenhouse Academy, usually jammed with chewing gum, spitballs, dead flies, and unrecognizable foreign objects. I scratched away as The Gawgon dictated fairly rapidly. Finished, I handed over the sheet of paper.

"Almost legible. We'll work on that." The Gawgon leaned her head against the back of the rocking chair. "Enough for today."

Glad to get off so easily, I collected my things. I had started for the door when The Gawgon called me back. She took something from her lap.

"This is for you." She handed me a large hank of yarn as tangled as Dr. McKelvie's beard, knotted, twisted in such a confusing mess I could see neither the beginning nor the end of it.

"Take it home," The Gawgon said. "Untie the knots, unravel it — as much as you can. Bring it next time."

6

Percy-Us and The Gawgon

If all I had to do was scribble down a few lines of poetry and untie some knots, I reckoned The Gawgon and I might get along very well indeed. To forestall my parents finding someone who would actually make me work, I gave my mother an enthusiastic account of my lesson. When my father came home, I had to describe it to him all over again, including the tangled yarn.

"Chuh! Lawmigawd!" My father lapsed into a Jamaican accent whenever he found Philadelphia English not expressive enough. "Knots? When I was your age, I had to study Euclid."

Sitting in the living room after dinner, I overheard him say to my mother, "If you ask me, old Annie's gone 'round the bend."

"Oh, Alan" — my mother usually began her comments with "Oh, Alan" — "you shouldn't say things like that. Let her do what she wants, for now."

"But we're paying to have him educated," my father protested.

"I told you there's nothing to pay," my mother said. "I offered, she wouldn't hear of it. No matter how much I insisted. You know how she is when her mind's made up. Too bad. Dear soul, she certainly could have used a little money. She's poor as a church mouse."

Satisfied at the financial arrangement, which amounted to zero, my father went back to the stock-market pages of the newspaper, which he studied as intensely as Uncle Eustace studied the death notices.

Sprawled on my bed, I picked at the knots as The Gawgon ordered. My sister had been entertaining the Tulip Garden. When they disbanded, of course she had to come and poke her nose into my occupation.

"If you were a clever blighter, you'd just take a pair of scissors and cut them," she said, watching me struggle. "Like somebody, whoever it was." My sister was more devoted to her toenails than to classical antiquity.

"Alexander the Great and the Gordian knot," I said. "I read how he chopped it with a sword. I'm not supposed to do that."

My sister soon got bored and left me

with the tangled skein. At first, I thought it would be easy, but the knots were tight, the strands twisted every which way. I undid only a couple of them; then I, too, got bored and, grumbling about The Gawgon, tossed the whole thing aside.

Lacking anything better to do, I rummaged out the paint box and amused myself making colored pictures. The details about the hero Perseus were dim in my mind and as complicated as my knotted yarn. I found an easy solution: I ignored most of them.

PERCY-US AND THE
TULIP GARDEN

Percy-Us was sitting on a boulder, gloomily polishing his shield, when along came a young man wearing a cap with wings on it, and another pair of wings on the heels of his sandals. He carried a stick with a couple of snakes coiled around it, and still more wings at the tip.

"I am Hermes," he announced, "messenger of the gods."

Even Percy-Us, not the smartest hero in the world, recognized Hermes. Who else dressed like that? "You've got a message for me?"

"Not exactly," said Hermes. "I happened to be passing by. You look like you need cheering up."

"I do," said Percy-Us. "King Polly Deck-Tease is getting married. He's mean, murderous, with Vaseline in his hair. Who'd want to marry him? But that's beside the point. I'm invited to the feast. There's where the trouble comes in. I have to bring a wedding present."

"Napkin rings?" suggested Hermes. "A king always needs napkin rings. State banquets and such. Solid gold is very elegant. I can put in a word with King Midas. He's got plenty. In fact, everything he has is gold. He'll sell cheap."

"I already told the king what I'd give him. I promised" — Percy-Us looked all the more unhappy — "I promised him the head of The Gawgon."

"You what?" cried Hermes. "Fool! Why, for Zeus' sake, did you do a stupid thing like that?"

"I don't know what came over me."

Percy-Us sighed. "We were sitting around in the king's hall, his warriors bragging about the gifts they'd bring, all better than any I had. I couldn't stand it. I had to think of something really amazing.

"So, it just popped out," Percy-Us went on. "I swore in front of the king and everybody I'd give him The Gawgon's head. It seemed like a good idea at the time. I'd be a great hero —"

"The first thing about being a great hero," put in Hermes, "is knowing when to keep your mouth shut."

"Too late now," said Percy-Us. "If I fail" — he shuddered — "you can't imagine what he'll do to me."

"Yes, I can," said Hermes. "I don't envy you, my lad. All right. Here, take this sword." He produced a blade from his cloak and handed it to Percy-Us. "You'll need it."

"Call that a sword?" Percy-Us stared in dismay. "It's bent. It looks like a sickle."

"Of course it's bent," said Hermes. "It's a Gawgon-hooker. By the way," he added, "make sure you never look at The Gawgon. You'll turn to stone. Now listen carefully. You'll need a few more things I don't have with me."

Percy-Us only grew more downcast as Hermes explained what had to be done.

"Good-bye," said Hermes after he finished. "Oh — keep polishing that shield."

Following the directions Hermes gave him, Percy-Us set off. At the end of many days of trudging along twisting pathways, floundering across rivers, and clambering over craggy mountains, he came to a forest grove. There, as Hermes had foretold, he saw a circle of long-stemmed flowers: the sacred Tulip Garden.

It was guarded by beautiful nymphs. As soon as they caught sight of him, they began screaming, shrieking, throwing gravel, and making unfriendly gestures.

"Go away, silly blighter!" yelled Elysia, the head nymph.

"I only want to borrow some of your treasures," protested Percy-Us, "to help me cut off The Gawgon's head."

"We're busy. Can't you see we're painting our toenails?" retorted Elysia. "Get out of here."

"No," declared Percy-Us, despite the

nymphs all squealing enough to burst his eardrums. "Give me what I ask or I'll sit here until you do."

"I think he means it," said one of the nymphs as Percy-Us squatted down on a mossy hillock, folded his arms, and showed no sign of moving from the spot.

After a whispered conversation with her sister nymphs, Elysia came up to Percy-Us. She carried several objects.

"Here," she said, handing him a leather bag. "You can stuff The Gawgon's head in it. And here's a pair of sandals."

"I have sandals already."

"Not like these. Strap them on and you can fly through the air whenever you want.

"And this cap . . ." She held up a leather headpiece with long earflaps. "Wear it and you'll be totally invisible."

Percy-Us heartily thanked Elysia and the nymphs and promised to return the items once he finished with them.

"Never mind," said Elysia. "Just go away. Put on that cap. We don't want to see any more of you."

The Gawgon seemed a lot brighter than she was after Dr. McKelvie's visit. She had stacked up several books on my card table. When I came in, she was at the rolltop desk picking through some papers. She motioned for me to sit down.

"Show me what you've done with those knots," she said, without further ceremony, and took her place in the rocking chair.

Suddenly wishing I had worked harder at them, I held up the yarn. It looked, if anything, worse than when she gave it to me. The Gawgon snorted something like "Phrumph."

At Rittenhouse Academy, we spent each class period on a separate subject. As I would come to understand, The Gawgon's method — if method it was — mixed everything together, as much a hodgepodge as the knotted yarn. That afternoon, for no particular reason, she had me do arithmetic, which started her talking about Euclid, who invented geometry.

"Do you know geometry? The value of pi?" said The Gawgon. "If you don't, you should."

When I explained that was for Upper School, The Gawgon made another snorting noise. "What nonsense. Why lose time? I have none to waste. Nor do you, for that matter. You have a brain, don't you? You're the paragon of animals."

"The what?" My aforementioned brain, by then, was going in circles.

"William Shakespeare," she went on. "While we're at it, write this down:

"What a piece of work is a man! how noble in reason! how infinite in faculty! in form and moving how express and admirable! in action how like an angel! in apprehension how like a god! the beauty of the world! the paragon of animals! . . .

"As for that," she said, "Captain Jack might hold a different opinion.

"It's from a play called *Hamlet*," she added. "Bloody, violent, brutal" — she saw she had caught my attention — "so all the more reason to read it, would you say? Apart from being the best play ever written."

She glanced at the little round watch pinned to her black bodice, a signal for me to leave. "Time goes quickly. For me, if not for you."

"It does," I sincerely admitted. "Quicker than school. Really, Gawgon —"

The word was out of my mouth before I realized I had spoken it. No way could I get it back; it seemed to hang in the air, floating in huge capital letters tormentingly beyond reach.

The Gawgon stiffened in the rocking chair and raised an eyebrow. "What was it you said?"

I expected to be turned to stone even as I sat there. I mumbled, "Gawgon."

"I suppose you mean 'Gorgon.' Where did you lick that up?"

I stammered that I must have heard it somewhere from somebody.

"Rosie, no doubt. It sounds like her. That's how you think of me? Next, I daresay you'll want to cut off my head."

I had never hurt an adult's feelings, never, in fact, imagined it was possible that adults had feelings to be hurt. I did not know how to apologize or beg forgiveness. I hung my own head, wishing it had been cut off before I had made such a blunder.

From the corner of my eye I saw her shoulders trembling. I feared she had burst into tears, which would have been still more unbearable, and I was ready to do the same.

She was rocking with laughter.

"Gawgon?" she said, catching her breath. "That's a good reputation to have. Better a Gawgon than a silly old goose. I like it. I like it very much. From now on, that's what you shall call me."

She raised a finger. "But only in private between the two of us. We can enjoy our small secret."

I recovered enough to grin, and asked if I, too, could have a special name.

"Very well," said The Gawgon. "I shall call you — Boy. *The* Boy. With capital initials. The capitals make all the difference."

Happy with that, I got up to leave and started to hand back the yarn.

"Keep it," ordered The Gawgon. "You could stand to learn a little patience and perseverance. If you think those knots are hard, they're nothing compared with the kind you'll have when you're older. Those you'll be untangling for the rest of your life."

The Gawgon pointed to a bowl on the desk. "Take a gumdrop. I recommend the licorice."

7

Captain Jack

The Saturday of my promised overnight visit turned out to be more of a treat than I expected. Yet another aunt and uncle had stopped by the boardinghouse. I did not see them often; they were always very busy, but I adored them nonetheless.

Aunt Florry, my mother's younger sister, worked as a paid companion for a Mrs. Heberton, who owned a big estate on the Main Line. To measure up to the elegance of her surroundings, Aunt Florry had to spend a good bit of her salary on clothes, and we all admired her for being a nifty dresser. When I saw her that day, she looked fashionable indeed, trim and neat in a white linen suit, a Panama hat with a red feather in the band.

Nifty dresser though she was, I always thought of her as my dancing aunt. She especially loved the Charleston and tried to teach me the steps. I had difficulty knocking my knees together and wiggling my legs, and she finally gave up. Still, it was a delight to see Aunt Florry in motion.

Along with her came Uncle Will, my mother's youngest brother. He worked for the same Mrs. Heberton as chauffeur and gardener. To me, he was my handsome uncle. I had, on occasion, seen him in his stiff cap with a shiny visor, leather gaiters, and gray tunic, like a dashing cavalry officer. With his wavy black hair and ruddy cheeks, he was the idol of the family. Making him still more romantic, he had a secret sorrow.

"The way that woman treated him absolutely broke his heart," I once heard my grandmother remark to my mother. "I'm not one to go against the law — Prohibition and all that — but I make allowances. Do you wonder the poor boy takes a drop of something now and again?"

On that Saturday, Uncle Will wore civilian clothes, which took nothing away from his air of gallantry. From time to time, he would briefly vanish into the storage shed at the rear of the kitchen and reappear bright-eyed and high-spirited. When my grandmother and Aunt Florry finished making dinner, I took up a tray to Captain Jack's room. His gramophone was going full tilt, playing one of the opera arias he dearly loved, and he did not answer my knock. Obeying standing orders, I left his tray on the floor.

The Gawgon, by then, had come downstairs to the dining room. She gave me an almost imperceptible wink, our secret unspoken and delicious. The Gawgon, like all of us in the sunshine of Uncle Will's presence, was in a fine mood, even joined in a game of Parcheesi — and won.

At the end of the evening came the ceremonial winding of the cuckoo clock, and we trooped into the parlor. The cuckoo lived behind the door of a Swiss chalet carved all in curlicues. To keep the clockwork mechanism going, large iron pinecones hung at the ends of two long chains. It was my honor and privilege to pull them up.

Uncle Will cheered me on as if the pinecones weighed a ton apiece:

"Heave-ho, Skeezix!" he called out. "Hoist the topsail! Haul away, splice the main brace! Steady as she goes!"

Aunt Florry laughed; my grandmother told him, "Oh, Will, you are a caution."

When I finished — making the operation look as strenuous as possible — Uncle Will clapped me on the shoulder.

"Good work, Skeezix," he said. "That

should get us through another day."

We waited for the big hand to reach twelve. The door flew open, the cuckoo appeared before its admiring audience, cuckooed the time, then popped back into its cottage and the door snapped shut; all in all, a dramatic event.

Nora, not to be outdone by a mechanical bird, did cuckoo imitations and never let up until I draped a cloth over her cage.

The Gawgon retired. Uncle Will left soon after, saying something vague about an important engagement. The boarding-house was like an accordion, expanding and contracting according to the number of residents. Now, with lodgers occupying the other bedrooms, the accordion was stretched to its limit, so Aunt Florry doubled up with my grandmother. I was assigned to an old army cot, unfolded and set in a corner of the dining room. I lay full-length on the musty-smelling canvas sling. The cuckoo diligently announced the hours until I lost track of them and my thoughts turned to Percy-Us. I had originally planned to have him cut off The Gawgon's head. But I had grown too fond of The Gawgon herself to allow such a fate, so I relented and made some adjustments.

PERCY-US BRINGS THE GAWGON'S HEAD

Percy-Us put on the cap and sandals the nymphs of the Tulip Garden had given him. Next thing he knew, he was high in the air — a thrilling sensation, except he was flying upside down and backward. Kicking his heels and flapping his arms, it took him some time to get the knack of soaring through the clouds as if he were belly-flopping on a sled.

Since the cap made him invisible, flocks of birds kept bumping into him until he finally took it off.

Soon, Percy-Us saw the mountain range that Hermes had described and swooped down to land at the mouth of a cave, where The Gawgon sat in a rocking chair.

"I've been expecting you, Percy-Us," said The Gawgon. The serpents that covered her head instead of hair had been snoozing; but now they perked up, darted out forked tongues, and fixed him with beady eyes.

Percy-Us made sure not to gaze directly at The Gawgon. Following the advice of Hermes, he used his polished shield as a mirror.

"Speak up. I can't hear you," said The Gawgon. "Stop mumbling into that shield. When you talk to people, it's polite to look at them. Don't you know anything at all about being a hero?"

Percy-Us, too clever to be caught in such a trap, only tightened his grip on the sword. The Gawgon kept on calmly rocking.

"I assume you're here to cut my head off," The Gawgon said. "Very well, get on with it."

Holding up his shield, observing The Gawgon in its reflection, Percy-Us walked backward to her. When he was close enough, he swung his sword in a great, glittering sweep.

Percy-Us miscalculated. He had forgotten that everything reflected in a mirror was reversed. Instead of smiting The Gawgon, he nearly sliced off his own ear.

"Try again," The Gawgon suggested.

Percy-Us made another swipe with his sword, but eyes on the polished shield, he still got mixed up over which was left and which was right. He kept swinging at empty air until he was out of breath.

"This is getting tiresome," said The Gawgon, who kept on rocking while Percy-Us slashed around in all the wrong directions. "You'll do better if you can see what you're trying to chop off.

"Put down that shield and go straight about your business. Don't worry," she added, "you won't be turned to stone. I'll give you something to make you immune."

The Gawgon tossed Percy-Us a licorice gumdrop. "Here, eat this," she said as Percy-Us eyed it distrustfully. "Go on, it will protect you. Gawgons never lie."

Percy-Us chewed up the gumdrop and took a quick peek at The Gawgon. He was glad to find he had not turned to stone.

"That should make things easier," The Gawgon said. "But, before you start chopping, let me review the situation. You need a present for a wedding you don't want to go to, for a king you don't like to begin with. So you blurt out the first thing that comes into your head and promise something you know perfectly well you can't deliver.

"Furthermore" — The Gawgon sharply eyed Percy-Us, who shuffled his feet uncomfortably — "what you promised was at the expense of an innocent by-stander who never did you any harm. All for the sake of saving yourself embarrassment, making yourself a hero, and gaining the good opinion of that oaf Polly Deck-Tease. Am I correct so far?"

Percy-Us sheepishly admitted she was.

"That strikes me as utterly selfish," The Gawgon said, "with no regard for anyone's feelings but your own. Stupid, into the bargain. What do you say to that?"

Percy-Us stuttered and stammered and came up with no answer. He finally admitted The Gawgon was right.

"Good," said The Gawgon. "Now you're beginning to think straight even if you can't smite straight. Nevertheless, I recognize you've gone to some effort. That's commendable; I give you credit. So, I'll tell you what I'm going to do."

The Gawgon explained her plan, to which Percy-Us heartily agreed. Hand in hand with The Gawgon, he soared into the air, and the two of them flew quickly to the palace of King Polly Deck-Tease.

While The Gawgon waited outside the door, Percy-Us strode into the great hall. The bride had not yet arrived, but the impatient Polly Deck-Tease and his warriors had already started feasting and reveling, gobbling refreshments by the handful.

"Aha!" shouted Polly Deck-Tease. "There you are! About time. You brought me The Gawgon's head?"

"Yes," Percy-Us replied, "I certainly did."

"Let's have it, then," Polly Deck-Tease ordered. "So far, my only wedding presents are a lot of napkin rings."

Percy-Us tossed him the leather sack. Sucking his teeth in gleeful anticipation, Polly Deck-Tease opened it. His jaw dropped.

"Empty!" he burst out. "Nothing! What kind of joke is this? You broke your promise, you boasting, bragging, pathetic excuse for a hero! I don't like being disappointed, especially on my wedding day. You'll regret trifling with me. I'll have you diced up and deep-fried in boiling oil."

"I didn't break my promise," Percy-Us

replied. "I told you I'd bring The Gawgon's head. So I did."

Having put on the cap of invisibility, The Gawgon stepped into the hall.

"And all the rest of her, too," said Percy-Us.

The Gawgon took off the cap and glared at the revelers. Instantly, they turned to stone. Polly Deck-Tease, shaking a fist, stood literally petrified. Some of the warriors had stayed seated, others climbed to their feet, still others held goblets in upraised hands, motionless as marble statues.

"Nice garden ornaments," The Gawgon said. "Someday, no doubt, they'll be in the British Museum."

Percy-Us, delighted everything had ended so well, flew The Gawgon to her cave, thanked her, and was about to leave when he stopped and turned back.

"For a Gawgon," he said, "you're not a bad sort."

"For a hero," said The Gawgon, "you're not a bad sort either."

🌀 🌀 🌀 Thuh End 🌀 🌀 🌀

Sunday morning, Uncle Will had not come back; no one had heard anything from him. The rest of us ate the traditional Sunday pancakes. After stuffing myself, I carried a breakfast tray to Captain Jack's room.

His dinner, untouched, was on the floor where I had left it the night before. I feared his breakfast might suffer the same fate, but when I knocked, he called me in.

A nose-prickling haze of Turkish tobacco smoke hung in the air. The canvas window shade had been pulled down to the sill; sunlight filtered through it in a yellowish glow. A bare bulb, unlit, hung from the end of an electric cord in the middle of the ceiling. Captain Jack's bed was rumpled, the bolster and half the covers on the floor. The most prominent piece of furniture was his gramophone: a tall cabinet with a hinged lid, and on one side, a handle to crank the mechanism. Captain Jack himself, unshaven, still in his BVDs, sprawled in an armchair. He grinned at me and gave a loose kind of salute:

"First Sergeant. Report."

"Company all present and accounted for, sir." I straightened to attention, then marched forward to set the tray on his lap.

Captain Jack picked up the tin shaped

like a log cabin and watched the syrup pour out. It seemed to fascinate him.

"Been on the sick list, I hear," he said at last. "Returned to duty? Good. And that bloody bird strong as ever?"

I assured him Nora was fine.

Captain Jack grimaced. "She ought to be roasted for Christmas. She'll drive me 'round the bend with her bloody screeching."

I felt sorry Captain Jack hated Nora, but let it go. My grandmother always told me never to worry over anything Captain Jack said or did; he had his good days and bad. Now, though he had drenched his pancakes with syrup, he only picked at them.

I mentioned that Aunt Annie — I almost said "Gawgon" — was giving me lessons. I told him she recited something about man being the paragon of animals and that he might have a different opinion.

"Paragon?" Captain Jack said. "Not the ones I've seen. Not in the trenches. Only animals. Live like pigs, die like pigs. There's your paragon."

It sounded gruesome but interesting. I asked him to tell me more about the Great War.

"The war to end all wars?" Captain Jack said. "It's loud, it's dirty, and it stinks.

Horses scream worse than anybody when they're hit. Over and done with now. Just thank God you'll never have to go through anything like it."

Captain Jack was staring past me into the distance. I asked him if he wanted to play some records.

"Eh?" He focused on me again. He knew I loved to crank up the gramophone and open its wooden shutters, like venetian blinds, to make it louder. "Whatever you please, First Sergeant."

He enjoyed his operas, so I put the quartet from *Rigoletto* on the turntable, carefully lowering the arm with its steel needle onto the first groove. Captain Jack settled into his chair and shut his eyes. For variety, I put on a comic song we listened to occasionally, very bright and jolly. A man's voice came through the shutters; it sounded as if he were singing from the bottom of a bucket with a tinny brass accompaniment.

"*Keep your head down, Fritzie boy,*" he taunted, while the trombone brayed impudently:

Keep your head down, Fritzie boy.
Late last night in the pale moonlight,
I saw you, I saw you.

You were fixing your barbed wire
When we opened rapid fire.
If you want to see your father
In the Fatherland,
Keep your head down, Fritzie boy.

"Enough of that," Captain Jack snapped. "Not in the mood for it."

I hurried to lift the needle before the band started a second chorus.

"It's true, you know," he said, less harshly. "Moonlight — almost bright as day. You can see a man's face at a hundred yards."

He held out the tray. "Bloody song soured my stomach. Take this away. You're a good boy, First Sergeant. Dismissed."

I closed the door behind me. Captain Jack had put on *Tosca* and was singing along with the tenor. In the parlor, Nora was hanging upside down from the top of her cage and, as if taking revenge on Captain Jack for his remarks, screeching her head off.

8

The Gawgon and the Sphinx

"The nose of the Sphinx is missing," said The Gawgon. "Most of it. Blame that on the Emperor Napoleon — no, not yet emperor then. Only General Bonaparte."

"Bones-Apart," I said.

"Sometimes, Boy," said The Gawgon, "you can be very silly. Well, in any event, he let his troops use it for target practice. A pudgy little man, Napoleon, with that spit curl on his forehead and a hand in his jacket as if he had to scratch. Small, for an emperor."

The Gawgon had been following her custom of exploring odd byways, more exciting than my plodding classes at Rittenhouse Academy. That afternoon, she had started me on penmanship exercises to improve my deplorable handwriting.

"The trick is in the wrist," The Gawgon said. "You'll get the hang of it. Be glad you don't have to write in Egyptian hiero-glyphics."

That had set her off on a detour to ancient Egypt. The Sphinx and Napoleon wandered in, along with statuary and wall carvings.

"The old pharaohs built things to last," The Gawgon said. "Temples, pyramids — still standing, mostly. A little the worse for wear; impressive, nonetheless. I'll never forget the first time I saw them."

"You were there?" I never imagined The Gawgon being anywhere but in her room.

"Long ago. A couple and their young daughter were touring Egypt, Greece, Italy. They hired me as a governess." The Gawgon smiled. "Governess? I was hardly more than a girl myself."

I could believe The Gawgon was ancient enough to have seen the Pyramids under construction. But — a girl? Never.

"Oh, yes," The Gawgon said, as if reading my thoughts. "Does that surprise you?"

She went to a pigeonhole in the rolltop desk and sorted through a packet of papers. "There was another Philadelphian in that gaggle of tourists. A young fellow who thought himself quite the photographer."

The Gawgon handed me a fragile picture. "He took this of me on the pyramid of Cheops. I wanted to climb to the top, but everyone kept shouting at me to come down, afraid I'd break my neck. Scandalized, more likely. I had on riding breeches, shocking for a female."

I peered at the photo, wafer-thin and brittle. Yet the image was sharp. Perched on a block of stone halfway up the sloping wall, a beautiful, bright-eyed girl gazed straight at the camera, grinning all over her face. I did not recognize The Gawgon at first. I glanced at her. The girl's features showed faintly behind The Gawgon's, like the lines of a drawing badly erased.

"When the photograph was ready," The Gawgon continued, "he made a great show of presenting it to me in front of all the other tourists. 'For the intrepid lady explorer,' he said. 'As fair as she is fearless.' He was a cheeky rascal — but I was the one who got scolded. My employers said I'd been flirtatious." The Gawgon chuckled. "Perhaps they were right.

"I never did see inside the tombs. Most were empty, anyway, ransacked by grave robbers. A fellow named Howard Carter found the biggest treasure a few years ago. Marvelous things. He dug into the burial chamber of Tutankhamen, a boy king about your age. 'King Tut,' the newspapers called him."

We had gone well past our time. Instead

of my mother driving me, I was able to walk home by myself. So, I would have stayed longer, but looking wan, The Gawgon dismissed me.

"You've hardly touched those knots, Boy," she said.

Exactly when, I could not be sure, but it was during one of those summer afternoons that The Gawgon captured my total devotion and allegiance. Because she saw me for whatever I was. No longer the Amazing Invisible Boy, with her I had nothing to hide. She made me feel my mind was free to do as it pleased. A mystery of the heart? I could not solve it, nor did I care to.

In any case, I came to imagine her as mistress of time and space, expert in all disguises, who went wherever she chose, did whatever she chose, knew all that was to be known. To me, she was capable of everything and anything.

For the simple reason, no further explanation required, she was: The Gawgon.

THE GAWGON AND NAPOLEON BONES-APART

Unbeknownst to the Turkish overlords of Egypt, unsuspected by the authorities in Cairo, The Gawgon and I had set up headquarters underground between the paws of the Sphinx.

The Gawgon, convinced that most of this colossal statue lay beneath the desert sands, thought it would be interesting to explore what she suspected was a maze of chambers and galleries untouched for thousands of years.

We had hired a pair of expert grave robbers and highly competent ransackers to do the digging and heavy lifting; their loyalty and devotion were assured by generous cash payments from The Gawgon's unlimited financial resources. While Mustafa and Ali stood awaiting instructions, The Gawgon bent over a folding table and, by the glow of an oil lamp, sketched out a plan. For the occasion, she wore a French army officer's uniform and disguised herself as a young girl, her long red-gold hair tied with a tricolor ribbon.

"There is a logic in architecture, Boy, as in everything else," she said. "If a chamber is — here, logically a passage should be — here."

The Gawgon stopped. Her keen ears had detected noises aboveground. A moment later, I myself heard them: a series of crackling explosions like a string of firecrackers on the Fourth of July — although the Egyptians did not celebrate our glorious national holiday.

We cautiously made our way up to the desert floor. Some yards distant, a regiment of French infantrymen lounged about, tunics unbuttoned, cocked hats askew. Some were drinking from wine bottles or playing cards on drumheads; others were firing their muskets at the Sphinx. Half the nose had already been shot away; another volley sent chips of stone raining on our heads.

"Halt, you idiots!" cried The Gawgon. "*Cessez* and *désistez* immediately!"

Dumbfounded to see a beautiful young girl in military garb snapping orders at them, the soldiers gaped and lowered their muskets. The Gawgon strode up and began tongue-lashing them for being worse than their ancestors, the barbarian Gauls. The shame-faced troops hung their heads. An angry figure came stamping through the ranks.

"*Parbleu!* A thousand thunders! What is it that this is?"

The pudgy little man wore a blue jacket dripping with gold braid, epaulets thick as hairbrushes; in his cocked hat, a blue, white, and red rosette; plastered on his perspiring brow, a curl like an upside-down question mark. He thrust his jaw at The Gawgon, who calmly observed him.

"How dare you to overrule my authority, monsieur?" he cried. "But — but a thousand pardons, I mistake myself. It is a most fetching mademoiselle!" He reached out and tweaked The Gawgon's ear. "Who is it that you are?"

"This is Le Garçon — The Boy." The Gawgon, reclaiming her ear, indicated me. "And, General Bonaparte, I am: The Gawgon."

"La Gaugonne!" Napoleon caught his breath. "Le Garçon! I have heard of your astonishing capabilities. Your fame precedes you. Do me the honor of joining me for a glass of champagne in my tent."

"We aren't thirsty," said The Gawgon. "The Boy and I have other things to do. As for yourself, General, allowing your troops to vandalize the treasures of antiquity, you should be ashamed."

"*Moi?* What will you of me?" Napoleon shrugged his shoulders and spread his hands in that exasperating gesture the French have so perfected. "It is but an old and badly damaged Sphinx. The Turks, the Arabs, all the world shoots at it. How else to pass the time in this abominable desert?" He stopped to insert a hand between the buttons of his waistcoat. "*Pardonnez*. Ah, these accursed sand fleas! They attack me in battalions without mercy. And, as well, my digestion suffers in this heat.

"Mademoiselle, we do not vandalize" — he scratched awhile longer — "we preserve. Accompany yourself with me. I shall demonstrate."

We followed Napoleon to the rear of the encampment. He pulled away a canvas cover and proudly pointed at a heap of objects: statuettes, golden bowls, elaborately painted jars, a mummy case with a reclining figure carved on the lid.

"*Voilà!*" he declared. "I am rescuing

these from the unworthy hands of the enemy. They will be safely transported, now that I have captured Egypt for La Belle France."

"Captured?" retorted The Gawgon. "Who captured who? Let me say two words: Royal Navy."

Napoleon's face went pale as Cammembert cheese. The Gawgon pressed on:

"At Abukir Bay, the British fleet devastated you. Even now, you are blockaded, bottled up, your Egyptian campaign a disaster."

"A small setback," protested Napoleon. "It shall be rectified."

"I doubt that," said The Gawgon. "Your government feared you were getting too big for your breeches — so to speak. They secretly wished to see you defeated, your reputation ruined. They sent you to Egypt, certain you would fail miserably. As indeed you have done."

"Those swine! Those cows!" burst out Napoleon. "I shall foil their treacherous plot and revenge myself on them. I remain in Egypt until victory."

"That could be a long time," said The Gawgon. "Meanwhile — I do not repeat gossip and tittle-tattle, but there has been talk of the beautiful Madame Bonaparte and certain handsome young officers."

"Joséphine! *Diable!*" Napoleon's cheeks went plum-colored. "No sooner do I turn my back than she cavorts herself!"

He shouted for his adjutant, gave him command of the army, and ordered him to make the best of a bad situation. "I depart to Paris immediately!"

"You can't escape, General," I warned. "The British blockade —"

"A fig for perfidious Albion! A nation of shopkeepers! I must keep the eye on that charming but naughty Joséphine. I shall hire a sardine boat, a felucca, a raft if necessary."

An orderly led up a prancing white horse. Without another word, Napoleon leaped astride and galloped off in a whirlwind of sand.

The regiment hurriedly broke camp, tossing away knapsacks, blanket rolls, and other gear that would slow their hasty withdrawal. Even the pile of looted treasure was abandoned.

As Mustafa and Ali joined us, The Gawgon went to examine the objects. "If I read the hieroglyphics correctly, this sarcophagus holds the remains of young King Tut."

"Where did it come from?" I asked. "We have to hide it safely. These other things, too. We can't just leave them lying around in the desert."

The Gawgon turned to Mustafa and Ali. "Take it to the Valley of the Kings. Find an empty tomb and haul everything into it. After that, wall it up so no one will suspect the chamber exists."

She fixed an eye on our attendant grave robbers. "Listen, you two. If you breathe a word of this, if you so much as think about sneaking back and rifling the tomb, I promise I'll hound you into your graves and make mummies of you."

The Gawgon's threat, accompanied by handfuls of gold coins, so deeply touched the hearts of Mustafa and Ali that they salaamed, groveled, and swore every oath to seal their lips for eternity.

"Nothing like terror and bribery to encourage good moral conduct," The Gawgon remarked as we set about loading King Tut and his trove onto our camels. "I'm confident those bazaar ruffians will keep their mouths shut. I'm also confident some reasonably intelligent person will, in time, find these treasures and treat them with proper respect."

The Gawgon smiled at the Sphinx looming in front of us. "There's someone, at least, who'll never tell our secret."

The Sphinx smiled back at her.

9

The Gawgon Walks Abroad

In late summer, Mr. Digby, one of my father's Jamaican chums, stopped off during a business trip. Looking very tropical in a cream-colored suit, a planter's straw hat, and a bristly mustache, he was installed with great excitement in our spare room. To make a grand occasion, my mother cooked a dinner featuring rice and peas, mangoes, fried plantains, and other delicacies.

Aunt Marta and Uncle Eustace were, of course, invited. He, my father, and Mr. Digby had not seen each other for some while. Suddenly they were all boys again, laughing like mad, drifting into Jamaican dialect, calling each other by their old nicknames: "Mackerel Fat" for Uncle Eustace, "Dog Flea" for my father, and, for Mr. Digby, "Diggers."

After dinner, Diggers brought down a glass jar from his suitcase. The object of his trip, he explained, was to recruit salesmen for a miraculous new product.

"Palm-Nutto," Diggers declared. "It cleans. It scrubs. Anything, everything. Carpets, pots and pans — you can do the laundry or wash your face with it." At this, he unscrewed the jar and fingered out a dollop of yellowish paste.

"Completely harmless," he said, gulping down the Palm-Nutto. "Good for the bowels, too."

My father and Uncle Eustace declined this chance at a fortune. Palm-Nutto did not fit in with Oriental goods or tombstones, and Diggers dropped the subject.

My mother proposed driving to Atlantic City next day. Uncle Eustace had an appointment with a grieving widow, but the rest of us thought it was a wonderful idea.

Then I realized next day was my Friday lesson. On the one hand, I loved the seashore, amusement piers, splashing in the surf, and an opportunity to pee in the Atlantic Ocean. Irresistible charms. On the other hand, The Gawgon had taken me to Moscow, Napoleon's disastrous retreat through howling Russian blizzards, and left me deliciously agonized in suspense when he was exiled to a rocky island. I knew, from school, that he was defeated at the Battle of Waterloo. But The Gawgon had some magical way of turning mind-numbing history into new adventures, equally irresistible.

When I explained my difficulty to my mother, she simply said the choice was mine. My sister, surprisingly, came out in favor of Atlantic City. And that was what tipped the balance.

"Give Aunt Annie a rest," she said. "She's had to put up with you all week. She'll be glad to get rid of you for a day."

"She won't be glad," I flung back angrily. "She won't be glad at all. Neither will I."

I decided to stay with The Gawgon.

THE GAWGON AND
MAMMA LETIZIA

We were relaxing on the terrace of The Gawgon's villa on the Riviera. For the time being, she had assumed the guise of an older lady of quality, certainly very rich. We had spent the evening in Monte Carlo, whose elegance and sophistication were matched only by Atlantic City's. In the glittering casino, The Gawgon and I had won so much at roulette that the tearful manager implored us to leave before we broke the bank, and we graciously complied.

One of the servants came to announce a caller who declined to reveal her name. The Gawgon, always curious about unidentified visitors, agreed to receive her. Moments later there arrived a massively stout, elderly woman with swollen ankles and a gold tooth. In voluminous, shiny black skirts, a black shawl over her head, she dropped with difficulty to her knees and begged The Gawgon's help.

"My boy, *mon enfant!*" she wailed in a heavy Corsican accent, more Italian than French. "His enemies have put him on an island. Exiled, forbidden to leave —"

"I take it," broke in The Gawgon, "you are Madame Bonaparte, mother of the ex-emperor."

"Please, call me Mamma Letizia," said Madame Bonaparte. "My Napoleone — I warned him he one day would go too far. Yes, a naughty boy, fighting wars with everybody. But always kind and loving to his mamma. Now his little heart breaks with unhappiness. He will surely die of boredom and misery."

The Gawgon agreed to do all she

could, and Mamma Letizia left after showering her with blessings.

"In principle, I'm not fond of emperors," said The Gawgon. "Troublemakers, most of them. Worse than spoiled brats. Napoleon? I haven't decided if he was a good emperor who did some bad things, or a bad emperor who did some good things. But, compared with Louis the Eighteenth, that nincompoop who took his throne, Napoleon looks better and better."

The Gawgon quickly dispatched a number of secret messages and made other preparations. Within a matter of days, we were aboard a fishing boat in the Mediterranean, sailing past the tip of Corsica to the tiny isle of Elba.

In the first light of dawn, we made out a figure with a telescope observing us from the shore. The Gawgon instructed the helmsman to make for a sheltered cove. Moments later, we tied up at a rickety pier. Napoleon clambered aboard, and we cast off for the open sea.

Wrapped in a threadbare greatcoat, a sailor's knitted cap on his head, Napoleon did not immediately recognize The Gawgon, who wore a sea cloak and had pasted on a false beard and mustache. When he realized her identity, he was pathetically grateful:

"Ah, La Gaugonne! Angel of mercy to extract me from this shabby, third-rate island! It has been insupportable, *morbleu!*"

"Ordinarily," said The Gawgon, "I prefer to let the high and mighty get themselves out of their own messes. I'm only doing this for your mamma's sake."

"My beloved mamma!" Napoleon clasped his hands. "To see her son brought so low! *Non, non,* that is not just. A thousand devils and *zut, alors!* Why did I sell the Louisiana so cheap? I could have gone there and built a new empire of the Western Hemisphere."

I suggested he might yet reach New Orleans, an easygoing town that asked no questions. He could surely find a job of some sort.

"*Moi?* Do you see me as, what, a sauce maker? A pastry cook?" Napoleon thrust his fingers into his vest. "Impossible! Being emperor spoils one for any other trade."

That instant, cutting through the sea mist, a British warship sped toward us.

We were hailed, commanded to heave to, and encouraging us to obey, a cannon blasted a warning shot across our bow.

The Gawgon drew Napoleon aside, whispered quickly, then ordered him and the crew amidships to start cleaning tubs of fish. The captain's longboat, meantime, had come alongside; the captain and half a dozen sailors climbed a rope ladder to our deck.

"Jolly good of you to stop without making us blow you out of the water, haw, haw!" declared the officer. "Got wind of a bit of a plot to spirit away Bony-Party. Deuced inconvenient, sorry, but I'm to search all vessels hereabouts."

"Search away. We have no emperors aboard." The Gawgon's answer was hairsplitting although technically true, since Napoleon had been deposed. "Only a cargo of fish, as you see."

"And smell, too, by Jove!" The captain pulled a scented lace handkerchief from his sleeve and waved it under his nose. He glanced sharply at the crew busily gutting fish, and stepped closer. "Fine lot of villainous rascals, wot? This one especially. You there, let's have a look at you."

It was all The Gawgon and I could do to keep silent as the captain went on:

"Well, you're as scurvy and scrofulous a fellow as I've ever seen. No emperor, that's for sure. Unless you're the emperor of sardines and anchovies, haw, haw!"

The captain added other scornful comments, then gaped as the object of this bullyragging leaped to his feet and began shouting insults in return. The knitted cap fell off the man's head, revealing an unmistakable lovelock on his brow.

"Egad! Good heavens, 'pon my word — Bony himself!" The captain immediately ordered his men to seize the fishgutter, who roared and cursed furiously. While the sailors shackled their raging captive, the officer strode to The Gawgon, accused her of being part of the conspiracy and threatened to clap her in irons.

"Why blame me?" The Gawgon innocently replied. "I use whatever crew I can hire, no telling who they are. You know how difficult it is to get help these days."

"All too true." The captain sighed. "Can't even find a decent butler. What terrible times we live in! Well, then, sail on about your business. Pip-pip, cheerio."

When the warship was out of sight, The Gawgon whistled through her teeth. From his hiding place in the hold, soaking wet and reeking of fish, climbed Napoleon.

"An impostor to take my place! A ruse worthy of myself!" he cried. "Those fools will ship him back to Elba before they realize he is not me!"

"Thank your mamma," said The Gawgon. "I asked her to find someone to pass for you. In case of emergency, it's always good to have a spare emperor."

"A perfect resemblance," I said to The Gawgon as Napoleon strutted up and down the deck, "but I was worried when he started yelling at the captain. He wasn't speaking French, he was speaking Italian."

"The British can't tell the difference," The Gawgon said. "If it isn't English, it's all Greek to them."

The Mediterranean turned choppy; a contrary wind kept us from making rapid headway. But, at last, we sighted the French coast and climbed into the boat's dinghy. The Gawgon and I rowed for shore while Napoleon stood in the bow congratulating himself and scoffing at the English for being such dupes. Too impatient for us to beach our little craft, he jumped out and went sloshing through the surf.

"I march to Paris *immédiatement,*" declared Napoleon. "My veteran troops, my loyal and adoring people of France will join me along the way. My empire will rise again. *C'est magnifique!*

"I shall put up statues of you both," Napoleon added, "and name our grandest thoroughfares 'Avenue de la Gaugonne' and 'Boulevard du Garçon.'"

"Don't bother," said The Gawgon. "You'll have enough on your mind."

"Do you know a town called Waterloo?" I put in.

"Of course. In Belgium." Napoleon shrugged. "A mere nothing of a place."

"Yes, well," I said, "don't go there."

☻ ☻ ☻ Thuh End ☻ ☻ ☻

"I hear you gave up a trip to the sea-shore," The Gawgon said, next morning. "That surprises me."

My mother had dropped me off at the

boardinghouse. Since everyone would be home late, I was to sleep over. I told The Gawgon I didn't want to go to Atlantic City and would rather stay with her.

"I take that as a high compliment," The Gawgon said. "Yes, Boy, I'm very touched.

"But fair is fair," she added, after a few moments. "You gave up one holiday. You'll have another."

The Gawgon got to her feet. "Lessons can wait. Come along, Boy. We're taking a ride."

When I understood what she meant, I still could hardly believe it.

The Gawgon was going out of the house.

ht*10*

In the Pale Moonlight

"Annie, do you think it's wise? Do you really think it's sensible?"

My grandmother and The Gawgon were talking quietly in the downstairs hall. A closet had produced a wide-brimmed straw hat and a pair of white gloves long unused, smelling of lavender. The Gawgon skewered the hat to her bun of white hair with the longest hat pin I had ever seen and examined the effect in a mirror. Had she been my sister, I would have called it primping.

"Mary, can you tell me," The Gawgon said, "have I ever been wise? Have I ever been sensible?"

"Dr. McKelvie —" my grandmother began.

"Pshaw!" The Gawgon made a final adjustment. "What does he know? The boy's given me a new lease on life, which is more than that pill-roller's done."

My grandmother watched us from the

111

parlor window as we crossed the porch and The Gawgon picked her way down the front steps. She had armed herself with a cane from the umbrella stand; an ordinary walking stick, but it would not have surprised me to see her unscrew the handle and snatch out a sword blade.

For the promised ride, I believed The Gawgon capable of summoning a coach and four, maybe a chariot. What she had in mind was: a bus.

We waited on the corner. Double-decker buses ran on Larchmont Street. I loved the upper deck, with the wind whistling, the bus lurching as if about to capsize. When it arrived, I expected her to prefer sitting below, but gripping her cane, The Gawgon climbed the narrow spiral stairway to the heights.

"Excelsior!" cried The Gawgon as we settled ourselves on a wooden bench. "That means 'higher' in Latin."

Ignoring the raised eyebrows of our fellow passengers, she began declaiming:

The shades of night were falling fast,
As through an Alpine village pass'd
A youth, who bore, 'mid snow and ice,
A banner, with the strange device —
Excelsior!

"It goes on and on," said The Gawgon. "I've forgotten most of it, which I count as a blessing. I'm sure it had deep meaning for Henry Wadsworth Longfellow; he was always partial to deep meanings. I happen to think it's one of the silliest poems in the English language."

The poem "Excelsior," The Gawgon explained, told of a youth with sad brow and flashing eyes hauling a big flag up the Alps. Everyone warned him against avalanches and raging torrents. A village maiden urged him to stay and rest his head on her breast.

"But no," said The Gawgon, "he kept climbing, holding up his flag, and shouting 'Excelsior!' at every whipstitch. A Saint Bernard found him frozen to death. Now, it's all very commendable trying to reach the heights of anything. But only an idiot would go mountaineering with a flapping big piece of cloth. Nonsense! The fool ended up dead, no use to anyone including himself."

We climbed off the bus at Fifty-second Street and plunged into a delicious stew of pretzel carts, hot-dog stands, cigar stores, crowded sidewalks, and not one but two movie houses. Aunt Rosie complained it was a loud, impolite street with a lot of

113

suspicious riffraff. I thought it was the most exciting place in the world. I was delighted that The Gawgon chose to take me there.

"Off we go to seek our fortune," declared The Gawgon. "To El Dorado, realm of gold."

I had no idea what she meant, which only made it more mysterious, and, of course, I would have followed her anywhere. It took The Gawgon a short while to find a shop just off Fifty-second Street. The only things close to gold were three brass balls hanging over the door.

Before we entered, she swore me to secrecy:

"I could have asked your father to sell my little trinket in his store, but he'd have fussed at me and bought it himself — charitably. This is nobody's business but mine. So, not a word to anyone."

I solemnly swore and we went inside. The Gawgon held up her skirts to keep them off the sticky floor. The place smelled like old mushrooms. Yet it was a kind of El Dorado, jam-packed with guitars, banjos, fiddles, racks of clothing, bins of household goods. The showcase displayed watches, jewelry, and a number of military medals.

From her purse, The Gawgon took a small brooch and motioned me to move back. She stepped up to a heavy-jowled, flinty-eyed man who did not look friendly. Without knowing why, I felt embarrassed for her, and for myself, a little queasy. Their conversation was some sort of business between adults, and I should not be listening. The Gawgon, undaunted, rapped her knuckles on the countertop:

"My dear sir, I'll thank you not to take me for a fool," she said. "The gold alone is worth more than that."

The man grumbled, but under The Gawgon's unwavering eyes, he finally shrugged and took some dollar bills from his cash drawer. The Gawgon handed over the brooch, accepted a receipt, and we left.

"That, Boy, is a pawnshop," The Gawgon said as we headed back to Fifty-second Street. "Not a nice kind of place, but sooner or later, you'll find there's a seamy side of life. It's where poor people borrow money and leave something behind. When they come to repay, they get their property again. Otherwise, the pawnbroker sells it. I don't intend coming back.

"What I do intend," she added, "is spending it all like a drunken sailor."

Of everything I could imagine The

Gawgon being, drunken sailor was not one. As for spending, she indeed led us on a daylong spree.

First, we went to the fancier of the two picture palaces. It featured a vaudeville show: a magician, a dancing dog, and spangled ladies kicking up their legs to the boops and yawps of the Wurlitzer organ. I made little sense of the movie that followed: mostly men in tuxedos and women in slippery gowns gazing at each other through drooping eyelids. Nobody got killed or maimed.

"I'd forgotten they talk now," The Gawgon said behind her hand. "More's the pity. There's too much yammering already."

Still, that would have been treat enough in itself. But The Gawgon had more in mind. After the movie, she found a combination bookstore and stationery store. There, she bought some books — their titles were unfamiliar to me, but she assured me I would like them and we would read them together later. As well, she bought a deck of cards with letters instead of jacks, queens, and kings.

"Anagrams," The Gawgon said. "You deal them out and try to make words."

The spending spree ended when we went

to a hot-dog and orange-juice stand. The Gawgon drew some attention from the other customers. Seeing her straw hat with its huge pin, her long black skirts, white gloves, and cane, they probably expected more genteel behavior, but The Gawgon chomped her hot dog with carefree abandon.

"McKelvie should see me now." The Gawgon had a mischievous glint in her eyes. "Pass the relish, Boy, if you please."

We rode the bus back to Larchmont Street, belching triumphantly in the gathering dusk.

My grandmother was as relieved to see us as if we had been on a perilous expedition up the Alps or down the Amazon. The Gawgon went to her room for a nap. I was too excited to rest. True to my word, I said nothing of the pawnshop, yet alone with my grandmother, I wanted to ask about something that lingered, troublesome, in my head.

I had the impression Dr. McKelvie would not have approved of our outing. I was curious to know why. But I did not ask. The young did not question the mysterious lives of their elders. Instead, that night, I stretched out on my cot and drifted away to Switzerland.

THE HEIGHTS OF
THE MATTERHORN

The shades of night were falling fast when The Gawgon and I reached a little village high in the Alps. Lamps already glowed cozily; the villagers were snug indoors. The Gawgon, brushing ice pellets from her cloak, stepped through the door of the local inn. I followed, carrying the long staff and its huge banner embroidered with a single word in fancy curlicues: EXCELSIOR.

During our ascent through mountain mist and drizzle, the banner had grown so damp and heavy we were obliged to take turns carrying it. The Gawgon, outfitted like myself in leather breeches and hobnailed boots, coils of rope at our shoulders, ice axes at our belts, called for hot cider. I looked around for some place to park the cumbersome burden and finally leaned it against the serving counter, where it dripped a large puddle of ice water.

"Mein Gott!" The innkeeper paled when The Gawgon told him our destination. "The peak of the Matterhorn?

This time of year? Not possible!"

"Possible or not," The Gawgon declared, "The Boy and I have an urgent mission. We must accomplish it at all cost."

As the innkeeper warned against this foolhardy venture, mentioning avalanches, raging torrents, and gaping chasms, his beautiful daughter approached me.

"O youth with flashing eyes," she said winsomely, "what signifies this banner and its strange device? An advertisement for some new product? Breakfast cereal, perhaps, like Swiss muesli?"

At a loss to offer satisfactory explanation, I could only say our task was of utmost importance.

"Ach, nein!" The maiden clasped her hands. "Do not to your doom go! With me here stay and rest." She batted her eyelashes and cast me a sidelong glance. "I will let you my cuckoo clock wind up."

Though tempted, I politely declined. The Gawgon finished her cider and we set off again, climbing ever upward through the night. The peak glinted icily in the pale moonlight, bone-chilling gales swept from the heights. Barely halfway up the slope, The Gawgon halted. Before us yawned a deep crevasse.

"We can't climb down one side and up the other." The Gawgon, chin in hand, made mental calculations. "A little too wide to jump across. Very well, Boy, furl that silly flag. Give it here."

I did as she asked. The Gawgon took the flagstaff and, with perfect precision, tipped it lengthwise across the chasm, where it lay like a bridge — but a bridge no wider than a tightrope.

"No, we won't dance across like acrobats," she said, when I asked if that was her intention. "More like a couple of monkeys."

As she ordered, we flung away our rucksacks and other gear to lighten our weight. The Gawgon then leaped into the crevasse, deftly caught hold of the flagstaff, and hand over hand, swung along its length and heaved herself up on the far edge.

I tried to do likewise, but a frosty film already covered the staff. One hand slipped. I hung, dangling and kicking, until I regained my grasp then swung my way across, never daring to look down until The Gawgon pulled me safely to my feet.

Retrieving the flag, I clambered after The Gawgon, ever higher. Despite the bitter cold, I was drenched with sweat, which quickly froze. I crackled with ice inside and outside my clothing. All that night, we pressed upward. One last assault and we would gain the pinnacle.

Our perils had not ended. Deep rumblings shook the mountainside. Snow-drifts as big as Swiss chalets careened downward. We scurried out of their path as they roared by. But no sooner did we think ourselves safe than a giant snowball hurtled straight at The Gawgon.

She had no time to dodge as it bounced down the slope. Without a moment's thought, summoning all my strength, I flung the flagstaff like a spear.

The tip of the staff struck the sphere on its upward bounce. The impact jarred the titanic snowball off its deadly course, and it landed harmlessly a few feet away. With the flagstaff sticking out of it, it looked like a huge vanilla lollipop.

"Well, Boy, I do believe you saved my life," said The Gawgon as I pulled the staff loose. "I appreciate that. Hurry along now. One avalanche is enough."

Just before daybreak, we made our final ascent. Stars filled the sky, but they began winking out as pink streaks rose above the Alpine range.

A figure stood at the top of the Matterhorn. Wrapped in an overcoat, its collar turned up to his ears, he stamped his feet and beat his arms against his sides. His bushy white beard had frozen stiff. Despite the muffler around his neck and the hat jammed down tight on his head, I recognized him from a portrait I had seen in one of The Gawgon's books.

It was Henry Wadsworth Longfellow.

"What took you so long?" he called out in a peevish voice. He pointed his frozen beard accusingly at us. "I've been waiting all night; I could have caught my death of cold."

"Don't take that tone with me, Henry," retorted The Gawgon. "You asked me to do you a favor, and I did. Here's your flag. Good-bye. The Boy and I are going home."

Without so much as a word of thanks, Longfellow impatiently unfurled the banner. One hand behind his back, the other clutching the staff, he cast his eyes heavenward, lost in solemn contemplation of the vast panorama.

The Gawgon motioned for me to begin the downward climb. I hung back.

"As long as we're here," I said to her, "I want to ask him: Really, what does all this mean? I don't understand the point of it."

"Let him alone," said The Gawgon. "Poets don't like to be questioned, especially when they don't know the answers."

✵ ✵ ✵ Thuh End ✵ ✵ ✵

Something woke me. I must have been tossing and turning on the cot, the sheets were tangled around my legs. Moonlight shone through the parlor windows. With a cloth draping her cage, Nora slept peacefully. I heard a soft shuffling; a floorboard creaked in the upstairs hall.

I got up and went cautiously out of the dining room. The flight of stairs led directly into the parlor. It was bright enough for me to see a white shape on the landing. It halted for a few seconds, then floated down the steps.

It was Captain Jack in his underwear.

My grandmother had warned me never to wake him up when he was having one of his spells, so I stood there holding my breath. I hoped he would turn around and go back upstairs.

Captain Jack moved steadily through the parlor, heading straight for Nora's cage. Frozen to the spot, I could do nothing to stop him. He took another pace and lurched against the stand. It toppled over; the cage crashed to the floor.

11

Toys in the Cellar

Nora beat her wings against the bars of the overturned cage. Her water cup spilled, her sunflower seeds scattered over the rug. She screamed at the top of her voice. Captain Jack began screaming, too. Upstairs, someone switched on the parlor lights. My grandmother and The Gawgon, in their summer nightgowns, came down the steps. I could only think of setting the cage upright and covering it with the cloth. It did not quiet her.

Captain Jack crouched on the floor amid the sunflower seeds, knees tucked under his chin, hands pressed against his ears. He was howling like a wolf. My grandmother, in tears, circled around him, begging him to be calm. She seemed afraid to go any closer.

The Gawgon moved quickly. White hair unbraided and hanging every which way, she went straight to him, knelt, and held him in his arms.

"Call McKelvie," she said sharply to my grandmother, and to me, "Go stay in the kitchen."

I obeyed, partially. I stopped in the middle of the dining room. Despite myself, I could not turn my eyes away. The Gawgon was stroking Captain Jack's head and rocking him back and forth.

It was dawn by the time Dr. McKelvie came, tousled, coat unbuttoned, without a cravat. Still in The Gawgon's arms, Captain Jack had stopped screaming and was merely sobbing. Dr. McKelvie opened his bag; I glimpsed a hypodermic needle in his hand.

"That's all I can do," he said to my grandmother. "I'll call the ambulance."

I ventured to the edge of the parlor. My grandmother went upstairs to fetch a bathrobe for Captain Jack. He was quiet now, but in spite of the injection, his eyes were wide open, the whites showing all around. When he happened to turn his head in my direction, he stared as if he had never seen me in all his life. I kept hoping he would at least recognize me; it had not been long ago when we listened to opera arias, when he called me "First Sergeant" and poured pancake syrup from a tin log cabin.

The men from the ambulance apologized, they were sorry to buckle him into a canvas straitjacket, but it was for his own good. Captain Jack did not struggle when they led him out of the house. He was well behaved and looked tired. In the street, he glanced around, squinting in the sunlight. The ambulance took him away

Later, my grandmother went through the motions of fixing breakfast. None of us wanted any. We sat at the table for a while. I understood that Nora's squawking had set him off, but as I said apart to The Gawgon, I didn't see why Captain Jack got so upset. Nora, after all, was only a bird.

"She made him think of the war," The Gawgon said.

But that, I said, was over long ago.

"Not for Jack," The Gawgon answered. "He never talked about it to us. But his sister knew. She told us when she brought him to live here. She had to work all day, you see, so your grandmother promised to look after him. Something had happened that he never got out of his head."

I asked what it was.

The Gawgon did not answer right away. Then she said, "He was fond of you, and I know you were fond of him. Try to under-stand this. He shot his friend —

"No, it wasn't murder," The Gawgon quickly added, seeing the look on my face. "They were ordered out on a night patrol. A stupid order, no point in it. No doubt some general was bored and wanted to stir things up. The trenches were so close, the Germans saw them in the moonlight and opened fire.

"Jack was badly wounded; his friend, worse. The rest of the patrol were dead. His friend kept screaming for Jack to shoot him, he couldn't stand the pain. Jack wouldn't do it. As his sister told us, they lay there a long time, with Jack's friend crying and begging to be put out of his misery.

"Jack hoped his friend would die soon, but he didn't. At the end, Jack shot him in the head with his revolver.

"When it was daylight, the Germans waved a flag of truce and let the Americans carry back the bodies. They all stayed in their own trenches after that. Jack was taken to a field hospital, and they sent him home."

I never thought of Captain Jack having relatives, but next weekend, I was at my grandmother's house when a plain-looking woman in a summer frock came to collect his belongings. She was his sister; my grandmother talked with her out of my earshot. Then a man came with a horse and cart to haul out the gramophone and records. The empty room still smelled of Turkish tobacco. The canvas window shades had been rolled up. I did not go in.

There was nothing else beyond some bundles of clothes and a few cardboard boxes in the cellar. I helped carry them up.

"I don't think he'll need any of this," my grandmother said.

"They're his things, even so," Captain Jack's sister said. "They're all he has."

Taking away the bundles left a gap like a tunnel in the heaps of odds and ends stacked against the cellar wall. One of my privileges was to root through whatever came to hand. Some days later, when things calmed down, I set about probing the tunnel.

Our cellar on Lorimer Street was too tidy to be interesting. My mother even dusted the chute, like a sliding board, that the coal man used to pour down chunks of coal into the storage bin. My grandmother's cellar, in contrast, was so disarrayed I could always find some surprise or other.

Most often, it was something with a vital

129

part missing: a sewing machine treadle without the sewing machine; a reel of old movie film but no projector to show it; a couple of headless golf clubs; a gadget for clamping metal caps on homemade root beer, but no caps or bottles. Clues that my elders must have gone around playing golf, watching movies, drinking root beer, and leading glamorous lives of their own before I existed.

That morning, when I thought the vein of this particular mine was exhausted, from the deepest level I pulled out a wooden box. It rattled intriguingly. I, of course, lifted the lid. Inside lay a dozen or more toy soldiers; cast in lead, their paint still bright.

I immediately claimed possession. Leaving everything else strewn about the floor, I seized the box and galloped upstairs to show The Gawgon what I had unearthed.

The Gawgon was sitting at the rolltop desk. When I held out the box, she stiffened.

"Where did you get that, Boy?" she said in an odd voice.

As I began explaining, she took the little figures and stood them one by one on the desk.

"Union soldiers," she said. "There used

to be Confederates, too, and horses.

"They all had their own names. I forget what they were." She picked up a blue-jacketed rifleman and turned it back and forth. "You found them, you can keep them."

I asked if they had been her toys.

The Gawgon gave a quick shake of her head. "My son's."

12

The Gawgon's Other Boy

"You didn't know? I'm surprised," she said, though I doubted she was half as surprised as I was.

"I assumed you already heard about it," The Gawgon said. "Family gossip — or so it used to be. Gossip, I suppose, goes out of date like everything else."

I expected her to change the subject, as my elders did when they caught me eavesdropping. Instead, she went on:

"His name was David, the same as yours. A quick, bright boy. You never knew what he'd be up to. He had a wild streak, like his father.

"He was close to your age when he died," The Gawgon said. "Influenza. They couldn't save him. That was the last time I saw his father. I wrote to him when it happened — he was always off to someplace or other. A wonder he came back at all."

The Gawgon's chin went up, her eyes flashed for an instant. Then her face softened. "No, I shouldn't say that. He did what he could. I was angry at him — for a little while. I could never stay angry at him very long. He was a charmer. And I? What did he call me? Intrepid? Fearless? Foolhardy, more like it.

"Yes," The Gawgon said, "he was the cheeky fellow who took my photo at the Pyramids. He kept trailing after me like a long-legged, overgrown puppy. I couldn't get rid of him. And didn't want to.

"We parted company in Cairo. When the tour ended, my employers didn't keep me on as a governess. I went home to Philadelphia.

"A few months later, that rascal came and found me. I was teaching school then. I had just come out of class and there he was, sitting on a bench in the hall. He asked if I remembered him. Oh, yes" — The Gawgon smiled — "I remembered him very well indeed.

"He wanted to be a photographer. That was the great new career in those days. He was going to Paris on the wild chance of studying with a Frenchman named Nadar, very famous at the time.

"He asked me to go with him," said The Gawgon. "Can you imagine? The nerve of the fellow! Standing there shuffling his feet, pretending to be shy — which he never was — with that loopy grin of his. I should give up my work and run off with a total stranger?

"I did, of course," said The Gawgon. "Yes, he was a charmer. A footloose charmer. He thought staying in one place was a crime against nature; and I went along with him.

"He never did study with Nadar. He set up his own portrait studio in Paris. No sooner did we start doing well than we dashed away to look at castles in Spain or ride gondolas in Venice. Between times, I gave English lessons. He wrote travel articles for the newspapers — when he felt like it."

The Gawgon broke off and went to sit in the rocking chair. I waited, saying nothing. After a time, she looked up at me:

"When I knew I was expecting our child, I went home. He promised to join me later. He never got around to it. Mary — your grandmother — took me in. I've lived with her ever since.

"That was the last I saw of him until Davy died. He came back for three days. He wanted to stay longer, but he had started working as a foreign correspondent, always caught up in one thing or another. Good at his job, I'll say that much for him.

"He had gone gray by then, but as big a charmer as ever. He was too old for it, but when the war started he grinned his way into being a frontline photographer. Sometimes I'd have a letter from him. He was killed in France, in the Argonne Forest."

This was more than any adult had ever seen fit to tell me. I felt somehow blessed and grateful. And heartbroken for her. I expected to see her grief-stricken by her memories.

"What young fools we were," The Gawgon said. "If I had it all to do over?" She paused and shook her head. "I'd do exactly the same. No, Boy, I don't regret one minute of it."

Her face was shining like a girl's.

I knew The Gawgon's opinion of Dr. McKelvie as a pill-roller and cheerful undertaker. He was, to me, a saint. The question came up again, at the end of summer, about my going back to Rittenhouse Academy. Dr. McKelvie strongly warned against it. So I was spared again, and I blessed him.

"Thank God for Annie," I heard my father say to my mother one evening.

"That's a saving. Elise is taken care of, for now. At least, her term's paid in advance."

Much later, I understood why he seemed relieved. The store had not been doing well. Customers were not flocking to fill their houses with Oriental goods. On the contrary, they were staying away in large numbers.

"It's beyond me," my father said. "What are they doing? Buying cars? Playing the stock market?"

He did try something he was sure would excite public interest: Mexican jumping beans.

From one of his suppliers he bought a bushel of what looked like old peanuts with the reddish-brown skin still on them. They did not actually jump into the air, but they did twitch from time to time; some quite lively, others just sat there unwilling to do much of anything. He put a big platter of them in the store window and a bowlful on the counter next to the cash register.

"What it is," my father said — he had brought some home for our amusement — "there's a little worm inside. When it moves, the bean jumps."

"What do they do all day?" my mother asked. "Suppose they eat their way through the shell? They're going to come out and crawl all over the house."

"Don't worry," said my father. "It's never been known to happen."

Nevertheless, my mother did not like the idea of the worms being sealed up in a bean dungeon without air and sunlight. Tenderhearted by nature, she felt sorry for them. She wondered if she should slice open the beans and liberate the prisoners. They could live outside in the areaway.

"They're happy where they are," my father said. "Let them be. They're better off in Philadelphia than in Mexico."

The Mexican jumping beans had no connection with Oriental goods. But, my father pointed out, he was now the only source of jumping beans in Philadelphia; in effect, the jumping bean king.

He reckoned the beans would lure passersby into the store, giving him the chance to sell them other, and more expensive, merchandise.

After a couple of weeks, he realized his scheme was not working. The Mexican jumping beans made no difference at all; but having paid for them, he was not going to throw them out. He carried them home in a sack. He planned on keeping them for a return engagement in the spring, when he was sure they would do better.

To accommodate the beans, my mother put them in bowls and saucers throughout the house. They kept quietly to themselves, twitching occasionally.

The only excitement they produced was on an evening when Uncle Eustace stopped by to commiserate with my father. Uncle Eustace was having difficulties with tombstone sales. People were not dying as often as they should.

Uncle Eustace sat gloomily on the sofa. He kept dipping absentmindedly into a dish of beans on the end table. In his morose frame of mind, he no doubt mistook them for salted peanuts.

"Stop! Stop!" My mother gasped when she saw what he was doing. "They're full of worms!"

Uncle Eustace sprang to his feet and spat his mouthful of beans onto the Oriental rug.

"That's not funny, Dog Flea," he shouted at my father, who had burst out laughing.

Despite explanations from my mother, Uncle Eustace was still convinced my father meant to play a joke on him and went away in a huff.

The beans seemed comfortable in their new environment. My task, each morning, was to sprinkle them with water to keep them moist. I did this chore promptly and hurried to my lesson.

At my own request, we would now have longer sessions every weekday. My mother, astonished and delighted that I actually wanted to study, was also concerned that it would be too heavy a burden for an elderly person. But The Gawgon wholeheartedly agreed with the new plan.

" 'Summer's lease hath all too short a date' — that's Shakespeare," The Gawgon said. "We have a lot to do. We haven't even touched geometry —"

The first thing I knew about geometry was that my sister and the rest of the Tulip Garden flunked it. Second, it had to do with circles, triangles, and arithmetic. The simplest arithmetic was, to me, an inscrutable mystery. Throwing in circles and triangles made it horrifying. Since we had not yet touched geometry, I suggested not touching it at all.

"Oh, we'll touch it," said The Gawgon. "Whether you'll grasp it remains to be seen. When you come right down to it, geometry's really learning how to think. If you can learn how to think, you can learn how to learn. If you can learn how to learn, you can learn anything."

So, through autumn, The Gawgon began working me harder than ever, not forgetting to chivy me about the still-untangled yarn. During these longer sessions, her face would gather a few more wrinkles, she would stop and shut her eyes; then, taking a long breath, pick up where she left off. When I was especially dim-witted or The Gawgon especially tired, we put everything aside.

" 'Much study is a weariness of the flesh,' " The Gawgon said. "That's from the Bible — Ecclesiastes, if I'm not mistaken."

No longer confining herself to her room, The Gawgon decreed an occasional recess. Early autumn was warm and sun-gilded. Those days we strolled a couple of blocks to Elm Park, as it was called, though not an elm was to be found.

"There used to be elms, but they died off and had to be cut down," The Gawgon said as we sat on a bench. "There were still a few when Davy — my Davy — and I came here."

She opened a brown paper bag of bread crusts that my grandmother had given us and we tossed them to the resident pigeons. The Gawgon, since first telling me, had said nothing more about her son. But I had thought about him. On the one hand, I wished I had met him; on the other — yes, I admitted to myself I was a little jealous.

"You'd have liked him," The Gawgon went on as the pigeons flocked around. "Two of a kind — no, I take that back. He was one of a kind. Just as you're one of a kind."

I felt reassured by that. I had wondered if The Gawgon volunteered to teach me because I reminded her of the other Davy. I hesitated, then ventured to ask.

"Bless you, no," The Gawgon said. "What's gone is gone. Sometimes we lose what we love best. The way of the world, Boy. We always keep loving and remembering, but the past isn't a good place to live in, only to visit from time to time.

"No," she said, "I wanted to teach you because I suspected you had the makings of a good mind. What you may do with it, I can't guess. But you deserve a chance to make something of yourself. I'll see that you get one."

The pigeons had been flapping all around us. One brazenly perched on The Gawgon's shoulder, and she let it peck crumbs from her hand.

When the bag was empty, our recess

ended. We started back with the pigeons trailing hopefully behind. A street cleaner in a white uniform was sweeping up the leaves with a long-handled brush and piling them into pyramids of red and orange.

"I see nothing sad about falling leaves," The Gawgon remarked. "New ones always come along. What did that poet — Oliver Wendell Holmes — say about the last leaf on the tree?

> *Let them smile, as I do now,*
> *At the old forsaken bough*
> *Where I cling.*

"And I," said The Gawgon, "intend to cling for a good long time. It may take a good long time to squeeze any sense into you."

It always made me uneasy when my relatives spoke politely to each other. It usually meant something serious was in the wind. One rainy night at the end of October, Uncle Rob, without Aunt Rosie, came to Lorimer Street. My father helped him off with his coat.

"Thank you, Rob, for coming out in this weather." My father ushered him into the dining room, where my mother already sat at the table. "We can't rightly talk about this on the phone.

"It could have some effect on your mother's situation," my father went on. "Some effect on all of us, for that matter. You should know what I'm thinking. I'd be glad for your opinion."

They murmured back and forth under the glow of the chandelier. My mother jotted figures on sheets of paper.

Something had gone wrong with the stock market. I did not know what the stock market was, except my father found it intensely interesting. It had collapsed, crashed, or some such.

I could get no mental picture of a market crashing, apart from shelves in the grocery store falling down and canned vegetables rolling around, so I could not follow the conversation.

"Sound reasoning, Alan," Uncle Rob said at last. "I agree. But, as you well know, it's unwise to move too quickly. The market will bounce back. President Hoover will make sure it does."

Uncle Rob and my mother embraced, my father shook hands, thanked him again, and he went home.

Uncle Rob, for the first time, did not slip me a quarter.

13

The Consulting Detective

Mrs. Jossbegger died in November. My grandmother and The Gawgon did not feel up to a funeral. Leaving me with them, my mother and my aunts attended the service. They had put on the black dresses they kept available for sad occasions. Afterward, my mother reported it was nicely done. Aunt Rosie thought it was skimpy.

"I'm sure they did the best they could," my mother said. "Everyone's cutting back, these days."

"Cutting back? On funerals?" Aunt Rosie said. "Heaven help us, where will it all end?"

Mrs. Jossbegger's absence ended the corn-cutting sessions. As for the stock market crash, Uncle Rob's visit troubled me. I privately asked my sister about it.

"If you paid attention to something besides drawing those dumb pictures, you wouldn't have to ask," she said — which meant she understood no more than I did.

What, I wondered, had it to do with our grandmother?

"You really are the stupidest blighter," my sister said. "Don't you know anything at all? Grandmother counts on Father to help out. She has to. She doesn't make enough money from the lodgers. The house doesn't even belong to her."

I had never heard about that. "Whose is it?"

"Father's," my sister said. "That's right. He owns it. He lets her live there free, but it's still his house. He buys stocks for her, too. That must be what he and Uncle Rob were talking about.

"Father will take care of everything," she went on. "Anyhow, it's got nothing to do with blighters. It's none of your business."

My sister knew the hallways and back stairs of the adult world, so I believed her. But if it was none of my business, all the more reason to make it so.

Next time I saw The Gawgon, I asked her to explain the puzzling crash. She tried her best; still I did not grasp it, only that it was not good.

"No, it isn't good," The Gawgon said. "Something like it happened before, years ago, and that was very bad, too. It all worked out in the end. I hope it works out

145

again. President Hoover says it will. But when politicians promise everything's going to be rosy, I start feeling my pockets."

I let it go at that. I would make it my business some other time. I had enough crowding my head. As threatened, The Gawgon dipped me into geometry. If this was supposed to teach me to think, it felt more like frying my brain. The notion of pi, a number that could stretch out endlessly, bewildered me. But at least I was good at drawing circles.

The Gawgon could sense when my mind wandered hopelessly beyond her reach. To give me some relief from theorems and propositions, she handed me a book of mystery stories.

"Better than just mysteries," she said. "Sherlock Holmes can show you how to pay attention to details and figure things out logically.

"Arthur Conan Doyle started out as a doctor," The Gawgon said. "He wrote to pass the time between patients. Since he didn't have a lot of patients, he ended up writing a lot of stories. His old professor was his inspiration for Sherlock Holmes, the world's greatest consulting detective."

It wasn't long before I was so captivated by Sherlock Holmes, I half believed he and his companion, Dr. Watson, really existed.

"They do," she said. "In your imagination."

Though devoted to him, I decided Holmes was not the world's greatest consulting detective. Second greatest. First was: The Gawgon.

THE AFFAIR OF
THE SEATED KING

The dense fog, which makes London infamous throughout the world, was so heavy as to be impenetrable. The entire city lay immobilized. Horses balked at pulling their hansom cabs. Police constables, attempting to walk their beats, became hopelessly lost and confused. The crowded streets were now deserted. Thieves and pickpockets, who normally thronged Belgrave Square and Piccadilly Circus, remained within their sordid lairs.

Unusual even by London standards, the fog discouraged us from taking our afternoon stroll in Kensington Gardens, and so The Gawgon and I chose to stay in our apartments, with a cheery coal fire in the grate, and amused ourselves by solving problems in geometry.

The Gawgon found the square of the hypotenuse to be especially droll and entertaining. We were chuckling over it when Miss Florry, our smartly attired housekeeper, announced the arrival of a gentleman identifying himself as Mr. Hemlock Soames.

Without waiting for permission, this individual brushed past Miss Florry and entered our sitting room.

"I pray you will forgive this unconscionable intrusion." The unexpected visitor removed his black bowler hat and made a courteous bow. He was tall and lean, almost gaunt. A pair of pince-nez spectacles bridged the high arch of his nose. His pale brow seemed to radiate a cool inner light.

"It is all the more unpardonable" — his quick eyes scanned the papers on the writing table — "since I observe you and your colleague are deeply engrossed in the square of the hypotenuse, which I myself always find a most enjoyable diversion.

"Be sure," he added, "only a matter of

extreme urgency brings me to impose my presence so rudely upon you."

The Gawgon, in a watered-silk dressing gown, approached him and shook his hand, and with her usual graciousness, invited him to sit in our best upholstered armchair.

"Before you reveal your difficulty," said The Gawgon, "it is essential to deal with each other in total frankness.

"You, I have reason to believe," she went on, offering him a goblet of soda water, "are endeavoring to practice a small deception upon us."

The gentleman startled and choked on his soda water as The Gawgon continued:

"I detect a slight West Indian accent in your speech. Jamaica rather than Trinidad; Kingston rather than Montego Bay. But, as well, I hear a charming musicality unique to that great American metropolis Philadelphia. Curious combination. It is possible, of course, that you have traveled or resided in those areas. A diplomat? A statesman? No, I discern too much intelligence in your features. You have, perhaps, assumed these accents for misleading purposes.

"Also, you appreciate the subtle joys

149

of the square of the hypotenuse; therefore, I doubt that you are an ordinary
plainclothes policeman in the employ
of Scotland Yard.

"More conclusively," went on The
Gawgon, "I notice an odor — I refrain
from calling it a stench — of pipe tobacco about your person. A private
blend of Latakia and Egyptian? Further,
when shaking your hand, I felt a small
callus near the second knuckle of your
index finger, caused, I hypothesize, by
long use of the bow for a stringed in-
strument. Were I to examine your left
hand, I am convinced I should find
other calluses on your fingertips. You
play the cello, violin, or viola — most
likely, the violin.

"Finally, with the exception of myself,
only one person knows every inch of
London so well that he could make his
way blindfolded — or, in this case, fog-
bound.

"For the sake of accuracy, I prefer to
address you by your true name: Mr.
Sherlock Holmes."

"Touché!" exclaimed Sherlock Holmes.
"My compliments. I consider myself — I
do not indulge in false modesty — a
master of disguise. I should have known

The Gawgon would see through my masquerade."

"Now that your identity has been established," said The Gawgon, "allow me to inquire: Why did you come disguised in the first place?"

"I was obliged to do so," replied Holmes. "There are always watching eyes and listening ears. If it became known that you were associated with me in any way, or that we have so much as spoken together, your life would be at risk as well as mine. For your own protection, I dared not take the chance of being recognized. I must warn you in advance: This affair is dangerous in the extreme."

"Risk, my dear sir, is what makes life interesting," said The Gawgon. "Now, I trust, you will explain the nature of this perilous situation."

"To put it briefly," replied Holmes, "after long and difficult negotiations, the Greek government has finally consented to lend the British Museum, for exhibition, its rarest and greatest treasure.

"It is a lifesize statue, the ultimate masterpiece by that sublime sculptor, Phidias. You are familiar, of course, with the mythical hero Perseus, who brought the head of Medusa to King Polydectes. At sight of it, the king was instantly turned to stone.

"The statue represents the king, seated on his throne, reaching out a hand to receive Medusa's head. The throne, alas, has not survived the ravages of time, but the figure is intact.

"It is superb," Holmes went on. "A glory of classical antiquity, a consummate work of art. Its value — beyond price. The ministry in Athens, reluctant to lend it in the first place, is profoundly concerned for its safety."

"Understandably," said The Gawgon. "If any harm were to befall this treasure, I foresee that Greece would be outraged, even to a point of threatening war. The Balkans, naturally, would be drawn in; the Russians would take a hand; the French could not resist meddling, which would stir up the Austrians and Prussians. In effect, a catastrophe. The object must be protected at all cost."

"You analyze it perfectly," said Holmes. "One thing I have not mentioned: The statue has already been stolen."

☾ ☾ ☾

14

My Uncle Santa Clause

The following Thursday, everyone ate Thanksgiving dinner at my grandmother's: a very good dinner, as it always was. My mother declared we had a great deal to be thankful for: We were better off than a lot of people; we were indoors eating instead of outdoors starving; and things could be worse. This, of course, was absolutely true and we were grateful. Still, nobody was having much of a laughing time.

My father and Uncle Rob sat deep in conversation. My sister, bored, would rather have been with her Tulip Garden. Aunt Marta dozed in a chair, never attempting even a chorus of "Sari Marais." The Gawgon, suffering a touch of indigestion, went to her room. Uncle Will, who had another engagement, left right after the mince pie. The only one in good spirits was Uncle Eustace. The raw weather had perked up the tombstone business; he was close to being lighthearted, and he had for-

153

given my father for feeding him the Mexican jumping beans.

In the kitchen, my mother, grandmother, Aunt Rosie, and Aunt Florry did the dishes. My work was to dry the silverware, a task that for some reason I disliked, and I was impatient to be done. Aunt Florry, usually brisk in washing up, was slow about it and, at one point, stopped altogether.

"I'll tell the men later." Aunt Florry kept wiping her hands on her apron. "Will can explain more when he comes back.

"Mrs. Heberton had to let us go."

"What? Fired?" Aunt Rosie burst out before my grandmother could say anything. "Both of you? After all these years, just like that? Ha! There's your high muckety-mucks, riding roughshot over everybody!"

"Oh, Florry, this is too bad." My grandmother put her arms around her. "Why? What happened? I never thought for a moment —"

"She couldn't help it," Aunt Florry said. "She certainly didn't want to. She's been talking with Mr. Ormond at her bank; he takes care of all her business. He's doing his best for her, but she'll have to close the house and try to sell it when the market's better. She can't afford to keep it up, least

154

of all paying a companion and a chauffeur."

"With her money?" retorted Aunt Rosie.

"Not anymore," said Aunt Florry. "She'll be lucky if she comes out with a penny to her name. Until things turn better, she's going to live with her son in New Jersey."

"Serves her right," Aunt Rosie declared. "That's mean, firing people at the holidays."

"No, she was very generous," Aunt Florry said. "Mrs. Heberton paid us to the middle of January. She didn't have to do that. She knows a lot of people, she promised she'd ask around and see if she could find jobs for us.

"I feel so bad for Will," Aunt Florry went on. "He was happy there, driving the car and looking after the grounds. He never touched a drop when he was working."

"If you need a place to stay —" my mother began.

"You'll stay here," my grandmother told Aunt Florry. "In Jack's room. I still don't have the heart to rent it to strangers. I'll fix up something for Will, too."

Everybody went home soon after. We walked the few blocks to Lorimer Street;

my mother thought the exercise would be good for our digestion. My father and mother talked between themselves. My sister, sulking, trudged behind.

It began to drizzle; the streetlights were pale smears. Most of the neighborhood street lamps, in those days, were gas. Just before sundown, a man came with a lighter on the end of a pole; mornings, he came back and snuffed out the flame. Now, with the mist swirling around the alleyways, it was the ideal place for lurking assassins; and Sherlock Holmes's mortal enemy, Professor Moriarty, was probably stalking us. I turned into the shadows of Lorimer Street as if I had never been there before.

AN EXPENSIVE TAILOR

"Yes," Holmes said flatly, "the priceless statue of King Polydectes has been stolen. It was stored in the basement of the British Museum for minor cleaning and restoration. Now it has vanished. The theft, so far, has not been made public, but you understand the consequences if its disappearance is revealed."

"And you, sir," I put in, "must find out who stole it."

"Of course not," said Holmes, with some asperity at my naive remark. "I know that fact already.

"I have, an hour ago, received a message from the perpetrator," Holmes went on. "A taunting communication, indeed. He boasts that he has planned it all in advance. He chooses to toy with me and play a vicious game. He challenges me to recover the statue within twenty-four hours.

"Otherwise, he will send an open letter to the *Times* and all foreign embassies, thus lighting the fuse of the European powder keg. Worse, when the disaster is revealed, London's thousands of painters, poets, novelists, and other devoted art lovers will riot in the streets. A terrifying prospect.

"Scotland Yard is incompetent to deal with the case," Holmes continued. "The blame will be laid on my failure."

"Diabolical!" I exclaimed. "What fiendish intelligence conceived such a plot?"

"One man," replied Holmes. "That individual who tirelessly seeks my destruction, who has already tried to murder me: Professor Moriarty."

The Gawgon nodded. "The Napoleon of crime."

"None other," said Holmes. "When you observed that only you and I could make our way through London's worst fog, you should have included Moriarty and his hirelings. Nothing keeps them from their loathsome business."

"Very possibly he means to draw you out and strike at your person," The Gawgon said, "but it would merely add a little icing to his poisonous confection: desirable but not essential. Destroying your reputation is far crueler than destroying you corporeally."

"I am aware of that," said Sherlock Holmes. "Alas, my staunch companion, Dr. Watson, has been called away for a fortnight in Wolverhampton. My brother Mycroft, though a genius, is preoccupied with philosophical speculations. Nothing, not even the fate of the world, could induce him to venture from the reading room of his club. And so I turn to you for any suggestion or advice you may wish to offer."

"My suggestion is this," The Gawgon said, after a few moments of reflection. "Return immediately to your Baker

Street apartments. Do not, in any circumstances, leave them until you receive word from us. My advice: Put this matter entirely in the hands of The Boy and myself."

Although Holmes protested, unwilling for us to risk our lives, he at last, and most reluctantly, agreed. Once the great detective had left our premises, The Gawgon went to her filing cabinet, where she riffled through the folders.

"Ah, yes, here it is: the key to a secret entrance of the British Museum." She winked at me. "I doubt that even Mr. Sherlock Holmes has such a means of access."

From her wardrobe of disguises, she outfitted us with black bowler hats, dark suits, tightly furled umbrellas, and Old School ties.

"From among the thousands of merchant bankers and stockbrokers wearing this identical garb," she said, "it will be impossible for Moriarty to pick us out."

I mentioned she had neglected to take revolvers from her extensive arsenal.

"If my hypothesis is correct, firearms will not be necessary," she said. "Come along, Boy. The game's afoot."

In the streets, we made our way unerringly through the enveloping fog. Arriving at the rear of the British Museum, The Gawgon produced her key and opened a narrow door. We went swiftly down the empty corridors lit by the occasional gas jet. As familiar with the bowels of the British Museum as she was with our own apartments, The Gawgon entered a room where various implements covered a worktable.

"Yes, the statue was brought here and set on this bench." The Gawgon lit a gas lamp, took a magnifying glass from her pocket, and scrutinized the area.

"I see traces of parallel lines on the floor," she said. "As Euclid points out, parallel lines do not meet, and so I assume these tracks continue —"

I had, in the meantime, noticed a crumpled scrap of paper under the worktable. I hurried to pick it up and hand it to The Gawgon. She smoothed it out and studied it closely.

"Well done, Boy. This is a better stroke of luck than I could have hoped. Even a master criminal has moments of carelessness. It makes my work much easier, for the pieces of the puzzle now

begin falling into place. This may confirm what I privately theorized from the
start.

"It is a bill, quite a large bill," said The
Gawgon, "from Houndstooth & Son, the
most elegant and expensive tailors on
Savile Row. I believe, Boy, it tells us all
we need to know."

☾ ☾ ☾

"Will wants to be Santa Claus," my
grandmother said, later that day.

My mother and Aunt Florry were back
from shopping on Fifty-second Street. I
had just come down from The Gawgon's
room and was as surprised as they were.
Uncle Will had not been Santa Claus for
several years now.

"If he'd like to," my mother said, "of
course, let him do it."

"Do we still have the suit and the
beard?" asked Aunt Florry.

"Packed away. I'll air them out," my
grandmother said. "It was Will's idea," she
added. "He wants this to be a good Christmas."

When I still fervently believed in him
and loved him, Santa Claus always came to

visit. We would gather in my grand-mother's parlor to wait for him on Christmas Eve. Uncle Will would always be there, eager as the rest of us, but he kept looking at his wristwatch.

"He's late," Uncle Will would say at last. "I have to run an errand. I'll be right back."

"Better hurry," my grandmother warned. "You don't want to miss him."

Uncle Will put on his hat and coat and left the house. I was fidgety, afraid he might not come back in time. But — and it happened fatefully every year — after about twenty minutes, there were loud knockings at the door.

"Santa Claus? My goodness!" My grand-mother clapped her hands to her head. "And Will's not here!"

She opened the door. Santa Claus came rolling in, red-suited, with bouncing belly, a white beard up to his eyes, a sack over his shoulder. He boomed out some ho-ho-hos, then suddenly stopped.

"Someone's missing." Santa Claus glanced around. "I don't see Will."

My grandmother explained that Will had gone on a short errand. Santa said he would catch up with him later. He heaved himself into an armchair; my sister and I sat on his knees while he fished out small presents from his sack, which looked suspiciously like a pillowcase.

We begged him to wait, Uncle Will would be here at any moment. But Santa had other stops to make; he bustled out with a flurry of *ho-hos* and *Merry Christmases.* Soon after, Uncle Will came back. When he found out he had missed Santa Claus, he sighed with huge regret.

"Next year," he said. "Next year for sure."

It did not happen. He missed the visit every Christmas. But except for Uncle Will's annual disappointment, these were always magical evenings. In addition to the smells of mince and pumpkin pies, the sage and onions of turkey stuffing, another aroma floated in the air, the very essence of Santa Claus.

Years later, when I was grown up, I still remembered that marvelous fragrance and recognized it as Scotch whisky.

15

Simple Gifts

When I was about seven or eight, Uncle Will stopped disappearing on Christmas Eve and Santa Claus stopped visiting. By then, I learned that Uncle Will's annual errand was a quick trip next door to the Noonans. Santa's costume and sack of presents were already there; he simply dressed up in the red suit and beard and hurried back.

I missed his visits. Now that Uncle Will decided on a return performance, even knowing what I knew, I was eager to see Santa Claus again. Though he was not the genuine article, it made no difference. As The Gawgon had said about Sherlock Holmes, Santa lived where he should: in my imagination.

As for Holmes, amid all the Christmas preparations I had neglected him; he was still cooling his heels at Baker Street, where The Gawgon had sent him.

THE PANJANDRUM CLUB

By the time The Gawgon and I left the British Museum, the fog had lifted and the skies had cleared to their usual sooty gray, the nearest thing to a sparkle that London could produce. Carefully pocketing the tailor's bill from Houndstooth & Son, The Gawgon directed me to return to our chambers. "On the way, would you be so kind as to take a message to Mr. Sherlock Holmes?" she said. "If he is interested in learning the whereabouts of the stolen statue of King Polydectes, he is invited to join us at high noon.

"He need not disguise himself," she added. "Also, assure him tea will be served."

The Gawgon declined my offer to accompany her. "Time presses. Professor Moriarty is surely gloating, impatient to set his diabolical scheme in motion. Some tasks remain, I can accomplish them more promptly alone."

She vanished into the throng of bowler-hatted, umbrella-bearing stockbrokers. Much as I wished to observe her brilliant analytical mind at work, I followed her instructions, then waited for the appointed hour.

Sherlock Holmes arrived a few moments early, for which he apologized. He wore his famous cape and the cloth cap of the style known as a deerstalker. No sooner had he entered than Big Ben boomed out noon. Before the echoes of the twelfth stroke died away, The Gawgon appeared.

Holmes sprang to his feet. "Dear lady, I am relieved to see you unharmed. Your message led me to hope —"

"Do you take milk or lemon in your tea?" The Gawgon deposited her umbrella in the Ming vase at the door. "Ah, yes. The location of the statue? Set your mind at ease, Mr. Holmes. King Polydectes is exactly where he belongs."

"Good heavens!" exclaimed Holmes. "That would be — ?"

"On proud display in the British Museum. Even as we speak, crowds are gathering to admire this treasure. Europe has been spared a conflict and Professor Moriarty foiled again."

"A brilliant accomplishment! As to be expected from The Gawgon and The Boy," said Holmes. "My gratitude is beyond expression. Let me ask one thing more: Your method of solving this most difficult and puzzling case?"

"Elementary." The Gawgon handed him the tailor's bill that I had found. "Thanks to The Boy, this was my first significant clue. All else followed logically.

"It immediately occurred to me," The Gawgon continued, "that the humble employees of the British Museum are in no financial position to patronize expensive tailors."

"Certainly not," agreed Holmes.

"Therefore, my suspicions were aroused," said The Gawgon. "I went immediately to Houndstooth & Son. They recalled making the suit, but what engraved it indelibly on their mind was something altogether bizarre.

"The customer did not come personally to be fitted. Instead, an arrogant, sneering sort of individual — by now, I was sure it was Moriarty — brought a list of measurements: waist, height, inside leg, and so on. Mr. Houndstooth showed me the specifications. They corresponded exactly to the dimensions of King Polydectes.

"At that moment, I grasped the nature of Moriarty's scheme, fiendish in its simplicity, simple in its fiendishness."

The Gawgon turned to me. "Do you remember the parallel tracks on the floor? Close examination showed me they had been made by a wheelchair, probably what is called a 'Bath chair,' fitted with a small hood or canopy.

"For the rest" — The Gawgon shrugged — "a matter of logical deduction. Moriarty had several of his henchmen wheel him into the museum; a common enough sight, an invalid being taken on a cultural outing, nothing to arouse suspicion. They concealed themselves until the museum closed, then entered the basement, dressed the statue in its custom-tailored suit, and set it in the chair. Next morning, mingling with the crowd, they wheeled King Polydectes out of the building. The theft was accomplished."

"So it must have been!" cried Holmes. "A magnificent reconstruction of the crime. But, my dear Gawgon, the crucial question is: What did Moriarty do with the statue?"

"Easily answered," said The Gawgon. "You are, of course, familiar with the principle: The best hiding place is in plain sight."

"Correct," said Holmes. "When an object blends so naturally with its surroundings, it becomes, in a practical sense, invisible. But a marble statue wearing a Savile Row suit?"

"You know the Panjandrum Club, the oldest gentleman's club in London," The Gawgon said as Holmes nodded. "Its members are as ancient and decrepit as the institution itself, their average age, according to my research, is ninety-seven.

"Moriarty and his henchmen simply wheeled the statue only a block away to the Panjandrum Club and into the reading room. I interviewed the doorman and the steward, both doddering and dim-eyed, who swore they recognized King Polydectes as a member. The equally aged waiter, glimpsing the king's outstretched hand, automatically put a glass of brandy in it, brought a copy of the *Times* and spread it on his lap. There was, then, no observable difference between the statue and the rest of the Panjandrum's members, most of them already petrified in Bath chairs.

"I confirmed this for myself," said The Gawgon. "Once I explained what was at stake, I was allowed to enter the reading room. Since the club's iron-bound rule is never to disturb a member, Polydectes still sat there, glass in hand, apparently reading a *Times* editorial, and from his stony glare, disagreeing with it.

"I then notified the museum staff. With utmost discretion, they sent custodians to wheel out the statue and bring it to the exhibit hall, where it now resides in all its glory. The custom-tailored suit, naturally, was removed.

"And so, Mr. Holmes, the case is closed. It was our pleasure to be of some small assistance."

"For me, more than a pleasure," said Holmes, rising to his feet. "It has been the highest privilege." He bowed to me and bestowed a gallant kiss on The Gawgon's hand.

"You are, of course, uniquely The Gawgon," he said, with something warmer than admiration. "But, to me, you will always be: The Woman."

"I take that as a compliment," said The Gawgon.

"Elementary," I said.

☾ ☾ ☾ Thuh End ☾ ☾ ☾

Next day was Christmas Eve. At Uncle

Will's request — and since he was to be Santa Claus again, it was happily granted — we rearranged the usual order of events. This year, we would not exchange gifts on Christmas Eve. Santa would arrive on Christmas Day, after dinner, and distribute everybody's presents from his pillowcase.

Uncle Will, meantime, had bought a handsome Christmas tree and trimmed most of it himself, with some added help from Aunt Florry and me. Nora got more and more excited at the shining ornaments, the ones we used every year; whooping and whistling, she tried to flap onto the top of the tree and had to be put in her cage. She made me think of Captain Jack, who once said she ought to be roasted for Christmas. I missed Captain Jack, but from what I understood, he was in some kind of hospital and would be there a long time.

Aunt Rosie was, at first, leery of the new plan.

"I don't like changing things around," she confided to my mother. "I hope it doesn't do something to my digestive track."

Nevertheless, she got herself into the spirit of the occasion and forgot about her digestive tract. Aunt Marta, carried away by the festivities, spontaneously burst into song, pleading to be taken back to the old Transvaal. Uncle Eustace, instead of grumbling, called for an encore. He was in fine fettle, selling more tombstones than he expected.

Uncle Rob, in addition to taking care of family legal matters, served as official turkey-carver and did it very well. It was, all in all, the liveliest and best Christmas feast I remembered.

Now the secret was known, I thought Uncle Will would simply go upstairs after dinner and put on the Santa Claus suit, but he claimed his usual errand and ducked out of the house. Soon after, Santa arrived. We cheered like wild and clapped our hands. He plumped into the armchair, I sat on one knee, my sister — grown long-legged since his last visit — perched awkwardly on the other. Again, the cloud of marvelous Santa Claus aroma enveloped me.

Uncle Will opened the pillowcase. This time, it held everybody's presents wrapped and tagged. He picked them out one by one and called our names. Before handing them around, he made a great to-do, shaking them, turning them upside down, pretending to guess what they were.

"This looks like a radio." Uncle Will held up a narrow box that could only contain a necktie. He hefted another package. "What's this? A new car?"

I had neither money nor access to department stores, so my mother bought gifts on my behalf. For a long time, I believed older ladies yearned for bags of sachet and jars of potpourri. That was what I always gave my grandmother and The Gawgon, and they were enraptured. I was also led to believe my aunts could wish for nothing finer than a slip, which I gave them. As it turned out, they all gave each other slips, were overjoyed, and held these undergarments in front of themselves for everyone to admire.

Two gifts came as no surprise. A couple of years before, my father had given Uncle Eustace a wooden bowl of shaving soap, and Uncle Eustace had given my father a straw-covered bottle of bay-rum face lotion. My father hated bay rum, even though it came from the West Indies. The following Christmas, he rewrapped the bottle and gave it back to Uncle Eustace.

"He won't remember," my father assured my mother.

That same Christmas, Uncle Eustace gave my father the wooden bowl of shaving soap.

Neither one said a word about it. From then on, they kept exchanging the bay rum and shaving soap, thanking each other and declaring it was just what they always wanted.

My sister and I already had our major presents at home on Lorimer Street. Here, I mostly received the dreaded underwear. But The Gawgon gave me a spectacular gift: one of her own books, a large-sized history of the world, filled with engravings of Egyptians, Greeks, and Romans. It was the first of three volumes. From the Sphinx-like smile on her face, I had reason to hope the others would someday be forthcoming.

I had my own extra, secret present for The Gawgon. I handed it to her when no one was looking and whispered she should unwrap it later.

When the pillowcase was empty, Uncle Will stood up and declared he had a lot of other visits to make. He embraced each of us. His white beard had gone crooked, but nobody minded.

He stopped at the door, blew kisses, and waved his arms.

"Ho-ho-ho!" he boomed. "Merry Christmas, God bless us every one!"

Next morning, Uncle Will packed a valise and left. It was the last we would see of him.

16

A Present for The Gawgon

"I knew Will was leaving," my grandmother said. "He told me two weeks ago."

My mother and I had come for the usual after-Christmas lunch of leftovers. With Aunt Rosie, we sat around the kitchen table while Aunt Florry made up platters of cold turkey and stuffing. The Gawgon was still in her room.

"He didn't have the heart to tell anyone else," my grandmother added. "It hurt him too much. He simply couldn't do it. That's why he wanted to be Santa Claus again. It was his way of saying good-bye. He's right, there's nothing for him here. He's going west."

My mother and Aunt Florry looked choked up; Uncle Will was their favorite, as he was everyone's. Aunt Rosie flung down the turkey wing she had been nibbling:

"West? And be a cowboy buggaroo? What's he thinking?"

175

desk. "You're a clever boy. You might end up being an artist — though I'm not sure I'd wish that on you. It can break your heart. It usually does."

Since no one was in the mood for it, we did not celebrate New Year's beyond listening to the radio and staying up until midnight. The Gawgon put off our lessons for a couple of days. Next time we met, her face was chalky, she was in a flannel bathrobe and out of sorts.

"McKelvie, that fool! What does he expect me to do?" The Gawgon muttered. "Live like a vegetable?"

She brought out the postcards she had talked about, and we picked through them. She held up a picture of a woman doing nothing in particular except sitting and vaguely smiling.

"Her name is Lisa del Giocondo. Mona Lisa, for short," The Gawgon said. "The most famous portrait in the world. An Italian painted her, something like four hundred years ago."

The Gawgon, growing more animated, went on about the artist, Leonardo da Vinci. Not only his pictures but, as well, his botanical and anatomical studies, plans for buildings, canals, even a flying machine. It amazed me to think he had designed an airplane hundreds of years ahead of anybody else. Still, I kept glancing at Mona Lisa, who smiled back as if she knew something important and wouldn't tell me.

"She does tease you," The Gawgon said. "She teases everybody. Leonardo, greatest genius of his day, had a thousand things on his mind. But she haunted him. He never got free of her."

TIC-TAC-TOE

We were in Venice, in The Gawgon's palazzo overlooking the Grand Canal, when a nice letter arrived from the Pope.

The Gawgon, beautifully regal in a gown decorated with seed pearls, scanned the page.

"He invites us to have dinner with him," she said. "Well, why not? He isn't a jolly table companion, but he has a first-rate cook.

"I'd thought of going to Rome anyway. They've discovered a rare ancient mural; it should be interesting. Better yet, we'll stop off in Florence. That's the real city for artists. They have more painters than pigeons. We can see the Pope when we get around to it."

We set off, next day, in The Gawgon's splendidly outfitted coach and four, reaching Florence by leisurely stages. I had never seen the city before. However, instead of admiring its many picturesque tourist attractions, The Gawgon drove to a large, handsome house, with courtyard and gardens. The housekeeper was happy to see her, but when The Gawgon asked if Ser da Vinci was at home, her face fell.

"In the studio," she said. "He won't come out. He sits, he stares. *Malocchio!* I tell you someone put the evil eye on him."

"We'll see about that," said The Gawgon.

She left her traveling cloak and floppy velvet hat with the housekeeper, and we made our way to a big, airy room at the back of the house. I expected to find paintings and sketches covering the walls. They stood bare. The studio was empty of furnishings except for a chair and a nearby easel.

The artist himself sat hunched at a

table covered with papers, scratching away with a stick of charcoal. He was fair-complexioned, with a curled mustache and neatly trimmed beard, a generous, noble brow, and a receding hairline.

"*Ciao,* Leo," said The Gawgon.

He started, ready to throw something. Recognizing The Gawgon, he jumped out of his chair and hurried to greet us.

"La Bella Gaugonna!" he exclaimed, embracing her. "*Ben-venuta!* It's been too long already. This is The Boy, Il Ragazzo? Aie, *misericordia,* you find me not at my best."

"How so?" said The Gawgon. "What's wrong?"

"Don't ask," said Leonardo.

"Come, now," said The Gawgon. "I hear you've been doing pretty well for yourself. You're the most famous artist in Florence."

"City of jackals!" Leonardo made a gesture with his fingers that only an Italian can fill with such intense emotion. "And the worst of them — that ham-fisted stonecutter, that butcher with a chisel! Michelangelo? Michel Diavolo! He stabs me in the back, he slanders me, insults me in the street.

181

Pazzo! A crazy man! Let him go carve tombstones, that's all he's good for.

"And that simpering, beardless boy Raphael, gawking around trying to copy me. His pictures? They give me a toothache. He should paint with sugar water."

"Pay him no mind," The Gawgon whispered to me as Leonardo ranted. "That's how artists talk about each other."

To draw Leonardo's attention from his colleagues, The Gawgon turned the conversation to his own work. I dared a glance at the sheet of paper on his table, eager to see what brilliant new masterpiece the greatest genius in the world had been pondering.

The page was covered with tic-tac-toe games. Leonardo had been playing against himself and losing.

"I promised Isabella d'Este a painting. Still not begun." Leonardo pulled at his beard. "The town wants a war memorial, a battle scene to cover a church wall. I tore up my sketches. I wanted to do a bronze horse, the biggest ever cast. I haven't even begun the model.

"I don't need this aggravation." Leonardo paced back and forth. "I'll go into

some other line of work. I can build for-
tifications, sewer systems —"

"Did you ever make a cootie-
catcher?" I asked.

"I invented it," Leonardo said. He
went on with his grumbling. "Earn my
bread? Worse comes to worst, I can always play the lute in taverns.

"Painting? No more." Leonardo seized
a brush and snapped it in two. "I give it
up. *Finito!*"

✻   ✻   ✻

17

La Gioconda

Leonardo cast around for something else he could break. He snatched up a palette and tried to snap it over his knee. When he did not succeed, he threw it across the studio, where it went sailing into a wall, leaving messy paint stains.

"Stop that nonsense," ordered The Gawgon. "What's the matter with you? What are you telling me, giving up painting? Ridiculous!"

"I've lost my knack." Leonardo's shoulders slumped. "I was doing a portrait. I can't finish it."

"Of course you can," said The Gawgon. "A simple picture? You could dash it off with your left hand."

"I *am* left-handed," Leonardo retorted.

"I forgot," said The Gawgon. "All right, you could do it in your sleep."

"Not this one. Besides, who sleeps? I

haven't had a decent night since I started this disaster. You want to know?"

"I'm sure you'll tell us," said The Gawgon.

"All right, if you insist," Leonardo said. "I'm here in the studio, going about my business. I'm thinking of my bronze horse. How to cast it? Interesting technical problem, it would have to be in sections. Yes, and that *pazzo* Michelangelo got wind of the project. He mocked me, right in the middle of the piazza. He said I didn't have the nerve, the gall to try anything so colossal —"

"Enough horse, enough Michelangelo," said The Gawgon. "Then what?"

"So, I'm sitting doing calculations for the molds when in walks a puffed-up idiot. I knew of him: Francesco del Giocondo, retired with a fortune, money pouring out his ears, but a miser nonetheless. He just got married, he wants a portrait of his wife — his third. The first two must have died to escape him; it would have been a pleasure for them. The new one didn't have a ducat of her own, no dowry, no property. Why did such a skinflint bother with her?

"Anyway, I tell him I have better things to do. 'Go ask Raphael,' I say. 'He'll make her look like an angel and do it on the cheap.'

"But that won't answer. It has to be me, no other. He takes out a purse and jingles it under my nose. He's talking cash, gold, a lot of it."

"And you agreed," said The Gawgon.

"What else?" Leonardo shrugged. "An artist has to live. 'Good,' he says. 'Only the best for my little Lisa. You make a nice picture. Understand?'

"Next day, he brings her to the studio. My eyes popped. I see why he didn't care if she had no dowry. *Bellissima!* Beautiful, you can't believe. She's, what, twenty something? And married to that ancient goat? Ah, well, I tell myself, this is Florence and what's a poor girl to do?

"She sits calm and relaxed, very sure of herself, no wiggling, no complaining she's getting a stiff neck. Only the best for little Lisa? Who could do less? I was inspired, I began to work. It went well, so easily. Then — catastrophe!"

"What happened?" asked The Gawgon as Leonardo paused to sigh.

"She smiled," he said.

"So?" said The Gawgon. "Everybody smiles when they have their portrait painted."

"Not like she did," Leonardo said. "She knows secrets, past anything I could understand. Little Lisa? No, with that smile she's every woman in the world, every woman since time began. I had to catch her smile; my life depended on it.

"I couldn't. She never smiled that way again. I try everything to bring it back. I recite poems to her, pile flowers in the studio, sprinkle perfume. I have musicians come and play. No use. I think she's teasing, daring me to make her do it.

"For how long?" Leonardo spread a hand and counted the fingers. "Three, four, five —"

"Who paints a portrait in less than a week?" The Gawgon broke in. "Not even you. Give it a few more days."

"Not days! Years!" cried Leonardo. "Close to six years I'm working on it. I put everything else aside, turned down commissions, gave up my bronze horse."

Leonardo stamped over to the easel and pulled away a sheet covering his painting. "*Ecco!* Defeat! Ruination!"

The Gawgon stared, hardly breathing. I did the same. Leonardo had worked mostly in rich, dark tones. In the background, the landscape alone was a masterpiece; it looked as if it had come out of a dream. But it was the figure itself that so bewitched us. Lisa sat quietly, hands at rest, without rings, bracelets, or any other jewelry, in the simplest of gowns; the most miraculous picture I had ever seen.

Only one thing was missing: her face.

Not entirely. To be more accurate, Leonardo had finished everything but the lips. It was all there except the smile.

"See what I mean?" Leonardo burst out. "Hopeless!"

The Gawgon had stepped a little away from the easel. She stood silently, lost in her own thoughts, on her features a mysterious look I had never seen until this moment.

Leonardo was glooming around and muttering to himself. I took his arm and pointed at The Gawgon.

"Is that the kind of smile you were talking about?" I said.

Leonardo stared at her. His jaw dropped, he nearly fell over backward. He ran to get the palette he had flung against the wall, snatched a new brush, and began working like a madman, all the while yelling at The Gawgon to hold her expression and not to move a muscle.

It did not take him long — after all, he was a genius. When he finished, he tossed brush and palette in the air and capered around the studio.

"That's it! At last!" he cried. "All right, you can move now."

The Gawgon went to study the finished portrait. "Yes, Leo, you've pulled off another miracle as usual. Lisa won't notice somebody else smiled for her. Or, what's the difference? Women all know the same things and smile the same way over them. So, it's done. You can deliver it only six years late —"

"Deliver what?" Leonardo protectively spread his arms. "Deliver nothing! *Niente!* I'm keeping her for myself.

"I'm leaving town," he added. "Enough of Florence. Lisa's coming with me. I still have a few little touch-ups to do."

"Somehow, Leo," said The Gawgon, "I'm not surprised."

"Good luck with the big horse," I said.

❋ ❋ ❋   Thuh End   ❋ ❋ ❋

My twelfth birthday came at the worst of a Philadelphia winter. We were housebound, ice coated Lorimer Street, snow drifted into the areaway and back alley. My father tied his derby to his head with a muffler, armed himself with a coal shovel, and made threatening gestures at the drifts. My mother took over and did a little better, but finally gave up. I volunteered — Admiral Peary hacking his way to the North Pole — but my offer was declined. Deprived of her Tulip Garden, my sister moped in her room and did not volunteer at all.

"God put it there," my father said. "Let Him take it away."

"Oh, Alan," my mother said, "you shouldn't talk like that. He might hear you."

Instead of the usual birthday party with my aunts and grandmother, there were only the four of us. My mother baked a cake, as she always did; I blew out the candles in one breath, as I always did. For gifts, I received handkerchiefs and underwear.

My father, all that week, did not go in town. He left the store closed and did not worry about business. There had not been enough business to worry about since his failed hopes with the Mexican jumping beans. The beans themselves had stopped twitching altogether. He told my mother to throw them out.

"Certainly not," she said. "They'll be all right. They're hibernating."

My sister was kept home from school, although given the equipment, I believe she would have hitched a sled to a team of huskies and mushed her way to rejoin the Tulip Garden. As far as I was concerned, I might as well have been quarantined without the distinction of a Board of Health sticker on the front door.

Lessons with The Gawgon had to be suspended. Even after the weather cleared, I did not go to see her. My grandmother had telephoned, saying it was better to put things off a little while. I stayed in my room and drew pictures of Leonardo tramping along the roads, with a sack tied to the end of a pole and the *Mona Lisa* tucked under his arm. In the distance, Michelangelo flung Italian gestures at him.

It was another week before I went to Larchmont Street. My mother walked with me. The sun had come out bright enough to blind us. It was almost warm.

"Don't stay long," my mother told me. She, Aunt Florry, and my grandmother talked in the kitchen. I went upstairs.

The Gawgon was in bed, sitting up with her back propped against some pillows, the flannel bathrobe wrapped around her. The curtains had been pulled back to let in a big shaft of sunlight with motes dancing in it.

"Happy birthday, Boy." The Gawgon looked in good spirits, so I knew Dr. McKelvie had not been there today. "Better late than never. What's that you have?"

I had brought my drawings of Leonardo and the *Mona Lisa*. I handed them to her. "You can keep them if you want."

The Gawgon laughed and said, "Heaven help us, what will you think of next? I have something for you, too. On the desk."

I picked up the package and tore off the wrapping paper. She had given me a treasure: the second of the three-volume set of history books.

"When you've chewed through that," she said, "you'll be ready for the third. I'll save it for an Easter present."

Hardly able to take my eyes off the book, I waited for her to start our lesson. She seemed content to scan the drawings.

"You've got a little better at it," she said, "but you still need to look harder at things. What I'm thinking," she went on, "suppose we go to the park. Not now. When it's warm enough so we won't freeze. Try sketching from life — the trees, pigeons, people sitting on benches. It might do you good."

I offered my own sudden inspiration. I could draw The Gawgon's portrait. That, I said, would be sketching from life. As a further inducement, I told her I could put the Pyramids in the background; she could be sitting on one of them, the way she did when she was a girl.

"I dread to think how I'd come out now." The Gawgon chuckled. "That would be quite a sight. We'll see, we'll see. All right, then. You can start tomorrow."

She leaned back her head. I understood she wanted me to go. I thanked her again for the book. When I left, she was smiling at the pictures in her hands.

The Gawgon died in her sleep that night.

18

The Legatee

"I think," my father said to my mother, "you'd better take him home."

My mother nodded. She put an arm around my shoulders and led me into a dim corridor so deeply carpeted our footsteps made no sound. She sat beside me on a hard-cushioned sofa that smelled of disinfectant. I knew I had behaved badly.

We were, that afternoon, in J. Robert Rockamore & Sons funeral parlor, a tall building in center city between a travel agency and a ladies' dress salon. All the rich and fashionable dead went to Rockamore's. Not that we counted among them, but Uncle Eustace managed to get us squeezed in. He knew people there, professional courtesy was involved. Not only was he supplying the tombstone at cost, he had also worked out some kind of cut-rate transaction. He was proud of his accomplishment.

"It wasn't easy," Uncle Eustace said.

"They have a waiting list."

I had never been to a funeral, let alone to Rockamore's. We entered the lobby through a pair of massive bronze doors sculpted with acanthus leaves and twisted vines. That, I thought, was what the gates of Hell must look like. Inside, Egyptian-style lamps stood on pedestals. The elevator, also with bronze doors, hissed gently as the operator took us to the top floor. No one spoke to him, but he evidently knew where we were supposed to go.

The parlor, one of Rockamore's smallest, seemed a little cramped. Since we did not have enough men in the family, Uncle Eustace had to pay extra for pallbearers. They took up as much space as we did. They stood mute against the wall, six broad-shouldered young men glad for part-time work, black-suited, white-gloved hands clasped over their groins — a posture I would see in later life taken by wedding ushers and politicians on solemn occasions.

Though Uncle Eustace had not contracted for an organist, strains leaked out from someone else's parlor down the hall, and we had the benefit of secondhand music free of charge.

Our vicar, Mr. Granville, was there to

conduct the ceremony. Uncle Eustace had first thought to scout around for a Presbyterian.

"That's what she was," he said.

Aunt Rosie put her foot down. "No, Eustace, that just won't do. We can't have some stranger coming in and mumbling who knows what kind of prayers. No, she'll have to go as an Episcopalian."

My mother and aunts were in the same sad dresses they wore for Mrs. Jossbegger. My sister and I had no official mourning costumes, so we made do with Sunday best. There was one basket of flowers from all of us.

Mr. Granville, at some point, made a gesture and we lined up. I had no idea what we were supposed to do. I saw my grandmother bend over and kiss the figure in the casket; then, one by one, the rest of us followed.

When my turn came, I could not do it. I broke away, choking and crying. I knew, shamefully, I was making a scene.

That was when my mother took me into the hall, where I quieted a little. After a time, Mr. Granville appeared in his white cassock, the pallbearers following with the casket, and I started up all over again.

There was some quick conversation between my mother and father. The upshot: I should not go to the graveside. My mother agreed she would have to take me home, which she did.

I was sick to my stomach but thankful I had not thrown up at Rockamore's. My mother put me to bed and gave me some tea. I tossed and turned and finally dozed off.

The night-light was on when I opened my eyes. It must have been late; the house was quiet. I raised my head, more asleep than awake. In a corner of the room, I saw a rocking chair.

The Gawgon was sitting in it.

"You didn't kiss me good-bye," she said.

"I couldn't," I said. "It wasn't you."

"Quite right," she agreed. "It wasn't."

"Are you a ghost?" I said. "A duppy?"

"Of course not."

"But — but," I said, "what are you? Where did you go after —"

"Nowhere. I never went away from you. Did you suppose I would?"

I did not know what to answer.

"I'm in your imagination," The Gawgon said. "You're making me up as you go along."

"Then," I finally said, "you're all right?"

"Yes, I'm all right," The Gawgon said.

"And so are you."

"That's good," I said. "I'm glad."

The Gawgon was still watching me as I turned over and went peacefully to sleep.

The following Sunday afternoon, Uncle Rob and Aunt Rosie stopped by. They brought some cardboard cartons and shoe boxes into the dining room and put them on the table. Uncle Rob's face had the same official look as when he carved turkey, so I assumed adult business matters were involved. It surprised me when Uncle Rob motioned for me to sit with them.

"Annie made a will. Did you know that?" he said, more to my mother and father than to me. "I'd been at her for years, but she kept putting it off. Well, a few weeks ago she got around to it."

"Why, for heaven's sake, did she bother?" Aunt Rosie said. "She had nothing to leave anybody."

Uncle Rob, meantime, had tucked up his sleeves and consulted figures on a piece of paper. There were, he said, some stocks and bonds, but the companies had gone bankrupt. There was a savings account, not enough to cover expenses. He calculated everyone would have to chip in to make up the difference when Rockamore's bill came. The few pieces of furniture in her room might as well stay there; no one would buy them, and they would be useful when the room got rented out.

"Now, you, Skinamalink." Uncle Rob finally spoke directly to me. He waved a hand at the boxes. "These are yours. That's what the will says."

"Well, well, Bax," my father said, "you're a legatee."

I asked if I could open the boxes. Uncle Rob nodded:

"They're yours, you can do anything you want with them."

The first thing I saw when I opened one of the lids was the third of the three-volume history; under it, Shakespeare's plays; a thick, gilt-edged anthology of poems; some Sherlock Holmes; the drawings I had given her at Christmas and the last ones of Leonardo and Michelangelo. In the shoe box were postcards of famous paintings; snapshots of her son; the photo of the Pyramids and The Gawgon with her girl's bright face.

These were treasures beyond any I could have imagined. I thought I had better take the boxes to my room, where I could look into them privately. I began hauling them upstairs.

"Just what I meant," Aunt Rosie was

saying. "Poor dear, she had nothing."

My father, that spring, seldom went in town to the store. I stayed mostly in my room. I had no heart to read the books or draw pictures. The tangled yarn lay untouched on the night table. I felt bad that I had not undone more knots. The Gawgon would have been disappointed in me, as I was disappointed in myself.

No one said anything about another teacher. I did not ask. Several times a week, my mother visited my grandmother. I went along and talked to Nora, but without much enthusiasm.

The Gawgon's room had been rented to someone named Mr. Vance. I saw him once or twice: a tight-faced man who wore wing-tip shoes. Uncle Eustace had somewhere struck up an acquaintance and recommended Mr. Vance as a reliable lodger. Men in dark overcoats and gray felt hats often came to visit him, carrying packages in and out. His door was usually closed.

My grandmother occasionally received penny postcards from Uncle Will. He was living in a boardinghouse in Detroit and, miraculously, had found part-time work in a factory.

"He sounds happy. He deserves to be."

My grandmother studied his latest message. "It seems he has a lady friend."

"He writes that on a postcard?" exclaimed Aunt Rosie, who was there when the news arrived. "Where the mailman and anybody else can read it?"

"I'm sure the mailman isn't interested," my grandmother said.

Aunt Rosie snorted. "I'm sure he is."

Going down the hall one evening, I saw my sister's door was open and the light on. She was sitting on the edge of her bed. Neck bent, shoulders drooping, she looked so forlorn and miserable I thought she might have broken a fingernail. I stood a few moments in the doorway. When she noticed me, she did not yell at me to go away. This was extraordinary. I ventured in and asked what was wrong.

"I'm not going to Rittenhouse Academy anymore," she said.

That, I said, was wonderful news. I congratulated her on being so lucky.

"You stupid blighter," she said, "I'm not going back and neither are you. Never."

That was a happy relief. I had feared, without someone to give me lessons, I might be returned to the clutches of Dr. Legg. I had planned, if such a disaster threatened, on trumping up some new and horrible sickness.

"Didn't they tell you?" she said.

Generally speaking, no one told me anything right away. If it was important, they would get around to it sooner or later.

"Father's closing the store," she said. "He's selling our house. Grandmother's, too."

At first, I wondered if she was just making it up to torment me, but she looked so awful she had to be sincere. Still, it made no sense. Where would we live?

"We're moving," she said. "Grandmother and Aunt Florry, too. Father bought a new house.

"Don't you understand?" she flung at me. "We have to go away. All of us. To some stupid place."

I was so dumbstruck I sat down beside her. She had, thus far, been speaking bitterly and resentfully. Now she started crying. So did I. We actually put our arms around each other.

19

The Irish Shillelly

My sister's information about unpleasant things was, as always, right. By the time my parents got around to telling me, it came as no surprise. Late that spring, with my grandmother, Aunt Florry, and Nora, we moved to a place called Rosetree Hill, a dozen or so miles from Philadelphia.

We called it the new house, but it was a very old one. It stood at the far end of Lakeview Avenue. Though I saw no lake to view, I learned there had been one, filled in when the neighborhood was built up. There were reminders of its presence when it seeped through the cellar floor, setting the basement awash at regular intervals.

"It looks like the Ming Dynasty," said my father, standing in the middle of the living room after everything was installed. He had closed his store and sold the contents, salvaging as much as he could in the way of lamps, screens, wall hangings, and some lacquered tables. The effect was definitely Oriental. The Mexican jumping beans had been lost in the shuffle.

I never understood my father's business dealings. I could only guess he had sold or rented out the houses on Lorimer Street and Larchmont Street, calculating we could live on that money until he went into a new business.

He had bought the house as soon as he saw it. Dirt cheap, he said. Understandably, for it was falling apart. The faucets dripped with continuous tinklings, like wind chimes. The floors sagged, the plumbing moaned and gargled when anyone flushed the toilet. The stairs sloped at an acute angle, strenuous to climb up, perilous to climb down.

"It's a fine house," my father said. "You won't find another like it."

"I'm sure not," my mother said.

"Now, that's what I call a property." My father held out his arms in an all-embracing gesture. "Land."

What he meant was the house had a front lawn. It was covered with bald spots as if the grass had a skin disease. Instead of an alley and areaway, there was an equally afflicted yard in the back, where sturdy clumps of weeds flourished. A porch and wooden railing ran along the front of the house. Chains dangled from the porch ceiling where once had been a swing. They looked like equipment from a medieval torture chamber.

It was the last house on Lakeview Avenue. Farther down were vacant lots. Still farther, at the dead end, some woods began: spindly trees and thickets. Our neighbors' neatly trimmed lawns seemed to pull their skirts away from us, leaving our property to itself in a sort of real-estate Hell.

My father was proud of the new house. I hated it.

If my grandmother's boardinghouse expanded and contracted like an accordion, our new house was more like a rabbit warren, with closets, cubbyholes, a pantry with lopsided shelves. Nora, with her cage and pole, held pride of place in the Ming Dynasty living room. We had not enough bedrooms to go 'round, so I was assigned to the attic — partly finished, it was called, which meant that one side was bandaged with wallpaper; the other, a skeleton of rafters. I was warned never to walk on the area in front of the eaves or I would crash through to the floor below.

I tossed and turned most of our first night in the new house. My old familiar bed felt as if we had never met. I had no idea what time it was when I woke again.

The Gawgon was sitting on my unpacked boxes.

I was surprised but happy to see her. "We moved," I said. "How did you find the house?"

"I can always find you," The Gawgon said.

I blurted out that I hated the place.

"Understandable," she said. "Nobody likes being uprooted. You'll get used to it."

I said I doubted that.

"Where's your imagination, Boy?" she answered. "You can turn this house into anything you please. King Arthur's castle, if you like. Or Dracula's, with bats and a vampire's coffin in the cellar.

"Or a Parisian garret," she went on, "with starving artists running in and out. A beautiful model having her picture painted — you're old enough to be interested in that sort of thing."

I began cheering up. Before The Gawgon could continue, I heard doors banging open and my father yelling. I jumped out of bed and stumbled down the attic steps.

Everybody was awake. My father, in striped pajamas, was heading for the landing, my mother behind him, telling him to

put on his bedroom slippers.

"Nobody move! Stand where you are!" my father commanded. "I've got a gun!"

Sleep-fuddled and confused, I called out the first thing that came to mind:

"Don't shoot The Gawgon!"

"Oh, Alan, you don't have a gun," my mother said. "If anybody's there, why tell them to stay?"

My father paid no attention. He was waving his arms and hurrying down the stairs while my mother tried to hold him back. He managed the first couple of steps, but lost his footing and went skidding down the rest. It brought him to the living room faster than if he had walked.

All the lights were on by now. We clattered after him. Unruffled by his rapid descent, he inspected the living room. He was sure, he said, he heard prowlers. He found none and stepped through the dining room into the kitchen.

The cupboard was open, so was the icebox. The latch on the pantry door had been broken. A cracked egg lay on the linoleum floor.

"Burglars," my father said. "I told you so."

My grandmother and Aunt Florry came to look around the kitchen while my sister observed from a distance. My mother surveyed the shelves and icebox. Missing, along with our eggs, were bottles of milk, some pork chops, a box of cornflakes, sugar, coffee, and a bag of flour.

"They only took the food. They didn't touch anything else," my mother said. "God help them, that's all they wanted."

She sat down at the table and began to cry.

Aunt Florry and my grandmother tidied up. My father toured the backyard to see if the burglars were hiding amid the weeds.

I went back to the attic. The Gawgon was not there.

"What we really need," my father announced, "is a tree."

"Oh, Alan," my mother said, "whatever for?"

"Landscaping." My father stood on the front porch and surveyed the property. He narrowed his eyes as if scanning a vast expanse. "We need one" — he pointed at a bare spot in the middle of the lawn — "right there."

When my mother asked where he expected to get a tree, he motioned beyond the vacant lot at the end of Lakeview Avenue. "In the woods."

"Steal one?" my mother said.

"Who'll notice?" Without further discussion, he formed us into a raiding party. He walked ahead, as pioneer and pathfinder; I followed, carrying a spade salvaged from a heap of rusty tools abandoned in the cellar. My mother, holding a burlap sack, brought up the rear.

In the woods — I had begun thinking of it as Sherwood Forest — the only trees he liked were too big to dig up. He had to settle for a tormented-looking sapling with skinny branches and barely any leaves. None of us knew what kind; my father said it didn't matter. We wrapped the straggly roots in the sack. He carried it like a baby in his arms. At the house, he called out for my grandmother, Aunt Florry, and my sister. We took turns excavating a hole. Then he went inside and came back with a pair of scissors.

"For good luck." He ceremoniously snipped locks of hair from everyone's head, including his own. He laid them, with one of Nora's feathers, in the bottom of the hole.

"We can plant it now," he said. "It's our family tree."

Later in the afternoon, Aunt Rosie and Uncle Rob drove out to see how we were getting on. Aunt Rosie stared at the addition to the yard:

"What, for heaven's sake, do you call that?"

"I call it a tree," my father retorted.

"What's that crookedy stick the Irish carry to hit each other?" Aunt Rosie asked Uncle Rob.

"A shillelagh," he said.

"That's it," Aunt Rosie said. "It looks like an Irish shillelly."

We all went to the porch, where my father had us stand to get a better perspective on the sapling. If we squinted a little, he said, we could see traces of green.

A dog, just then, came wandering past the house and sighted our family tree. Wagging his tail, an eager grin on his face, he trotted up and peed on it.

Each day after that, dogs of every size and ancestry showed up. Some I did not recognize as belonging in the neighborhood; they must have traveled from miles away, all members of a widespread network, a peeing society with its meeting place at the Irish shillelly — its permanent name, thanks to Aunt Rosie. We chased them off whenever we saw them.

My father did not worry about the dogs. The Irish shillelly showed signs of actually growing a little. As my father saw it, we were getting free fertilizer.

20

A Swimming Party

I nearly drowned, that summer, and also fell in love. The drowning part came first, but both events happened at practically the same time. I very sensibly did not mention either one to my family.

In any case, they were all occupied with other things. Now that we had settled into the new house, my father concentrated on making a living. He thought about it a lot, mainly while sitting on the porch, eyes closed in meditation, sometimes glancing up to admire the Irish shillelly. He still read the financial pages of the newspaper, more out of habit than anything else, for there were no finances to read about.

"All in due course, all in due course," he assured my mother when she asked what he had in mind. "I'm planning my strategy."

Aunt Florry, it turned out, was the first to get a real job. Her old employer, Mrs. Heberton, had been as good as her word.

She did ask around on Aunt Florry's behalf. Through her influence, Aunt Florry was hired as a clerk in the mortgage department of the biggest bank in Philadelphia. Always a nifty dresser, she looked especially nifty when, each morning, she walked the quarter mile to the trolley. Not only an old and most distinguished institution, the bank also provided free lunches to its employees. When she came home in the evening, Aunt Florry often brought some buttered rolls, a slice of pie, or other portable tidbits saved out of her meal and wrapped in paper napkins.

My grandmother had news from Uncle Will. Instead of a postcard, this time he wrote a letter, saying he was getting married.

"I'm glad," my grandmother said. "I only hope she treats him better than" — she rolled her eyes — "you know who."

I did not, but everyone else did. All agreed it was a good thing for Uncle Will, so I was happy for him.

My sister was too busy to pay much attention to any of that. She cultivated another Tulip Garden.

Our first week or two in Rosetree Hill, she had been sullen and brooding. Then, almost overnight, a Tulip Garden sprang up. I never learned whether she grew a new one or got transplanted into one already flowering; nor did I understand how she managed it so quickly. But all at once, there they were, looking the same as the previous group though noticeably blossomed out.

On hot afternoons, they clustered, long-legged in their summer frocks, in languid attitudes on the porch steps. Most of the time, along with the standard whispering and giggling, they gossiped about the young men of Rosetree Hill; in particular, someone called Nick Ormond. The very name carried enough magical power to send them swooning in rapture. Nick Ormond, I gathered, was the local hero. Like my sister and her companion tulips, he was going to be a senior at Rosetree High School that coming fall. A foregone conclusion, beyond any doubt, he would be captain of the football team, head of the student council, class president, and, later, king of the world.

As with the previous Tulip Garden, their company was forbidden to me.

"Make him keep away," my sister warned them. "He'll try to look down your dress."

This was true, but I thought nobody no-

ticed. And so I could only ogle and eaves-
drop from a distance.

My father, meanwhile, had struck on a
plan to make a fortune.

"The River Jordan," he said. "I'm going
to buy it."

"Oh, Alan, that's ridiculous," my mother
said. "I'm sure it's not for sale."

"Not the whole river," my father said.
"Just some."

His plan involved importing Jordan
water by the barrel. He would then re-
package it in small bottles, like perfume,
and sell them — along with a fancy certificate — for baptisms. The Jordan water
would get babies off to a good start in life.

He proposed using regular tap water and
adding a few drops from the Jordan.

"A little," he said, "should go a long way."

My mother wanted no part of the
scheme. Diluting water with water, even
Jordan water, seemed dishonest. And who
knew what kind of trouble he could get
himself into, especially with God Almighty?

My father said he would take his
chances, we needed the money. Since he
was unsure who actually owned the river
and how he might buy some from a spot
nobody cared about, he wrote letters to

kings, prime ministers, and various ambassadors. Awaiting their answers, he went back to studying the financial pages.

For myself, idle, I scuffed around the house and halfheartedly chased dogs away from the shillelly, which persisted in putting out a couple of leaves from time to time. Most often, I holed up in the attic with The Gawgon's books.

The Gawgon still came to visit, although irregularly. Once, poking at the clutter on my table, she gave me a quizzical look:

"What, Boy, you've stopped drawing pictures?"

I nodded. I had, indeed, given that up; nor had I bothered to think of any foolish stories. I told her I hadn't felt like it.

"As good a reason as any," The Gawgon said. "You'll start again, sooner or later."

No, I said. Things weren't the same.

"Nothing stays the same," The Gawgon said. "Not you, not anything else. Don't worry, you'll find what you need."

"I don't care," I said.

The Gawgon left. I was sorry. It was the first time I had been any way snappish to her.

Occasionally, for the sake of getting away from the house, I wandered the neighborhood, hoping to find boys my own age. The only ones in the vicinity were several years older than I. They were cordial enough; they simply had their own interests.

I ventured, one day, past the end of the street, beyond Sherwood Forest, where it turned into serious woods, thick with trees and heavy underbrush, outcroppings of rocks, gullies that fell away so suddenly I nearly tumbled into them. I pressed on and soon came to a creek bubbling over a stony bed.

I followed it a while. Farther along, I heard whoops and yells. The creek had widened into a modest river with sloping, pebbly banks. Half a dozen older boys were swimming, splashing, and ducking each other with a lot of merriment and horseplay.

I picked my way closer to stand and watch. They noticed me but neither chased me away nor invited me to join them. One, sandy-haired, with a pair of athletic legs and black swim trunks, was clearly the leader. When he jumped into the water, so did everyone else; when he sunned himself on the shore, they all squatted around him.

Had my sister been there, she would have gone berserk, for one of his entourage addressed him as "Nick." It dawned on me

I was in the very presence of that paragon of animals and future king of the world: Nick Ormond himself.

I hung around the fringe of this activity for a time. When they tired of swimming, they all traipsed off together and left the creek to me. It looked so inviting, with the sunlight flashing on the green ripples, I thought how pleasant it would be to go for a swim. I glanced around, making sure I was unobserved, then peeled down to my underwear.

The water, when I stepped into it, was chillier than I expected; gooseflesh erupted all over me. I got used to it after a minute or so, and launched myself into the current.

There were only two difficulties. First, I had never been in water this deep; second, I did not know how to swim.

These had not seemed insurmountable problems. I had watched Nick and his friends. It looked simple and easy enough. I followed their example. And sank like a stone. By the time I realized I should have kept my mouth shut, I believed I had swallowed half the creek while the other half poured up my nose and into my ears. I thrashed around, which only made matters worse. I assumed I was drowning, and that could get me in serious trouble at home.

In the course of kicking and flailing, and yelling when I found enough breath to do it, my feet scraped the bottom. It occurred to me, in some dim instinct for survival, to stand up. When I did, the water came barely to my shoulders. All I had to do was walk out. Gasping and coughing, I lumbered against the current, which felt like crawling through molasses. Torn between gratitude for my salvation and fury at my idiocy, I sprawled on the bank.

After a few minutes, I put my clothes on. My head pounded; water filled my ears and made fluttering noises as if moths had nested there. I still shook, frightened and freezing. I thought I had better go home.

As a shrewd and canny woodsman, I followed the creek in the direction I had come from. I had, by then, dried out, warmed up, and started feeling pleased at my conduct. The creek, in my adjusted recollection, became much wider and swifter, with high waves and a treacherous undertow. I had dealt with it well.

Busy congratulating myself, I must have made a wrong turn. Instead of reaching Lakeview Avenue, I found myself deeper in the woods. I recognized nothing familiar. The faster I walked, I reckoned, the sooner

I would be out of the place, which had begun looking suddenly weird and sinister. This led me nowhere. I had to admit I was hopelessly lost, never to be seen again until someone eventually tripped over my skeleton. The most sensible reaction was blind panic. I went scrambling straight through the underbrush.

21

My Sweet Gloria

Euclid claimed, as The Gawgon taught me, the shortest distance between two points was a straight line. I was not able to apply that principle. I kept zigzagging as brambles maliciously sprang up and got in the way. I lost track of where I had been and where I was trying to go. I did, soon, come to a dirt road. A stone bridge spanned the creek, which had either looped back on itself or I had been running around in a circle. Lacking any better idea, I crossed over it. After a dozen more yards, the woods ended and I burst through into civilization.

This was a part of Rosetree Hill I had never seen before: large, handsome houses, tall trees lining both sides of the street. I headed for the nearest house, hoping to find other human beings.

What I found was Nick Ormond. Still in his black trunks, the future king of the world was pushing a lawn mower. I dared to approach. I called to him by name. This did not surprise him. He may have recognized me from the creek; perhaps he took for granted that everybody knew him. He stopped mowing the grass — I hardly believed the paragon of animals was doing such a humble chore — and looked me up and down. I tried to be properly respectful, all the while wondering how to ask directions without shamefully confessing I was lost. I told him my name and where I lived.

"Don't you have a sister?" he asked, before I could get around to my own questions. "Elise?"

Amazed that he was aware of her existence, I admitted I did. He nodded and grew almost cordial. I hinted I was on my way to Lakeview Avenue, wherever that might be.

Meantime, a substantial, silver-haired man with a neatly trimmed mustache had come from behind the house. He wore white duck pants and a short-sleeved shirt with crossed golf clubs embroidered on the breast pocket. Nick, who seemed to know we had just moved into the neighborhood, told him who I was, adding a mention of my sister.

The man — Nick's father — courteously shook my hand. "Lakeview Avenue? Well, son, you've got yourself all mixed up." He eyed the scratches on my arms and legs. "Been hacking around the woods? They can fool you if you don't know them."

He turned to Nick. "Ready for lemonade?" Nick declared he surely was. The two started down the driveway. Mr. Ormond glanced back. "Come on, you have some, too. I think you could use a good stiff drink." He laughed good-naturedly. "Nonalcoholic, of course."

I accepted gratefully. I followed them down a driveway to a big backyard lined with flower beds. Nick went and stretched out in a hammock slung between two trees. Mr. Ormond motioned for me to sit on a wooden bench at a trestle table. Mrs. Ormond, a pleasant-looking woman of my mother's age, came out the back door. She brought a tray with tall glasses and a chrome-plated ice bucket. Beside her, carrying a pitcher, walked a slender girl in a sundress.

"We need another glass, my dear," Mr. Ormond said to the girl. "We have an unexpected guest."

With a curious glance at me, she disappeared into the house. By the time she came back, Mrs. Ormond had taken up a pair of tongs and dropped ice into the tumblers. Mr. Ormond made brief introductions as Mrs. Ormond poured out the lemonade. Gloria, so their daughter was named, turned closer attention on me. Whereas her brother's hair was close-cropped and yellowish, hers was golden brown, long, with lighter streaks in it. She had wide-set, blue-green eyes, and they made me ill at ease, for she seemed to be studying me with secret amusement.

"Hey, sis, where's mine?" Nick, without raising himself from the hammock, held out an arm and wiggled his fingers. "Bring it here, twit."

"Lazy lump," Gloria called back. "Get it yourself."

Nick made a great show of protesting he was tired, ordering her to be a good little brat and do as she was told, and they tossed insults back and forth. Mr. and Mrs. Ormond, evidently used to this, paid them no mind.

Gloria sighed and shrugged. With a wicked little curve to her lips, she went to the hammock. Instead of putting the glass in Nick's hand, she poured the contents, ice and all, onto his head. Nick, roaring, tipped himself out of the hammock and sprawled full-length on the grass. He started after his sister, on her smiling way to the table.

"Enough. Stop it," Mrs. Ormond said. "No more nonsense, either of you. We have company."

Nick refilled his glass, which Gloria had let fall to the ground. He took it to the front yard. He was more than a little vexed; no doubt he had his reputation to uphold in front of strangers.

Gloria, unruffled, sipped her drink, as I did my own. It was nectar of the gods; even the ice was delicious — in glittering cubes, not slivers, which meant the Ormonds had one of the new electric refrigerators. More than all that, Gloria handed me my lemonade with such a graceful motion, and looked full at me over the rim of her tumbler. That was probably when I fell in love with her. People, I suppose, have fallen in love for less reason.

Mr. Ormond, meantime, had been asking about my family, how long we had been in Rosetree Hill, and what my father did. I was reluctant to explain about buying the River Jordan; I only said he imported things. I added that my aunt worked at the biggest bank in town.

"What a coincidence," Mr. Ormond said. "So do I."

It was a pleasant enough conversation until Mrs. Ormond began talking about school, as adults do when they know nothing better to say to children. Gloria, she mentioned, would be going into seventh grade at Rosetree Junior High.

"You look the same age," she added. "I imagine that's where you'll go, too."

Junior high? From what my mother had calculated, I would, in the fall, go to elementary school as a sixth grader.

So besotted with Gloria, I had not given a thought to school and grades. This was monstrous. The elementary school and the junior high were miles apart, geographically and every other way. I knew the iron-bound, unbreakable system of class and caste. I had seen and lived it myself at Rittenhouse Academy.

It was unthinkable, unspeakable, maybe illegal, for anyone in a higher grade to have anything but scorn and contempt for anyone in a lower. I could already see Gloria's lovely face fill with horror. Her fond glances — as I was sure they were — would turn to disgust, as if I had been transformed into a slithering reptile, a warty toad, a less than human creature covered with oozing sores and trailing clouds of poisonous dandruff.

Between now and autumn — who knew what might happen? Before being unmasked as a wretched sixth grader, I could be lucky enough to get squashed by a truck.

And so I took the only reasonable course: I lied.

I said I wasn't sure what grade. I had been reading *Tom Brown's Schooldays*, one of The Gawgon's books, and I grasped at that straw.

"Because, you see," I went on, "it's different in England. They don't have grades, they have forms."

"England?" Mr. Ormond raised an eyebrow.

"To Rugby," I said. "It's a famous school."

I prayed for a thunderbolt to blast me. It did not. I floundered on, explaining that my parents were thinking of sending me there. To assure Gloria our separation would not be long, I added I would be home for the holidays.

"Interesting," said Mr. Ormond. I wondered if he knew I was lying.

"How exciting," said Mrs. Ormond, as if she believed me. "You must be looking forward to it."

Gloria did not comment. I was only looking forward to going home before I dug a deeper pit for myself. I stood up —

staggered up, rather, under the burden of my preposterous claim. Mr. Ormond gave me directions to Lakeview Avenue. It was not far, less than a mile; he told me to cross the trolley tracks, turn left there and right someplace else.

I was not keeping any of this straight in my head. I asked him to repeat. Convinced, no doubt, I was an idiot, he finally asked Gloria to take her bicycle and go with me.

"We don't want you getting lost again," Mr. Ormond said.

I was already lost. Gloria went to the garage. I walked down the driveway. Nick Ormond stopped pushing the lawn mower long enough to call, "Say hello to your sister."

Gloria came pedaling into the street. She tossed her long hair and waved for me to follow. I trotted along the pavement, wondering if she meant to make me run all the way. She kept glancing back with the same air of secret amusement she had when we were drinking lemonade, as if teasing me to catch up with her.

Before I lagged too far behind, she circled back, wheeling graceful spirals and figure eights. At last, she dismounted and rolled the bicycle to the pavement. She pushed it along; we walked side by side. She smelled of sunlight and perspiration. She was marvelous.

"We have a parrot," I said.

By then, we had reached Lakeview Avenue. I pointed to our house and asked if she wanted to come in and see Nora. A couple of dogs were sniffing around the Irish shillelly. I chased them away. When I turned back, she was gone.

I had come home just in time for dinner. As we all sat down, my mother looked at me closely and with some concern and asked where I had been all afternoon.

This time I did not lie — except for leaving out the parts about drowning, getting lost in the woods, and falling in love. I offhandedly remarked I had a nice visit with the Ormond family, after happening to run into Nick.

My sister sat bolt upright, as though galvanized by a powerful electric current. I smiled and charitably threw her a crumb.

"Oh," I said, "I almost forgot. Nick was asking for you."

I left her choking and gulping and turned to Aunt Florry. Mr. Ormond, I told her, also worked at her bank.

"He certainly does," Aunt Florry said.

"Good heavens, he's a vice president."

My father laughed. "Bax, old sport, you've been hobnobbing with the upper crust."

Aunt Florry reminded us that Mr. Ormond had been her old employer's financial adviser. Mrs. Heberton had spoken to him and recommended her for a job. Everyone was surprised I had been face-to-face with him; underlings at the bank caught only glimpses of Mr. Ormond. They went on to talk about other things.

I ate my dinner quickly and started for the attic. My sister ran after me. I beat her to it and locked the door behind me.

"What did he say?" she yelled. "Exactly."

"I can't remember it all," I said, taking a dumb-ox attitude which she hated. "Something like 'hello to your sister.'"

She squealed and smacked the door as if it were my head. I climbed the rest of the steps to my garret, as I had begun calling it, and flopped on the bed, relishing my thoughts — most of them circling around Gloria. Finally, I rummaged out a sketch pad and soft pencil, meaning to do a portrait of her. I had drawn nothing for such a long time, I could not catch the likeness. I crumpled sheet after sheet and tossed them on the floor.

"Well, Boy, I believe you've gone and lost your heart."

The Gawgon was looking over my shoulder.

I did not answer. I was happy to see her; but I said nothing.

"I'm glad," The Gawgon said. "In fact, I rather hoped you would. Sometimes, the best way to heal a heart is to lose it. But I'm sorry you told such a terrible whopper. It was silly on top of being a lie. Ah, well, it's not the last silly thing you'll ever do."

The Gawgon peered at the sketch I had begun for about the seventeenth time. "That's your little Gloria? Yes, she's a lovely child. It will be a nice portrait."

"I wish I could have drawn yours," I said. "I'm sorry I didn't have the chance. It's not that I haven't been thinking of you. I can still try —"

"No, no," The Gawgon gently said. "We've had our adventures, you and I. Wonderful adventures. I'm glad of them. You go ahead now with your own."

"You don't mind?" I asked. "About Gloria and me?"

"Of course not," The Gawgon said. " 'Summer's lease hath all too short a date.' "

"Shakespeare," I said.

"Correct," said The Gawgon. "Be happy. Good night, Boy."

After breakfast next morning, I went on the porch to stand sentry duty, ready to defend the Irish shillelly. No dogs hove into sight. I was about to climb to my garret and work some more on the portrait. I stopped short. Swift and graceful as an antelope, Gloria came pedaling her bicycle down Lakeview Avenue. She coasted up to the steps.

"You wanted me to see your parrot?" she said.

22

Summer's Love

Gloria and I were sweethearts that summer. We never talked about it. I wondered if she knew. I believed she did. That was good enough.

We were together from that first morning she came to see Nora. I warned her Nora sometimes nipped, but Gloria went straight to the perch and held out a finger. Nora, charmed, stepped onto it.

She charmed the rest of my family, as well. My mother patted her head and said what a pretty child she was. Gloria had no grandmother. Mine happily substituted, and within a week or two, Gloria was calling her "Grandma Mary."

My sister sweetly fussed over her — Gloria's brother, after all, was king of the world — offering to paint her nails and do her hair. And my sister never called me a stupid blighter — when Gloria was there.

My father was delighted when Gloria oohed and ahhed over the Ming Dynasty living room. Beaming, he explained what all the curios were and where they came from.

"I want to go to China," Gloria said to me later. She had a distant, dreamy look in her eyes. "I want to sail all around the world."

Offering my own adventures on the high seas, I told her I had visited relatives in Jamaica. I made it sound as if the voyage had been marked by hurricanes, threats of shipwreck, and mutiny. I went on about coconuts and mangoes, palm trees and pirate coves.

"Yes," Gloria said. "Oh, yes. I'll go there, too. I'll go everywhere."

If Gloria charmed my family, our house charmed her. She loved the cubbyholes, the Alpine stairway, the wooden icebox with all its doors. She showed tender feelings toward the Irish shillelly and helped shoo the dogs away. Our house looked better to me after she had been there. I did come to love it, and loved it, no doubt, because she did.

We saw a lot of each other during those summer days, though I could never be sure when. Gloria would simply show up on her bicycle, or I would walk to the Ormonds' house and hope to find her. Sometimes she was there, sometimes not. I wondered if she kept company with other boys. No, that was too horrible to imagine. I uprooted that idea from my thoughts. But I never knew where she went, and never asked.

My father, meantime, had received no letters from any kings or ambassadors. Annoyed at them, he gave up trying to buy the River Jordan and turned to a brighter prospect.

"Palm-Nutto," he said to my mother. "Diggers wanted me to sell it. He ate some, remember? To show how pure it was."

My father wrote to his boyhood chum in Kingston. In due course, several cases of the household cleanser arrived. Convinced he could sell anything to anybody, he foresaw no difficulties.

His first morning of door-to-door salesmanship, he wore his straw boater with striped hatband and his white summer suit — an ice-cream suit, my mother called it. He stowed a dozen jars in the trunk of our car and drove off with a gnashing of gears.

He came home before noon. He carried his straw hat in his hand, his complexion was a delicate green. No one had bought any. Besides, eating the Palm-Nutto to show its purity made him nauseous. One lady seemed a good prospect but lost interest when he threw up on her floor. He renounced Palm-Nutto then and there.

My mother took over the business and brought home small amounts of cash. She assured my father he was a fine salesman; it was simply that she could talk about housecleaning better than he could. She did not eat any Palm-Nutto.

Uncle Eustace was prospering. While the Depression kept getting worse, his tombstone business kept getting better. It was, he said, thanks to Mr. Vance, who had been a lodger in my grandmother's boardinghouse.

"He's a good sort of fellow, is Vance," Uncle Eustace said. "He never talks about what line of work he's in, but he sends a nice bit of business my way. His friends buy a lot of stones."

"His friends keep shooting each other, if you ask me," my father said. "You're probably selling tombstones to half the gangsters in Philadelphia."

"So?" Uncle Eustace shrugged. "It's a living."

"Gangsters or not, they should have a decent burial," my mother said. "They're just as dead as anybody else."

Gloria, that summer, taught me to ride a bicycle. At her request, Mrs. Ormond let me borrow Nick's outgrown vehicle. It was small for me as well, and I had to be cautious about banging my knees on the handlebars. Gloria never made fun of me when I fell off. Even when I caught the knack of balancing, pedaling, and steering, I never matched her spirals and loops. Still, I could ride to her house quickly; it was as good as having an automobile.

Being in love with her made me shrewd and calculating. I was always afraid she would, one day, glide away on her bicycle and vanish. I kept thinking of schemes to snare her interest.

Not only had I begun studying in earnest, I had also started drawing again. I proposed doing her portrait. That would keep her with me a long time. I would make sure it did. She agreed, and from then on I brought my sketch pad.

My cunning knew no limits. I began a story to be revealed when the time was right. Seeking inspiration, I burglarized Shakespeare from the book The Gawgon left me. Shakespeare had plenty of ideas. He would never notice any missing.

WONDERS OF THE WORLD

Under the cloak of darkness, Davio Aldini strode happily and eagerly to what might cost his life. The clock in the piazza tolled twelve. He quickened his pace and slipped noiselessly through the lavish gardens of the Ormondi estate.

Since that morning in the marketplace, when a street urchin pressed a scrap of paper into his hand, Davio had counted the hours. His heart leaped with joy at the words that could well be his death sentence:

My dearest Davio,
We must no longer be apart. Come to my chambers at midnight. Second balcony, east wing.
Yours truly, and truly yours,
Gloria Ormondi
P.S. I'll leave the light on.

He had glimpsed her only from time to time when the beautiful Gloria and a train of servants bought baskets of lemons for her family's lemonade. Between them, however, passed the melting glances of love at first sight. They had never spoken, nor dared to. The Ormondis and Aldinis, richest and most powerful families in the hill town of Rosamonte, had been mortal enemies for centuries. They had forgotten why but did remember to hate each other.

Davio made his way to the east wing of the Ormondi mansion. Thick greenery covered the wall. A lamp glowed from the chamber casement. He flung aside his cloak nonchalantly as he risked his life and climbed athletically up the vines.

As he was about to swing over the stone balcony, a figure loomed from the shadows.

"My darling!" Davio whispered. "I'm here —"

"And so am I, you sneaking swine!"

Davio stared into the furious face of Mr. Ormondi, whose mustache convulsed with a life of its own.

"You wretch! You dog! You — you Aldini!" roared Mr. Ormondi. "How dare you! What are you up to? Answer me!"

"Aggag," replied Davio, unable to explain further with Mr. Ormondi's hands clamped around his neck. He had resigned himself to death in exchange for a moment with his beloved. He had not reckoned on his tonsils exploding. With all his strength he peeled away Mr. Ormondi's fingers, but, in the desperate struggle, tumbled backward and crashed down through the shrubbery

Mr. Ormondi bawled for his army of lackeys and retainers. Davio sat up and held his spinning head. He staggered to his feet and lurched away with no clear idea where he was going. A hand seized him by the collar. He flung himself around to face his attacker.

It was Gloria, dressed in the leggings and leather jerkin of a stable-sweeper.

"Quick, my dearest," she urged, while torches flared and angry Ormondis swarmed from the mansion. She hustled the still bewildered Davio through the gardens and into the shadows of the olive trees.

"No time to warn you," Gloria hurried on. "That treacherous little guttersnipe! I shouldn't have trusted him with my letter. He blabbed to my father. I'm sure he was well rewarded."

By now they had reached what looked to Davio like an abandoned toolshed. He stumbled through the door after her. With flint and steel from her jacket, Gloria struck a spark and lit a lamp on the cluttered workbench. Even in her coarse garb and these dilapidated surroundings, she appeared still more radiantly beautiful. He held out his arms to her.

"Alone at last!" cried Davio.

"Not for long," said Gloria. "They'll find us here if we don't get a move on."

"My dearest, we have no escape," Davio said. "But at least we shall spend these final moments together. They will be all the sweeter because of their brevity.

"Then let your father stab me with a bodkin!" Davio snapped his fingers. "I care not a figgo! Let him run me through with a rapier —"

"You?" said Gloria. "And what do you think he'll do to me?"

"We shall have the joy of dying together," Davio pointed out.

"Not a good idea," said Gloria.

She stepped to a corner of the shed where a canvas-draped object leaned against the wall.

"My father's cousin Leo gave him this to try out," Gloria said. "Cousin Leo's a genius at inventing things — and a pretty good artist, too. He only made one of these, then got interested in painting somebody's portrait — Lisa something-or-other — and that was the last we saw of him.

"My father thought it was ridiculous," Gloria went on. "One more of Cousin Leo's harebrained schemes. Useless, my father said. Who'd want it when we have horses?"

Gloria, during this, had untied the cords that secured the canvas and pulled aside the covering. "I think it's wonderful."

Davio blinked at the strange contraption, unlike anything he had seen before. A slender framework had been crafted of polished wood. At the front was what looked like a pair of gracefully curving horns and, at the rear, another pair. Two narrow leather pads had been set on a crossbar. There were two large wooden wheels studded with tiny nailheads.

"Cousin Leo called it a 'velocipedia,'" Gloria said. "I've practiced, I know how it works."

"What's it do?" Davio eyed the machine with mingled curiosity and distrust.

241

"Gets us away from here." Gloria rolled the velocipedia through the door and motioned for Davio to follow. "The back gate won't be guarded. They're sure an Aldini will be too proud to use the tradesman's entrance."

Gloria was right. They passed quickly through the olive grove and the gate and continued on to a well-paved road. Except for the crowd of vengeful Ormondis, Davio would have enjoyed the moonlit outing with his beloved; but Gloria, after a moment, halted.

"Get on that saddle thing in the back," she directed. "Hold those curved bars. Put your feet on the pedals. I'll do the steering."

Davio did as she instructed. "Now what?"

Gloria swung lightly to the seat in front of him. "Just keep pedaling."

Next thing he knew, the velocipedia shot forward. He found himself pumping like mad as Gloria, likewise pedaling, guided Cousin Leo's vehicle as expertly as the helmsman of a ship. They skimmed along at a breathtaking rate. The wind whistled in Davio's ears. They would have made rapid progress and been well away from Rosamonte if

Davio had not lost his balance every few yards and sent himself, Gloria, and the velocipedia into a roadside ditch.

They had picked themselves up for the tenth or twelfth time when Davio, about to remount, paused and cocked his head. From behind them came thundering hoofbeats. Under the moon, in the clear and starlit night, Davio could make out Mr. Ormondi on horseback, galloping at the front of his retainers, all brandishing pikes and swords.

"Quit staring," ordered Gloria. "Climb back. And keep on pedaling."

For one hopeful instant, Davio believed they might outdistance Mr. Ormondi. His heart sank. Word must have spread like wildfire, for, some distance down the road ahead, galloped his father and every other Aldini in town.

"Trapped between our families!" exclaimed Davio. "All is lost!"

"Keep on pedaling," said Gloria.

From what little he could see, Gloria had taken both hands from her steering bars and begun pulling at several rods and levers.

"I told you Cousin Leo was a genius,"

she called over her shoulder. "He knew it would take a lot of strength to make this thing go. That's why he made room for two. I never tried this part by myself, but I trust Cousin Leo."

Fearless enough to face a thousand Mr. Ormondis, Davio suddenly felt as if the top of his head were coming off while his terrified stomach sank to his kneecaps. Cleverly folded into the frame of the velocipedia, a pair of light but sturdy wings deployed and flapped steadily. The vehicle began rising. Moments later, it was airborne and rapidly climbing.

"My dearest," cried Davio, "what do we do now?"

"Keep on pedaling," said Gloria.

Below, the galloping Aldinis and Ormondis collided, but instead of hacking and stabbing, they craned their necks skyward in dumbstruck disbelief.

Davio, overcoming his first fear, was developing a taste for soaring into the stars.

"You realize, my darling," he said, "after this, we won't dare go back to Rosamonte."

"Who wants to?" said Gloria. "We'll fly on to China, India, Samoa —"

"What about Jamaica?" Davio said.

"There, too," said Gloria. "Keep on pedaling."

❧ ❧ ❧ Not Thuh End ❧ ❧ ❧

"I like your house better than mine," Gloria said. "At home, it's boring. My father has everything decided ahead of time, all planned out. Nick's going into politics when he gets out of college. It's what my father wants."

We were, that afternoon, sitting on the porch at Lakeview Avenue. I had put down my sketch pad to chase a dog away from the shillelly.

"Nick," Gloria said. "He's my brother and I love him. But he's not nice with girls. He thinks he has — privileges."

We both knew Nick and my sister had been seeing each other. In the end, my sister would have her heart broken. For the moment, she was blissfully happy.

I asked Gloria what her father planned for her.

"He hasn't told me yet." She had the same wicked curve to her lips I saw when she doused her brother with lemonade. "I probably won't like it."

"Then don't do it," I said.

Gloria grinned at me. "I won't." She added, "What are you going to be?"

My answer — I didn't know if it had been stewing in the back of my mind, or, if so, for how long. In any case, it popped out and there it was. I felt as if I had untied one of The Gawgon's knots.

"I'll be an artist," I said. "I'll write stories, too."

Gloria nodded. "You'll be good at that."

I went back to her portrait. I planned, eventually, on adding color as another way of stretching out the project. Gloria asked when it would be finished. I warned her it could take a long time. Leonardo da Vinci, I told her, spent six years on the *Mona Lisa*.

"I don't mind," Gloria said.

"I don't, either," I said.

That evening, The Gawgon was waiting in my room.

"So, Boy, you seem to have made an interesting decision. You lied to that lovely girl about going to England. Were you telling the truth this time? Do you really want to be an artist?"

I said I believed I did, and asked if she thought that was what I should be.

"My opinion is beside the point," said The Gawgon. "Don't do something just because somebody else thinks it's a good idea."

I remarked that my father hoped I might work for the Pennsylvania Railroad.

"It's up to you," answered The Gawgon. "If you don't want to, then don't. That's what you told Gloria, isn't it?"

"Yes," I said, "I guess it was."

My father came up with yet another scheme to make our fortune: deodorizing public lavatories in office buildings, restaurants, gas stations, and department stores.

He designed a hollow cone that could be attached to the wall, and found someone to make plaster-of-paris castings of it. He bought a jug of concentrated perfume and, with a turkey baster, dripped a little into the cone. The perfume would seep out of the plaster and spread its aroma throughout the lavatory He proposed selling the fixtures and charging for the service of going back and refilling them.

Each morning, he packed plaster cones, the jug of scent, and the turkey baster into a satchel and went into town hunting customers. Amazingly, he found some, and for a time, did make a little money. But he came home reeking of gardenias and had to change his clothes. Even then, the odor hung around the house.

"Phew! It smells like a New Orleans bardello," Aunt Rosie said, next time she visited.

"How would you know that?" my father said. When she turned her back, he goosed her. Aunt Rosie gave a whoop.

"Oh, Alan," my mother said.

While my father grew heroically optimistic, I grew more agonized. Gloria's portrait was coming along well; coming along, that is, very slowly, so that we saw each other almost every day. Fourth of July passed without much celebration. Summer's lease was getting shorter, my vile secret would soon be revealed and nothing I could do about it. What I did, in fact, was: nothing. I did not breathe a word of going to England, what school, in what grade. Still, my preposterous lie gnawed at me; the calendar made my fate inescapable.

Worse, my mother had been talking with Mrs. Woods, the principal of Rosetree Elementary. I knew nothing of it until she sat me down at the dining-room table.

She began by telling me not to be upset, a good clue I was going to be extremely upset. There was, she said, some question about my grade when school started. My marks at Rittenhouse Academy were — she did not use the word "appalling," but it hovered around the edges. I had been out of school for such a long time, followed no approved studies, and as far as the official world reckoned it, I was deeply uneducated. A "savitch," as Aunt Rosie said.

"Mrs. Woods is a lovely person," my mother went on. "Very kind and sympathetic. But — and she was frank — she doubts that you'll qualify for sixth grade."

My mother gently exploded another bombshell:

"It's likely you'll have to repeat fifth grade. Possibly" — she hesitated, seeing my expression — "possibly you may go back to fourth. Mrs. Woods wants you to take a special test and she'll see."

I was, blessedly, too numb to remember much of what happened after that. My mother did take me to Rosetree Elementary. Mrs. Woods, as my mother said, was kindly and considerate, a smiling executioner. I sat at a desk along with some other victims. A couple of them were big, hulking boys who looked as if they had grown to manhood in fourth grade. We all had the hangdog air of educational felons.

Mrs. Woods passed out booklets and pencils and personally supervised the torture. It took a long time, though I marked down my answers as quickly as I could. At home again, I slunk to my garret. I wanted to see The Gawgon. She was not there.

I could only try to put the whole sorry affair out of my mind and fill my remaining days full of Gloria. I kept working on her portrait, which would never be finished. We rode our bicycles, we walked through the woods, we laughed, it was all wonderful and doomed.

For a time, I was able to forget what lay in store, but the closer we came to Labor Day, the heavier my secret weighed. I knew I would soon be forced to decide: wait like a coward until she found out, or bravely tell her myself. I preferred cowardly; for, if I said nothing, I could still hope to be run over by a truck.

That afternoon, Gloria and I were sitting on the Ormonds' lawn swing. It was warm yet. The Ormonds' big trees hadn't started changing.

I tried working on her portrait but erased what I had done. I had brought my story about the Aldinis and Ormondis. "For you to keep," I said. "You can read it when I'm not here." Then I said:

"I'm not going to England."

I did not confess out of heroic nobility. I couldn't carry the lie around with me anymore. I knew I would not be saved by a careening truck.

Gloria said she was glad I didn't have to go away.

Quickly, before I could change my mind, I said I was never going to England in the first place, not to Rugby or anywhere else. I wasn't even going to junior high. I'd be in elementary school and lucky if they put me in sixth grade instead of fourth or fifth.

Gloria stared at me. "You made it all up?"

I looked away and nodded. I did not try to explain. I had no idea how or what to explain.

Gloria got out of the swing and ran into the house. Mrs. Ormond was looking at me from the kitchen window. I got on the bicycle and went home.

I hardly slept that night. I had one more thing to do. In the morning, I rode back to her house. I had forgotten they would be getting ready for a weekend at the seashore. They were all in the driveway. Nick and Mr. Ormond packed things in the car. Gloria had just come out of the house. I wheeled the bicycle up to her.

"I'll put this in the garage," I said. "You'll want it back now."

"You don't have to do that," Gloria said. "I was mad, at first, because you lied to me. It doesn't matter. You were just being silly. The story was silly, too." Then she grinned. "I loved it."

She went on to tell me she didn't care what grade I'd be in. If we were in different schools, we could still see each other afternoons and weekends.

Mr. Ormond was calling for her to get moving.

"It won't make any difference," Gloria said.

I knew it would.

On Friday, my mother sat me down again at the dining-room table. She had a call from Mrs. Woods about the test. Mrs. Woods was troubled.

I said I guessed I had flunked. It did not surprise me.

My mother shook her head. "You got a good score. Better than good." That, my mother said, was what troubled Mrs. Woods. According to the test, I belonged in junior high. She didn't want to hold me back, but it was a big jump and Mrs. Woods worried I might not be ready for it. She thought it would be easier on me if I spent the year in sixth grade.

"She did say," my mother added, "whoever taught you must have been remarkable. That would have pleased Annie."

But, my mother added, I was the one to decide what I wanted to do.

For the sake of appearances, I thought it over for about three seconds. Seventh grade, I said, was fine with me.

Gloria would be glad to know. I would tell her as soon as she was home.

I went to the attic later. The Gawgon was sitting in her rocking chair.

"I'm glad you confessed to that ridiculous whopper," she said. "You at least cleared your conscience. Now there's room for the next foolish thing you do. And, I gather, you're moving up in the world."

I told The Gawgon I didn't care what grade I was in as long as Gloria and I could be together, sweethearts forever.

The Gawgon smiled. "Nothing is forever. But some things do last longer than others."

We sat quietly for some time. The Gawgon stood up.

"I'll go now," she said.

I asked when I would see her again, and hoped it would be soon.

"No, not soon," The Gawgon said fondly. "I did what I could for you. From now on, it's up to you. You have your own life to live. And I?" She laughed. "I'm dead, after all."

"Yes," I said. "I know that."

"Good." The Gawgon's face lightened. She had her same bright look of a girl.

Before she was gone, she turned and said:

"I'll not be back. Don't forget me."

"I won't," I said.

The Gawgon kept her word. She never came back. I kept mine. I never forgot.

About the Author

Lloyd Alexander is the acclaimed author of more than thirty books for young people. His many honors include a Newbery Medal for *The High King,* a Newbery Honor for *The Black Cauldron* — both in the Chronicles of Prydain — and National Book Awards for *The Marvelous Misadventures of Sebastian* and *Westmark.*

Mr. Alexander's best-loved work features strong heroines, as found in *Gypsy Rizka,* the Westmark Trilogy (*Westmark, The Kestrel,* and *The Beggar Queen*), and the Vesper Holly Adventures (*The Illyrian Adventure, The El Dorado Adventure, The Drackenberg Adventure, The Jedera Adventure,* and *The Philadelphia Adventure*). Now The Gawgon joins this bright company.

Lloyd Alexander and his wife, Janine, live in Drexel Hill, Pennsylvania, not far from where he was raised.